Reporting the Firs
Charles Repington, *The Times*
and the Great War, 1914–1918

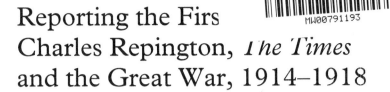

A. J. A. Morris

University of Ulster

CAMBRIDGE
UNIVERSITY PRESS

CAMBRIDGE
UNIVERSITY PRESS

University Printing House, Cambridge CB2 8BS, United Kingdom

One Liberty Plaza, 20th Floor, New York, NY 10006, USA

477 Williamstown Road, Port Melbourne, VIC 3207, Australia

314-321, 3rd Floor, Plot 3, Splendor Forum, Jasola District Centre, New Delhi-110025, India

79 Anson Road, #06-04/06, Singapore 079906

Cambridge University Press is part of the University of Cambridge.

It furthers the University's mission by disseminating knowledge in the pursuit of
education, learning and research at the highest international levels of excellence.

www.cambridge.org
Information on this title: www.cambridge.org/9781107512856

First published 2015
First paperback edition 2017

A catalogue record for this publication is available from the British Library

Library of Congress Cataloging in Publication data
Morris, A. J. A.
Reporting the First World War : Charles Repington, The times and the Great
War / A. J. A. Morris, University of Ulster.
Cambridge ; New York : Cambridge University Press, 2015. | Cambridge military
histories | Includes bibliographical references and index.
LCCN 2015022171 | ISBN 9781107105492 (hardback)
LCSH: Repington, Charles à Court, 1858–1925. | War correspondents – Great
Britain – Biography. | World War, 1914–1918 – Journalists – Biography. |
Times (London, England) – History. | Great Britain – History, Military – 20th
century. | BISAC: HISTORY / Military / General.
LCC PN5123.R47 M58 2015 | DDC 070.4/499403092–dc23
LC record available at http://lccn.loc.gov/2015022171

ISBN 978-1-107-10549-2 Hardback
ISBN 978-1-107-51285-6 Paperback

Reporting the First World War

Charles Repington was Britain's most influential military correspondent during the first two decades of the twentieth century. From 1914 to 1918, Repington's commentary in *The Times*, 'The War Day by Day', was read and discussed by opinion-shapers and decision-makers world-wide who sought to better understand the momentous events happening around them, and his subsequently published diaries offered a compelling portrait of England's governing class at war. This is the first major study of Repington's life and career from the Boer War to the end of the Great War. A. J. A. Morris presents unique insights into the conduct of the First World War and into leading figures in the British high command: French, Haig, Robertson, Wilson. The book offers modern readers a rewardingly fresh understanding of the conflict, and will appeal to scholars of the First World War and British political and military history of the period.

A. J. A. MORRIS is Emeritus Professor of History at the University of Ulster. His publications include *Parliamentary Democracy in the Nineteenth Century* (1967), *Radicalism Against War 1906–14: The Advocacy of Peace and Retrenchment* (1972), *Edwardian Radicalism* (1974), *C. P. Trevelyan: Portrait of a Radical* (1976), *The Scaremongers, 1896–1914: The Advocacy of War and Rearmament* (1984), and *The Letters of Lieutenant Colonel Charles Repington CMG: Military Correspondent of 'The Times', 1903–18* (1999).

Cambridge Military Histories

Edited by

HEW STRACHAN,
Chichele Professor of the History of War, University of Oxford and
Fellow of All Souls College, Oxford

GEOFFREY WAWRO,
Professor of Military History, and Director of the Military History
Center, University of North Texas

The aim of this series is to publish outstanding works of research on warfare
throughout the ages and throughout the world. Books in the series take a broad
approach to military history, examining war in all its military, strategic, political
and economic aspects. The series complements Studies in the Social and Cultural
History of Modern Warfare by focusing on the 'hard' military history of armies,
tactics, strategy and warfare. Books in the series consist mainly of single author
works – academically rigorous and groundbreaking – which are accessible to both
academics and the interested general reader.

A full list of titles in the series can be found at:

www.cambridge.org/militaryhistories

For CIS

LVII

Grow old along with me

For the best is yet to be.

Contents

Figures

Preface

Colonel Repington's war was the Great War of 1914–1918. His contemporaries referred to it as the Last, or European War. Quite deliberately he chose 'The First World War' as the title for his wartime diaries, and so provided that dreadful engagement's lasting, most familiar name. Critics claimed it was unduly cynical of him to imply there would be other world wars. He retorted, history had taught him nations were unlikely to stop waging war one with another. He preferred to acknowledge reality rather than indulge in wishful thinking and millennial rhetoric.

For the first two decades of the twentieth century he was the most influential military writer in the country. On questions of defence he was unmatched as a critic and communicator. From 1914 to 1918, his commentary in *The Times*, 'The War Day by Day', was read, dissected and discussed by opinion shapers and decision makers world-wide. A familiar coterie – ministers, statesmen, civil servants, soldiers and sailors – provided him with a constant supply of reliable information. His military informants were for the most part friends or acquaintances from his army days. Sir John French was a close personal friend, but his relationship with Douglas Haig, who succeeded French as C-in-C of the British Expeditionary Force, was never better than reserved. Haig knew that Repington questioned his capacity to command. He resented particularly the military correspondent's effrontery in daring to question his decisions.

Repington generally enjoyed excellent relations with the British and Allied high commands, but he thoroughly distrusted and disliked Henry Wilson. Had Repington not been obliged to leave the army, for which he blamed Wilson, many believed he, not Wilson, would have become Chief of the Imperial Staff.

Much of his writing received extravagant praise and was widely cited with approval. However he never lacked critics, as eager to censure the man as they were contemptuous and disdainful of his opinions. The publication of his wartime diaries in 1920 became the catalyst of this critical opprobrium. Did he really deserve either approval or censure in such immoderate measure? Were his critics justified in characterising him

as a too clever by half, unpatriotic scoundrel? Was the messenger disparaged simply because his message was disapproved? Neither friend nor foe
lightly ignored or forgot what Repington chose to say about them. He was
well named 'Io's gadfly', for his criticisms were intended to goad and
sting.

The Radical Liberal editor Henry Massingham, in an attempt to
diminish the influence of a troublesome and persistent critic, characterised him as a narcissistic dandy, 'the gorgeous Wreckington'. The
Unionist editor J. L. Garvin, in the course of a mendacious, abusive
tirade, scornfully dismissed Repington as 'the Duke of Yellington'.
Lloyd George did not scruple to question the military correspondent's
patriotism, shamelessly asserting that Repington had been prepared to
put his country's security at risk to satisfy his own selfish ends. Why
should an ex-prime minister indulge in such bitter, slanderous recrimina-
tion a decade after the journalist's death?

A happy coincidence – gaining access to *The Times*' archive that contained many of Repington's letters, and the simultaneous discovery of a
battered, second-hand copy of his wartime diaries – persuaded me the life
of this soldier turned journalist offered the possibility for an unusually
well-documented account of military–press relations in the first decades
of the twentieth century.

Over the years many friends, far more knowledgeable than I, have
generously and readily responded to my requests for help and advice.
Were I to list them all, their number would challenge the number of
names in a typical index of one of Repington's books. I hope, therefore,
it will be understood why I mention only those who have helped most
directly. The greatest debt I owe to Michael Chapman, who, ever uncomplaining and patient, has provided detailed answers to my endless questions. Celia Lee first pointed out to me the treasure-trove of Jean
Hamilton's diaries, which I otherwise would most certainly have missed,
and kindly provided me with the relevant transcripts. Michael Ackroyd
generously volunteered facts and photographs from his unrivalled collection of materials pertaining to Amington Hall and the Repington family. I
also thank those friends and colleagues who at different times have read
early drafts of chapters and patiently pointed out the mistakes and
blemishes: Bruce Murray, Noel Garson, Andrew Porter, Michael
Howard, Keith Jeffery, Roger Stearn, Samuel Hynes and Alistair Irwin.
The late John Grigg was always a present help and unfailing source of
excellent advice, as were the late John Keegan and my much missed,
lifelong friend and mentor, John Griffith. Anthony helped pick up the
pieces when I faltered in my task and first introduced me to the
undoubted benefits of the computer. For saving the text, and on occasion

my sanity, as a consequence of unplanned 'adventures' caused by the transfer from my familiar, battered typewriter to modern technology, I owe much to the skills of my saintly friend, Jay Diamond.

Finally, as ever, my heartfelt thanks to Cis. Without her constant support I doubt whether this book would ever have been completed.

A. J. A. Morris
Clun

Abbreviations

AC	Army Council
AEF	American Expeditionary Force
AG	Adjutant General
BEF	British Expeditionary Force
C-B	Sir Henry Campbell Bannerman
C-in-C	Commander-in-Chief
CD	Defence Committee
CID	Committee of Imperial Defence
CGS	Chief of the General Staff
CIGS	Chief of Imperial General Staff
DAAG	Deputy Assistant Adjutant General
DGO	Director General of Ordnance
DMI	Director of Military Intelligence
DMO	Director of Military Operations
DNI	Director of Naval Intelligence
GHQ	General Headquarters
GOC	General Officer Commanding
GQG	Le Grand Quartier Général/French General Staff
HQ	Headquarters
LG	David Lloyd George
MP	*Morning Post*
NDA	National Defence Association
NID	Naval Intelligence Department
NSL	National Service League
PHS	Printing House Square
PM	Prime Minister
psa	pass staff college
QMG	Quartermaster General
RA	Royal Artillery
RE	Royal Engineers
RFC	Royal Flying Crops

SWC	Supreme War Council
TF	Territorial Force
USN	United States Navy
UVF	Ulster Volunteer Force
VC	Victoria Cross

Introduction

Charles à Court[1] was born 20 January 1858. He was proud of his family pedigree and his ancestors who had rendered distinguished service to church and state. His father, Henry Wyndham à Court Repington 1819–1903, was by nature gentle and retiring; his mother, Emily (neé Currie), was the dominant partner in the marriage. Both parents indulged their attractive and clever only son, which might explain the wilfulness sometimes apparent in his adult character. His education was conventional for someone of his social class. After preparatory school, from 1871 to 1875 he attended Eton College. A want of interest and effort, not any lack of ability, explain his school years' lack of distinction. After Eton he was sent for a year to a military crammer at Freiberg. There he forgot much and learned little. In 1877 he entered Sandhurst. It proved a hugely enjoyable experience. Commissioned as a sublieutenant in the Rifle Brigade, he was sent to India in 1879, where he joined the fourth battalion at Nowshera. He had scarcely time to master the fundamental disciplines required of a regimental officer before joining the Peshawar Field Force. He judged his personal contribution to his first campaign, the Second Afghan War, 'supremely unimportant', yet it taught him a significant, never to be forgotten lesson. The army's political masters seemed blissfully unaware that a successful campaign required detailed, advance planning, and so were quite unconcerned that troops were left in blank ignorance about the country in front of them, that transport arrangements were miserable, hospital equipment wretched and that inadequate numbers had been provided for all units. The army was accompanied by Archibald Forbes,[2] the outstanding military correspondent of his day. He, however, had seen no reason why he should report any of these obvious failings. Despite the inadequacies of equipment and lack of preparation, the fortitude and courage displayed by the troops ensured the assault mounted upon the formidable fortress of Ali Musjid succeeded. Shortly afterwards, Repington collapsed with a violent and prolonged attack of enteric fever and was invalided home.

When his health finally recovered, he resumed his military service in Ireland. Ceremonial guards and a richly agreeable social and sporting life

Fig. 1 Major Charles à Court, 1898 (aged 40)

contrasted with helping to put down and control agrarian riots. During this period he began a self-imposed, arduous programme of military studies. His monograph, *Military Italy* (1884), enjoyed a *succès d'estime* that encouraged him not only to pursue his professional studies with even greater determination but fostered an ambition to secure a place in Staff College. He entered Camberley in 1887 where, for the next two years, he was extremely happy. Significantly he acquired a wide circle of friends, many of whom were to enjoy distinguished military careers. Of this company he was generally acknowledged to be the most brilliant. The one teacher who impressed him was Colonel Fred Maurice, who lectured on strategy and tactics.

After Camberley he was posted to Burma to resume his regimental duties, but to his delight almost immediately was transferred to the Intelligence Department. France was then considered the power that posed the greatest threat to British security. It became the particular focus of his study and interest. He spoke and wrote the language fluently and through frequent visits gained a thorough knowledge of the country's topography and communications' systems. He compiled a series of handbooks on the French Army that covered a wide range of subjects and was written in a style more lively than any previous departmental publication. By the end of his five years at Queen Anne's Gate he was firmly established as a staff officer of outstanding potential. He rejoined his regiment and served first at Aldershot, then Dublin, never missing an opportunity to impress his seniors with his competence and dash. In August 1897 he was chosen as one of two British officers to serve as DAAG on the staff of Sir Francis Grenfell, Sirdar of the Egyptian army. Subsequently he served on Kitchener's staff during the Atbara campaign and at the Battle of Omdurman (1898). He was impressed by Kitchener and the great man clearly thought well of him. Á Court was twice mentioned in despatches. Later that same year during the Fashoda crisis he was recalled and sent to Brussels from where he first set up and then supervised a highly successful secret service system throughout France.

In November 1898 he was appointed the first British military attaché to the Low Countries. Temperament and knowledge ideally fitted the Major (brevet Lieutenant Colonel) for his new posting. This was necessarily enhanced by his father's deep purse, upon which he was encouraged to draw generously. Repeated requests for detailed reports on his hosts' military plans at first threatened to overwhelm him, but they were successfully executed to the declared satisfaction of his various chiefs at the Foreign and War Offices. At the First Universal Peace Conference at The Hague (1899), he was attached to the small British delegation as a technical military expert. He took full advantage of the opportunity this afforded him to become closely acquainted with the Great Powers' most influential military, naval and diplomatic representatives. Most importantly, he became convinced that Germany, not France posed the greater threat to the security of Britain and her empire.

A Court returned to England in September 1899. Within two weeks he had sailed for South Africa as DAAG on Buller's Headquarter's staff. Arriving in Cape Town, he soon discovered that bluff and hard work were insufficient to compensate for earlier miscalculations and inadequate preparations. Disappointingly, the heroic Buller proved to be an unimaginative, overcautious C-in-C. But à Court perceived the army's greatest weakness was the want of a properly functioning General Staff. He was engaged in the thick of the fighting at Spion Kop, Vaal Krantz and Pieter's Hill. Shortly after the relief of Ladysmith, he was once more struck down by a violent attack of enteric fever, developed serious complications, and his life was despaired of. More dead than alive, he was invalided home where, after a long period of recuperation, eventually he recovered. For his 'thoroughly good services as Commandant of Headquarters' he was twice mentioned in despatches and in September 1901 gazetted a Companion of the Order of St Michael and St George.

He returned to his old posting at The Hague and Brussels to discover circumstances were much changed and far from easy. The British were extremely unpopular and sentiment at every level in Dutch and Belgian society favoured the Boers. Repington was involved in unofficial peace negotiations, but it was at this point that his private life collided disastrously with his military career. On 14 January 1902 the *London Gazette* gave notice of his immediate retirement from the army. In a quarter of a century's service he had demonstrated ability, industry, ambition, boldness, bravery and tenacity. He had been both a popular member of his regiment and a staff officer of outstanding promise. His virtues as a soldier were many, but there were undoubted faults. He was extravagant and impetuous, could be decidedly cavalier in his attitude to routine and authority, and made it very apparent, whatever their rank, he did not suffer fools gladly.

In February 1882 à Court married Melloney Catherine Scobell (1860–1938). Of their four children, two daughters survived infancy. He was an amusing, generous but never faithful husband. Army life offered him many opportunities for frequent, unexplained absences, a temptation he did not resist. He enjoyed several, mostly short-lived, amorous liaisons. Just how many exactly must now be largely a matter for conjecture. What is certain is, though his behaviour was inexcusable it was no worse than that of many another young army officer. The faster set in society winked at marital impropriety, the only solecism to be found out. For his part, this never seemed to concern him.

In 1897 while serving in Egypt, he met Mary Garstin (née North, 1868–1953), the wife of Sir William Edmund Garstin, a distinguished and successful engineer. They fell in love and their affair flourished. As he never conducted any of his amours with discretion, his wife soon learned of his latest adventure. When discovered, invariably he would promise his wife in future he would desist from such conduct, but sooner rather than later his head would be turned by some pretty creature and once more he would be up to his familiar tricks. Quite out of character, he remained 'loyal' to Mary Garstin and despite numerous discoveries and enforced estrangements their affair continued. Less than a week before his departure with Buller, his wife discovered they were still 'carrying on'. He promised, as so often before, he would never stray again, but this time, to ensure he kept his bargain, he was required to sign a document before witnesses promising 'upon his word of honour as a soldier and a gentleman' he would never again meet or communicate with his mistress. Mary's cousin, Georgina, Countess of Guilford, was actively involved in these negotiations and it was she who formally demanded à Court's written parole. Before signing, however, he insisted his undertaking was given 'on the under-standing [Mary] will be spared all future indignities and humiliations on my account'. He always maintained this condition 'formed part of the transaction'. When signed, his parole was given to Major Henry Wilson 'for safe keeping'. Apparently Wilson was involved, not only as a friend of Garstin and Georgina but also as à Court's colleague.

Three months after leaving England à Court received a pathetic letter from Mary telling of the bitter reproaches and cruel taunts she had constantly to suffer at the hands of her husband and her cousin Georgina. He had kept to the letter and spirit of his agreement, but their behaviour was a clear breach of the understanding he had signed. He considered himself no longer bound by his parole. However, when told Wilson this he refused to acknowledge that Garstin and Georgina had broken the agreed terms repeatedly asserting, 'You know this will end in divorce.' Shortly after this meeting with Wilson, à Court was struck down with enteric fever and his life despaired of. It was months before he was fit enough to be invalided home. Soon after his eventual recovery he resumed his affair with Mary. He asked his wife to divorce him on the grounds of his admitted adultery. She refused but Sir William showed no similar reluctance. He sued his wife for divorce on the grounds of her adultery and cited à Court as co-respondent. An undefended suit was heard in December 1901 and Garstin was granted a *decree nisi*. The case was reported in considerable detail in the London and national press.

The day following the trial à Court received a letter written at the direction of the Commander-in-Chief, Lord Roberts from the Adjutant General, Sir Thomas Kelly-Kenny. His attention had been drawn to the report of the divorce proceedings in *The Times*. A Court was asked to submit a 'statement of explanation' as to why he had not kept his parole. His detailed explanation was duly sent to Kelly-Kenny. Wilson was also sent for, interviewed, and asked to submit an account of his conversation with à Court about whether the terms of the parole had been broken. There are clear inconsistencies of fact between what Wilson wrote and what he had actually said as recorded in à Court's sworn statement. Because the Adjutant General had a good opinion of Wilson but thoroughly disliked à Court, he was not inclined to examine à Court's account carefully, and neither did he address the inconsistencies in Wilson's evidence. He simply advised Roberts, 'Lt. Colonel à Court has broken a solemn written promise made to a brother officer.' A Court's explanation he described as 'far from satisfactory' and proposed, 'not withstanding his past services I advise he be called upon to retire from His Majesty's service'. Roberts concurred. 'He has not behaved like an officer and gentleman.' The Minister for War formally signed his approval and à Court was immediately ordered to retire. There was no formal appeal.

Á Court blamed his dismissal, not upon Kelly-Kenny, as he might well have done, but entirely upon Henry Wilson, an opinion shared by many of his colleague in the Rifles. They too distrusted the eccentric Irishman and thought him not only inordinately ambitious but also extraordinarily devious. Nor did it escape their notice that à Court's enforced resignation would ease Wilson's professional advancement. The rumours concerning Wilson persisted, and because the army could ill afford to lose an officer of à Court's calibre it was supposed he would soon be reinstated.[3]

Obliged to earn his living, he chose journalism as his new vocation and rapidly established a world-wide reputation as Britain's leading military commentator. His advocacy of the reformed defence arrangements introduced by Esher and Haldane made a significant contribution to their success and public acceptance. The changes he canvassed and advocated so enthusiastically were designed to strengthen and protect Britain and her imperial defences against Wilhelmine Germany. When war with Germany was declared, he kept a critical, day by day watch over the nation's military fortunes as, with her major allies, France, Russia (until 1917) and latterly the United States of America, Britain engaged in a life and death struggle with Germany and her associates.

In September 1920 Constable published *The First World War, 1914–1918: Personal Experience of Lieutenant-Colonel C. à Court Repington CMG.*[4] Priced two guineas, the first impression of the two-volume set sold out almost as soon as it appeared. Nine further impressions swiftly followed as sales on both sides of the Atlantic remained buoyant. The diarist's declared purpose was to provide a reliable source for future historians. He also wittingly provided the conflict with its lasting title.

The historical value of a record written by an informed commentator who knew so many of the leading military and political participants was immediately acknowledged. Repington was compared with Pepys, 'as much at home in the War Office and Whitehall as Mayfair. He knew everyone worth knowing and heard everything worth hearing'.[5] His daily war commentaries afforded neither individuals nor governments any opportunity to be complacent. Inside Westminster it was widely mooted he was more influential than many ministers.

The same month as Repington's war diaries appeared, Margot Asquith published her autobiography. 'I fear the next journalistic enterprise that unlikely pair might inspire,' declared Esher to the king's secretary, 'could well be a weekly causerie in a Sunday paper by "Leaders of Society".' Margot cheerfully admitted that want of money had been her reason for writing. Repington's diaries had been similarly inspired. This motivation was by no means unique. Thoughts of financial gain plus the opportunity for vindication of their actions inspired most of the war's early memorialists and historians.

Within a decade of succeeding to a life interest in a large and valuable estate, Repington had managed to dissipate a good part of his inheritance. Yet, he insisted, he dreaded bankruptcy. One meaning of his former unadorned surname, *à court*, is 'to be short of funds'. The irony did not escape him. In earlier, prosperous, carefree times he had frequently avowed money meant little more to him than counters. He continued to look after neither pounds nor pence, deliberately eschewing Micawber's sound financial advice. He decided the speediest, most sure way he might solve his financial problems would be to write a best-selling book. In *Vestigia*, a memoir he published in 1919, he had strolled through his family history as preface to his life as a soldier. He offered no explanation as to why his army career had ended so abruptly. Nor did he say anything of his broken marriage or of Mary, who, as his de facto wife, adopted his surname and had borne him a daughter. His brief account of his pre-war years as a military correspondent, first with the *Westminster Gazette*, then *The Times*, concluded with Britain's declaration of war against Germany, on 4 August 1914.

Critics generously praised *Vestigia*. It sold well but made no more than a modest, short-lived dent in his huge debts. He concluded, had he not written the book with deliberate discretion, he would have sold many more copies. The better to attract the guineas of future readers, he promised his friend General Sir Ian Hamilton, 'My next book [a diary of his wartime experiences] will not be discreet.'[6] From September 1915 onwards he reordered materials into a daily account of the war. He included letters and notes of conversations with politicians, soldiers and friends, anything he considered likely to attract the widest possible constituency of readers, for only huge sales of his book could ensure his freedom from the toils of bankruptcy. The odds against success were long, but Repington, an instinctive and habitual gambler, always found heroic wagers irresistible.

When published in 1920, an early critic, the former premier, H. H. Asquith, remarked how the diaries were a 'strange mélange of social gossip and military criticism'.[7] Shane Leslie, though an extremely hostile critic, nonetheless began his review with the unqualified assertion that there could be no doubt this was 'a great book of the war written by a central and typical figure'.[8] But some critics who sought to undermine Repington's credibility insisted he had been deliberately mendacious, indiscrete and had betrayed confidences. Their ill-informed judgments would soon have been forgotten had not certain members of the establishment eagerly chosen to play wilful chorus to their misrepresentations.

Derby, Minister for War, 1916–18, was one such disgruntled grandee. He complained, Repington had 'betrayed' him by 'revealing' their frequent discussions. This had succeeded in making him 'appear disloyal'.[9] Derby and his ilk were enraged at Repington's 'revelations'. They believed the *hoi polloi* should never know what their social superiors thought about anything. It was none of their damned business. Admiral Sir Reginald 'Porky' Bacon wrote, 'It would have been far better if the public had been told nothing.'[10] It never occurred to these critics that Repington's supposed indiscretions had been prompted by *their* revelations. The messenger alone they supposed worthy of blame. They had supplied the brickbats but wanted no part in any blame for the consequent shattered window panes.

Esher, as befitted a royal confidant and political fixer who preferred power without responsibility, was a much wilier bird than Derby. He loftily dismissed the diaries as 'very indiscreet, much very dull, all very vulgar'. Those who had 'unburdened their souls ... when they knew they were talking to a journalist', were not deserving of sympathy. They had only themselves to blame. He smugly claimed *he* had never said anything to Repington he had not been prepared to see in *The Times* next morning. He permanently guarded his privacy behind the marmoreal barriers of his discretion. He claimed Repington was 'thoroughly untrustworthy', but conveniently forgot how eagerly he had once canvassed and applauded his support. Nothing was ever allowed to shake Esher's fine opinion of himself. With untroubled conscience he knowingly misrepresented the diaries' purpose. They were merely intended 'to rehearse the diarist's social triumphs'.[11]

The addressees to whom these condemnatory communications were sent were as important as the tone and content of the messages. Esher chose Stamfordham for that best guaranteed the credulous attention of the king. The Dean of Manchester chose Field Marshal Sir Henry Wilson, knowing him to be Repington's sworn enemy. He sent the CIGS a catalogue of the diarist's supposed moral shortcomings, salaciously emphasising the diarist's delight in the company of handsome women. Lubriciously he pronounced, to 'judge by the number and description of the lovely ladies who flit across his pages, Repington would certainly have moved heaven and earth to get Turkey in on our side so that when he was *dégommé* he might be received into everlasting harems!'[12] Grandee politician, courtier, cleric; their eclectic choice of Repington's supposed failings delineated not *his* but *their* moral perturbations.

The official historian of the war, Sir James Edmonds, noted how it had been the gossip and intrigue Repington related in his narrative, that lost him his social position. Another distinguished historian, Cyril Falls, on the evidence of the diaries, supposed Repington to have been an elderly thruster living in the greatest comfort, dining and wining all the prettiest and most charming ladies, while from the vantage of Hampstead continually calling for more sacrifices. This characterisation of Repington is as far from the truth as *Punch*'s spoof, 'War to the Knife & Fork' that portrayed the hero, 'after putting things right at Downing Street and showing everyone at the War Office how their work ought to be done, lunching at Claridge's with six leading ladies, all of them cheery souls'.[13] Shane Leslie noted there was nothing Repington would not blurt out 'like an honest fish-wife. When he is most outspoken he is most true'. There was the rub for those who supposed themselves to be the 'victims' of Repington's portraits: they were too disconcertingly honest!

Repington's judgment of men and what motivated them was both astute and unsparingly honest. He affords his readers an immediate, compelling portrait of England's governing class at war. Members of the establishment waged or avoided the war after their own fashion; Repington merely provided an unvarnished record of their actions. He never surrendered his duty to dine in company any more than he ever forgot to record the interminable lists of his fellow guests and diners. But whatever his critics then and since have thought, his social vignettes were included not because he was a snob. They were simply literary stage setting intended to amuse readers and attract potential purchasers. To disingenuous middle-class moralists, they presented a novel, otherwise inaccessible, social scene. To the familiars of his social circle, what he described was commonplace. Their interest was arrested by the possibility they, their friends or acquaintances might be mentioned or to discover whether they had ever said something indiscreet that he had recorded for posterity.

Repington's critics insisted that the threnody informing his personal experience of the war was a shameless lamentation for his privileged, overindulged, social set; the self-pitying whines of an older man urging the young to pointless sacrifice. But what we read is the frequent angry revelation and denunciation of shortages of munitions and men; the confusions, the avoidable reprehensible mistakes of politicians and governments; the wasteful *contretemps* and misunderstandings between allies; the endless, destructive interference of certain politicians, most particularly Lloyd George, in matters that would have been best left to the military. Repington's was an early, compelling exegesis on the battle between the frocks and the brass hats.

Repington 'saw' the war as a 'Westerner', determinedly opposed to 'sideshows' dreamed up by 'amateurs' without experience or knowledge of war and the military arts. At the same time, he seriously doubted whether Haig initially had really been aware of the true cost and consequences of entrenched warfare any more than he really acknowledged the disadvantages of fighting in a sea of mud. Sir Douglas, maybe because he was persuaded he was divinely inspired, for long seemed to think he could win without acceding to the same dreadful imperatives as other commanders. He insisted he would find a way to break through the enemy lines and gallop on to victory. Repington early acknowledged and understood why the German Army had to be battered into complete humiliating submission. The majority of his post-war critics accused him of being heartless and uncaring of the human cost.

As a reviewer in the American press pointed out, due to the short-sighted enthusiasm of biographers, the reputations of many of the war's leaders were in danger of being ruined. He instanced Henry Wilson whose immediate reputation as a clever soldier was largely destroyed by his biographer's injudicious use of extracts from his personal letters and above all his diary, 'the most sensational self-exposure in all literature'.[14] Wilson could not be blamed for the posthumous publication by others of his private papers. Repington, however, deliberately designed the diaries of his war experiences to attract the maximum attention. He hoped the consequent expected huge sales would repair his finances. Instead he succeeded in offending many, and particularly Lloyd George. The former prime minister was angrily intent, at almost any cost, to justify his reputation as 'the man who won the war'. Malignly, unjustly and dishonestly his *War Memoirs* besmirched the correspondent's patriotism.

Despite the obvious prejudice and self-interested animosity of Repington's contemporary critics, historians, for the most part,[15] have accepted their judgments. Repington has been dismissed as an intriguer, an untrustworthy, dishonest, scoundrel, and his journalism, books, published diaries of the war unduly neglected. Yet, they remain what they have always been – an honest record of one man's opinions. The conversations he recorded and published that caused such a social and political furore, illuminate brilliantly that boundary where publicity and politics merge and so often collide.

Was Repington a far-sighted, honest military analyst – a trustworthy, informed commentator on the First World War – or the evil Manichaen figure his detractors have made him out to be? Just who was Repington? What is the true measure of his influence and work? These questions, like the paradoxes they embrace, deserve careful consideration.

Part I

The years of preparation, 1903–1914

1   A new profession

In January 1902 the *London Gazette* announced Repington's immediate retirement from the army. With his income suddenly disastrously reduced, the need to find paid employment was urgent and compelling. He decided journalism offered the most likely prospect, although previous literary endeavours scarcely suggested an ability to generate a fraction of the income he had previously enjoyed. Whatever others might have thought, it never occurred to him he would fail as a journalist.

His time on Buller's staff had earlier prompted an unexpected offer from *The Times*. Leo Amery had proposed a multivolume *History of the War in South Africa* hoping to expose the army's all-pervading atmosphere of stupidity, a proposal the foreign editor, Valentine Chirol, enthusiastically supported. However, he wondered whether readers might not suppose Amery too young and inexperienced to be taken seriously? Perhaps it would be wise to acquire 'a good military man'? Amery agreed, but when he chose Repington, Chirol immediately opposed the appointment. It was 'not for personal reasons' he insisted, but to secure the reputation of *The Times*. It was not 'creditable' they should hire someone 'so morally shabby'.[1] As it was Moberly Bell's responsibility to hire staff and he approved of Repington, Chirol's objections were ignored.

Repington, who knew nothing of Chirol's opposition, plunged into his task, but soon entertained reservations about endorsing Amery's harsh judgments of commanders in the field. A crushing assessment of Major General Sir William Penn Symons prompted a note to Sir George White VC. Repington did not know that White, like Field Marshal Lord Roberts VC, had been advised by the Secretary of State not to help Amery. Repington was as anxious as Amery to see the army reformed but questioned the value of learning from the past when the facts chosen were doubtful, deliberately nuanced or even withheld. He judged that any commander outside Roberts's charmed circle was unlikely to receive a fair assessment. He knew how much military reputations owed to their press image and so was concerned that his former chief, General Sir Redvers Buller VC, notoriously contemptuous of journalists, would be unfairly compared with Roberts. The little field marshal had always enjoyed excellent relations with the press and assiduously practised all the arts of self-promotion. The public, knowing nothing of 'the many difficulties under which commanders in the field labour', would perceive Buller as a blundering buffoon when compared with Roberts, who would appear wise and heroic. But for Repington to address White was a waste of time. His only concern was to vindicate his own leadership; he could not have cared less about Buller's reputation. As a new boy at Printing House Square (and temporary at that), Repington was scarcely in a position to insist upon changes. He salved his conscience by observing the impossibility of writing a *complete* history of any war, for 'in this world it is a doomed ideal'.[2]

In December 1901 Chirol again objected to Repington's appointment. This time Bell acceded to Chirol's request. He sought to spare Repington's feelings by telling him there were insufficient funds to retain him. 'I would have been happy to continue the work for nothing had you thought that would be of help,' Repington responded, and went on to say he intended 'to write a great deal on foreign, naval and military matters in general'. He was certain it would 'be of interest to *The Times*'.[3] Whenever his fortunes were at a low ebb, he had the happy knack of conjuring up an optimistic vision of his immediate and future prospects. So he imagined himself as a latter-day de Blowitz, the famed foreign correspondent. Should Bell happen to hear of a suitable English newspaper seeking a regular Paris correspondent, Repington would be obliged if he mentioned his name. Either the Foreign or War Office would happily confirm he knew France better than anyone.

In his search for employment Repington produced a torrent of words upon disparate topics that he submitted to various newspapers. Happily for him, an imaginative effusion concerned with Westminster politics caught the fancy of the outstanding Liberal editor, J. A. Spender, who immediately accepted it for publication. Typically, the next day Repington presented himself at the editor's office and an hour later left Tudor Street with an offer to write regularly for the *Westminster*. Spender's influence upon his writing would be wholly benign. The editor was impressed by Repington's 'extraordinary range of knowledge combined with great facility as a journalist'. A shrewd judge of character, Spender thought him 'honest, clever and possessed of discretion and good sense ... brave and principled'.[4] Repington's good fortune was to have presented himself at Spender's office just when the editor was seeking a replacement for W. E. Cairnes, the *Westminster's* former, military correspondent. While this might explain why he attracted Spender's attention in the first place, to have retained his respect for more than two decades implies he possessed outstanding journalistic qualities. At Spender's suggestion he concentrated upon contemporary problems of military reconstruction and reform.

Repington sincerely believed journalists could effect significant changes in the army, a notion General Sir John Ardagh thought absurd. Ardagh insisted the satisfactory solution of any military problem required technical knowledge and expertise. Newspapers might talk glibly of educating their readers, but on technical subjects they scarcely knew what they were talking about. The real purpose of a newspaper was not to instruct its readers but to drive up circulation figures and thus accrue ever greater profits. Increased circulation was best guaranteed not by instructing readers but exciting, entertaining and amusing them. Ardagh had in mind the popular press, the 'new journalism' successfully pioneered by Alfred Harmsworth that Salisbury had patronisingly dismissed as 'written by office boys for office boys'.[5] Repington understood the arguments and reservations of both the Prime Minister and the general, but the press embraced much more than the half-penny dailies. The *Westminster Gazette*, for one, could never be accused of chasing profits, or sacrificing facts in the name of entertainment. Men of any or no political party respected its editor while its readers were drawn from the political elite. What the *Westminster Gazette* thought about current political, economic or social problems was of interest to all opinion makers and legislators. Never was this more true than when the Liberals were in government.

Tom Macaulay, the historian, started a most interesting hare before the passage of the first Great Reform Act of 1832. He claimed the press constituted a fourth estate of the realm. Thereafter, every Grub Street hack enthusiastically endorsed the truth of that assertion. The conceit was afforded substance and verisimilitude by Westminster politicians, who eagerly recruited publicists and allies to cajole the public into agreement. Successive instalments of reform continued to extend the numbers of the newly enfranchised, but other than the press there was no alternative practical means of shaping, instructing and informing the ever-increasing body of public opinion.

Among those newspapers that aspired to influence opinion *The Times* was generally acknowledged uniquely important. Chirol explained why this was so to a junior colleague. *The Times* would always retain its primacy because it understood the nature of political power. At sixpence a copy, it was too expensive to go directly to the masses so instead it sought to influence those who possessed political power. Chirol advised Amery, the most effective way to influence and change opinion at the War

Office was to focus upon 'the *men* in whom you can put your faith and then run them for all your worth'.[6]

Such advice might have been tailor-made for Repington, who relentlessly censured the proposed reforms of the Secretary of State for War, St John Brodrick. Self-righteous and opinionated, the minister generated hostility in the House. His friends considered him honest, sincere and principled; others saw only his smug inflexibility. He believed the war in South Africa had revealed nothing seriously wrong with the army. This put him at odds with Repington, who was now closely associated with a group of young Tory back-benchers as intent as he upon army reform.

The minister was not without experience as a journalist, but his autocratic behaviour towards the press matched the worst traditions of his predecessors at the War Office. George Clarke, a fomer military correspondent of *The Times*, fairly observed, 'No government department behaved wisely all the time. But of all departments, the Admiralty and the War Office invariably were the most stupid and impolitic.'[7] Hapless and inefficient, the system promoted needless offence, encouraging a constant drip of rumour, scandal and official secrets. The more secret and embarrassing the information, the more gleefully and swiftly was it published. Bureaucrats and generals alike were infected by the contagion. Information was disseminated more frequently and efficiently through unofficial than official channels. Like any competent journalist, Repington took advantage of the system's weaknesses, but his enterprise was distinguished by the importance of the information he gratefully received. Those who leaked information did so not for altruistic reasons but supposed it best served their own interests.

Brodrick seemed quite incapable of dealing sensibly with Fleet Street. He had been fortunate to get away with a gross misjudgment of government–press relations during the Boer War. He was convinced the proper relationship between a minister and the press was for journalists to demonstrate grovelling gratitude for the smallest mark of ministerial favour. Those were not the sort of terms Repington or any self-respecting journalist would accept. He ladled opprobrium over Brodrick, swiftly establishing himself as the minister's most persistent and effective critic. Bell, much impressed, deemed it worthwhile risking Chirol's disapproval and so asked Repington once more to contribute to *The Times History of the War in South Africa*. Unhesitatingly Repington accepted, although he admitted the extra work involved made it 'a pretty tough job'.[8]

Winston Churchill, who had won widespread attention and general acclaim for his adventures in South Africa and had recently secured in the Tory interest the parliamentary constituency of Oldham, recruited Repington to serve as an adviser to the Army Reform Movement, a group of young Tory MPs intent upon ambushing the war minister's proposed legislation. In his memoirs, Repington was unduly dismissive of this pre-ntice venture, but his alliance with a dissident parliamentary coterie made this campaign the forerunner of many in which he later engaged. He did not fall into the error made by many journalists closely involved with politi-cians, who often believed erroneously the press rather than parliament was the better arbiter of the nation's fortunes. He never forgot that Westminster and Fleet Street undertook disparate tasks and responsibilities.

Although he enjoyed acting independently, Repington was neither reluctant nor unhappy to disguise his individuality. He would strive, devil, research or prompt as assiduously for Churchill and his Army Reform Movement as he would later for Kitchener, Roberts, Esher, Haldane, Lloyd George and a dozen and one others. He was never slow to put his shoulder to whatever wheel seemed to him might best serve the general purpose. He joined the Army League and the Imperial Defence Association, but wearily confided in Churchill that he did so because, 'We must make use of the tools that God sends us and must hope to bend them to our policy.'[9]

Briefed by Repington, the Army Reform Group's parliamentary cam-paign in 1903 slated Brodrick's proposals as too expensive, impracticable and unsuitable. Churchill led the assault in the Commons, but his fine rhetoric proved no more than a stirring prologue to failure. In the Lords, the promised vigorous opposition to the minister's proposals entirely failed to materialise. Furious, Churchill urged Repington not to desert the cause, an unnecessary plea for it had never occurred to him to surrender. 'I will keep on shooting until the enemy retires,' he assured Winston. Nor was he convinced all was lost, for were London discounted, 'Three in every four people supports us.' For his part he intended to keep up 'a steady and persistent fire even after your heavier guns fall silent'. He would continue sniping each day in the press.[10] True to his word, in the *Westminster, Spectator, Blackwood's* and *National Review* he defended the opinions of his friends and scorned the minister's proposals. Little by little the spine of opposition to the minister's plan stiffened. Repington was now among the loudest, most cogent, persistently persuasive voices chal-lenging Brodrick. Amery, in a series of articles, proposed his own list of army reforms that at an estimated cost of 23 million pounds was a third less than the minister demanded. The merest hint that Brodrick planned to spend wantonly upon the army was sufficient to excite the opposition of the tax-paying electorate.

By October 1903, to everyone but Brodrick it was evident his scheme was a failure. He had successfully increased the size of the reserve but had failed in all else. He had envisaged three years' service and an army made up of a mixture of Regulars, Militia and Yeomanry, making six corps in all, yet had failed to fill more than three corps. The minister's efforts, particularly concerning the auxiliary forces, redounded to his discredit as Auxiliary strengths steadily declined throughout his time at the War Office. As Volunteers and Militia fell below their establishments, questions on defence topics pushed to the forefront at Westminster. Suddenly it was apparent Brodrick posed a serious threat to the health and future of the Unionist government. As soon as he might, Balfour shuffled him into Lord George Hamilton's berth at the India Office. Repington refused 'to shed even crocodile tears over the departure of such a hopeless creature'.[11]

The outbreak of war between Japan and Russia in February 1904 offered an unexpected opportunity Repington eagerly grasped. Amery deemed it impossible both to cover the war adequately and do justice to his other work at *The Times*. When asked if he would consider reporting and commenting in Amery's stead, Repington happily agreed. In less than two years he had already established a reputation as a knowledgeable, influential and distinguished commentator on military affairs. His public renown would soon reach far beyond the confines of Fleet Street. The book he later compiled from his collected articles, *The War in the Far East* (1905), was widely and generously acclaimed. Reviewers described him as 'the Prince of military writers', 'the Clausewitz of the occasion', and other like exaggerated compliments.

His first article on the Russo-Japanese war concerned *Bushido*, the ancient Samurai code of honour. It made an immediate and deep impression with his readers. Previously, the general public's perception of Japan and the Japanese owed much to the characters and verses of W. S. Gilbert's Savoy comic opera, *The Mikado*. Repington's description of the Japanese as a virile, self-reliant people dedicated to the service of their nation, proved an effective antidote to Gilbert's caricatures. He hoped Englishmen would ask themselves, were they as fit and determined as the Japanese to pursue their imperial destiny?

Writing from London, like a spider sitting at the centre of its web, Repington could pick and choose the best of the available information, and unencumbered by military censorship he wrote what he wished. From the beginning of the war he supported the Japanese and predicted they would be victorious for their troops were better trained than the Russians, were better led and believed in their own destiny. He would later admit his support for Britain's Asian ally had been a matter of duty. The claim is entirely plausible. Swifter and more clearly than most he acknowledged how the shifting sands of diplomacy dictated different strategic priorities to the Powers.

Not everything he wrote earned universal acclaim. H. O. Arnold-Forster, who had succeeded Brodrick as Secretary of State for War, reminded Balfour that Admiral Mahan, the American naval historian and theorist, had described Napoleon as 'a wizard whose power ceased the moment he came into contact with the water'. The same, he suggested, might be said of Repington. 'He knows nothing of the sea and, so far as I can make out, resolutely refuses to learn.'[12] But Repington had long taken a particular interest in amphibious warfare and was well versed in naval history and naval strategic studies. His writings on the Russo-Japanese war emphasised the useful parallels that might be drawn and the lessons Britain might with profit learn from a conflict that had matched a maritime with a vast land power. Despite the repeated assertions of naval advocates, he never suggested undermining the navy's dominance. Only the obtuse and prejudiced assumed to strengthen one service necessarily meant to weaken the other. Admiral Jack Fisher, ever watchful in defence of his naval fiefdom, had grown increasingly suspicious of the military correspondent's intentions. He claimed Repington's attitude towards new weapons was over cautious. What Repington had pointed out was the defeat of the Russian fleet should give pause for thought to those who had earlier dismissed torpedoes fired by small, mobile craft as ineffectual. Exaggerated hopes inspired by the undoubted destructive capacity of modern weaponry might well be disappointed if the weapons were not deployed intelligently. He had an uneasy feeling that rapid, technical advances had outdistanced the ability of naval and military commanders to make the best use of their splendid new toys. Fisher found such opinions particularly distasteful, expressed as they were on the eve of the revelation of the *Dreadnought* battleship, the First Sea Lord's own pet project.

Technical innovation in weaponry raised questions about tactics as much as about strategy. The speed with which in the decades before 1914–18 new, ever more powerful weapons emerged, necessarily meant sound tactical theories to maximise their effective use were often delayed. Wars of the future would be fought in the air as well as on land, beneath as well as above the waves. The difficulties of assessing a new weapon's potential were made more complex by the political problems inseparable from defence: the endless rivalry between manufacturers and designers, the claims and counter-claims for their inventions aired by publicists and protagonists in the press. The resultant controversies were invariably heightened by the constant quibbling and competition between the two armed services over money. Weapons and tactics were often retained long after they had become redundant, even dangerous. Those who sought guidance or legitimacy for future actions from the lessons of past campaigns were frequently confronted by confusing, contradictory or misleading examples. Repington played an eager, often significant part in the debates.

In September 1904 Repington published his seminal essay, 'A Plea for History'. From the beginning of the war he had consistently argued that Britain needed to learn the lessons the war offered. Knowledge had been lost because of government penny-pinching. The same knowledge had to be painfully reacquired at a later date. The governing class never initiated change 'unless pressure was applied by the force of public opinion or the lash of the press'.[13] Repington scorned many of the official histories of past campaigns and dismissed them as written exclusively for internal consumption. Their dark secrets were kept forever from prying eyes. Critical reports were mislaid, then forgotten in some musty War Office archive, but despite these efforts 'to lose, delay, bury or forget', sometimes official histories created controversy. The *History of the Second Afghan War* was twice suppressed, was abridged and bowdlerised. Finally it emerged, not six volumes as originally planned but as one. George Henderson's account of the recent war in South Africa provided a good example of how *not* to conduct an historical inquiry. His death in November 1903 allowed the politically inconvenient first volume to be scrapped leaving what remained, so Repington believed, 'deprived of half its human and all its political interest'. He concluded, if the intention were to write a worthwhile history of the Russo-Japanese war, then there would have to be a full account given of the 'pre-war, bilateral expansion of national forces'. This would provide a political chapter of the greatest value and interest. If left out, however, the account would be of no value 'for the Army, the Navy, or the leaders of the Nation'. There were some hopeful signs. Esher's committee had given history 'a modest place in the back seat of the pit'. Few subjects escaped the beady eyes of Fisher, Clarke and Esher, the three members of the War Office Reconstitution Committee. Repington proposed in future the best seats in the house should be reserved for 'an historical section of the Great Imperial General Staff', so that the public might 'confidently anticipate reading history not hucksterage'.[14]

Ostensibly intended to arouse interest in the writing of imperial history, he knew that his essay could not fail to draw attention to the author. Esher wrote promising his support. Obsequiously Repington responded, it afforded him 'very great satisfaction to win the approval of such a good judge'. It was not the first time he had broached the subject of official history. Despite Roberts's support, an earlier sortie had failed. 'Some idiot at the War Office', he told Esher, had seen fit 'to bury the effort'.

Fig. 2 C. B. Moberly Bell (1847–1911) (*The Times*)

Nothing Esher had said implied he supposed Repington had been angling for an official appointment. Nevertheless, there were rumours he might well be the man best qualified by ability and experience to co-ordinate the writing of official histories. His response had been to insist nothing in the world would ever again induce him to work for the War Office. Whatever the cost, before all else what he wanted was independence. Was he being entirely honest? A few months earlier, Intelligence had recklessly proposed the publication of a new journal as a forum for professional debate but available for sale to the general public. Repington had agreed to contribute a monthly article on the Russo-Japanese war. He asked to see the reports of the official war observers.

When permission was first granted then withdrawn, he swiftly rescinded the offer of his services. 'The germs of sheer, stupid secretiveness,' he observed contemptuously, 'have as fast a hold in Pall Mall as the bugs in the barracks in Upper Burma.'[15]

Repington blithely chose to ignore how his ambitious scheme for imperial history was to be financed. Anyone familiar with the casual, chaotic conduct of his personal financial affairs would not have been surprised. The Historical Section he had proposed was created and given as its first task the compilation of the official history of the Russo-Japanese war. It was agreed, political as well as military issues would be fully discussed and that military and naval strategy would be integrated rather than treated separately. In June 1908, in *The Times*, Repington wrote: 'History alone affords a treasury of principle that allows us to study and learn from the experience of the great masters.' In his memoirs he noted with regret, 'cabinets did not look at the larger defence issues involved in the understanding of the conditions of modern war' for they supposed such 'subjects unfit to drag into the sun ... Honest investigation would have entailed a radical change in the military policy of the country that no Party was prepared to face.'[16] By this he meant the adoption of conscription, but that was much too soon for that word even to be pronounced.

Immediately upon his arrival at Printing House Square, Repington tacitly had been given the mantle 'our military correspondent' previously bestowed upon George Clarke and Lonsdale Hale. However, when asked to confirm his status formally, Buckle would never give an unequivocal response. Only after an exchange of letters with Moberly Bell in December 1904 was his status as military correspondent and a staff member of *The Times* formally confirmed. His services were required, preferably exclusively, and all military and defence news would be his. He was offered as salary nine hundred pounds a year. That was remarkably generous and some measure of how highly *The Times* already rated his work.[17]

Repington, with deliberate casualness, suggested he might employ his War Office and army contacts and thus 'secure information from all the best sources'. So far he had merely 'scratched the surface'. Artlessly he wondered would it be worth his while 'to dig, for digging is a laborious affair and takes time and organization'. Like a conjurer revealing a trick he was certain would please, he told Bell that the design of the improved field guns had been settled behind the back of the Secretary of State for War and without consulting the Army Council. Since 1901 there had been a continual technical debate about improving the field guns that had failed in South Africa. A final decision had been delayed for reasons of economy. No decision would have been made had not Esher, fearing French's

'Striking Force' at Aldershot would be ill-provided with artillery, anxiously pressed Balfour. He then told the king the Cabinet had resolved unanimously to proceed speedily with the new design. Repington's source clearly had been Esher. Repington knew that raising the question of the guns would open a can of political worms that would have been devastating for the government.[18] It was the kind of story to tempt any editor. Someone who could elicit such stories would be worth his weight in gold. Repington insisted, a War Office 'in a state of chaos' and an army 'very ill at ease' would afford countless opportunities to preach change. He would make it his business to seek out the reasons for this malaise, before prescribing his own patent medicine providing a certain and satisfactory cure.[19] Buckle and Bell must have rubbed their hands with glee at the prospect.

2   Kitchener's champion

At last the Russo-Japanese war was over. Repington assured Bell there would be sufficient time to investigate the state of the British army thoroughly. In the past he had neglected issues other newspapers had covered; now he intended to cut them down to size. Repington's rapidly growing influence and distinction as a military commentator afforded pleasure to all senior staff at PHS, save Valentine Chirol. He particularly deprecated Repington's support of Kitchener. Chirol was Curzon's leading advocate in his quarrel with the Indian army's C-in-C. The clash of the two Indian titans envenomed the already soured relations between the two *Times'* men.

After the 1857 Mutiny, the rule of the East India Company had been replaced by that of the Crown. The Indian army was responsible for internal security and the reinforcement of external policy. On India's North-West Frontier British suspicion of Russia's territorial ambitions had already prompted two disastrous Afghan wars as government and military determinedly pursued a policy designed to keep the Russians at arm's length. It was feared that India's other land boundary to the east of the Ganges was threatened by French territorial ambitions. There, three wars were fought between 1824 and 1887 before Burma had finally been annexed.

Curzon had been warned Kitchener could be an awkward customer. Nevertheless he had insisted on Kitchener's appointment as Commander-in-Chief. This meant that Kitchener was responsible for the army's organisation, training and its conduct in wartime. The Indian army's administration was the responsibility of Major General Sir Edmund Elles. The military member in the Viceroy's Council he had charge of the non-combatant services and the preparation of the military budget. This division of executive and administrative functions, the so-called 'Dual System', had been devised to ensure that should the C-in-C ever happen to be absent from Calcutta, the Viceroy would always have a senior military adviser to consult. The system had worked well enough under Kitchener's mild-mannered predecessor, General

Power-Palmer, but Kitchener wanted sole control of everything to do with the army. He did not like Elles personally and this added to his determination to get rid of him. Repington assured Buckle, his support of Kitchener's opposition to the Dual System was based solely 'on the great abiding principles of administration'.[1] Doubts about the validity of that claim were reinforced by a more than sneaking suspicion the army opposed the Dual System in order to pay back old resentments against the civil government.

Repington had not long been with Spender's *Westminster* when he first mentioned a wish to 'write a warm article' on the subject of the military member. He asked his friend Raymond Marker, who was at the time a member of Kitchener's staff, to provide evidence to demonstrate how 'Elles and his muddlers [were] still playing the garden ass'.[2] He shared Kitchener's aversion to Elles.[3] The case against the military member had seemed straightforward until Roberts intervened with an argument that contradicted the 'facts' Marker had given Repington. What made Roberts's involvement difficult and embarrassing was that he was 'the effective head' of the East Indian county families. They 'hated intruders or outsiders within their sacred domain', and so wished nothing changed unless they had indicated their approval.[4]

Repington assured Marker, it was not his intention to renege on his promise to write an article condemning the military member. However, in the new circumstances he thought it not unreasonable they should accumulate 'more evidence'. Kitchener should realise, if the article was to be convincing then Repington needed to be told *everything*. This theme he returned to constantly. He desired there to be 'No more hocus of official secrets where none exist.'[5] He knew his demand would not endear him to Kitchener. Curzon had earlier warned Repington it would be naive to suppose everything Kitchener's messengers told him was accurate. Despite denials, he had to admit, what Curzon had said was true.

Chirol had complained to Moberly Bell that, as editor, Buckle never took the time to examine any question independently. Too frequently he deferred to the opinions of colleagues who claimed to be 'experts'. 'Of course,' Chirol disarmingly admitted, 'if one happens to be the expert one doesn't mind.'[6] At PHS, Repington readily acknowledged that on India, Chirol's opinion held sway. If he were to wage an effective campaign against Curzon, he would need to undermine Chirol's influence and recruit Buckle as his ally. By October 1905 he judged he had achieved this. However, he warned, they still needed to be 'armed at every point to resist the onset from all quarters of all old Indian hands'. To this end he sounded out Brackenbury, who had served on the Viceroy's Council for five years. No one was better fitted by experience to tell them what

Fig. 3 Sir Valentine Chirol (1852–1929) (*The Times*)

arguments their opponents might use. Then Repington sketched out an article but still counselled delay. If at all possible, he thought, it would be better not to clash with Curzon. The Viceroy's power and influence in Tory Party politics was such that a mere word from him would be enough to cause the government's collapse. Repington believed Kitchener should make one more attempt to persuade Curzon to his view.

Chirol insisted Repington had agreed to be employed as Kitchener's tool because he had been promised reinstatement in the army.[7] Repington contemptuously dismissed this claim as a 'cock and bull story scarcely credible to any right thinking person'. He was his own man. 'I prize my liberty too much,' he insisted, 'to give it up. £10,000 a year and a peerage would not again make me the slave of the d—d fool class that misgoverns this benighted country.'[8] But that did not stop detractors whispering behind his back, 'There can be no smoke without a fire.' Repington had been cautious and careful but Chirol perversely insisted the case against the military member had been made 'recklessly and furiously'.

There was a coda to this episode when, in early 1913, questions concerning the suitability of India's C-in-C prompted a suggestion from Lovat Fraser in *The Times* that the former military department should be re-established. Repington hastened to inform Dawson, 'Nothing could be more fatal to the efficiency of the Indian Army.' With relish he recalled how they had succeeded: 'Our argument not our numbers won the day. I have never been more proud of anything.' He suggested Dawson search in the newspaper's archives for a printed copy of a secret letter from Kitchener to the India Office explaining in great detail the crimes of the old military department. Should his editor wish to study the issue in more detail, Repington directed him to 'all my arguments in *The Times*'.[9]

In his autobiographical fragment, *Fifty Years in a Changing World* (1927), published two years after Repington's death, Chirol's resentment against the military correspondent burned as brightly as ever. He claimed to have accused Kitchener, 'to his face', of lowering himself by entering into confidences with a man like Repington. Kitchener retorted, in a fight one 'could not afford to be too squeamish about the instruments used'.[10] He told Chirol he had hated writing to Repington because of the moral offence he felt at 'his disgraceful behaviour with Lady G'.[11] His assertion was pure humbug. He later admitted he could not have cared less about Mary Garstin's fate.[12] In Kitchener's universe he was the sun about which all lesser planets revolved. He would shamelessly use others to serve his purpose. Repington was no one's fool, and well aware of this. He championed Kitchener convinced that to do so best served the army's interests. His partisanship raises questions about his frequently claimed independence, for it took the war of 1914–18 before Repington finally acknowledged his superman had feet of clay.

Repington and Chirol were constantly 'at daggers drawn'.[13] Chirol was frustrated by Buckle's refusal to heed his warnings and complaints. Repington found addressing George Clarke's constant carping altogether easier than coping with the permanently intransigent Chirol. Clarke's criticism he supposed to be fuelled solely by injured vanity. His ego had been bruised for he did not like to think Repington enjoyed that same influence with the War Office that he had once commanded. Writing to

Esher, Repington poked gentle fun at Clarke by quoting from Ecclesiastes.[14] Clarke bitterly resented being usurped by some Johnny-come-lately. Admittedly the fellow had a certain facility with words, but he believed he lacked real conviction and was inclined to employ his talents to serve essentially selfish ends. He dismissed him as superficial, vain and a trimmer. But Clarke would very soon realise, Repington always argued his case tenaciously, cared not a jot for the opposition his views might excite, and was not inclined to waste his time either rebutting false charges or trading insults.

More often than he cared to admit, Clarke found he agreed with Repington. India's defence, however, was a different story. He once complained to Balfour of those writers (he was thinking particularly of Repington) who encouraged Simla to make absurdly ambitious plans. The one issue guaranteed to prompt angry debate between the two protagonists was India's railway system. Kitchener had planned a network of strategic railways aimed at Russian communications. The plans were fully discussed in the Viceroy's Council and rejected, then finally set aside on the grounds of cost by the new Liberal administration. Repington insisted Clarke grossly underestimated the number of troops required to rebuff the Russians. Repington was convinced the Russians could rapidly transport many more men and supplies by rail than Clarke by his calculations allowed. To resist the Russian horde he required many more troops to resist them. Clarke warned Esher, the number of troops Repington demanded was absurd. His use of differential calculus to compute the supplies required to keep that number of troops in Afghanistan was quite beyond Repington's mathematical comprehension.[15] But to Clarke's fury, his mastery of geometric ratios and the faultless logic of his arguments were ignored. His enviable mastery of higher mathematics bemused and confused rather than enlightened his audiences while his brusque, irascible manner caused great offence. On every issue he insisted he knew best; he sought to bludgeon rather than persuade others to his point of view. Repington's less hectoring, presentational style undoubtedly served him better.

Clarke was convinced Kitchener recklessly enhanced the case for a Russian invasion of India and accused Repington of knowingly lending himself to a calculated scare campaign designed to flush out extra funds from the Treasury to finance unwanted reserves of troops and armaments. Repington supposed Clarke had given away the real source of his argument – the old, familiar enemy of every, imaginative, military scheme – Treasury economy. He was certain India was being more highly charged for defence than England and infinitely more than the Empire as a whole. He wanted Marker to extract the necessary figures from the

Indian budget, but to leave the analysis and presentation of the figures to him.[16] What made finance such an irresistible subject to Repington? Did he suppose he possessed Kitchener's talent for financial calculation?

In December 1905 John Morley was appointed Secretary of State for India. The new minister's reputation as a Radical scarcely suggested he would make a comfortable, political bedfellow for Repington, but he believed he could persuade Morley to see the frontier question through Kitchener's eyes. He sensed this new Secretary of State was disposed to seek a compromise over frontier policy. In their private correspondence he adopted a discernibly friendly tone. 'Honest John' would certainly not be the sort of Secretary of State to act rashly. He found particularly disarming Morley's admission he knew little about the North-West Frontier question Repington was flattered to be asked to bring a map with him to explain the question the next time they met. Morley pronounced it the kind of conundrum that 'either finds a man mad or leaves him mad'.[17]

Repington was convinced he could convert Morley to his way of thinking. To make the best of the circumstances, he wrote to Marker urging him to get Kitchener to tell him everything he might require. The letter suggests a degree of uncertainty in Repington's mind whether Kitchener's strategic imperatives served India's and the Empire's best interests? Morley after all was nobody's fool, and he seemed to think tact and diplomacy alone might be sufficient to sort out India's problems. To provoke war unnecessarily was not a sensible use of resources, especially when the Kaiser was making a nuisance of himself so much nearer home. He passed on the Secretary of State's reflections but without any comment of his own. As always, whatever reservations he had, when push came to shove the familiar loyalties of the old soldier took over. He arranged a luncheon party for Morley and the minister was seated between Generals Hamilton and Smith-Dorrien who had been instructed by Repington 'to ply Morley hard'. Thereafter, Morley could not fail to be thoroughly apprised of the military viewpoint. He wrote of this to Marker, 'I fancy you are smiling.'[18] But he had ignored one vital consideration. No matter how spiritedly the generals might have insisted Kitchener knew best, Morley was the last man to be bamboozled into an unqualified belief in the C-in-C's transcendent military genius.

In putting his money on Kitchener, Repington made a grave mistake. Though the Foreign Secretary was a Liberal imperialist, in the negotiations for the Anglo-Russian Agreement he found the Radical Secretary of State for India to be much his most useful Cabinet ally. Both were equally and deeply concerned about German political and territorial ambitions. That was why Morley impressed upon Minto, the new Viceroy, 'Germany seeks only coolness and a quarrel between us and Russia.'[19]

When, at an intimate supper party he gave for Morley, Esher and Knollys at Claridges, the minister spoke freely of his concern about German intentions, Repington was genuinely surprised. He observed, the views of a supposed Radical 'were almost those of a Jingo'.[20] Once signed, the Anglo-Russian Agreement did have far-reaching consequences for the future of Central Asia and the Middle East, not excluding the defence of the Indian subcontinent. It also changed diplomatic relations in Europe. It could not be otherwise since Britain's familiar, long-term opponent in 'the great game' was now her diplomatic partner.

This reversal of the familiar diplomatic scene afforded Chirol a new opportunity to pursue his vendetta with Repington. The ink was scarcely dry on the Anglo-Russian Agreement when he insisted the *raison d'être* for Kitchener's forward policy, formerly vigorously championed by Repington, no longer existed. Now he deliberately sought to discredit the military correspondent both at Printing House Square and the India Office. The early moves were rather petty. He managed to keep some of Repington's writings on India's defence out of *The Times* and then planted a hostile review of *Imperial Strategy*, Repington's latest book, in the columns of the *Pioneer*. But newspapers as politically disparate as the *Westminster Gazette* and the *Morning Post* published glowing reviews. A particularly favourable review that Amery had drafted for *The Times Literary Supplement* was, at the last minute, altered by Buckle. Repington supposed Buckle, 'trembling at Chirolean objurgations ... cut out all Amery's supporting paragraphs inserting twaddle in their stead'. He complained, this was the sort of thing he had to contend with all the time. In a note to Buckle he pretended not to know that at the last minute the editor had altered the review. Much enjoying the joke, he censured the 'ignorance and dishonesty of the reviewer'.[21] If the book had made Chirol angry, it made Curzon incandescent. He complained how even on holiday he was not free of Kitchener's 'irritating and compliant scribe'. On finishing *Imperial Strategy* he wrote post haste to General Barrow, Elles's deputy. 'I daresay you saw Repington published Kitchener's essay on foreign policy [to suppress and replace the policy for which I was responsible] as the concluding chapter of his book ... The voice was the voice of Jacob but the hands were the hands of Esau – and very hairy too.'[22]

Repington, Chirol and Kitchener remained bound in a fateful trinity. The focus of their endless debate and differences was not any longer who should have final charge of India's military organisation, for that had been settled in Kitchener's favour, but how much should be spent upon the Indian army. As a direct consequence of the signing of the Anglo-Russian Convention, changes were expected in Kitchener's plans. His modified military ambitions were expected to reflect the changed diplomatic scene and the likely future international outlook. These changes, Liberals assumed, ought to deliver considerable economies. What Chirol now told Morley left the Secretary of State with little regard and less respect for India's C-in-C. But why should he have believed Chirol so readily?

Morley, a most distinguished and experienced journalist, was acknowledged as the doyen of that profession. Thus he naturally took a particular and informed interest in the press and attached the greatest importance to what *The Times* said on any issue touching the condition of the subcontinent. He considered it 'the only journal that follows Indian Affairs in a consecutive manner and that is read by the very limited class of public folk who take a real interest in India'.[23] Much of the credit for this he gave to Chirol. He profoundly respected the foreign editor's unrivalled and intimate knowledge of the subcontinent, its administration and the senior personnel of the Raj. Chirol was the last journalist Morley would have wished to offend by questioning his reliability or integrity. Consequently he had not questioned his unqualified claim to have seen a letter written to Repington by India's C-in-C. This had stated categorically the signing of the Anglo-Russian Convention would make *NO* difference either to military policy or the preparations for India's defence. As this was contrary to Morley's declared wishes, it had come as a surprise. Recently Kitchener had seemed prepared to lower his demands. He had given the distinct impression Afghanistan no longer played so important a part in his thinking. That should have been enough to have given Morley pause for thought. But he had been incensed by Chirol's revelation. To Minto he despatched a private, confidential note berating Kitchener for forgetting he was the government's servant. Morley assured Minto, what he said about Kitchener was no conjecture. He had learned the Commander-in-Chief's exact thoughts from 'an absolutely reliable hand who must know'. He could only have meant Chirol.[24]

Despite Morley's injunction to keep the information to himself, Minto told Kitchener. Immediately he dismissed the accusation as a 'stab in the back ... delivered in the dead of night'. Minto informed Morley he was 'absolutely certain' Kitchener had been 'misrepresented with a view to making mischief'. It could not be doubted the C-in-C 'strongly approved the Convention'.[25] Minto's assertion received further confirmation from a most unlikely source. Recently appointed Governor of Bombay, Sir George Clarke wrote to tell Morley that upon his arrival in India Kitchener had made a point of telling him he approved of the Convention. This unsolicited confirmation carried considerable weight with Morley, for he highly esteemed Sir George.[26] Minto now insisted Chirol could not have seen a letter Kitchener had written to Repington. Minto's military secretary, Lieutenant Colonel Victor Brooke, who had charge of the C-in-C's letter book, knew with absolute certainty Kitchener had *not* corresponded with Repington.

Morley valued Chirol's support and confidences. He could not bring himself to admit, in the same 'rough' words Kitchener employed, that Chirol had told him a 'deliberate lie'. The minister insisted he 'always meant to be straight', but conceded the foreign editor could be 'extremely hard to move in his opinions'. His 'political character poses very real difficulties. It is almost impossible to shake his stubborn prepossessions'.

Repington's triumph over Chirol consolidated his position as an authoritative and influential senior staff member of *The Times*. With good reason, he still kept a wary eye upon him and was quick to take the field when, in the following year, a dispute suddenly flared into life over policy on India's North-West Frontier. On this occasion, Repington saw himself as 'checkmating' Chirol, who, in cahoots with several retired Indian Army warriors, most notably Lieutenant General Sir Edwin H. H. Collen, had suggested Kitchener once more wished to pursue a forward policy in Afghanistan. The same incident afforded Repington the opportunity to remind another old Indian foe, Curzon, that he was more than ready to curb his tricks. He told Marker he had imported into an article for *The Times*, 'a venomous paragraph . . . just to make GNC sit up and take notice'.[27]

In April 1909 Kitchener delivered to the Legislative Council a statement explaining and justifying his military administration, recounting the reforms he had initiated: his reorganisation schemes, the complete rearmament of the Indian Artillery and the rearming of all Indian troops with new, more efficient rifles, all achieved at considerably lower cost than expected. Repington, who had been leaked a copy of Kitchener's speech by Raymond Marker, recognised how well it would serve 'the interests and reputation of Lord K'. He persuaded the acting editor to publish it in full in *The Times*. At the same time, he suggested when Buckle returned to Printing House Square, the newspaper should pay 'a handsome tribute' to Kitchener for his work in India. 'Then we shall see whether Buckle will be man enough to brave the Chirol–Nathaniel combination.' Thus it was at Repington's instigation and very much as a consequence of the unrequited feud with Chirol that *The Times* would play a key part in establishing the legend of Kitchener's rule in India, a massive contribution to the pantheon dedicated to his military genius.[28] In the autumn of 1911 Kitchener left India to become proconsul of Egypt. Chirol, as reluctant as Repington to leave old scores unsettled, admonished Morley for 'promoting a legend' that Lord K's administration had been the last word in economy and efficiency. 'Need I tell you how little that corresponds with the facts ... you have incurred a very grave

responsibility by your silent acquiescence in the growth of that legend.'
Without comment, Morley passed on Chirol's malediction to Crewe.[29]

Clarke, so long Chirol's ally in attempts to undermine Repington,
found his new position in India absorbed all his energies. He had more
immediate and significant things to do than point out for the hundredth
time the error of the military correspondent's ways. When Clarke published his autobiography, *My Working Life*, he made no mention of
Repington. The military correspondent had said nothing of Clarke in
Vestigia. The omissions effectively concealed an important relationship
concerning military and defence policy in the early years of the Liberal
government. Regrettably much of their correspondence is lost, but what
remains tells a story very different from that suggested by both men's
memoirs. Repington always retained a certain wry affection for Clarke,
even when the apoplectic Sir George was determinedly doing everything
in his power to disabuse Esher, Buckle and an assorted host of politicians
and soldiers, of any idea Repington could ever be a reliable guide on
matters of defence.

Chirol's influence at Printing House Square was so formidable
Repington could never afford to ignore him entirely. Yet in his memoirs
Repington devoted only two sentences to him. He described Chirol as 'a
man with a wide knowledge of foreign affairs' before concluding abruptly,
'I appreciated his competence in his own branch.'[30] Chirol waited to have
his say about Repington and the Curzon–Kitchener altercation until two
years after Repington's death. He saw no reason to revise his original
estimate. The only reason Repington succeeded was because he had
always been 'a week ahead [of him] with fuller materials supplied by
Indian Army headquarters'. The truth was Chirol could never forgive or
forget that Repington had once bested him.[31]

3   Esher's War Office reforms

Repington first became acquainted with Esher when writing for Spender's *Westminster Gazette*. Both men hoped the recent war against the Boers had taught the nation an important lesson; from humiliation might emerge a period of unprecedented military reform. In November 1903 Esher had been appointed chairman of a Reconstruction Committee charged with examining the workings of the War Office. It was acknowledged that Esher's task was extraordinarily difficult, but one for which he was particularly well suited. He was a close friend of the prime minister, Arthur Balfour, and also enjoyed an unique relationship with the king. Edward could be awkward and inordinately sensitive if he supposed his prerogative powers in relation to the army were threatened, but better than anyone else, Esher knew how to humour him. His career became a dazzling demonstration of 'how finely tuned obsequiousness could be instrumental in gaining social status and political power'.[1] He cultivated the social connections he had first made when at Eton and Cambridge and thereby created an informal, constitutionally nebulous yet influential position in the state. He determined many of the army's reforms but made sure he never bore direct political responsibility for his actions or advice. When offered official posts that bore such responsibility, generally he rejected them. The power, influence and patronage he exercised behind the scenes was in no way diminished by this apparent reluctance to accept high political office. If anything, it made him even more formidable. Norman Angell, the pacifist publicist, best described the inherent paradox of Esher's public persona; strangely unaccountable, approachable yet impenetrable, the go-between of the king to his ministers and of the king to other rulers.

Although Esher spent his days in the company of the powerful and privileged, he never forgot the political potency of public opinion and so carefully cultivated his friendships with newspaper men. He had soon learned the press could misinform and misrepresent as easily as promote and enhance. His journalistic mentor had been the uniquely gifted editor,

36

W. T. Stead. Among leading contemporary journalists, Esher counted J. A. Spender, J. L. Garvin, J. St Loe Strachey and Leo Maxse as particular friends giving him ready access to the *Westminster, Observer, Spectator* and *National Review*. All were very different but important journals of opinion. He was also closely associated with George Clarke, Repington's irascible predecessor as *The Times*' military correspondent. He still retained influence on defence issues at Printing House Square. Amery also shared Esher's interest in the army. But of all *The Times* fraternity, Esher's most useful ally was undoubtedly Repington. They were to develop an almost symbiotic relationship.

James Lees-Milne, Esher's biographer, has suggested Repington was for Esher never more than a 'great busybody, a bore who wrote interminable letters',[2] but it was not so. In pursuit of a common end, each after his own fashion sought to influence very different audiences. Each dominated in his own demesne: the one, a *habitué* of the shadowy corridors of the establishment, the other, a prince of the Fourth Estate. Their professional worlds, otherwise dissimilar, were alike in their amorality, lack of sentimentality and scruple. Both were conscious of how much each gained from alliance with the other. Theirs was a marriage of convenience designed to promote those causes both espoused in common.

In the decade before the Great War, though Esher's only military experience had been the year he served as a lieutenant in the Duke of Rutland's Regiment of Militia, he entirely reshaped the War Office. He had culled his military knowledge entirely from books and conversations so Repington's professional experience was invaluable, particularly his knowledge of the rising generation of officers. Although Repington insisted he was no longer interested in 'individual' or 'personal matters', he demonstrated neither reluctance nor reticence when Esher asked him to assess a candidate's suitability for promotion. For all his disclaimers Repington canvassed vigorously on behalf of any officer he considered had been unjustly passed over or ignored. With the exception of Henry Wilson his estimates were fair, often astute. Upon first meeting Repington Esher wrote, 'I have just spent two days in the company of a very clever soldier . . . who knows everyone in the Army by experience of war . . . He was very open about events and men.'[3] What had particularly impressed Esher was Repington's detailed criticism of the quality of the generals in South Africa. Gratifyingly it confirmed his own thinking, a fortunate congruence that disposed him to suppose Repington's was a voice worth listening to. Repington particularly admired Esher for his 'wonderful ability to get things done swiftly'.[4] This quality, he believed, suited him admirably to chair the War Office Reconstitution Committee.

The faults and failures of the army in the South African War had been identified by the Elgin Committee,[5] a commission of record not advice. In the face of widespread opposition, reform schemes promoted in Parliament were emasculated, delayed or lost. Seemingly less ambitious, the triumvirate of Esher, Fisher and Clarke sought to answer three questions: How many men did the regular army require? Upon what terms could they be enlisted? What would it cost? Esher determined their answers should rest upon first principles.[6] War Office departmental responsibilities would be logically divided. Roberts as C-in-C would go and be replaced by an Army Council. A directorate would help the military members of the new council, while an Inspector General would report regularly upon the troops' state of readiness for campaigning. The desired General Staff would not be achieved until wholesale changes were made among the senior ranks. Finally, a permanent secretariat was proposed to serve the revivified Defence Committee that was already engaged in examining the larger questions of home and imperial defence. Upon Balfour's insistence all these recommendations were executed immediately. The Army Council was created by Letters Patent. Eight senior generals were removed from post and four military members appointed, directors assigned to their directorates and an Inspector General nominated. Each proposal was enthusiastically endorsed by Repington in *The Times*. Kitchener wanted to know why a body without any experienced military man should impose its designs upon the army authorities. Surely Esher would never have got away with exceeding his mandate if the army had not been so discredited in South Africa?[7] Upon further reflection Repington had second thoughts he expressed privately. Initially he had unreservedly supported root and branch reform because at the time his thoughts were set exclusively upon the future. He was convinced Esher's reforms would strengthen the army in its dealings with the politicians. He had been unreservedly impressed by the Reconstruction Committee's rapid completion of its tasks, comparing it most favourably with 'the emasculated responses of an ordinary committee's report'.[8] At Printing House Square it did not go unnoticed how often Repington was spoken of most favourably. Consequently, his in-house status was greatly enhanced. When the time came to comment on the army's administrative reform, where he led *The Times'* editorials unhesitatingly followed.

A. L. Haliburton and R. H. Knox, two former permanent undersecretaries at the War Office, natural allies of Sir Henry Campbell Bannerman, questioned the constitutional propriety of Esher's suggested changes, frequently expressing their trenchant opposition. Repington had hoped advocates of the new rather than apologists for the old would have been more in evidence, but instead Knox and Haliburton, with scarcely a dissenting voice, mounted a determinedly effective defence of the civil branch of the War Office against Esher's incursions. Esher having effectively promoted himself as the sole begetter of the triumvirate's recommendations deservedly bore the brunt of their criticism, although the real villain of the piece was George Clarke. He had caused the government considerable embarrassment by his bitter attack on the Finance Department. Although there had been no real evidence to support Clarke's allegations, Esher stood by everything he had written. When Haliburton mounted a further powerful attack upon Clarke, he characteristically urged Buckle to employ Amery's acerbic skills promising to furnish him with all the necessary information.

Not everything had gone as Repington had at first hoped and expected. Called as a witness by the triumvirate, he told them exactly what he thought. They had listened politely, but he gained the inescapable impression that the committee served only Esher's interests. Concerning Intelligence, Esher had taken particular notice of what Repington had to say. Preparing his evidence, Repington had been amazed then appalled by the number of 'fifth rate men' who, somehow or other, had inveigled their way into his former department. He concluded, twelve only of the thirty-two in post (he listed their names) were worth keeping.[9] He insisted nothing worthwhile would ever be achieved until Kitchener was made Chief of the General Staff. To appoint anyone else to the key post of CGS would be 'an utter disgrace'.[10] Repington chose not to believe Esher's explanation that Kitchener had not been considered because he refused to make himself available. Repington believed the truth was Esher had taken against Kitchener and the other committee members had been obliged to accept his conclusions.

The members of the Army Council had already been assigned their places, yet Repington continued to question their suitability. To Esher, he listed those few merits he discerned but stressed rather their many faults. He knew them all well, none better than Lyttelton, his former fag master at Eton, now designated Chief of the General Staff. As a man he could not have liked or admired 'NG' more. No officer in the British army was a better cricketer. Unfortunately the question was not what the general knew about cricket but what he knew about imperial defence. The answer was *very little if anything at all*. Esher had chosen as the Chief of Staff someone generally acknowledged to be 'quite hopeless', an absolute duffer. No member of the triumvirate would have disagreed with that estimate. All had favoured French as CGS because he believed 'in joint Naval and Military operations'. The king, however, had not shared their admiration.[11]

Repington considered 'NG's' appointment to be beyond the pale; Charles Douglas's appointment as Adjutant General also caused him concern. Douglas possessed much 'the strongest character' of the four generals and so would inevitably dominate the rest. The Army Council would 'never get beyond the regulations for they are his Bible and his God'. Repington, who had served with Douglas, knew him to be shy, reserved and not particularly imaginative. But this was altogether to miss the point. The quality Esher sought in his ideal Adjutant General was a conspicuous willingness to question nothing, to play the game strictly according to the rules. These requirements Douglas fulfilled exactly.

Of Wolfe-Murray, Master General of the Ordnance and fourth member of the council, Repington entertained fewer reservations. They had once been colleagues in Intelligence and he thought him 'much the best and the most worth having' of the four. At least he had spent some time contemplating the great problems of national defence, though, like all the rest, he knew nothing about naval planning. Wolfe-Murray's greatest failing was his cautious and reserved nature. 'His opinion,' Repington warned, 'would have to be dragged out of him.'[12]

Repington said nothing of 'Plum', the Quartermaster General. He knew Esher kept himself well informed about old Etonians. Presumably he already knew Plumer in his college days had been a 'scug', scarcely promise of intellectual brilliance. Repington's damning critique of all four appointees was, as they were accustomed to run in blinkers they would be only too happy to continue to do so. He feared their mediocrity posed a severe threat to the success of the reforms. They lacked the capacity to break the mould. Their ordinariness was guaranteed to frustrate the most brilliant initiative.

Esher did not need to be told that the four men were undistinguished. The same could have been said about the candidates he had earlier considered and then discarded. But their collective lack of distinction was unimportant. He believed a well-designed administrative system ought to run efficiently whatever the qualities of those who temporarily happened to be in charge. Repington frequently sternly censured Esher for always thinking in terms of systems rather than personnel. 'Men make success as much if not more than systems,' he would urge.[13] He forecast Esher would soon be disillusioned by his choice of CGS. His insistent mantra from the very beginning of the triumvirate's reform exercise had been, Kitchener is the only man of the front rank. A year later and it was Esher who pleaded with Kitchener to accept the post, for now he believed only K of K's titanic presence sufficient to ensure an ill-disposed incoming Liberal administration would not dismantle the military reforms he had so carefully devised and put in place. But despite all verbal blandishments, the offer of a greatly increased salary and a Field Marshal's baton, Kitchener refused to change his mind. He would not have anything to do with the General Staff, whom he considered a hopeless, hapless bunch.[14]

Repington stubbornly refused to acknowledge the suitability of anyone other than Kitchener as CGS. He knew he favoured autocratic systems. Kitchener had demonstrated this trait both in his Sudan and South African campaigns. He also had good reason to remember K's prolonged, intransigent opposition to the military member of the Viceroy's Council. But Kitchener was the one military genius England possessed. Repington's intuition responded to romantic, outdated notions, and in Kitchener's case intuition altogether displaced reason. The model he had in mind was hopelessly antediluvian; the warrior monarch leading his troops into battle; Harold at Hastings, Henry at Agincourt, or a Captain-General, like Oliver Cromwell or John Churchill. So powerful were Repington's romantic yearnings for a Nietzschean-like military super-man, he could contemplate with equanimity the possibility of Kitchener dominating the rest of the military, even the Secretary of State for War. The navy afforded a convenient if not entirely persuasive paradigm in Admiral Jack Fisher. Repington was never entirely purged of this danger-ous delusion. He refused to acknowledge that although exceptional men are capable of achieving miracles, they are just as likely to perpetrate spectacular blunders.

To Raymond Marker, who shared his exaggerated estimate of Kitchener's worth, he would admit, as he never could to Esher, the full extent of his unbounded admiration. A detailed litany, he conceded, would require 'a small volume'. He was convinced 'for the good of the army' it was 'an absolute necessity' a place should be found for Kitchener at the War Office. The manner or place of the appointment did not matter. The overriding consideration was Kitchener's supreme quality as a leader: his brilliant flashes of intuition, his unrivalled capacity for improvisation, the immense force of his character that filled the hearts and minds of all who served under him with admiration and absolute confidence. Repington feared 'the powers that be' would resist Kitchener's appointment. 'They fear him because they fancy they will be overshadowed by his figure.' In the army confidence in authority had diminished and present discontents would only multiply. Kitchener's presence would guarantee the 'silencing of senior generals' jealousies', the direction of policy 'on purely military lines', the 'creation of a business-like atmosphere', and not least, the protection of the interests of all army officers. Everything pointed to the need for 'a strong controlling hand'.

There were times when Repington's grasp of political realities could be amazingly enfeebled. He seriously considered the possibility of Kitchener using the House of Lords as a suitable platform upon which to 'build a party of sturdy young men who want for a leader'. To suppose Kitchener might become the focus 'of all the conservative influences in the country already alarmed by the spread of Socialism', revealed, when blinded by his hero worship, that Repington could be as foolish a political pundit as the next man.[15] His exaggerated estimate of Kitchener's capacities, he extravagantly demonstrated in two short articles for Garvin's *Observer* in 1910. First he touted Kitchener as 'the ideal Indian Viceroy', next as 'the best man to succeed Haldane as Minister for War', then finally as the 'ideal Chief of the Imperial General Staff'. Repington insisted that Kitchener possessed in abundance the credentials to fill any of these exceedingly important appointments. 'He has all except self-seeking and self-laudatory oratory ... excels in statesmanship ... will never be made the instrument of any party, faction or clique ... Kitchener stands alone for England and England has need of such a man.'[16]

The old soldier in Repington was not always as unreservedly enamoured of Esher's proposals as might have been supposed from his comments in *The Times*. The urgencies of daily journalism did not always allow time for mature, leisured reflection. Appointments to the Army Council, he admitted, had meant the unceremonious dumping of some very senior army officers. In the army, respect for rank was exaggerated. When rank was slighted, memories could be notoriously long. He was not pleading for a return to the old days, merely expressing a cautious awareness that sensitivities and expectations were not to be ignored. Only a fool would heedlessly disregard them. The disturbance after the dismissal of the generals had been shattering. Nicholson, Kelly-Kenny, French and Brackenbury had gone at a stroke of Esher's pen. There was more than a whiff of jobbery in the air. Henry Wilson wrote, 'Our days pass like nightmares.'[17] But Wilson's particular nightmare was that his claim to promotion might be ignored and his ambition thwarted. It was the treatment of 'Old Nick' that had particularly shocked Repington, and he doubted whether it had been altogether wise of Esher to insist upon the appointment of Prince Arthur, Duke of Connaught, as Inspector General. Appointing a royal duke had made the slaughter of the generals look even more 'a gross job'. That was not the only possible cause of future contention concerning Connaught. He had been made a Field Marshal in 1902, which was all right so far as it went, but to pay him more than the CGS was 'absurd'.[18] It seemed to Repington that Esher needed to take greater care. Should they so wish, the many friends of the deposed generals could make life very uncomfortable for him.

Britain possessed 'no means for co-ordinating defence problems to deal with them as a whole'. This was the problem Esher's committee addressed in its first report. As was asserted, it was a complete waste of their time reforming the War Office unless their suggested reforms were associated with the means 'to obtain and co-ordinate for the use of the Cabinet all the information and expert advice required to shape national policy in war and to determine the necessary preparations in peace'. They proposed a Committee of Defence that in due time became the Committee of Imperial Defence, which would 'invariably' be chaired by the Prime Minister. He would have 'absolute discretion' in selecting his fellow members.[19] When Esher recommended the Defence Committee should have a permanent secretariat, it had not seemed particularly significant, but time would reveal its vital importance. The initiative had been prompted by Esher, who feared a Unionist defeat in the forthcoming general election. He thought a Liberal victory would leave them hostage to every woolly minded Radical, peevish pacifist and revolutionary Socialist in Parliament. It seemed exceedingly unlikely that Campbell-Bannerman, an avowed opponent of the committee, once he was prime minister would meekly act in Balfour's stead and change nothing. A permanent secretariat would provide at least some element of continuity. In October 1905 Esher was himself made a permanent member of the Defence Committee, the arrangement approved by R. B. Haldane, soon to be Secretary of State for War. What was more, Haldane pledged he would try to increase the committee's permanent element. At the beginning of the new Liberal administration, when the Defence Committee's future was most uncertain and vulnerable, Haldane successfully begged its life from Campbell-Bannerman. Once given remission for a year, the committee's future was never thereafter seriously challenged.

Repington had not been unduly concerned at the prospect of a Liberal government. His work for Spender's *Westminster Gazette* had brought him close to that party's heart. As a government the Liberals would face very different problems from those they had experienced as an almost perpetual opposition. As with any government, the nation's security would be their first concern: '*salus populi suprema lex*'.[20] Few seemed to remember Campbell-Bannerman had once been Secretary of State for War. Repington had already sounded out Sir Henry, a contact that in the near future he thought might prove useful.

He had never shared Esher's unqualified admiration for Balfour as a military strategist.[21] One might have supposed otherwise for the strategic problem that had particularly concerned Balfour was how best in future to co-ordinate Britain's defence plans. The navy was the nation's favourite service. The army enjoyed occasional moments of popular acclaim, but its familiar function was as the services' financial whipping boy. Therefore, searching for a 'sensible' defence policy, Balfour concluded that to economise on the army was the best way to meet unavoidable increases in the cost of naval armaments. To achieve such economies the army needed to be reformed. Its role should be limited to the defence of India and garrison duties in British overseas territories. Balfour, like all 'Blue Water' thinkers, confidently assumed the navy would permanently ensure Britain's freedom from invasion. Since the committee's members were all convinced Blue Water doctrinaires, they conveniently shared Balfour's prejudice. The Admiralty perceived no flaw in such thinking; the War Office was not similarly convinced. Occasionally they entertained the notion the Defence Committee might not know its business. They asked how it could be sensible or equitable always to suppose whenever the navy needed more money it was best provided by cutting the cost of the army.

At first, India's internal and external security had been the committee's prime concern, but eventually it chose to examine, if only briefly, an old, familiar conundrum. Was Britain vulnerable to invasion? This was the question the army always asked whenever threatened with another bout of retrenchment. They wished to remind anyone intent upon draining money from the army's coffers that their pre-eminent task was to protect Britain by hurling any invading force back into the sea. Admiral Fisher, never happier than when kicking lame army dogs, prevailed upon Balfour to publish the 1903 Invasion Inquiry's conclusion, information given the House eventually in May 1905. To wild approbation Balfour assured the Commons that the navy was overwhelmingly strong. *The Times* wrote an approving editorial but to everyone's surprise Repington dissented. He insisted it was neither prudent nor proper for the Prime Minister to discuss strategy in Parliament for then the Commons might be tempted to reduce the services' annual estimates. If funds were reduced any further, the army would not even be able to defend India's North West frontier effectively.

The case Repington had made was scarcely convincing and brought a torrent of criticism down upon his head. Esher was amazed and outraged. Until that moment Repington had been the staunchest, public advocate of the Defence Committee. Did he not realise the 'ill effect his comments would have'? For the first time he had missed the point of a great argument. 'How could [he] as a patriot employ the dissecting knife so thoroughly?'[22] In a further letter Esher rebutted each of Repington's arguments in turn. Between these two letters George Clarke spatchcocked an angry denunciation of Repington to which he did not respond.

The old bruiser Clarke's anger was to be expected, but at the same time Repington thought it a pity they should disagree so frequently. He did not like being at odds with him any more than with Esher. Both, however, had missed the crucial point. The annual parliamentary estimate debates horribly impinged upon the thinking of the two service departments, as fearing the worst they each hoped they would be the beneficiary of Treasury largesse.

Repington tried to forget the Balfour invasion statement but could not. It was still very much on his mind when, more than a year later, he wrote to tell Esher he was a strong supporter of the Committee of Defence, 'but when I am asked to express fidelity to my ideal, I can only think of faith, hope and charity'. Arthur Balfour's words had 'left much to be desired'. He had given a handle to all who sought to reduce the army to impotence by imposing ridiculous economies. The primary task of the Defence Committee was not to worship unthinkingly dangerous political shibbo-leths but to determine objectively 'the bases upon which the military organisation of the Empire would rest'. He assured Esher he would 'not write thus in *The Times*'. But at the same time, he could not be expected to conceal his anger and frustration with this 'hole in the corner business of political *alternativement*'. That made him 'sick unto death'.[23] Defence should stand above party-political considerations.

Esher's immediate response was to insist they both sought the same end, differing only on how best to attain it.[24] He wondered whether that would that be enough to guarantee Repington's public silence? A few weeks later he told off his bulldog, Clarke, to attempt to calm Repington, but Clarke was not too confident about the prospects of success. 'I will see what I can do,' he responded, 'but he is rather inflated.'[25]

The change of government had no deleterious consequences for the Defence Committee, since the Liberal leader happily left its future con-duct to Haldane who accepted Balfour's creation as a fait accompli. In two letters to Leo Maxse, Repington explained why he unreservedly supported the Defence Committee.[26] It was no excrescence but 'an indispensable part of the machinery of government'. Its greatest value was undoubtedly 'to co-ordinate the work of various departments'. It might enjoy even greater importance in the future as 'the nucleus of a great Imperial staff, with representatives on it from India and all our great colonies'. Repington well understood the importance of the Defence Committee as a co-ordinating agency but did not altogether perceive how Balfour, by means of the framework he had created, ensured that in future the Cabinet, and not Parliament, would determine defence strategy. He underestimated the Tory leader's mastery of civil military relations.

With the status of the Defence Committee greatly enhanced and Esher a permanent member, it was more than ever important Repington should remain his friend. He patiently instructed the irascible Maxse why it was their 'duty' to support the Defence Committee. There would otherwise be a danger they might revert to 'the old, disastrous system of government in compartments'. This last thought had been prompted by the behaviour of certain generals. Without reference to the Defence Committee they were busily planning the army's strategic response should there be war with Germany in the near future. The prospect of the nascent General Staff acting independently of the Defence Committee pleased neither Repington nor Esher. When they advocated the creation of a modern general staff they had not desired the generals to ignore the Defence Committee.

4   Arnold Forster lays the foundation for the General Staff

Repington enthusiastically greeted H. O. Arnold-Forster's appointment as Secretary of State for War.[1] He had been impressed by the short book the minister had published at the height of the South African War setting out the lessons he considered Britain needed to learn. However, what he did not appreciate was the minister suffered from an incurable affliction – an inability to appreciate, or tolerate, any views other than his own.

Repington had long been certain the creation of a General Staff offered a sovereign specific that would cure many of the army's ailments.[2] This opinion he shared with most up-and-coming young army officers; the top brass, almost without exception, thought otherwise. Repington observed, not a single, senior commander in South Africa had known how to make the best use of his staff. It was scarcely credible their confused, unprofessional endeavours should have occurred three decades *after* the Franco-Prussian war. That conflict ought to have impressed upon any thinking soldier one major consideration. Modern warfare required specialist staff officers to think critically about tactics, strategy and logistics. All the necessary preparations needed to be made in advance. This was a lesson all the other major European powers had long acknowledged, but the British seemed to assume they need do nothing, believing their naval predominance permanently guaranteed their inviolability. Britain's continental neighbours sought to buttress their safety and sovereignty by diplomatic alliances backed by massive conscripted armies. Britain behaved as though the world had not changed. Increasingly diplomatic isolation seemed more dangerous than splendid. Technological innovation and the constantly rising cost of armaments made world-wide naval dominance more difficult to sustain.

Spenser Wilkinson's book *The Brain of an Army* (1890) had described the constitution and work of the German General Staff. It had attracted little interest for the overwhelming British disposition was to show suspicion of new ideas and to cling tenaciously to the familiar and traditional. The alien idea of a General Staff was soon forgotten at the War Office.

Very few believed, like Repington, that professionalism would be instilled in the British army only when the need to create an equivalent of the German system was accepted. The reason he had wanted to join Intelligence was because he thought it 'the nearest approach we possessed to a modern General Staff'.[3]

After humiliation at the hands of the Boers, in the time-honoured British fashion, committees were set up to find out what had gone wrong hoping thereby to learn how to avoid a similar debacle in the future. Characteristically, committees spawned more committees, one of which was intended to determine the skills, knowledge and experience that best qualified an army officer for staff duties. To Repington's disgust Lieutenant General H. D. Hutchinson was appointed chairman. 'A tragedy,' Repington fumed, 'such a fool of a General should have charge of a task for which he is patently unqualified.'[4] Opinion in the army was hopelessly divided about what an officer's duties, remuneration and tenure should be. At the centre of this maelstrom of uncertainty and contradiction was Lyttelton, the recently appointed Chief of the General Staff, a man fit only to make 'confusion worse confounded'. Scarcely surprisingly, given such ineffectual leadership, the recently created Army Council had proved no better than its predecessor. The hoped for, clear, unambiguous advice had not materialised. Council members endlessly vacillated, procrastinated and bickered. They were set in their former ways, unable to break with the past. Repington likened them to a mule train.

The impasse was finally broken when the opposition asked if the public were getting value for money. It was now openly stated in the House that the Army Council and new Directorate were hopelessly inefficient. Repington feared, if incompetence were disclosed – something any businesslike, thorough inquiry would rapidly reveal – it might well prompt a subsequent witch-hunt. Unqualified amateurs would then feel free to dream up hopelessly impractical schemes. He, like all military men, thought it quite proper soldiers should point out their failings to one another, but it was no business of civilians to poke their noses into such matters. His anxiety was not feigned. When he had pressed Esher to send him examples of the council's work, what he received several months later proved to be 'rather jejune ... No question was considered from a sufficiently lofty standpoint'. His worst fears were confirmed. Esher now acknowledged Lyttelton was the greatest incubus to progress, but to perceive the inadequacies of the CGS as the fount of *all* their troubles did not alter one inconvenient reality; Lyttelton, limpet-like, continued to cling tenaciously to office.

In two articles published 18 and 25 May 1905, Repington directly addressed the Secretary of State. He insisted Arnold-Forster knew better than anybody why reform was urgently needed. Were he to establish 'a General Staff of the modern stamp', then his place in the pantheon of great military reformers was assured. Repington acknowledged the contribution made by those who had written about the General Staff and had demonstrated the German army's staff system was 'the most effective weapon in their armoury'. Some supposed Britain already possessed the framework of a satisfactory General Staff system. Repington assured them they were mistaken. It remained to be created.

In his second article, he demonstrated the January 1905 Army Order, setting out the duties of the General Staff, had been ill conceived and was much too narrow. He proposed a number of alternatives. To avoid an incomplete, insufficiently trained, inefficient, unpopular General Staff, 'The soldier of greatest ability and experience must always be appointed as Chief.' Then he insisted, 'No officer should be appointed other than upon merit.' Any General Staff candidate before appointment should have completed satisfactorily a task allotted by either the CGS or the C-in-C India. Alternatively, a candidate should have undertaken instruction or service at Headquarters. This would guarantee whomsoever was in high command would have received General Staff training. But if these suggestions were ignored, the army would drift back to its 1899 condition when generals 'had to be sifted and sorted out at the cost of many disappointments, the loss of many noble lives and the expenditure of two hundred and fifty millions in money'. He was well aware that what he had said would cause offence to the 'old guard'. Nevertheless, it was imperative they realise 'An aristocracy of talent is indispensable for success in modern war.' Buckle supported Repington with a powerful editorial. 'Any intelligent, serious nation should acknowledge, a trained General Staff is the condition precedent of success in war. Without it disaster is fore-ordained.'[5] Scarcely surprisingly, Esher fully agreed; they had been mulling the subject over together for months.

Repington doubted whether there was 'a single person in the War Office who had the least idea where he wanted to go or how to get there'.[6] Arnold-Forster knew better than that. He immediately sounded out Henry Wilson, the War Office's keenest advocate of a modern General Staff. The minister thought Wilson's response describing the purpose and duties of the General Staff, 'the most able, lucid and constructive paper he had read'.[7] Yet it took vigorous prodding from Esher and Clarke before at last he set down his own thoughts, effectively adopting Wilson's ideas and words. He asked Lyttelton to comment but, as might have been anticipated, heard nothing. When Repington enquired of Arnold-Forster whether he had drafted instructions for the formation of a General Staff, the minister's response was to insist he too was concerned about the delay. Whether unwilling or unable to wait any longer, Arnold-Forster finally gave his memorandum to Balfour. He attached to it a slightly hysterical note. If there were to be a genuine General Staff, Arnold-Forster insisted, it was either 'now or never'.[8] To this urgent injunction Balfour paid no heed. Another month went by.

On 11 November 1905 Arnold-Forster *ordered* Lyttelton to implement his instructions *immediately*. Still nothing happened. After another ten days Wilson was told to release the information to the press, at which Repington congratulated Arnold-Forster. He had made 'a serious attempt to graft the greatest product of the school of Moltke upon a somewhat rebellious British stem'. There was much he approved, but it would have been better had the minister's instructions been accompanied by a warrant or army order. Nor should it ever be forgotten, the proposed scheme's success would depend upon the appointment of the right person as Chief of the General Staff. He must be someone possessed of out-standing abilities; tactful, experienced and utterly ruthless. Such a man would not be found without a diligent search. Paraphrasing Hannah Glasse's familiar culinary instruction, Repington cautioned, 'First we must catch our Moltke before we put him into pickle.'[9]

The army order was drafted but never published. Within weeks the Unionist administration resigned. Repington was unconcerned about the resulting delay for he assumed it would be only temporary. After all the recent trials and tribulations he refused to be anything other than positive about the future of the General Staff.

Repington and the minister had engaged in many rough, tough exchanges in the columns of *The Times*, yet the correspondent never bore the politician any long-term resentment. He found much to admire even though he undoubtedly regretted Arnold-Forster's unwillingness to acknowledge any merit in ideas other than his own. In his private letters written after the politician's death in 1909, there was a note of genuine regret at his early demise. In 1910 Repington informed Esher he had been engaged 'in conflabs with the Tories' and trusted the 'venom' in his relationship with the Unionist Party had 'disappeared with poor AF'.[10] A decade later in *Vestigia*, Repington paid Arnold-Forster an handsome tribute. There was scarcely an unfavourable reference to what had often been a troubled, ill-tempered relationship. He insisted, the minister deserved acknowledgment and great credit for laying the foundations of the system that marked 'the beginning of real reform'.[11]

5   Anglo-French military conversations

The Unionist government resigned in December 1905. A month elapsed before victory in the general election confirmed the Liberals would form the next administration. During that period of political uncertainty a diplomatic altercation over Morocco between Germany and France threatened to involve Britain. Germany's actions had been designed to reassure Germans their interests were not being overlooked in North Africa. But the move had also been intended to punish and humiliate their arch-foe, the French foreign minister Delcassé. What anti-German circles in Britain feared was France might become too dependent upon a Germany whose bullying behaviour had seemed encouraged by the Russian's earlier humiliation at the hands of Japan. Germany's share of Moroccan trade was much less than that enjoyed by France or Britain, but in the kaiser's belligerent rant at Tangiers that marked the beginning of the crisis he had spoken not of economic imperatives but of diplomatic and military concerns. In *Vestigia* Repington claimed the crisis threatened the peace of Europe. Yet at the time he had virtually ignored the fluttering in the international dovecote prompted by Wilhelm's bombastic words and behaviour. Repington judged 'impossible' the likelihood of that particular 'bolt from the blue' leading to war.[1]

The Anglo-French Entente (1904) had effectively ended Britain's self-inflicted diplomatic isolation. Wilhelm feared the entente was intended as a stepping-stone towards a Triple Agreement with Russia. Were that to become reality, then encirclement, *einkreisungspolitik*, Germany's greatest fear, would have been realised. Repington was uncertain of how the diplomatic scene might develop, wondering whether older loyalties and enmities might not triumph. Until the signing of the Anglo-Russian Convention in August 1907, the defence of India's North-West Frontier against Russian territorial ambitions remained a key consideration in his strategic thinking. Despite the Franco-Russian Dual Alliance (1894), he warned Russia might yet join with Germany and Austria-Hungary in a recreation of the *Dreikaiserbund*.[2] But each year Repington had grown increasingly convinced Germany, more than any other nation, posed the outstanding threat to British security. England's diplomatic priority, he believed, should be to detach as many powers from Germany as possible.

Repington never tired of repeating, political decisions determined strategic choices. But what if politicians were confused, even unaware of the consequences their decisions might promote? There seemed a distinct reluctance to acknowledge that the Anglo-French Entente necessarily had military and naval repercussions. Of course, soldiers and politicians saw matters differently. Politicians, like diplomats, always wanted to retain their freedom of choice for as long as possible; soldiers wanted potential enemies or friends identified swiftly. The precise terms of an alliance appealed to soldiers more than the necessarily vague commitments of an entente.

Soldiers were inclined to underestimate, deny, or discount the difficulties politicians and diplomats faced. They would insist their conception was 'honest', 'straightforward', 'black and white' and 'in the national interest'. Those who rejected their 'simple', 'obvious', 'insignificant demands' did so from 'weakness', 'pusillanimity' or a 'lack of determination'. They claimed they had no political axe to grind but forgot how frequently they made common cause with the parliamentary opposition. On foreign affairs, most politicians, whether government or opposition, extolled the doctrine of continuity, while on defence they similarly concurred about the importance of an all-powerful navy. Consequently, few politicians chose to criticise in Parliament the conduct of foreign or defence policy. Those who did so were more likely to come from the back than the front benches. Press criticism usually was customarily confined to the smaller battalions of Radical journalism rather than the Tory or Liberal popular press.

During the 1905/06 crisis it suited the politicians to procrastinate whereas British military and naval planners insisted they could not. Repington told Marker, the French, anticipating a German attack through Belgium, were 'trooping back to their barracks [while] all the talk in Germany is of war'.[3] With uncharacteristic unanimity, naval and military chiefs decided, in the event of war, Britain must and would side with France. They insisted public opinion allowed for no alternative. That claim was most unusual. Service chiefs rarely if ever concerned themselves with what the public thought. For that matter, a feature of the prolonged general election campaign was the electorate's virtual silence on questions of defence and foreign affairs. A popular electoral slogan of the victorious Liberal Party had emphasised the priority of pursuing peace and economy in armament expenditure. Liberal politicians were ill-informed about foreign affairs. The minority who took any interest generally favoured Imperial, Protestant Germany rather than Republican, Catholic France. Whatever service chiefs claimed, their decision to support France clearly owed nothing to popular opinion.

When France agreed to convene an international conference at Algeçiras to adjudicate on the Moroccan squabble, the Germans immediately set out to win over British opinion. Repington feared they might 'pull the wool over the eyes of easy-going Britishers'.[4] *The Times* castigated pro-German, Liberal politicians as 'well intentioned, naive sentimentalists' while Repington warned them, they were hopelessly deluded if they supposed for a moment their words would promote peace when they were much more likely to persuade Germany to fight. He insisted, most Britons were resolved to fight side by side with France. Where was his evidence to support that assertion? He also talked up France's military capacity, her preparedness for war. He warned the Germans it would be foolish for them to think victory a certainty.[5]

Next day, Huguet, the French military attaché, invited himself to dine with Repington and did not leave until the early hours of morning. Immediately, Repington prepared a résumé of their conversation for Sir Edward Grey. He wrote that the French apparently sought reassurance. They were uncertain whether the new Liberal government would act as its Tory predecessor had promised but what exactly that was they did not disclose. Apparently, Cambon and Lansdowne, in earlier conversations, had 'made the situation perfectly clear'. Unfortunately, Grey had made no similar 'declaration'. Repington had told Huguet, 'so far as [he] could judge, public opinion in England would be solid on the side of France if she were the victim of unprovoked attack', but that was likewise insufficient. The French insisted, if the Germans were to be resisted then 'prompt action and immediate decision' were required. Effectively, what this amounted to was 'formal assurances'.[6]

The letter was despatched by express mail to Northumberland where Grey was electioneering. Later that day Repington met an agitated General Grierson, the DMO who insisted he was being deliberately excluded from meetings of a subcommittee of the Defence Committee. By right he ought to attend but French had been invited in his stead. What made matters worse was Fisher's presence. What exactly was going on? Repington promised to find out. He immediately wrote to Esher telling him he had met 'a flustered War Office dignitary' who had denounced him and his cabal for 'planning military coups ... in the case of war without consulting the General Staff'. He artlessly enquired whether they might talk about this. A furious Esher raged at the 'busybodies of the General Staff twisting an innocent discussion into something sinister', but well knew the 'discussion group' had been scarcely innocent.[7]

The strategic planning subcommittee, as the 'discussion group' was formally known, was Fisher's brainchild. His strategic plan – a joint, amphibious operation – was the first to be considered. Repington dismissed Fisher's idea to attack Germany's Baltic littoral. It could never be more than 'a side-show' when the 'heart of the war [would be] on the Meuse. All else would be mere tickling at the extremities'.[8] There was not a soldier who was not certain Fisher's scheme was quite impracticable but weeks elapsed before they finally pronounced it unsuitable. In truth, had it been the most brilliant scheme they would not have accepted it. Had they done so, effectively they would have ceded hegemony in all future strategic planning exercises to the Admiralty. Even at a time of supposed grave national danger, selfish, myopic departmental imperatives determined the attitudes of senior naval and military personnel. There was no co-ordination, certainly no agreed strategy for a joint response by army and navy. It was this impasse the meeting had been called to solve.

The navy's representative had not been Fisher, as Grierson had supposed, but Captain C. L. Ottley, recently promoted Director of Naval Intelligence. Ottley's military equivalent, Grierson, ought have been invited, but instead Sir John French, General Officer Commanding Aldershot attended, because he was thought to favour amphibious operations and unlike Grierson was not closely identified with the General Staff's obsessive concern for an independent, military, continental strategy.[9] The four men had gathered to consider *any* suitable response to a German attack upon France. The detailed planning would be undertaken by French and Ottley. The committee intended to reconvene on 6 January to discuss progress, but by that date Repington's thumb was well and truly stuck in the strategic pie.

When next Repington met Esher, Reggie was his customary, emollient self without any hint of displeasure or disagreement. His next port of call was the Admiralty where the First Sea Lord was in boisterous mood, reeling off their preparations in anticipation of a possible Franco-German crisis. These fortunately did not include his notion to 'Copenhagen' the German fleet. When he first mischievously advertised this idea, the king had wondered whether Jacky was mad.[10] 'Jack means to act upon his own initiative at the first sign of danger,' Repington told Marker. 'He is bringing home a lot more ships to form a new Western Fleet.' That was guaranteed to enrage the kaiser. What he chose not to tell Marker was that Fisher believed the German army would wallop the French. Nor did he disclose, when the French had attempted to discuss naval co-operation, Fisher had turned the idea down flat. All he wanted them to do was place their submarines at Dunkirk.

Repington still thought the risk of war negligible. The kaiser would fight only when he was certain Britain would not join the French. But there was always an incalculable element. 'We might drift into war owing to the d—d stupidity of German diplomacy.' He doubted the Germans possessed the military strength to crush France completely. He knew exaggerated accounts of the German army's strength owed much to the reports of Edward Gleichen the British military attaché. Repington had always thought him excessively gullible. He had probably been 'got at by the Berliners' and it was this that accounted for the 'extravagant forecasts of what Bill & Co. proposed to do'.[11]

First post on New Year's Day brought Grey's reply to Repington. He had been 'much interested' in the account of the meeting with Huguet and affirmed he had 'not receded from anything which Lord Lansdowne said to the French'.[12] Although Grey's tone was guarded, Repington thought surely he had said enough to remove any remaining doubts in French minds. Yet Huguet insisted some embassy staff were still concerned. The British government needed to state categorically it was prepared to take up arms in defence of France. Grey would never say as much. Quite simply, an entente was not an alliance.

Repington could not let the matter rest there. His 'sense of duty', he explained to Sir Edward, obliged him to point out 'certain dangers upon the horizon'. He assured Grey military conversations with the French would be more than useful. The speed of modern warfare made such preparatory exchanges a necessity. Sir Edward should be acutely aware of the congruence of military and diplomatic considerations, particularly when it came to the defence of the Low Countries. Repington rehearsed the history of Gladstone's 1870 signing of the guarantee of Belgian neutrality. By the time the guarantee had been signed, the first battles of the Franco-Prussian war had already been fought. A similar delay now would be fatal. Germany honoured treaty obligations only when they were backed by force. Therefore, now was the time to act. They must flush out the Germans and force them to reveal their true hand. Then he turned adroitly to consider domestic political pressures, asserting that in a national emergency a Liberal government would be subject to internal as well as external pressures. He had discussed with Huguet 'several alternatives respecting co-operative action with the French in time of war'. The French attaché had strongly advocated 'assistance to Belgium'. That, Repington insisted, was the best strategic option. It suited French as well as 'British naval and military needs'. Then he added shrewdly, 'I am inclined to think that [assisting Belgium] will be the easiest for the present government to assent to.'[13] Repington was not politically naive. He knew to talk to the French about military dispositions was a political act.

Politicians and diplomats might for convenience sake argue the contrary, but Anglo-French military conversations would effectively convert the 1904 entente into an alliance.

A letter arrived for Repington from Clarke: could he discover whether Huguet was prepared to sound out the French naval and military staffs about their intentions. The request did not imply that Clarke and Esher had abandoned their preferred strategy. They still prayed Ottley would come up with a suitable plan to take advantage of the navy's overwhelming strength and flexibility. Repington emphasised the merits of pragmatism. He would do anything 'to insure the French alliance'. His use of that word *alliance* was deliberate. Esher like the rest needed to be reminded; just as circumstances altered cases, so personal prejudice ought not to determine their final choice of strategy. To do so would be to risk their 'eternal condemnation by history'.[14]

That British strategic thinking was hopelessly sundered was confirmed for Repington the following evening. Dining at The Rag, Grierson and a former colleague from Intelligence declared their opposition to the navy's proposed scheme, insisting the army's was the better option. If Germany threatened to violate Belgium's borders the army would have two divisions in Namur within thirteen days of mobilisation. By the thirty-second day the whole British army would be at Antwerp. They confidently asserted this would be enough to turn the German tide but Esher and Clarke did not agree. They rejected all talk of Belgium. They were not prepared to abandon the naval option on the supposition that Germany *might* attack France through Belgium. Informed by Repington that Fisher had effectively dismissed the French navy as not relevant, Clarke concluded correctly the Admiral had failed to think through the strategic picture thoroughly. Esher, however, insisted it was Repington who was mistaken. Fisher had sound, strategic plans. He had simply not wished to discuss them with Repington.

The posturing over strategy went on unabated. On 5 January Repington again dined with the French attaché. Huguet complained the French had been told nothing. He warned, the British could forget ideas of an amphibious operation. All France required was a simple answer to a simple question. If Germany violated Belgian neutrality, did Britain intend to join the Belgians, or tag on to the French line of deployment between Verdun and Mexieres? Repington's attempts to reassure Huguet were unsuccessful. Then he bearded Clarke and Esher, who were also worried about Britain's vulnerability. The public, entirely engaged with the general election, offered the Germans an unprecedented opportunity to catch Britain off guard, a chance they were unlikely to ignore. Something needed to be done.

What they chose to do – prepare for future military conversations between British and French staff – strongly suggests they were motivated not by the immediate state of international uncertainty but by some as yet unknown future contingency. As Repington alone held no official position, they agreed that he should be the one to approach the French, employing Huguet as intermediary. Whatever information Huguet acquired, Repington would pass on to the British government. They drafted eleven questions for Huguet to pose to the *Conseil Supérieur de la Guerre*. He left for Paris on Sunday 7 January, returned late on 11 January and reported next morning to Repington.

The French had done everything to help make the mission successful. Clearly they wished the exchanges to continue, but *with* the British government's official imprimatur. To speed up this process, the French instructed Cambon, their ambassador, to seek a meeting with Sir Edward Grey. He had been told of Huguet's mission only the previous day. Cambon asked Grey a series of specific questions. It was soon apparent Grey would offer the French nothing other than non-specific generalities until the election was over and the Liberals were firmly installed as the government.

In a letter to Marker written some six months after these events, Repington conveyed the essence of what happened. 'When Grey learnt of my unofficial communications with France and the replies, he wired Haldane. They met in the throes of the General Election and decided to carry on with Paris from the point I had reached and to say not one word to their colleagues.' After this meeting, without either the knowledge or permission of the Prime Minister, Haldane 'authorised communications to proceed between the French Military Attaché and General Grierson direct'. Repington did not mention he had hoped to make a trip to Belgium himself but had not received the required Foreign Office sanction.[15]

Two items of news Huguet brought from France did not please Repington. The French army planned to deploy against the Germans in the same way that Napoleon had at Jena. Repington was greatly dismayed. If they did, the Germans would envelop and destroy them. Therefore, he strained every nerve to persuade the French their 'lozenge' was fatally flawed. He succeeded eventually, but it quite undermined his belief in French tactics. The other revelation was quite bizarre; a section of the French General Staff was planning to invade England. Only the previous week, Huguet had mentioned the existence of these plans but Repington had assumed they were of historic interest only. Now he learned, despite the immediate international outlook, the *Troisième Bureau* was not in the least inclined to abandon a problem that had occupied and fascinated them for years.[16]

All he had learned from Huguet, Repington passed on to Clarke and Esher. They later attended the subcommittee on strategy. This time Grierson was present. Despite Ottley's vigorous protests, naval plans were effectively jettisoned. The army's strategic thinking was totally dominant, reinforced by the French strategic preference that Fisher's scheme be abandoned and British troops committed instead to support the French army. But what if Fisher refused to ferry the troops to France?

The admiral behaved truculently but failed to hide his hurt. He insisted he neither cared what the French thought nor what they chose to do, for he had no intention of giving up his strategic plans at their say-so. He cared nothing for hurting their feelings and so would not co-operate with them on their soil. Concerning the French navy (he scarcely bothered to disguise the sneer), the Royal Navy would sort out matters for itself. Repington, who had long thought Fisher incompetent, argued the present crisis demanded the French be given *exactly* what they wanted. Fisher's duty was to guarantee the British army's safe passage to France. Seizing the political heart of the matter, Repington warned Esher, 'Unless we show a disposition to share in the real struggle at the decisive spot, then you can say good-bye to all ideas of the French Alliance!' That was the real issue wrapped up in agreeing to joint Staff talks. He did well to emphasise its importance in stark terms. If no British troops arrived in France, there would be no alliance. The Germans would have won before the first shot was fired.

In his letter to Esher, Repington addressed a central strategic issue the army planners appeared to ignore in their calculations. 'As to the employment of our troops on the continent alongside the French,' wrote Repington, 'I think we are most of us opposed to participation in a land struggle on the continent if we can avoid it.' Since the Middle Ages the small British army, whenever possible, avoided direct confrontation with the larger armies of continental enemies. Sheltering behind the overwhelming strength of the navy, Britain's wealth was used to subsidise their allies. 'Breaking foreign windows with our guineas' was how Pitt's critics described it. What the military now seemed agreed upon was that somewhere in northern France or the Low Countries the whole British army would be hurled into the balance on the side of her entente partner, hoping thereby to defeat the mighty German army at a single blow. 'The French authorities,' Repington emphasised, 'place most importance upon the *principle* of joint-co-operation not the *amount* of British military support.'[17] He was not so strategically naive as to suppose a small British military contribution would immediately and decisively tip the scales against the mighty German armies, but the British public would at once perceive the true scale of the military threat Germany posed. They would also come to understand that in modern warfare high losses were inevitable and this at last might prompt the necessary political will to support conscription. The frailty of the adopted military strategy was obvious. But until a better alternative emerged they must retain it.

Despite Repington's warnings concerning Jack Fisher, Ottley remained unconcerned about the First Sea Lord's stubborn intransigence. Fisher might insist to the contrary as much as he liked, the navy would not refuse to ferry troops to France. The old boy notoriously said the wildest things, but one learned to live with his daemon and ignore its violent impulses. This, Repington accepted as a realistic assessment by one who knew Fisher well, whereas Esher's guarantee Fisher had a number of alternative strategic plans but did not wish to reveal them to anyone, he had found not the least reassuring. He warned Esher, 'We need to confront reality. These sailors hold us in the hollow of their hand.' What was the point of agreeing to join the French army if the navy's co-operation was not guaranteed? 'We cannot go on unless they carry us.'[18]

The account Repington gave of these events in his published diaries was not absolutely accurate. He asserted that after meeting Grey, Haldane went to London where he spent the weekend of 14/15 January. He told the Prime Minister what had happened and Sir Henry approved the military conversations. Lyttelton and Grierson were instructed to pursue talks with their opposite numbers in France. On Tuesday 17 January Huguet told Repington the talks had begun that morning. In the circumstances, the French were entitled to believe the involvement of Lyttelton and Grierson had the authority of both Haldane and Campbell-Bannerman. Repington asserted categorically the Prime Minister had accepted Haldane's assurance that 'to talk in an emergency was a permissible measure of prudence'. Repington felt he needed to explain to his readers the Prime Minister's attitude given that Campbell-Bannerman's Radical sympathies were widely and well known. Radical publicists consistently represented Sir Henry as being opposed to secret military conversations.[19] Repington insisted the Prime Minister behaved as he did because he was 'a warm friend of the French', and, in matters that concerned the army, as befitted an ex war minister, he was 'a fine old Tory'. Haldane had not needed to emphasise the delicacy of the situation. Sir Henry had treated the military conversations as a 'departmental affair'.[20] Such a claim sounded plausible but was not what happened.

The actual sequence of events was as follows: Sir Henry, electioneering in Scotland, had not returned to London until the evening of 27 January. Consequently, he was nowhere near London on 14 and 15 January to discuss the military conversations. Repington's claim was a deliberate falsehood. At the time he had made his unease obvious that C-B should initially have been left out of the loop. It was for that reason he told Esher he regretted he had not been able 'to tell Huguet whether the inference he drew [the Prime Minister had been told everything by Haldane at the time] was correct or the reverse'.[21] That the account in his *War Diaries* is misleading is scarcely surprising. The published accounts of all British participants say as little as possible about the origins of the military conversations. Arthur Ponsonby and Francis Hirst, as good Radical Liberals, would later claim a Radical prime minister had been gulled by his two devious and scheming Liberal Imperialist ministers. But all three, Sir Henry as much as Grey and Haldane, while they wished to be as well prepared as possible for any imminent conflict with Germany, could not afford to risk arousing the suspicions of their Cabinet colleagues. Nor did they want to be tied by any permanent obligation to their entente partner. They both wanted to have their cake and to eat it.

Grierson was unhappy that Repington had anything to do with the antecedents of the military conversations. The French government, however, obviously thought it worth their while to maintain contact with him. In a wide-ranging conversation Cambon told the correspondent he hoped war with Germany would be delayed a year until Russia might count. The ambassador was advancing the right argument to the right man. Repington had always thought it had been Russia's weakness that had prompted German aggression. After her military defeat by Japan, Russia 'on sea and land had ceased to exist' and was now further weakened by internal disputes and revolution.[22]

When the military conversations were first mooted, George Clarke had warned Esher, the War Office's involvement guaranteed there was no hope anything could remain secret for long.[23] When the cat was let out of the bag, Repington justifiably pointed the finger at Paris. The conversations had scarcely started when Clemenceau was asked in the Senate to deny rumours in *Le Figaro*. He refused. 'It was the duty of any responsible government,' he insisted, 'not to answer.' The British Radical press, sniffing for the merest hint the entente was actually an anti-German alliance designed to embrace reactionary Russia, thought Clemenceau's response unconvincing. The Tory press said nothing. The German ambassador to St James's made enquiries on his master's behalf and was assured by Haldane and Sir Henry there were no military conversations. Their categorical denial did not impress the kaiser. 'Magnificent lies,' he scrawled in the margin of the ambassador's report.

Huguet remained involved with the military conversations up to the outbreak of war in 1914 all the while keeping Repington fully informed. Repington never questioned the special relationship between France and Britain. What caused him to bridle in private was the least sign of French pusillanimity. 'The trouble with the Froggies,' he wrote to Marker, 'is they are always afraid that something might offend the Germans or that Willy will raise objections. I reply, let the Germans object and be d—d.'[24] Timidity and an exaggerated respect for German military power among the French higher command at the time of the Casa Blanca Incident in November 1908[25] caused concern to Sir John French and Esher. They discussed their worries at a private dinner party with Huguet. He formed the erroneous impression, if attacked by Germany the British might not support the French militarily. Somewhat incongruously, their political masters, Asquith, Grey and Haldane, had decided if it were necessary, then Britain would assist France. Huguet compounded his false impression by repeating it to the French chargé d'affaires. Thereafter it took much effort on Repington's part to disabuse the attaché of his mistake. He hoped he had succeeded, he told Esher, otherwise the French Ambassador might seek the sort of formal assurance from the British Foreign Secretary he could not possibly provide. Repington concluded, 'None of us can afford to do anything to render the Entente less cordial.'[26]

General Ewart, was invariably circumspect in his dealings with the French. He admitted to Repington his puzzlement. Why should 'undoubtedly high-minded and sincerely patriotic men' like Grey and Haldane, well aware of the strategic implications of the military conversations, refuse to divulge this information to other Cabinet ministers? Consequently, 'some who were not in the know agitated for reductions that dislocated all preparations'.[27] Ewart and Repington discussed this subject on a number of occasions in the context of increasing the numbers of trained soldiers. The general professed to be puzzled and unconvinced by the arguments Repington employed. Ewart insisted, 'It would pay us better to tell the British public the whole truth.'[28] That said, he never revealed his disquiet in public. But his successor, Henry Wilson, suffered no similar inhibition as he never looked further than his own opinion. In 1911 he would force the Cabinet's hand.

Cambon recommended Repington be invested an officer in the *Légion d'honneur*. At this he protested official recognition might compromise his independence. Nonetheless, in September 1906 he was duly invested, together with French, Grierson and Esher's son, Maurice Brett. The cross and ribbon arrived a little before Christmas. Repington wrote to Knollys, he wished the king to know how much he prized his new decoration.[29] As a further permanent reminder of his contribution to the *pour-parlers* preceding the military conversations, the French government presented Repington with a flamboyantly ornate inkstand. Thereafter it always held pride of place on his writing desk, where it provided a splendid conversation piece.

Repington immediately recognised the month-long hiatus caused by the change of administrations from Unionist to Liberal afforded a convenient opportunity to make changes among senior army personnel. Plumer ought to go. He had been too close to Arnold-Forster and had failed to realise that his kind of personal loyalty was not as important as 'the loyalty he owes to the army and the country'.[1] There was no shortage of generals worthy of dismissal, but an over-large cull would make life difficult for the Secretary of State. Even a limited pruning would require Haldane 'to act the wary old party'. 'It would be unwise' to create unnecessary trouble for himself.[2]

Plumer was replaced by Nicholson who, so it was supposed, accepted because he had been promised that he would be the next Chief of the General Staff. Repington was not entirely sure about Nicholson. He was much the cleverest of the generals, but was he a team player? If Haldane had chosen him as a future CGS, he should beware. His strengths were critical and destructive whereas they needed someone who could build as well as destroy. He would require careful handling.[3] Some of Repington's reservations were scarcely fair. Nicholson had previously made many enemies and so Repington had assumed he must be on trial as QMG, to afford his peers 'the opportunity to see if they could get used to him'. There were few ideally qualified candidates for senior appointments. Haldane wanted a submissive leader for the Army Council; scarcely the quality one associated with Nicholson.[4]

Haldane asked Repington whether he thought 'Wully' Robertson would make a suitable replacement for Grierson as DMO. He refused to be drawn. He liked Robertson well enough and admired his many fine qualities but doubted whether his personality and background suited him for that post's very particular demands. 'Uncommonly few officers possess the necessary qualifications to make the ideal DMO,' Repington observed. The constant contact with Cabinet ministers 'demands certain characteristics that an old ranker seldom possesses'. When Robertson was made Assistant Quartermaster General at Aldershot and later replaced Archibald Murray as Smith-Dorrien's CGS at the Aldershot command, Repington applauded 'a most satisfactory solution'. He was accused by some of not speaking up for 'Wully' because he was a snob and disapproved of Robertson's lowly social origins. Nothing could have been further from the truth. No one more strongly supported the principle of promotion on merit than Repington. On this occasion, for the post of DMO he genuinely considered Spencer Ewart the better-qualified man.[5]

No one enjoyed the promotion game more than Esher. He was pushing Douglas Haig for all he was worth. Haig also impressed Haldane but this time he would have to wait. The immediate delay would not permanently damage his future prospects. Repington idly wondered whether Haig was the Moltke they all so eagerly sought but swiftly dismissed the idea. Haig had taken to serious study too late in life to satisfy such an exalted expectation. Once Haldane had conveniently shuffled off Lyttelton to some harmless backwater, Nicholson would be given his place. After that, who knew?

Repington never admitted as much to Haldane, but he was reluctant to abandon the idea of Kitchener becoming CGS. He was convinced his old chief was the one man supremely qualified for that onerous post. Had he thought about the whole question *de novo*, he would have had to acknowledge Kitchener was not formally qualified as a staff officer and had repeatedly demonstrated his unwillingness or inability to understand how best to deploy his staff. What Kitchener possessed was the capacity to inspire in those who served under him the certainty he was a genius. The immensity of his personality dwarfed everyone and everything about him. In the first year of the Liberal government Repington frequently discussed with Haldane and Morley what military appointment might best utilise K's towering genius. Every suggestion created problems. Repington was forced to concede that to accommodate the colossus would involve a general post of lesser military figures and that would create far too many personal and political difficulties.

Repington wrote that Haldane inherited all the pieces of a suitable framework for a General Staff. He was merely required to fit them together in the correct order and breathe a soul into them. But to say as much was to ignore the many unresolved differences that divided War Office opinion. The so-called 'Blue ribbon' advocates supported an elite group of specialists, separate from the administrative staffs of the Adjutant and Quartermaster Generals. Others thought this completely wrong-headed. As everyone determinedly stuck to their guns, Haldane was left with the unenviable task of adjudication. He was prepared to follow the Esher Committee's suggestions, but he viewed them as a guide, not as inalienable, holy writ. He had been impressed particularly by 'the fatal confusion that arose whenever the General Staff were tangled in administration'. His determination 'to impress the principle of division of labour on my Generals'[6] clearly indicated he favoured the 'Blue ribbon' solution.

On 8 March 1906, in an exceedingly long speech delivered at hectic pace to a somnolent Commons, Haldane spoke of the General Staff. He praised Arnold-Forster for pursuing the principles advocated by Esher's Committee and pledged to continue that work. Repington simply declared his satisfaction with Haldane's statement. He was among the first to receive a copy of a new draft order. One clause proposed the CGS might, if he so wished, add names to the General Staff list. Nicholson, almost certainly with an eye to his own succession, refused to see the Chief's patronage diminished. The trouble was that Lyttelton had hopelessly compromised his credibility. 'His idea of happiness', Repington insisted, was 'to have no questions asked'. He rated men according to whether they left him alone.[7] The order was withdrawn, revised and then reissued in July. Repington remained dissatisfied with 'NG and his friends' and accused them of being 'fit only to play at tin soldiers in a back nursery'. He ruefully admitted, NG possessed 'insufficient intelligence to fill a nut'.[8]

Lyttelton's lack of mental acuity and his reluctance ever to admit he was wrong did not make him unique among senior army officers. Most generals, Repington observed, were bloody-minded, self-opinionated, intransigent and hot-tempered. Lyttelton was nothing like as violent as some of his colleagues. Repington recalled with relish how a critical comment made by French after inspecting 'Curly' Hutton's division had stoked that readily combustible general beyond boiling point. Repington gleefully recorded, 'There had been the devil's own ructions . . . Hutton was never nearer being put under arrest in his life.' Arthur Paget was another who possessed a quick and fearsome temper, 'but at least knew where to stop'. Horace Smith-Dorrien was notorious for the volcanic ferocity of his temper. Generals, Repington concluded, were 'ticklish souls none too easily driven'.[9]

The General Staff issue was not making the rapid progress Repington had expected. He doubted whether the CGS and the rest of the crew would ever be able to run their own show. Esher feared the draft order might be approved without serious amendment. Adroitly he persuaded Knollys to involve the king. Edward was guaranteed to oppose anything that might trench upon his prerogative. Soon he was harrumphing his doubts and displeasure to Haldane.

Already in bad odour for planning to axe two battalions of the Guards, Haldane was not prepared to risk another bout of royal displeasure. He capitulated. The order was withdrawn. Its replacement did not materialise until September.

Repington, meanwhile, questioned Esher about the General Staff. Were they, he wondered, being sufficiently inclusive? If they wanted to secure a monopoly of the army's best available talent, why exclude all save those who did well in the General Staff billets detailed in the order? Surely it would be better to draw talent from the widest possible spectrum? Why exclude India and the self-governing colonies? Esher ought to consider whether the draft orders had been 'too narrow and inadequate'. He admitted to 'grave doubts'. As presently proposed, would the General Staff serve the army well? Surely it was a mistake to suppose you could ignore administrative experience or the ability to lead men in battle . . . If a successful General Staff were to be created, then those who aspired to be appointed should have had experience in the entire business of an army. Once in the field, 'their work would presume and demand all this previously acquired knowledge'.[10] His Military Notes in *The Times* for the end of October argued forcibly that peace conditions 'stereotype a division of duties and consequently of knowledge fatal to success in the field'. To produce 'a breed of generals ignorant of administration', would be to take 'the direct road to disaster . . . To take deliberate measures to propagate the species would be an outrage on common sense'.[11]

The qualities to be looked for in a general in command of troops in the field was a subject to which Repington repeatedly returned. His own campaign experience gave his words a particular authority and as well determined his arguments. 'Without bravery no general is worth his keep,' he wrote. He was not concerned simply with physical courage; moral grit was equally important. Unduly influenced by Buller's over-cautious tactics in South Africa, junior generals who were proven 'thrusters', elicited disproportionately glowing accolades, but by championing these bolder spirits he injected something very worthwhile into the debate. In peacetime there was a tendency to decry boldness as foolhardy, to abandon risk takers and to 'exalt those men who shone in conversation, or in Society, or on paper'. He insisted, 'The men who win battles are the Gatacres, Harts and Hunters . . . those I know and have seen in warm corners'. Repington acknowledged the faculty of commanding a great army in the field had changed in many ways, 'replaced by the more exacting if less brilliant but now indispensable art of managing and directing staff services'. Nevertheless, he concluded, 'an army will never be quite satisfied if its chief has not all the appearance, the manners and the prestige of a great general'.[12]

That General Staff officers should be well trained was the *sine qua non* without which success could never be assured. Relevant areas of expertise or character should neither be undervalued nor ignored. They would otherwise produce 'well meaning amateurs who in their ignorance w[ould] impose tasks upon the troops which they cannot carry out'.[13] Esher recognised he and Haldane were the object of these criticisms. Why else should Repington have written of the uncertainty whether 'some clever people realise all the different types we need in one Army'? Esher anxiously wondered if he would publish these misgivings. To do so could only compromise the case for securing a General Staff. But Esher's anxiety was misplaced. Nothing was further from Repington's mind. He had no desire to damage the public credibility of either the General Staff or its sponsors. Beyond doubt, the order was flawed, but it was never his intention to oppose it root and branch. He would judge its value by results. Now it was enough to play the gadfly; to test, to disconcert, to pry and poke at perceived weaknesses. Esher's complacency, like Haldane's, required occasional denting. Nevertheless he seriously questioned the wisdom of keeping command, administration and inspection as distinct functions. Where was the buckle designed to hold War Office and army together? 'I have yet to find the *trait d'union* ... you say it is not the business of the War Office to move about among the troops.' But surely Esher had not designed the Inspector General's office to ensure a desk-bound Army Council isolated from the army? And whatever Esher's intention had been, the War Office was making it obvious, it didn't care a two-penny damn what the Inspector General had to say.

Bringing the Duke of Connaught into play was a shrewd move. Repington knew Esher and Haldane were conspiring to banish the duke by marooning him in the Mediterranean Command. Esher had chosen to ignore Repington's repeated warnings when he appointed Connaught Inspector General in 1904. Repington had enquired if Esher really supposed the Secretary of State and the Army Council would be pleased to receive an unfavourable report from the Inspector General. As Repington had anticipated, the first report (1904) found the army wanting in a disturbing number of ways. Arnold-Forster had suggested it might be 'revised' to placate War Office displeasure. When Connaught angrily refused, the report was shelved. Effectively, a similar fate befell the second report (1906), which was ruled out of order and silenced upon entirely spurious grounds. Connaught made his indignation and exasperation known to Repington. First, his reports had been ignored. Now they wanted him removed. His treatment confirmed what others in the Inspectorate had previously told Repington. The War Office effectively ignored criticism. 'The IG & Co. are the only people in close touch with the army,' Repington informed Esher. Other than the Inspectorate, he scarcely ever saw anybody from the War Office at manoeuvres or on field days. Did War Office warriors, he wondered, prefer riding desks to horses? The Inspector General's influence ought to be increased. Could he not be given a place on the Army Council? When he made this suggestion he knew Esher would not like it any more than he was likely to approve the proposal to publish Connaught's unrevised report. But if the War Office followed these suggestions they could never again ignore the Inspector's General's criticisms. It would be a politically difficult stroke to pull off, but not impossible.[14]

Concern for Kitchener's future employment prospects, not Connaught's, had prompted Repington. His suggestion that the duke join the Army Council was intended to ensure 'a large number of court flunkeys' would make an effective brouhaha on his behalf. 'When there is a change his successor will have a chair in Pall Mall, and if the chair is filled as I hope it may be filled, the old Council will have to sit up.'[15] Repington had reason to suppose Kitchener would be the next Inspector General; Haldane had mooted as much most enthusiastically.[16] If Kitchener were one day to run the Army Council, it was not too early for him to fire a warning salvo. There would be a barrage of demands when that eagerly anticipated day arrived. How much would be gained if the Director of Military Training was kept constantly in touch with the Inspectorate rather than 'immured in the War Office spinning manuals, knowing ever less about what was going on'. Did Esher realise there were generals still in high command who had performed hopelessly in South Africa? Was it wise to allow them carte blanche to put their individual imprimatur on the troops they trained? The need for co-ordination was clear and urgent.[17] He would have liked to discuss these matters at greater length, but at least he had planted these ideas in the minds of those who made the decisions.

Although the last place to which Connaught wished to go was the Mediterranean, Haldane, Esher and the king willed otherwise. As the duke prepared for his departure, Repington fired a squib in *The Times* questioning whether a Mediterranean Command was really needed. In sending Connaught there, were they making the best use of his military experience? But at this point Repington chose to be diverted in order to score off an old adversary. He revealed that the duke's annual reports as Inspector General had been quashed on Arnold-Forster's order. Repington succumbed to the temptation to hurt Arnold-Forster rather than question the need for a Mediterranean Command.[18] George Clarke repeatedly condemned Repington as a clever but not fair controversialist, and on this occasion his criticism was deserved.[19]

Not Kitchener but French succeeded Connaught as Inspector General. Repington had long admired 'Johnny' French. He earlier told Marker that Kitchener apart, French was the only commander he supposed possessed the common sense and capacity to 'control the dreamers and schemers to keep the train on the rails'.[20] He had known for some time Esher was grooming French as a future Inspector General. Though French's friend and admirer, he nonetheless felt obliged to warn Esher of a possibly fatal flaw in the little man's character. It pained him, he wrote, to draw attention to 'the many growls'[21] within the army at the prospect of French's appointment. The question was, as President of the Selection Board, would his recommendations for promotion be sufficiently objective? Many senior army officers believed that in the past he had too often favoured his friends. Repington insisted he would not want French's appointment to give 'the least cause for the enemy to blaspheme'. Too many people lost the good opinion of the army by 'descending to jobs for their friends'. He did not wish to see Sir John's career wrecked for the same paltry reason. The emollient Esher rather than anyone else might best broach the subject with the fierce French.[22]

As evidence of French's supposed failings, the case of Major Algernon Lawson was frequently cited. French had secured the appointment of his aide-de-camp as Brigade Major of the 1st Cavalry Brigade, overturning the wishes of the Director of Staff Duties and the Secretary of State for War by the simple expedient of threatening his own resignation. French had supposed Lawson, who was not a Staff College graduate, was being victimised by Wilson and Rawlinson. He wanted Lawson because he believed he was the best man for the job. Repington did not consider the case against French by any means proven.[23] He was aware that behind the scenes Esher had been much involved in the Lawson case on French's side. Wisely, he chose not to instance another notorious case involving Esher's son, but pointed out that doubts alone could be sufficient to wreck French's future usefulness.

Appointed Inspector General in November 1907, French's powers as president of the Selection Board remained untrammelled. However, Repington's anxiety had not been entirely misplaced. In 1913 when CIGS, French presided over a selection board that passed over four generals causing widespread complaints of partiality. Stamfordham warned French, the board's decision had prompted 'animadversions by many senior officers in by no means favourable terms'.[24] But, as so often before, French survived the *sotto voce* mutterings and hostile grumbling of his fellows.

From his first moment in office he proved that he was not only a vigorous new broom but also the exact link between the War Office and the army that Repington had long advocated. Determined to act as the Army Council's eyes and ears, he demanded widespread changes. His top priority, to ensure the troops were ready and fit for immediate action. Senior officers were required to demonstrate professionalism of the highest degree. Harry Scobell, Repington's brother-in-law, was to become an early victim of this determination to raise standards.

In South Africa, Scobell, the ideal, independent column commander, was one of French's brightest stars. After the war he was given *the* plum cavalry appointment, command of the 1st Brigade at Aldershot. Scobell, who cared not a fig for army reform, would not pretend an interest in the tactical exercises French had recently introduced and keenly espoused. When French required his protégé to handle a force of cavalry greater than had ever before been gathered on Salisbury Plain, the gallant Major General's brilliant career was spectacularly and disastrously undone. As the exercise proceeded, French was by turns surprised, disappointed, angered and finally disgusted. He vented his spleen on the unfortunate Scobell, upbraiding his former friend in such extreme terms the meanest intellect on the field would have appreciated his career was blighted beyond hope of recovery. French's notoriously hot temper made it most unlikely any serving officer would dare criticise his behaviour. Repington wrote to Esher and suggested his letter might be shown to French, who must be made aware his treatment of Scobell was open to misunderstanding. No one who knew French well could ever suppose the violent expression of his innermost feelings had been prompted 'with anything other than the good of the Service at heart'. But the way French had exercised his authority had prompted great concern among the many senior serving officers present. Repington warned, if the affair were treated carelessly, French's reputation and his candidacy for the highest military command would be damaged beyond repair. The letter was wise and generous. It warned French not to endanger his future by another hasty public outburst. There was a widely rumoured notion that French had deliberately set up Scobell. Repington dismissed the idea. French, he insisted, would not act like that.[25]

In March 1912 French succeeded Nicholson as CIGS. The move neither surprised nor displeased Repington. Since 1910 he had been telling Haldane they could not go on much longer with a CGS so out of touch with the army. 'Mr H humorously calls Nick an eminent civilian and so he is.' He told Esher, he thought 'he [was] a bit fatigué'.[26] Nicholson had been an enthusiastic and early advocate of the German General Staff scheme and had pushed for its adoption when questioned by Esher's triumvirate. A gifted staff officer and administrator with a keen intellect, he never shook off the unfortunate impression that weighed heavily with Clarke, Esher and Repington that he was more difficult to handle than other generals. Repington had not taken the hint when Nicholson told him he was 'wise enough to recognise [his] own limitations'.

Assuming that Nicholson was long past his 'sell by' date in 1912, it was scarcely satisfactory to appoint as his replacement someone who did not believe wholeheartedly in the General Staff concept. Over the years French's doubts about the position of CIGS had been exacerbated by the performances, first of Lyttelton, for whom he felt nothing but contempt, and then Nicholson, whom he supposed was no more than a damn nuisance. His antipathy was further fortified by a complacent ignorance about what exactly the General Staff could achieve. The memorandum that accompanied Army Order 233 made clear the *raison d'être* for a General Staff. Long understood by continental armies, now at last it was fully acknowledged by the British. The General Staff would in future be the army's repository of strategic doctrine, its fount of strategic advice and its specialist planning corps.[27]

The Army Order had both addressed and acknowledged the reservations and criticisms of sundry critics. The compilation of the General Staff list, a problem that had long divided the membership of the Army Council, was resolved in favour of the 'Blue ribbon' supporters. At the same time, the value of administrative experience was fully acknowledged. The king was reassured; his prerogative, to be consulted about and approve senior military appointments, would not be undermined.

Upon that last issue, Repington thought it all very well to placate the king's sensibilities, but what about when his advisers foisted unsuitable promotions on the army? It was a question currently very much on his mind. He had been greatly exercised by 'Bully' Oliphant's appointment as General Officer Commanding-in-Chief Northern Command, a candidate he considered egregiously unsuitable. With the Defence Committee about to initiate an inquiry into invasion, Repington was anxious to keep Esher on side and not irritate him unnecessarily. Oliphant, he knew, had been Esher's choice. He wrote to Balmoral where Esher was in waiting upon the king. He admitted there could be no more charming companion than Oliphant, 'especially for a game of cards', but how could Edward have agreed to give him the Northern Command? Sadly, 'Bully's' was not the only doubtful recent promotion. He wondered whether the king enjoyed the benefit of advisers at all. Perhaps the time had come to 'throw a bomb ... explain why a man passed over four times for promotion was the obvious choice for a very important command'?[28]

Esher did not appreciate being the victim of Repington's heavy irony or the butt of his jesting threats. By return he read Repington a restrained but sharp lesson. Oliphant, he insisted, had been 'quite *excellent* in the London Command and should do very well at York'. He reminded Repington how he had recently enthusiastically approved Pemberton Leach's appointment as General Officer Commanding-in-Chief Scottish Command. 'He might have been dear to your heart but he is no more than a first class duffer.'[29] Repington never supposed it was a fix when he approved a candidate yet recommendations made by others with which he did not agree he would invariably condemn. Not prepared to yield entirely he said no more about Oliphant, but wondered whether clever men invariably know best about everything. 'Haldane crabbed Leach, and so do you ... Because his intellect is not on your level, you call him a first class duffer. I'm not saying he isn't ... but the army wants a good many subordinate leaders ... the sort of men who will take risks which the men of intellect would shy at.'[30] He believed neither Esher nor Haldane when considering promotions gave sufficient weight to the opinions of senior officers. He did not perceive the illogicality in his own position. If there were to be the sort of revolutionary changes to which he, as much as Esher and Haldane, was wedded, then they could not always go with the grain of established tradition. The claims of revolution sometimes had to outweigh those of evolution. A serving army officer for almost a quarter of a century, it would have been surprising if Repington had honoured the same tribal gods as Esher and Haldane. The perspectives and priorities of the three men were necessarily different. The paradox Repington did not acknowledge was his conservatism over senior appointments often contradicted the notion of a meritocracy he otherwise espoused.

Frequently impolitic, rarely serving his own best interests, Repington too often failed to suppress his disquiet or dissatisfaction at appointments Haldane or Esher had recommended. When Major General Charles Hadden, Director of Artillery, was promoted to the Army Council, Repington made no effort to conceal his anger and disapproval. When he bearded Haldane the minister unsuccessfully tried to convince him that Hadden deserved to be promoted. Repington promised, as it could not be undone he would not raise objections publicly. Now was not the time 'to cry down [Haldane's] credit when he was about to introduce a great reform'.[31] It did not, however, stop him complaining to Esher that 'Except Hadden rhymes with sadden and madden and suggests good nursery doggerel, I see no point in it.' He insisted, 'If you want the army to go with you and feel contented, you should get your Grenfells and Methuens on to the AC.'[32]

To Marker he wrote, 'It is of no significance whether Hadden is a good or bad general. What I am utterly opposed to is the appointment of junior men to the AC. If four of the present members were removed, who would you put in their place?'[33] Three of the names Marker had earlier suggested Repington had dismissed cursorily. The fourth, Douglas Haig, he admitted was 'a very smart officer'. But was he ready for promotion? Perhaps one day, 'when he has fully learned War Office business'. Doubtless Repington's caveat was repeated to Haig, who would scarcely have been delighted. Repington believed no army ever produced many men suitable for the Army Council. However, what mattered was 'At all times to pay due regard to the opinions of the higher ranks of the army.' Not to do so would mean that a divisional commander could well say of a Major General appointed as Quartermaster General or Adjutant General, 'What can one expect with that d—d Jack in office?'[34]

In August 1909 Nicholson had been given the title Chief of the Imperial General Staff. Repington applauded but it was too soon. The white, self-governing, imperial colonies jealously safeguarding their independence and autonomy suspected, and not without reason, that the Mother Country wished to use them to satisfy Westminster's insatiable appetite for men and money. Canada wondered whether Britain saw an Imperial General Staff as a means to commit them in advance to assist Britain in a war in Europe. In 1909 there was neither the will nor the trust to contemplate genuine strategic planning between all members of the Empire.

7   Invasion

On half a dozen occasions during Victoria's reign widespread public concern was expressed at the country's vulnerability to invasion. This recurring national neurosis was prompted by supposed French ambitions. The Admiralty insisted there was nothing to fear so long as Britain continued to rule the waves, but panic was never readily defused.[1] Where France had once generated fear Germany now prompted concern. Admiral Fisher laughed at such fears. He insisted the worst invasion risk Britain faced was five men in a dinghy. To suppose Germany might invade Britain was, he insisted, absurd. He, however, did not think it paradoxical to advocate a British naval-borne invasion of Germany, a strategy the army dismissed contemptuously. Repington did not agree with Fisher and deplored the lack of agreement between the two services. For this he did not entirely exonerate the War Office, but the greater share of the blame he allotted to the Admiralty, where Fisher reigned supreme.

Repington's once favourable opinion of Fisher, earned by the admiral's attitude during The Hague Peace Conference, had been entirely dissipated by his attitude during the 1905 Moroccan crisis, when Fisher had dismissed the possibility of invasion. Repington believed he had done so for no better reason than a selfish determination to secure for the Admiralty an unjustifiably bigger portion of the defence budget. Fisher constantly urged Balfour to rehearse the Defence Committee's finding that there was little real risk of invasion. He hoped the CID's conclusion would impose a crippling financial blow upon a 'bloated army'. Fisher never doubted it was better to spend money on the navy than 'squander it to keep 170,000 men kicking their heels in idleness as a supposed force for home defence'.[2] He condemned Repington as a 'turncoat'. He had deserted the Blue Water camp to join with those who constantly warned of a 'Bolt from the Blue'. But what better might be expected of a liar, a modern Captain Dugald Dalgetty, a pedant, a braggart, a soldier of fortune whose loyalty could be bought and sold?[3] Arnold-Forster did not charge Repington with 'apostasy, but with purposeless vacillation'.[4]

Fig. 4 Admiral Sir John 'Jacky' Fisher (1841–1920)

The military correspondent happily admitted he had changed his mind. For years he had mistakenly trusted 'Blue Water' theory. Britons were always being told the navy was all important. As he whimsically observed, that idea had seemed particularly risible when fighting the Boers among the Drakensbergs![5]

Blue Water theory, first articulated by the brothers Philip and John Colomb, was popularised and disseminated by Alfred Mahan, the American naval theorist and historian. Even the War Office, though it never entirely discounted the threat of invasion, eventually accepted the navy was Britain's primary defensive bulwark against such a possibility. At Westminster, Blue Water was the widely accepted orthodoxy. Both

major political parties cited it to justify the imposition of rigorous economies upon the army to release ever more money to satisfy the constantly
rising cost of maintaining a dominant navy. Blue Water doctrinaires were
supported and encouraged by the Admiralty and the great steel and ship-
building interests. Repington feared Haldane realised neither the strength
nor influence exerted by these politically and economically inter-related,
integrated interests. They had achieved dominance by exploiting a mistaken conception. The original thesis had been corrupted and altered by
ignorant doctrinaires into an inviolate axiom: a fleet in being was an
absolute bar to invasion. To rebut this grossly mistaken but superficially
attractive notion, Repington deployed his 'hearth-and-home' concept –
that at all times a strong military force is required to defend Britain. 'No
matter how strong the navy,' he insisted, 'the main deterrent to invasion is
a numerous and efficient army. It is an essential condition of peace,
security and public confidence.'[6] The better to prove his point he
gleefully informed Marker, in recent naval manoeuvres four battleships
under Admiral Sir William Henry May, C-in-C of the Atlantic Fleet,
'swept the Channel and landed at Scarborough quite unopposed'. This
clearly demonstrated the utter nonsense of the assertions Fisher and his
associates had so often made.[7]

No other prominent national figure so assiduously or successfully
cultivated the press as Jack Fisher. He insisted it provided him with the
only engine capable of achieving the vast naval revolution he desired.
'Without the Press it can not be done.'[8] Prodigal with his gifts of classified
information, he promiscuously pursued journalists. J. A. Spender, one of
the First Sea Lord's more clear-eyed newspaper friends, cheerily
admitted the admiral 'cultivated the Press unblushingly'. The shameless
old scoundrel was rewarded 'with such an advertisement of himself and
his ideas as no other seaman ever received from newspapers'.[9] With the
exception of Repington, senior staff at Printing House Square unquestioningly supported Fisher.

Repington determined to take on Fisher's supporters at *The Times*. He
would completely undermine the idea invasion was impossible and blow
those Blue Water sycophants right out of the water. Buckle promised,
when Parliament rose for the summer recess Repington could publish the
kind of article that would so rouse Fisher's 'furious acolytes they would
pelt him'.[10] Despite Buckle's generosity, he resented the editor affording
any space to any contribution that was favourable to Fisher's ideas,
especially if written by Thursfield, even though he was the newspaper's
acknowledged, leading naval expert. It was enough to induce an exaggerated rant from Repington accusing Buckle of betrayal, bias and victimisation. Such charges were as absurd as they were unfounded.

Repington insisted he could actually destroy the 1905 claim and give the Blue Water, or rather *Veltmarine* fanatics a nasty jolt'.[11] His articles created much interest and prompted a furious exchange of letters in *The Times*. 'I really can't understand Mr Buckle giving Repington his head in this way', Fisher complained to Esher. Simultaneously he urged George Clarke 'Fire a broadside at Repington and sink him.'[12] Clarke needed no encouragement. In the course of a violent personal attack he dismissed Repington as nothing but a damnable scaremonger. If the invasion bugbear were not set aside for ever, they would never have an efficient field army. But then, to his utter amazement, Clarke learned Balfour had been impressed by Repington's claims. Surely Balfour realised the correspondent's *real* intention in talking about invasion was to persuade people to think more favourably about conscription. Yet Balfour said his intention was to attend the National Defence Association's meeting to hear Repington give his paper. Clarke warned him, if the audience were persuaded the navy could not protect Britain against invasion in all circumstances, then conscription would be the only viable basis for military organisation.

Repington's paper successfully demonstrated naval supremacy was relative, not absolute; that Britain's supreme navy could not save the country from terrible and prolonged sufferings unless a national army confirmed and complemented the victories won at sea. Repington believed he had successfully gibbeted the Blue Water brigade. He genuinely regretted hurting Thursfield, but 'a hardened publicist who speaks his mind has to put up with these little sorrows. A military critic who does not lose one valued friend a month should reconsider his position.'[13]

Repington delightedly described Balfour's response to the paper he gave to the NDA meeting as 'the best speech he ever delivered'. The Unionist leader had agreed with every positive proposition he had advanced. Esher, always Balfour's admiring friend, was more than somewhat surprised that Arthur should have thought so well of Repington's paper. He had been far from impressed when he had read an earlier draft. He did not need telling by a cockahoop Repington that its publication in *The Times* would give George Clarke 'fits'. That prospect clearly delighted Repington, who gleefully anticipated it would bring 'the whole flotilla of Navalists' down on him. 'Until we have put an end to all their damned nonsense,' he asserted, 'we shall never get our National army.'[14]

Repington never despised using Leo Maxse's *National Review* as a vehicle for a more explicit statement of his views. The November issue boasted a lengthy and detailed article on invasion. George Clarke in a letter to *The Times* insisted all Repington's talk of 'Germany's Black

Treachery' and of 'Bolts from the Blue' was make-believe ... intended to force conscription upon us'. Unabashed, Repington countered, the question of *German* invasion had never been thoroughly examined. If any six intelligent soldiers and the same number of sailors were provided with the true facts about the naval and military strengths of Germany and England and were asked to prepare a German plan of campaign, 'they would all without exception advocate the imperative need for a naval surprise followed by invasion'.[15] There followed a further series of sharp exchanges with Clarke in Letters to the Editor of *The Times*. Repington insisted the nation deserved better than to be battered by the repeated accusations and recriminatory exchanges of ill-tempered, partial witnesses. The best solution, as he had repeatedly stated, was to reopen the invasion inquiry.

Working with Lord Lovat and financed by Sir Samuel Scott, a wealthy Unionist MP, Repington had gathered information designed to contradict and overthrow the 1902–03 Defence Committee's findings. The original initiative had been Lovat's, but Repington's knowledge and unremitting energy inspired the enterprise. Fisher described Lovat and Roberts as Repington's 'co-adjutors ... simply putty in his hands'.[16] To make Field Marshal Lord Roberts their titular leader had been Repington's idea. The old warrior made the ideal figurehead. Repington ensured that when the time came, Roberts had not only learned his lines perfectly but had been rehearsed to deal with all foreseeable contingencies. The care and energy with which this task was undertaken is apparent from the number and detail of the letters he despatched to Roberts in the period before and during the inquiry. Repington's industry and thoroughness was all the more remarkable for he was simultaneously engaged on a number of other tasks that made widely disparate demands on his time, energy and expertise.

With sufficient evidence gathered to make a persuasive case, Repington and his group approached Balfour. Repington was reassured by Balfour's immediate response that there could never be a final conclusion on invasion. The new evidence was embodied in a note to the Defence Committee. Repington was delighted.[17] His concern now was their work might be stymied by Fisher. As it happened, the admiral's exaggerated opposition to any investigation ensured the Defence Committee's involvement.

Repington asked Esher as Fisher's friend, 'to disabuse him of any notion we want to attack him. Our target is to expose an invertebrate and huckstering Government which fails to give the consideration to defence questions which circumstances require.' But Fisher was not to be so persuaded, especially after learning Repington was in close contact with Admiral Beresford, the sailor who publicly and privately had been grossly insubordinate to him. The mutual ill-will of both men was stoked and prompted by their subordinates. If Fisher was the greater man, Beresford was never far behind him in his love of self, country and the navy. To that service both men had unstintingly given the better part of their lives. At the heart of their most recent, bitter altercation was Fisher's decision to divide the Channel Fleet and reduce Beresford's command. It made little strategic sense. There was talk that Beresford might resign and stump the country, the better to advertise his complaints of victimisation and Fisher's strategic incompetence. Repington's anxiety was Beresford should 'attend the promised invasion inquiry as C-in-C of the Channel Fleet and Admiralissimo designate in war. I want the subcommittee to have his views while he is in a responsible position.'[18] It was imperative Charlie B, in a sudden temperamental outburst, did not resign.[19]

Repington asserted confidence could no longer be placed in the navy as a shield against an enemy who enjoyed the overwhelming advantage of initiative and surprise. Unfortunately, 'Most people will not allow for German wickedness because they will not read history, nor modern German teaching, nor understand the profound alterations brought about by the modern machinery of fleets which suggests, indeed imposes, a rapid knock-down blow at the start.' There was no good reason to accept the arguments of those who denied Germany would attempt a naval surprise. 'Any other form of naval hostilities would at present be an absurdity.' Britain had provided Germany with more than sufficient motive for such a surprise attack. There had been Fisher's own wildly indiscreet threat, still going the rounds, that he would 'Copenhagen' the German Fleet. Repington did not reveal Beresford had supplied him with evidence, clearly implying the navy would be hard pressed to contain the German Fleet, even if given advance notice of an intended attack.

Lord Charles alternated between confident claims that they would soon have Fisher gaffed and netted, and pessimistic assertions that the slippery old fish would get away with all his sins by packing the committee of investigation with his friends. At least he was pleased that Repington, and Admiral Sturdee, his Chief of Staff, were co-operating in the preparation of their case. All the while Charlie B insisted, Germany could certainly hold the Straits of Dover for forty-eight hours.

It pleased Repington that well placed friends of his at the War Office, like Harry Rawlinson and Spencer Ewart, were providing him with useful information for the inquiry. As Ewart was DMO he particularly valued his help and was anxious Moberly Bell should allow Ewart access to *The Times*' intelligence services, 'as a *quid pro quo* in recognition of his assistance to me'.[20] Repington mused upon which witnesses might be called, if the inquiry were to be thorough and really 'intended to probe the whole question to the bottom'. He drew up a preliminary list of suggested names. Fisher, when he saw it, declared it was 'absurd'. Replete with the names of diplomats, admirals, generals, financial and commercial experts, the list concluded with 'HRH, the Prince of Wales'.[21]

Asquith took the chair. Repington rather underestimated him. He excused his overfondness for holding hands with a woman young enough to be his daughter, but not 'Sozzle's' overindulgence in strong liquor.[22] He would later blame Asquith for some of the rough times he and Roberts suffered in committee when in fact they were entirely the consequence of their own failings induced by the questioning of Captain E. J. W. Slade. The committee would meet sixteen times between November 1907 and July 1908, finally reporting on 22 October 1908.

Roberts opened proceedings by reading a statement of general principles prepared by Repington.[23] Next, Repington described a hypothetical German attack, landing at Edinburgh and Leith, seizing the north, then moving south upon a broad front, living off the land. Then he posed a series of questions: How many troops were assigned to home defence? How long would it take to collect them? What arrangements were there for their transportation and supply? Was there a designated central authority concerned with the problems of home defence? This opening foray continued into the second day of the hearing.

When Repington left the room Fisher harangued the committee's members for an hour. Since the start of the inquiry, both the Admiralty's senior representatives had appeared impatient and unconscionably angry. Tweedmouth's patience had been tried beyond endurance before the inquiry by his unsuccessful attempts to hold the ring between Fisher and Beresford. In the circumstances, perhaps his querulous demeanour was understandable, but why was Fisher so blazingly angry? It seemed he might explode at any moment. Repington thought both men's behaviour effectively admitted the weakness of the Admiralty's case. Nonetheless, he warned a blasé Roberts to remain careful when cross-examined. He should not tolerate any nonsense from Fisher.[24]

Esher grew increasingly convinced by the 'mass of information and detail' Repington and his associates submitted, and when he suggested Clarke's *Imperial Defence* (1897) undermined their arguments, Repington refuted each proposition in turn. 'You can't take vague assertions like Clarke's in affairs of this complexity,' he insisted. When it came to knowing about sea-borne invasion, he judged Clarke to be 'a child' and slapped him down with rare condescension. Not all Esher's doubts had been entirely dispelled but he could not fail to notice Fisher's all too obvious, angry discomfort. Esher could only conclude from the Admiral's attempts 'to burke any further inquiry', he had something to conceal. Repington was invited to spend an evening at Orchard Lea, thus affording him a further opportunity to make and elaborate his case to Esher.[25]

Repington ought to have been elated. Instead he was irritated because Asquith treated them as though they were 'the protagonists in this affair'. Repington supposed their success – or otherwise – now depended upon Nicholson and French. It was certain they could expect nothing of Lyttelton and Fisher. They were 'unlikely to appear in the white sheets of penitents and repent of their past mistakes'. Indeed, in adversity they might well choose to 'combine against us'.[26] Fisher continued to fume and fret, vowing he would smash the invasion bogey and eternally discredit Roberts and Repington. Captain Slade, however, did not share all Fisher's prejudices against the army. He thought a closer, more detailed examination of the invasionists' case might well be worthwhile. Despite all the new evidence, in its essentials he was convinced it was the same story as had been told in 1903. Before their next meeting, Slade produced an Admiralty statement reflecting not Fisher's but his strategic appreciation of invasion. Only after hours of bitter debate had this been agreed with Tweedmouth and Fisher. What Slade argued for was a combined strategy and a reasoned understanding by the two services of their respective functions.

Slade impressed the inquiry members. Repington acknowledged he must find more evidence to rebut Slade's argument. He doubted he could finish the task satisfactorily much before the next meeting. His real 'facer' was that Slade's strategic conception was so similar to his own. Repington had never been guilty of supposing the entire fault lay at the doors of the Admiralty. What he had wanted was to shake them up, to stir them out of their complacency. He had hoped to make obvious, an army and navy in constant opposition to one another served no one's interest. Early in January 1908 he had enquired what Roberts thought about reaching a compromise with Fisher and the Admiralty, as both services had the same objectives in view. He thought a good time to approach Fisher was when the Admiralty was being vigorously assaulted by the Radical Liberals. In the face of their common foe might they not support Fisher in his battle for increased estimates provided he agreed to support 'our views for a strong Territorial army and withdraw his pretensions to play the part of both army and navy'?[27] Roberts, however, would not agree. It was a difficult call for Repington to make. Giving evidence to the inquiry, Roberts was the puppet and he the puppet master. Yet the old boy was essential to the success of their case. Without the magic of his name and his unfailing popularity, the facts and figures would seem stale.

Repington turned to Esher to sound out whether he favoured a compromise. Fisher would have to accept 'Mr H's general policy and that a large national army in the second line is indispensible. Until the Fisher folk acknowledge this we must fight. If they suffer as a consequence *tant pis pour eux*.'[28] Esher said neither yes nor no. Nor would he rise to the bait when Repington suggested, 'One word from the king ... would settle the matter at once'.[29]

Repington's offer was undoubtedly genuine. He had made a similar proposal a few months earlier that Fisher had peremptorily rejected. The First Sea Lord refused to consider any compromise that might mean even a modest amendment to his own carefully cherished prejudices. Intellectually and imaginatively he was insufficiently flexible to appreciate Repington's offer was genuine. As to the inquiry, he was certain it was intended to discredit him and to undermine the changes he had initiated in the navy. His paranoid suspicions were not limited to Repington. 'We must be careful what we do,' he warned Slade. 'Everyone is intent upon behaving in a most unprincipled way ... The crisis on the estimates has been manufactured ... the whole thing is dishonest in the extreme.' Slade had as much cause to be concerned about Fisher as Repington. He confided to his diary, 'Sir John has no idea how he confuses the issue when he launches out on one of his digressions.'[30]

For three sessions the invasionists were cross-examined, Repington bearing the brunt of the hostile questioning. He enjoyed the verbal jousting – which was just as well – but it drove Fisher almost to distraction. A typical exchange concerned the German fleet's ability to avoid detection. Fisher pronounced it impossible. If undetected by any other means, it would certainly be picked up and reported by Admiralty secret agents. Repington responded with a knowing smirk, the one thing he had learned about secret agents was they could never be trusted to provide certain assurance of due warning. Fisher was so stung by this rebuttal he bellowed, 'When I say something it *is* so', an explosion that did nothing for his dignity or credibility. Repington had the measure of his man, but knowing Esher would be anxious Fisher should not irredeemably blot his copybook, Repington observed, 'Naturally Sir John wishes to do as he pleases. All strong men do.' He did not spare Reggie the moral of his cautionary tale. 'In so vast a business as peace strategy ... it is not safe to confine the fortunes of our Empire to one man, however able.'[31] As he pondered this stark assertion Esher might have wondered why Repington never admitted as much about Kitchener.

Never obviously offensive to his interrogators, Repington nonetheless could be irritatingly petty and sometimes seem insufferably smug. Inevitably there came a time when his mask of apparent infallibility slipped. At the 27 January meeting, in the last quarter of an hour he wilted. Asquith rescued him to Slade's chagrin for he was certain given another hour he would have demolished Repington's case entirely.[32] The military correspondent's disenchantment was complete when, at the next meeting on 4 February, after an ineffectual cross-examination of Slade, he and Roberts were dismissed from the inquiry. Grey had asked whether they should be present when secret information on mobilisation was being discussed. Little if anything revealed would have been news to Repington for Huguet kept him constantly informed. Fisher, making the most he could of the incident, wrote to the king of how he had 'objected strongly to the way Repington was given access to secret documents'. Edward concurred wholeheartedly. It had been 'very foolish' to give secrets to the 'very clever but equally unprincipled military correspondent'.[33] Edward did not say so, but what had angered him was the brouhaha Repington had stirred up by his letter to Buckle, published in *The Times*, concerning an exchange of letters between the First Lord of the Admiralty and his nephew, Wilhelm.

In 1899 Victoria had appointed her grandson, the kaiser, an honorary admiral in the British navy. Politicians soon regretted the queen's generosity. Wilhelm demonstrated a manic enthusiasm for all things nautical, bombarding British ministers with memoranda on everything from gunnery to tactics, even ship design. A letter he wrote to Tweedmouth, dated 18 February 1908, described recent parliamentary criticism of the German Supplementary Naval Law as '*absolutely nonsensical and untrue*'. He enquired, how could the Germans be intent to challenge British naval supremacy when their fleet was 'built against nobody at all'? For Britain constantly to harp on about the German danger was unworthy of a great nation, especially as it possessed a navy five times the size of Germany's. Esher's recent assertion in *The Times* that Germany was anxious to see Fisher removed from the Admiralty was 'unmitigated balderdash written by the supervisor of the royal drains'.[34] It was an epistolary effusion typical of the All Highest.

Tweedmouth foolishly supposed he had been paid an enormous compliment: to receive a personal letter from the kaiser. At the time a guest of Alfred de Rothschild, he read the letter to fellow guests. A discreet silence would have better served everyone's interests, but this was the first of many impolitic public readings. The Foreign Secretary read and approved a draft reply to which he attached the naval estimates not yet debated by Parliament. Everyone seemed intent upon behaving with the maximum indiscretion. Scarcely surprisingly, journalists soon learned about these epistolary exchanges. With one exception they agreed, it would be best to keep silent. Only Repington insisted the kaiser's letter *ought* to be published. He persuaded Buckle, readers of *The Times* should know of Wilhelm's wicked impropriety, an 'attempt to influence in Germany's interests the minister responsible for our navy estimates'. Two very senior members of staff, Leonard Courtney, a constitutional expert, and James Thursfield advised Buckle it would be better not to publish a letter addressed to him by Repington. He chose to ignore this advice.[35] Churchill tried to persuade Repington that it was not in his interests to publish, but Repington, with the bit between his teeth, could not wait to tell Esher that a friend from his days as military attaché at Brussels, Colonel von Leipzig, had suddenly turned up in London with his countess and invited him to dine. 'You have to admit our William does things thoroughly. He will have to square the circle before he squares me.'[36] He was obviously highly excited and exceedingly pleased with himself. His letter to Buckle stated he considered it nothing less than his public duty to draw the public's attention to such a grave and important matter. Written 4 March, it was published two days later.

Buckle supported the letter with a trenchant leader that insisted the public were entitled to demand publication of both the kaiser's letter and Tweedmouth's reply because the First Lord had been written to not in his private capacity but as a public servant.[37] Repington, who had earlier spoken with Esher of his intention to advertise the kaiser's impertinence, had alerted him that his 'bomb' would be thrown the next day. Esher tried to persuade Buckle to hold back on publication because 'it might place Grey in a dilemma', but Buckle's enquiries at the Foreign Office revealed how much 'the permanent officials greatly resented the kaiser's interference'. Buckle determined in the circumstances he would publish. Repington confidently looked forward to 'a pretty racket'.[38] It made sufficient immediate stir to prompt a temporary fall on the stock market, the surest barometer of British middle-class sentiment. A Cabinet meeting was called to decide how best to respond in Parliament. It was agreed a statement would be made to the Commons while Tweedmouth offered his explanation to the Lords.

Repington had hoped opposition politicians, together with the Unionist press, would chase the hare he had raised and generate a fine old fuss in the country, enough to create sufficient pressure to ensure adequate funding for both army and navy. But the reaction of the Unionist press was a huge, unexpected disappointment. He had not bargained for the virulent attacks upon *The Times* widely condemning it for employing 'gutter press tactics'. Repington observed to Maxse, 'They seem to care more for their own than national interests.' That dig was aimed primarily at Northcliffe.[39] His *Daily Mail*, usually so swift to lash out at the government on behalf of the navy, on this occasion had not joined in the hue and cry. Instead the whole issue was dismissed as nothing more than a mare's nest. Leo Maxse, who had cast himself in the role of Repington's cheer leader, taxed Northcliffe with a lack of patriotism. The newspaper magnate unconvincingly responded, his actions had been dictated by his patriotic sense of what was right. The real determinant had been his concern for his business interests. It was not that he was uncaring of Britain's needs, but rather he loved his businesses more. His attention had been fully engaged with the negotiations to buy *The Times*. Repington was particularly disappointed that Garvin and the *Observer* had not come up to the mark. He was not then aware quite how much Garvin was Fisher's man. Only the *Telegraph* proved as patriotic as he might have wished, for they loudly condemned the kaiser.

His distress at the somnolence of the so-called patriotic press was as nothing compared with the anger he felt at the opposition's compliant inactivity. He grumbled to Maxse how he had 'presented them with an unequalled chance', but they had chosen to 'remain as tame as tom cats. What can you do with such a crowd?'[40] Once more, Repington was guilty of altogether failing to appreciate Balfour's skills as a parliamentary tactician. He supposed that Balfour, for the sake of a quiet life, had chosen to 'silence the rabble seeking office and rewards ... the Tapers and Tadpoles shivering for their shekels'. That explanation served to convince Leo Maxse, who was always eager to think the worst of Balfour, or for that matter, almost all MPs. Complacently Maxse and Repington comforted themselves with the thought that they at least had done their patriotic duty. They could not be squared or bought off with bribes. Repington told Charles Dilke he was 'quite indifferent to the maledictions' hurled at him by a bunch of 'Liberal office holders' who had been thrown into a panic by his 'imperial bomb'.[41] Later, Balfour's private secretary, J. S. Sandars, was pressed by Leo Maxse to explain Tory tameness when afforded such a splendid opportunity both to smite the government and support the navy. Sandars responded he was sorry but the party had treated the affair with philosophic indifference.[42] Balfour would later elicit an unequivocal pledge from Asquith as recompense for the opposition's co-operation in the government's cover-up. The promise was that a sufficient number of dreadnought battleships would be built to ensure Britain retained her naval supremacy over Germany. Esher was convinced Balfour would never have drawn such a declaration from Asquith had it not been for the exposure of the kaiser's letter. If he was correct in this surmise, then Balfour had brilliantly exploited an advantage initially secured by Repington's insistence upon the letter's publication. The following month, after a Cabinet reshuffle, Tweedmouth lost his post as First Lord. *The Times* rather sadly felt obliged to claim the credit for what at best was a poor consolation prize.

At a later date, Repington suggested several reasons why he chose to become involved in the incident of the kaiser's letter. The public ought to know when the head of state of a potentially belligerent power was given information not yet divulged to Parliament and had exercised undue influence over a minister. To Roberts he said he wanted to demonstrate the threat of a successful invasion was real, for it would promote the case for conscription. From the beginning George Clarke had insisted that had been Repington's actual purpose. If it was, then he failed. However, had his intention been, as he also claimed, to punish Tweedmouth for his impudence and impertinence towards Roberts, then he succeeded. But the odds had long been stacked against the exhausted First Lord, worn out by the impossible task of adjudicating between Beresford and Fisher and afforded no help by his two parliamentary aides, Lambert and Robertson, who, according to Arnold-Forster, were two 'congenital idiots incapable of telling the difference between a battleship and a cow'.[43]

Whatever Repington's real intentions had been, he had neither considered nor expected it might permanently damage his reputation. J. A. Spender, who formerly had the highest opinion of him as a journalist, had been astounded that 'A man [he] had thought to be of discretion and good sense' should have perpetrated 'one of the worst pieces of deliberate mischief I ever saw made even in the yellow press'.[44] He judged it to have been a single, rash act, quite out of character, so did not justify the correspondent's wholesale condemnation. Few were as generous as Spender. In the circumstances, Repington might well have concluded the game had probably not been worth the candle. To outward appearances he seemed not to care a jot what others thought of his reputation. Immediately afterwards, he was sharply critical of the king. He insisted Edward had no business summoning Asquith to Biarritz to kiss hands upon his appointment as Prime Minister. The king, angry at such insolence, was not disposed to forgive swiftly. Repington's profound mistake was to suppose royal displeasure was of little consequence. He failed to appreciate just how unremitting the royal household's collective memory could be; how the slightest supposed offence could be harboured, never to be forgiven lightly or forgot. Once pronounced, royal judgment became ossified. Repington sometimes positively welcomed unpopularity as 'proof' his opinion was right: 'When the majority of people in England think something they are generally wrong.'[45] But he could ill-afford to indulge such monumental complacency, especially when it came to telling the king to mind his constitutional ps and qs. Yet, like a cheeky schoolboy, despite the likely painful consequence, all too often he could not resist having the last word.

Meanwhile the naval manoeuvres intended by the navy to restore public confidence in their ability to defend Britain against invasion had quite the opposite effect. In the north of Scotland, a small force eluded the defending fleet and scrambled ashore. When the Admiralty attempted to conceal this by saying nothing, rumour filled the void. By December, when McKenna denied 70,000 men had landed at Wick, few believed him. His problem was compounded when it was learned the Territorials had proved entirely ineffectual. A further series of incidents excited wildly animated debate between Blue Water and Bolt from the Blue advocates. On 6 October 1908 Austria annexed Bosnia-Herzegovina while the Casablanca Affair, involving Germany and France, remained unresolved. Then a mixture of boastful, indiscreet and naive remarks made by the kaiser published in the *Daily Telegraph* intended to foster a good opinion of the All Highest amongst British readers, caused nothing but public anger, resentment and confusion. This was further exacerbated by accounts of his absurd posturing at the Berlin Opera when he flounced out of Mrs Cornwallis-West's box shouting the English would regret spurning his friendship. Over-excited press reports once more stimulated public concern about invasion. In the circumstances, those who believed in the threat of invasion could scarcely be blamed for seeking to make the most of their opportunity.

The invasion inquiry had completed taking evidence in May and by the end of July had finished consideration of the draft report. With the report signed Repington hoped the public would demand its publication, but the government was reluctant to release it. Balfour argued it was not expedient to publish at a time of acute international tension. The arguments raged, the letters flew between the parties with attention increasingly focussed upon the conclusion. The Invasionists' considered it vital the army for Home Defence should be sufficient to deal with an invading force of 70,000 men. Their hopes centred on Balfour's suggestion to Esher that the Repington–Roberts camp might be satisfied if 70,000 were to be released as the officially agreed estimate of the size of an invading force. The Prime Minister had been afforded an ideal opportunity in his November Guildhall speech to make such a statement. But Asquith said nothing to the point, chosing instead to rub salt in the wound by insisting the navy constituted sufficient protection against invasion.

Thoroughly exasperated, Roberts sought to force the issue by initiating a debate in the Lords. A motion in his name was already tabled but Repington worried this tactic might well misfire. Their carefully researched 'proofs' could be discredited by the unavoidable degree of statistical uncertainty, such as the number of troops required for garrison duty in Ireland as well as mainland Britain; or, how many should constitute the necessary field force to meet and repulse an invading force whose size was also a matter for dispute. Their calculations, never disproved, were for an invading force of not 70,000 but 150,000. How many Regulars would be surplus after the mobilisation of the Expeditionary Force? There would be seasonal variations in draft strengths, the number of untrained recruits, and so on. Could Roberts be trusted to cover all these issues without forgetting some or hopelessly confusing others? Repington suggested to Roberts, perhaps it would be best if he first 'cleared the air a little'. This would 'enable the public to appreciate what had gone before', so that the Field Marshal's speech need not be unduly overloaded. Repington trod warily. He was anxious not to upset the old boy. To reveal division now would be fatal.[46]

Provided the figure of 70,000 was admitted in the Lords, they promised to 'eat out of the government's hand'.[47] A large attendance for the debate was expected. Haldane's circumspect responses failed to satisfy Repington's associates. They threatened, if the government did not supply the required figure when the debate came off in the Lords 'every "I" would be dotted and every "T" crossed'.[48] The message could not have been plainer. In a letter to Lord Crewe, as the price of abandoning the debate Roberts demanded a definite statement – that the country needed to prepare to meet an invasion by 100,000 men. At Asquith's request Esher asked the king to intervene. Roberts refused to be brow-beaten by Edward. Repington, maintaining his reasonable man stance, told Ellison he was 'much exercised' at the thought of the approaching House of Lords debate, wondering how he could both hunt with the Robertian hounds and ride with the Haldanian hare.[49]

Roberts demanded a statement of the invasion inquiry's findings. Absurdly he claimed England harboured 80,000 Germans, almost all of whom were trained soldiers. He then made his usual appeal for a citizen force of a million men. The next day's newspapers were full of praise for him. At least in *The Times* the Blue Water advocates proved they were not entirely sunk. They managed to stifle an article Repington had prepared praising Roberts and answering his critics. Nevertheless, on the evidence of the opinions expressed in most newspapers, when he wrote to the Field Marshal to congratulate him he could convincingly assert, their 'shaft had gone home'.[50]

8   Repington helps Haldane

Repington blamed most of the army's failings on the hopelessly misguided efforts of politicians. Temperament, education and heritage disposed him to favour Tory men and measures. However, when it came to the army he found little to choose between the two great political parties and condemned both as hopeless. Scarcely an MP showed an informed interest in the army; many boasted of their ignorance and disinterest. There were a few 'capable young men', but they desperately needed 'guidance, advice, direction to utilise their energy ... a master to lay them on the right lines otherwise they were inclined to riot'. Nevertheless he continued to maintain Parliament was central and necessary to the process of military reform. Only there could the future army either be made or marred.[1] The Commons needed an infusion of experienced, thoughtful, senior army officers. That would be the easiest way to promote practical, military reform. However, to his surprise he was to discover very few senior officers made convincing speech-makers. A noteworthy exception Lieutenant General E. T. H. Hutton, possessed an acute brain and subtle tongue, but all attempts to persuade him to stand for Parliament proved unsuccessful.

Although Repington insisted Parliament was the principal forum for military reform, other journalists emphasised the superiority of the press. Though ineffectual as proponents of military reform, MPs nonetheless continued to refer complacently to the 1895 cordite vote as proof of their continued effectiveness.[2] The press highlighted Arnold-Forster's epistolary campaign that forced first Wolseley, then Brodrick, to admit the army was overstretched. They insisted they had replaced the Commons as the forum for military reform. Repington had been impressed by Lansdowne's early conduct as War Minister for he secured the army's largest peacetime establishment. Lansdowne's two immediate successors, however, failed to achieve the reforms they had so confidently advertised. Nonetheless, Repington believed success *would* attend the army reforms planned by the, as yet untried, Liberal War Minister, Richard Burdon Haldane.

Repington, well informed about Westminster, never failed to scrutinise Hansard carefully. Nor did he confine his reading 'to those set pieces where some great gun was due to make an especially explosive charge', but as diligently searched for 'those infrequent moments when members lapse into honesty and struggle for the truth'.[3] The trust he showed in the new Liberal Secretary of State surprised some. He admitted he was 'the willing victim of Mr Haldane's great gift of conquering all who approach him'.[4] The minister had inherited a department divided by distrust. Speedily he had established unity and vitality. After only one meeting Repington discerned that Haldane possessed very special qualities, 'a strong man ... difficult to humbug or jockey'.[5]

In his memoirs he described their relationship as scarcely ever ruffled by disagreement.[6] The dynamics cannot be satisfactorily understood simply in terms of a shared professional interest in the reform of the British army. Repington believed the tensions natural to any relationship between journalist and minister were in their case tempered by an unusual degree of mutual respect and genuine affection. Their friendship was not as intimate as that which Haldane shared with Grey and Asquith, or Repington with Cowans and Hamilton. Nor did it mirror Haldane's relationship with Esher, but the Fisher–Garvin partnership affords a useful, if not exact, comparison; the close association of two powerful, opinionated men from different professional worlds. Admiral and editor, like Secretary of State and military correspondent, were intent upon promoting a shared purpose. The difference was, when Garvin wrote about the navy his copy deliberately reflected Fisher's thoughts and sentiments, whereas Haldane never expected Repington to be his compliant echo.

Just as Garvin and Fisher, so Repington and Haldane both understood the game they played and the roles they were assigned. Repington believed to criticise some part or detail of a proposal would not necessarily damage Haldane. 'If I never disagreed,' he explained to the minister's mother, 'I would be dubbed a partisan and the effect of my general support ... would be lost.'[7] It would be amazing had this elementary political calculation altogether escaped Haldane. When considering or drafting an article for *The Times*, the natural consequence of their frequent discussions would have been a tacit understanding of what was better said or left unsaid and sometimes they would agree to disagree. Repington suggested, none too convincingly, the minister valued being chastised occasionally in *The Times* because it created a pressure that unified the parliamentary Liberal Party behind him, thus effectively marginalising the Radicals and their assorted allies.

At first, Repington had hoped Haldane would encourage the emergence of a central group of MPs divorced from political extremism and intent upon serving national not partisan interests. This coalitionist dream failed to acknowledge that Liberals and Unionists perceived the national interest differently. Haldane realised he would succeed only if he won over his own party. Repington underestimated the minister's skills as a parliamentarian. He supposed Haldane bent 'to the storm of political conditions in the House of Commons'.[8] But Haldane followed a clear strategy; first, to win over the Cabinet, then persuade the greater part of the parliamentary Liberal Party to join his side. He anticipated little interest or enthusiasm would at first be shown in his proposals. However, when the time came to vote, he was confident the great majority of Liberal backbenchers would troop through the government lobby.

Haldane's temperament and his professional training as an advocate meant that more readily and frequently than most other senior politicians, he was prepared to debate an issue. After exchanging views with a critic he would sometimes accept a procedural adjustment; more occasionally a substantive change. Even at his busiest he always found time to elucidate the more contentious or complex elements in his argument. His patient dealings with persistent, even ill-natured critics, never failed to amaze Repington. He recalled an occasion when he had expected censure for his opposition but had been disarmed after a meeting with Haldane. It was impossible to sustain angry differences for long with so reasonable an opponent.

At their very first meeting Haldane had assured Repington he did not intend to repeat Arnold-Forster's mistake. He *would* listen to army opinion. Despite this assurance Repington still fretted. He feared Haldane valued intellect at the expense of practical experience. 'It is one thing to lay down beautiful general principles, quite another to harmonise them with the daily tasks of the practical administrator.'[9] If Haldane's reforms were to be permanent then the army would need to rate them practical. Never having been in the army, he did not understand what it was to think like a soldier. That weakness was compounded by Esher's identical want of military experience. Their intentions might be the best, but inexperience could well betray them. Repington was oppressed by thoughts of the recent clean sweep of very senior army appointments. Initially he had been persuaded it was worth the pain and dislocation, but upon further reflection realised the folly of supposing it would not occasion long-lasting damage. The army, always reluctant to forget or to forgive, had an exaggerated respect for rank. These important considerations had been insufficiently weighed. Whenever afterwards there was talk of changing the membership of the Army Council, Repington would remind Esher 'feelings of soreness' left by the previous dismissals had still not subsided.[10]

The Army Council completely misconstrued Haldane's promise to consult them. Members had supposed he intended to listen to them exclusively, but that was never his intention. It would, for example, have meant excluding the valued advice of Ellison and Haig.

From 1905 to 1908, with single-minded devotion, Ellison served as Haldane's principal private military secretary. Repington once mused whether Ellison would not have made as good a minister as Haldane for without his help it was certain that much the minister achieved would never have been realised. 'It is a pleasure to think,' Repington wrote in a valedictory letter to Ellison, 'you and I were in agreement throughout in supporting the best War Minister of modern times.' Both of them agreed, modern military regeneration was only beginning. 'The one advance on a great scale likely to occur in our day,' wrote Repington, 'is the substitution of compulsory for voluntary training.' Knowing it to be an optimistic estimate he added reluctantly if realistically, 'A modern army system is a plant of slow growth and *festina lente* is a good maxim.'[11]

When it came to Haig, Repington recognised Haldane appreciated and respected his political judgment. His own relationship with Haig he admitted was at best guarded. The truth was each man sensed as they warily circled each other like two great cats, their latent antipathy. Haig had returned from India somewhat sooner than expected. The Indian army's former Inspector General of Cavalry was appointed successively to two key directorates; Training, 1906–07, and Staff Duties, 1907–09. Because Repington remained cautious rather than enthusiastic about the long-term prospects of this rapidly ascending star in the military firmament, he always hedged his praise about with caveats. He sensed rather than knew that Haig disliked him, but supposed this was because he was a journalist. What Haig particularly distrusted and feared about Repington was his ready access to powerful people and especially his intimate relationship with the Secretary of State for War. He was also concerned with what he considered was the correspondent's demonstrable lack of moral probity. Modest and discreet in the conduct of his own private life, imbued since childhood with a latent religiosity, he neither understood nor had the least sympathy for the way Repington lived openly with his mistress. Particularly mindful of his own professional advancement – even his marriage had been contracted with that very much the foremost consideration – Haig sought as little contact with Repington as possible.[12]

When asked upon whom Haldane relied for his advice, Repington would respond, he was leaning upon the right people. The clear implication was that he was one such right person. There was a widespread misunderstanding about the function of advisers and their relationship with the minister. Haldane had neither the experience nor military knowledge to be aware of every practical difficulty. After his roles as teacher and publicist, Repington saw his task as making good that deficiency.

In seven memoranda he published during his first six months at the War Office, Haldane set out his proposed reforms together with the principles underlying them. When circulated in advance for comment, Repington angrily denounced them. The most glaring flaw was the omission of Kitchener's name. Why had he not been sent a copy? The want of co-operation between London and India was ridiculous. India's C-in-C should be encouraged to express his views freely and continuously. He would send Kitchener his draft copy. This idea was instantly slapped down. The War Office went to absurd lengths to keep India in the dark. Haldane insisted they had no duty to tell the government of India that the Defence Committee had decided the Indian army could not be guaranteed reinforcements. Repington promised to raise Cain if India continued to be kept in the dark. He told Marker everyone at the War Office seemed 'terribly frightened by what Lord K. might say'.[13] Not a single person with worthwhile recent Indian experience sat on the Committee of Defence. There would never be progress until this was changed. Repington was convinced, to involve Kitchener could only strengthen Haldane's hand. He was confident it would instantly highlight those weaknesses in the plans to which he had frequently drawn attention, particularly the want of any strategic base. Contrast this, he implored, with Kitchener's recent speech on India's military policy. At the same time he reassured Marker the Indian army had no reason to feel unduly aggrieved. They were not alone: for instance, there had been 'no discussion whatsoever with the Army Council'.[14]

Repington's deliberately casual tone belied his deep anxiety. He had told Haldane repeatedly it was foolish to suppose any scheme could succeed without the backing of the best senior officers. He reminded the minister, his success in the House depended upon Campbell-Bannerman. It was he who guaranteed the Radical Liberals would not unduly endanger army reform. To ensure his continued support, Haldane should follow the precedent set by Cardwell. Simply to mention the name of the former war minister under whom Sir Henry had once served was enough to guarantee the Prime Minister's enthusiastic support. Haldane ought to submit his proposed scheme to a committee like MacDougall's (1872), which would ensure a clear, logical plan worked out in detail by practical men. If he did not, Repington was convinced, the scheme was as good as dead.[15] Haldane chose not to accept this advice. A too great dependence upon frequent consultation with the Army Council, he suggested, would only alienate members' affections. He was not being deliberately disingenuous. Arnold-

Forster had consulted the Army Council no less than thirty times in 1905. The frequency of their meetings had served only to emphasise how little the minister had valued their advice. Members had grown cynical and dejected. Instead of summoning the Army Council, Haldane preferred to tackle particular problems with individual generals.

Repington dismissed this proffered rationale as worthless. Haldane had to allow the Army Council to draw up the report and to sign it, otherwise his ideas would remain 'airy, impossible, impractical and certain to be torn to pieces'.[16] Repington declared further debate served no useful purpose. Haldane had been at the War Office less than seven months yet faced failure unless 'someone dragged [him] back to mother earth from the clouds'.[17] Esher resolutely insisted the minister's schemes were 'clear and definite'. Repington refused to concede.[18] Where was the detail to address the many practical difficulties? Haldane *must* consult the Army Council. Surely this was the logic of his whole approach to army reform? The minister should set out the general principles and determine the boundaries of discussion while those with practical military experience would provide the necessary detailed adjustments.

By January Repington appeared to think only a miracle would resolve matters. Esher was now his only hope, 'the *deus ex machina* who would put things right'. The directors knew what had been going on and 'deserved to have their ears pulled'. The military members of the Army Council rarely saw Haldane, but were aware he was in daily close conclave with Ellison and Haig. The seventh and final memorandum promoted widespread fury. It was all too clearly the work of Haig, so Council members protested loudly insisting it would never be accepted. They had found no fault with the main proposal; they were angry and resentful because effectively they had been reduced to no more than the executors of others' ideas. That was *not* how the Army Council was supposed to work. It was *not* how Haldane had *promised* it would work, but clearly he did not care what they thought. A member told Repington, 'If we are worth our salt we ought to give our opinion. If not, then better men should be put in our place and made to give one.' These and similar sentiments Repington rehearsed unsparingly to Esher. He hoped the nonsense of non-consultation would now cease. Haldane had given him the distinct assurance he would assemble the *Conseil en Séance plénière*[19] and consult them about the general principles of his plan.

Repington, despite a hopelessly lengthy catalogue of complaints, insisted everything was still not beyond redemption. Haldane, when the full Army Council was assembled, should allow the military members to 'talk until they are tired of the whole plan, principles and details ... a few hours of boring sitting and the expenditure of liquid fuel should solve the problem'. Repington emphasised Esher needed to exert all his powers to ensure Haldane did not break with Council members. A rupture would be fatal. The problem was Haldane refused to acknowledge he was a civilian. He could not behave at the War Office as Fisher did at the Admiralty. He did not appreciate Council members were 'the trustees of the army's interests. Any rough measures with them might turn the whole army into his embittered enemies.' The task of impressing these truths upon the minister was best left to Esher. Repington declared he no longer wished to be involved.[20]

Repington's mistake was to have listened too attentively and too often to the complaints of the Council members. Consequently he blamed Haldane for needlessly putting their noses out of joint. But Haldane had not ignored Repington's advice so much as chosen to employ the expertise of Army Council members differently. He suggested a subcommittee of the Defence Committee should critically examine the military content of his planned changes. The members of this subcommittee, together with the witnesses called to give evidence, would embrace not only Army Council members but other senior army officers, not even excluding Lord Roberts. Once he knew and understood just what Haldane was intent upon doing, Repington insisted it was the same ploy as he had recommended the previous October. More accurately, it bore some passing similarity to a scheme he had suggested the previous May. Rather better than he supposed, the minister understood the strengths and weaknesses of certain senior army officers and had cleverly drafted the subcommittee's terms of reference to anticipate and nullify any captious objections the Adjutant General and the CGS might make. Repington rarely questioned Haldane's good intentions but often failed to appreciate the exact thrust of his strategy. His faith was now further tested by the cuts Haldane claimed needed to be made in the army estimates.

Repington frequently complained the public was interested only in how much the army cost, a subject about which they grumbled endlessly. He conveniently forgot how a few years earlier he himself had fought for cuts in military expenditure, forcing St John Brodrick to economise as an urgent priority. Arnold-Forster as Secretary of State had accepted financial restraints, but his attempted economies had failed. His financial miscalculation became Haldane's economic inheritance. Where other ministers had failed, Haldane *needed* to succeed; substantial savings had to be achieved. The strict parliamentary timetable meant estimates had to be prepared and presented in just three months. Westminster and Fleet Street waited to see how much the minister would demand.

During the general election campaign Haldane made two key speeches. They appeared to imply his priority would be efficiency rather than economy. Unionists approved, but it had provoked wailing, lamentation and motions of censure from Lib-Labs and Radicals. After their general election triumph, the Radical faction constituted such a formidable congeries it suggested their views would not be lightly ignored by the parliamentary Liberal Party. But Haldane's first speech to the new House stressed not efficiency but economy. It seemed he had decided to make cuts in the army's budget after all. In *Vestigia*, Repington insisted Radicals wanted the army estimates cut 'so severely reform would be out of the question'.[21] He deliberately chose to demonise the Radicals. This made more credible his subsequent claim that they, not the Unionist opposition, posed the greatest parliamentary threat to Haldane's intended reform programme. His earlier derisive dismissal of Radicals as ineffectual was forgotten.[22]

Given the hopeless stewardship of his own finances, Repington ought to have been reluctant to volunteer advice on economic questions. Nonetheless, he declared he was eager to help the minister. His readers had become accustomed to his occasional oracular pronouncements on the British economy, although financial detail was not his forte. He once told Marker, 'damned calculations' made him 'dizzy'. They were 'better ignored' as 'much too obscure. They served only to confuse the British public'. Instead he liked to repeat his favourite mantra: 'there was a right as well as a wrong way to finance the army'. Any soldier could have told the minister how to proceed. First, establish the army's strategic role. Next, calculate accurately the number of men and supplies needed to match the given strategic purpose. Repington wondered why Haldane failed to acknowledge what was so self-evident. Why was he hell-bent upon imposing arbitrary financial limits?

A further disturbing dimension puzzled Marker as much as Repington. Both men shared a high regard for Ellison, yet he had concurred with Haldane's decision. Together in conclave at Cloan, they had produced the first memorandum on the army estimates, suggesting 28 million pounds as the amount available to be spent on the army for the coming financial year. In the second memorandum the limit became mandatory. How could Ellison have agreed to such a wrong-headed proposal? It must have been against his better judgment. Repington thought this 'mistake' could be readily explained. Haldane had only recently begun his study of the army's problems. To demand he produce a draft memorandum on military expenditure so soon was as though Kitchener had been asked, after a few months' study at Lincoln's Inn, to codify English law. 'You cannot make a soldier or a lawyer in a few months,' Repington smugly asserted.[23] What he had altogether failed to grasp was, it was not Haldane's job to think like a soldier. Faced with an economic and political problem, not unreasonably he looked for an economic and political solution. In future *he* would determine how much money was available for the army to spend. The military might not like it, but better the War Office inflict the economies than the Treasury. From now on the War Office would be the master of its own financial fate.

The figure of 28 million pounds had not been pitched arbitrarily but astutely, to appeal to the Army Council. Members accepted the limit set with considerable relief. Haldane had anticipated their reaction. Council members had feared he would offer them much less. The Radicals had confidently predicted the army's estimates would not exceed 20 million pounds. Haldane had once more demonstrated he understood the mind-set of the military members better than Repington, who continued to insist the estimates were being cut against Haldane's better judgment in order to placate his rapacious Cabinet colleagues and assorted selfish loafers and cranks on the Radical and Lib-Lab benches. So enamoured was Repington with this invention, he maintained it in the pages of *Vestigia*, where he likened Haldane to a traveller in a snowy waste hurling hapless infants from his sleigh to delay the pursuit of ravening Radical wolves. It was, he insisted melodramatically, the only way their hunger could be assuaged.

Army finance was, Repington admitted, an 'infernally tricky wicket', but he believed in order to defeat Haldane's detractors, 'the financial stroke [was] much the best to employ'.[24] He was inspired by sentiments similar to those that had informed Sir Henry Newbolt's familiar poetic paean about playing the game, *Vitai Lampada*. Faced with the economic equivalent of 'a bumping pitch' and a 'blinding light', Repington supposed one judicious blow could win the game for England, Empire and army. It was a waste of time and effort to appeal to the patriotic sense of Radicals who would happily endanger the safety of the realm to pay the bribes, doles and pensions for which they constantly whined. They would 'beggar the army so as to squander funds upon Socialistic experiments'.[25] Their claims could be readily smashed by detailed economic analysis and argument and, so he would later claim in *Vestigia*, his arguments proved 'beyond any doubt' the country possessed more than sufficient funds to satisfy the simultaneous, contradictory demands of social *and* military reformers. He presented a persuasive case with panache. His conclusion pleased him, which he seemed to equate with convincing others! Britain's immense resources would 'entirely justify any expansion of our armaments our situation might demand'. He supposed he had provided Haldane with an unanswerable argument that would allow him to spend as much as he desired upon the army. Proudly he insisted, 'Not one of my figures was ever disputed.'[26] Surely, even in his most euphoric mood he must have known it was a delusion to suppose that one article in *The Times* would quash all future economic argument.

Repington might suppose what he liked, he never really understood Haldane's thinking on economics. The minister, a prudent, canny Scot, shared many of the economic ideas of the Radical reductionists. He deprecated waste or extravagance of any kind and disapproved of the army loan system. No previous minister had resisted the temptation to raid the loan fund, the most convenient way of borrowing in excess of the army's annual estimates. When Asquith had been Chancellor of the Exchequer, Haldane promised him he would not repeat his predecessors' unprincipled profligacy. He further pledged to cut the number of troops. These two measures would guarantee a substantial saving in the annual military budget. Had Repington known of this promise, he would have been horrified.

Haldane argued the cost of the army was determined by the decisions of those Cabinet colleagues who decided Britain's overseas policy. Thus, it was they who effectively determined the number of troops required to fulfil their policies. Political parties generally agreed, whenever international circumstances allowed, budgets ought to be cut. Haldane insisted, the day the India Office told the War Office fewer troops were needed to defend India, he would be only too happy to order a decrease. Repington had been in Haldane's drawing room when the recently appointed First Lord of the Admiralty had regaled the assembled company with an account of how the war minister had effectively trumped the demands of the reductionists in the Cabinet with his argument. When told it was their policies, not War Office extravagance that accounted for the ever-increasing military budget, 'the Secretaries of State for India, the Colonies and Foreign Affairs, each in turn held up their hands in horror and protested vigorously'. Repington preserved this pretty vignette in a letter to his editor, Buckle.[27] Both men were, therefore, well aware of Haldane's ploy but preferred to stick to the myth that the economies were the minister's reluctant response to unreasonable Radical demands.

Repington never sat easily or for long in anyone's shadow. At a private briefing designed to leak confidential information to Lloyd George's disadvantage, he had been expressly asked not to become involved. He said he would seek to persuade Buckle to keep *The Times* from making any comment upon the conflict. He failed to do this but his initial vexation soon turned to delight. 'The Winston–Lloyd George intriguers', he told Haldane's sister, 'deserved a good slap in the face',[28] and now he felt free to join in the slapping. Despite Haldane's clear proscription, the opportunity for a dust-up with Lloyd George and Winston was too good to ignore. In an article entitled 'The Cabinet

and the Army', he ordered the Radical 'twins' to cease making 'a colleague's life unnecessarily, indeed desperately difficult'. Their desire to
sate their appetites for plunder, 'to excite the demands of the least
intelligent fraction of the lower orders, [was] scarcely worthy of a shabby
parish councillor'. Higher standards of behaviour were required of
responsible ministers of the Crown. It simply was not good enough the
Chancellor and his sidekick pursuing their personal agenda, especially
when it put the safety of the realm at risk.[29] Esher told Repington he was
wasting his time. It was only Churchill up to his usual tricks, thinking he
was Napoleon, trying to push to the front of the Cabinet. Repington
preferred Balfour's explanation, that Winston was intent upon playing
his father's part. Churchill, to work up a case against Haldane, had been
given privileged access to the War Office and to its papers. Haldane
feared Asquith planned to promote Churchill to the War Office and
would offer him the Woolsack. Repington's stream of anti-Radical
vituperation, intended to help Haldane succeed, had only made things
more difficult. To calm an irate Churchill, Haldane was obliged to
disown everything Repington had written. Radical Liberals had always
doubted Haldane's good faith and his honesty of intent. They thought of
him still as a leading Roseberyite and an unrepentant Imperial apologist.
Repington's unbridled attack upon the Radical 'twins' could not have
been better calculated to stir up the latent hatred and factional distrust
at all levels in the parliamentary Liberal Party. He ought to have appreciated that once Asquith replaced Campbell-Bannerman as prime minister, Haldane was left without anyone to secure his credit among the
Radicals, either in Cabinet or among the backbenches.

The fate of the army estimates seemed to tremble in the balance;
Haldane even feared for the future of the Expeditionary Force.[30]
Churchill, apparently supported by the majority of the Cabinet, was
busy touting his own scheme insisting it would be more effective and
cost less than Haldane's plans. Repington joined with Esher to rubbish
this assertion. He assured Haldane he had nothing to fear, but Haldane
remained unconvinced that he could win the day. Only by bending every
ounce of his diplomatic skill and political will to secure his survival, did
Haldane eventually emerge triumphant from a very bruising ordeal. If
Repington had heeded Haldane's original injunction and succeeded in
muzzling *The Times*, or perhaps on this occasion, even more usefully,
chosen to make no contribution to the debate, most if not all Haldane's
problems would have been avoided. As it happened, the army estimates
were saved but *despite* and not *because* of Repington's involvement. The
one unlooked for and unexpected consequence of Haldane's success was
the army estimates would in future be settled directly with Lloyd George.

Having failed to sink Haldane, Churchill hauled off in pursuit of Reggie McKenna and the navy's budget.

Against considerable odds, Haldane had secured the army's 1908 estimates. There were good and sufficient reasons for him to have refused to have any more dealings with the correspondent whose involvement against his express wishes had so exacerbated his problems. This latest scrape was not the first, nor would it be the last time Repington blotted his copybook. Nevertheless, Haldane continued to confide in him, to listen if not always to act upon his advice. What outweighed all other factors was Repington's unique value as the acknowledged leading contemporary military journalist. In the battle for the minds and hearts of the public it was an inestimable advantage to have his support. No other critic better advertised and justified his reform proposals. Haldane understood advertisement came at a price. He willingly paid in the coin journalists most value: privileged, reliable information.

Haldane handled Repington patiently and dextrously, a courteous deftness he deployed in his treatment of all journalists; so different from the ham-fisted efforts of his immediate Tory predecessors. He created a special department regularly supplying information and favourable propaganda. 'Good writing carefully read', he believed, was the best way for his reforming intentions to be understood.[31] Repington sometimes suspected the presence of leading strings and then was inclined to overemphasise his own contribution to Haldane's reforms. There is no hint of this in his memoirs where he wrote, 'I hope I did some good ... I enjoyed the controversy ... I hope I gave as good as I got.' If anything justified his work for *The Times*, he insisted, it had been 'the consistency of [his] support for Mr Haldane's military children'. He believed Haldane deserved 'every ounce of credit for the creation of the force that withstood the Hun in 1914'.[32]

Repington had hoped Haldane would not change the Regulars. However, by early summer 1906 it was apparent he intended to cut the number of battalions to achieve parity between those serving at home and abroad. This would also help keep costs within the limits of his self-imposed budget. But even planned economies required to be circumscribed. Eight line battalions and two battalions of the Guards were to be culled. Repington insisted these economies were not made for sound military reasons but to obey arbitrary political demands.[33] Ivor Maxse suggested the 3rd Coldstream might be saved by reducing the Irish Guards, to which Repington responded that Maxse's suggestion was no use to him when he was 'opposed to all reductions'. Anyway, Maxse surely realised it was 'not really practical politics to get rid of the Irish Guards just after they have been formed'? What Ivor Maxse, or anyone else for that matter, had not known was Repington had discussed his article with Haldane while it was still in page proof. The exact figures of the reductions had been omitted at the minister's personal request. Nonetheless Repington had not pulled his punches and had expressed almost unqualified disapproval. Not that he supposed Haldane was in any risk of 'injury from the severity of [his] attack upon the policy of reductions'. Though it might seem paradoxical, the minister would find his hostility 'helpful as the reductions would then appear to have been dragged from him by *force majeur*'. To save the Guards, the best thing they could do was strengthen Haldane's hand. 'Now is the time to beat the big drum and to commandeer all the *guerilleros* who will fight.' Despite his belligerent words Repington doubted they would win, and wrote rather hopelessly to Marker, 'I suppose it would be something if we at least established a funk.'[34]

To Repington's intense embarrassment, St John Brodrick had been among those who declared unqualified approval for his attack on the minister's proposals. When Haldane gave the figures to the House on 12 July, Repington's tone became positively threatening. He had hoped the minister would 'raise the question of Imperial defence above the quagmire of party', but it seemed his intent was 'to alienate those who will not kiss the Socialist rod'.[35] Such absurd rhetorical flourishes were not his usual style, but in his private correspondence he was almost as wildly condemnatory of Haldane's plan. He dismissed the plan as 'pretty sorry', arguing with Marker that Haldane had not so much imposed his cuts as failed to save the army from unnecessary economies. He had given insufficient time and consideration to his scheme. He had told the Army Council he was a virgin and would take the usual nine months to conceive his plan. He was then delivered of it in less than seven. The explanation seemed obvious. 'He has been hassled at Cabinet and had a miscarriage.'[36] Surely Repington realised this vulgar explanation was scarcely credible? In the months that followed, his articles, like his letters, were replete with anti-Radical rant. The obvious intention was to blame reductions on the Radicals rather than condemn Haldane's judgment. He cautioned the minister's critics to be realistic in their expectations. He continued to rag Haldane about his economies, but, given the present temper of the Commons and the numbers and cocksureness of the Radicals and their allies, Repington argued the minister had no alternative but to cede to the majority in his party.

When Haldane announced he proposed to reduce the number of Regular battalions raised, there was an immediate, savagely partisan barrage of criticism from the Tory press. Haldane, while not over-confident, had carefully planned his strategy. He correctly anticipated the uncompromising ferocity of the Tory attacks. He described them to his mother as 'the

London Society Opposition and Conservative papers'.[37] Nonetheless, it was they who unwittingly would prompt the bulk of his own party to rally to his side. In playing the party card his game was not only wiser but longer and more realistic than Repington's hopeless and impractical desire to place the army above party politics. Forgetting his own earlier, intemperate criticism of the minister and seeing Haldane baited and scorned in Parliament and the press, Repington turned upon the minister's Tory critics to rend them. They had shamelessly abandoned the minister at the very first sign of difficulty. An attack by Leo Maxse in his *National Review* had been unforgivable. Leo was almost certainly beyond rational persuasion, but Repington considered H. A. Gwynne of the *Standard*, though among Haldane's loudest critics, not beyond redemption. 'Taffy' possessed sufficient political common sense to appreciate that merely to recycle the all too familiar, partisan slanders achieved nothing other than damage to the army's future prospects. Might Gwynne not be persuaded to play a more subtle, political game? Surely he saw it was in everyone's interest Haldane should remain at the War Office?

Although the Militia were not liable for overseas service, Haldane intended 40 per cent should join the Expeditionary Force. The War Office would need an Act of Parliament to extend its control. Auxiliary troops not required for the Expeditionary Force would be amalgamated into a Territorial Army. Raised and administered locally, they would undergo intense training at the outbreak of war before taking their place in the front line alongside the Regulars. Repington cavilled at certain details but generally supported the concept of the Territorial Army, commending the idea to his readers. At their earliest planning stage he had recommended the Territorial provisions to Marker. He recognised the idea would be stubbornly resisted by traditionalists as well as by a significant fraction of the parliamentary Liberal Party, whose hostility was aroused by the least sniff of militarism. He anticipated the Volunteer lobby would cause the most trouble. It would take them no time at all to perceive Haldane's scheme would undermine their vested interests. To placate them, Repington suggested Haldane change their terms of enlistment. From the letters he had received, he judged many Volunteers expected the future Territorial Force would be run by a Volunteer Advisory Board created at the War Office. 'The last thing you want,' Repington warned, 'is a pack of old, volunteer women at the War Office.'[38] The Volunteer COs would kick against the loss of their financial lever and there would be more opposition than Haldane anticipated.

Haldane admitted, although the army experts were on his side, it would be difficult to realise his plans; he would have to face down not only stupidity but also much prejudice. To reassure and disarm his critics, Haldane proposed a Territorial Forces Committee, soon more familiarly known as the Duma. Chaired by Esher, its members embraced a diverse spectrum of opinion. In May, Haldane, addressing the Militia leaders for the first time, tried to persuade them they had nothing to fear. In July he addressed the Yeomanry, and in September the Volunteers, but all three approaches proved unavailing. In the face of this intransigent antagonism, Haldane's optimism crumbled. He sought to appease them by modifying his original scheme. This process continued until the bill had passed all its parliamentary stages. Repington considered the minister had panicked unnecessarily. This, however, was said *after* Haldane's bill had negotiated its passage through the House. He conveniently forgot only months before he had forecast to Esher there would be stern opposition from the Volunteers, greater than the minister anticipated. On the Volunteer issue, Repington thoroughly indulged the freedom to change his own mind, while accusing Haldane of hopeless indecision. 'No one wants Haldane to succeed more than I do, but he cannot unless he takes a firm line. His friends scarcely dare put pens to paper because the saint they may vow themselves to may not prove to be *his* saint, and then they will be in the cart. Can you not get some lymph from a good, pig-headed priest from the Propaganda College in Rome,' he asked Esher, 'to inoculate the S of S with a single idea and purpose?'[39]

Haldane and Esher had both wanted Repington to join the Duma, but after careful consideration he refused. His initial explanation to Esher cobbled together his usual assertion – it might compromise his independence – with his publicly stated aversion to 'cuts in the Guards and the artillery forced upon Mr Haldane by circumstances that appear to me arbitrary'. He did not at first admit he thought the concept fundamentally flawed. Most members would serve only their own selfish purposes. When Esher admitted they were an odious team to drive, the news scarcely surprised Repington. Having to chair the Duma he likened to the Old Man of the Sea perched permanently upon Esher's neck. He would have unloaded the burden and told Esher as much, but was ignored. As Repington had predicted, none of the well-intentioned discussion served any useful purpose.

The Territorial and Reserve Forces Bill did not receive its second reading until after the Easter recess, 1907. Few in the House supposed the bill would become law. Like other 'experts', in his private correspondence Repington vacillated. To General Hutton he urged a non-partisan approach as most likely to succeed, but then singled out Balfour and Arnold-Forster and belaboured them for 'trying to queer the pitch for political ends'.[40] In Balfour's case the criticism was undeserved and to combine him with Arnold-Forster was particularly perverse. Writing to Esher, Repington anathematised *all* Unionists. They had allowed their political hostility to the government to determine their attitude on defence issues. When Arnold-Forster insisted Haldane's measures 'imperilled the safety of the country', Repington saw red. He dismissed the claim as 'a mare's nest'.[41] Marker was moved to defend his former political master, at which Repington immediately relented for his heart was never in making sport of Arnold-Forster. And as he and Marker both wanted the same thing, it was folly for them to wrangle.[42]

The expected, stern Unionist challenge to the Territorial Bill in the Commons never materialised. They seemed strangely distracted. Charles Dilke pointed out MPs on both sides were neither interested nor enthusiastic. Dilke, a dangerous and informed critic, was a potentially important ally for Haldane. He and Repington were never friends but respected each other. Repington had been more than usually disconcerted by the warm compliments he received in the course of the debate. Dilke had described him as Haldane's chief supporter in the press. Others suggested the minister's recent success owed much to the powerful articles of the clever military correspondent. Repington was irritated that Haldane should appear to be keen to conciliate his critics when their pusillanimous behaviour suggested they could have been ignored with impunity. Criticisms heard in the House had been 'piffle ... not one practical proposal ... in two days debate ... The Tories have been more stupid than I could have imagined possible ... They are a dead party in a military sense'.[43] He neither appreciated nor really understood how Haldane had ensured Balfour would deliver an acquiescent opposition. Haldane had been more than happy to make concessions as the price of co-operation in the Commons. There his tactic had paid off handsomely. The Lords, however, he feared might prove a tougher obstacle.

Relations between the two Houses of Parliament had deteriorated. To succeed in the Lords, Haldane's legislation required Unionist co-operation. Asked by Haldane to test the ground, Repington reported the Unionist leader was 'disposed to be friendly'.[44] Lansdowne admitted Haldane's bill contained some very good points, but warned, he was 'not sufficiently behind the scenes [to know] whether an attempt might be made to find a way out of impasse'. Lansdowne clearly was disposed to seek a compromise and Repington delightedly reported the progress of the bill would not be hindered. Haldane did not have to rely on Repington's estimate alone. That same day he had consulted with Esher, Ellison and Haig. Parliamentary victory was his highest priority. To achieve it he was prepared to concede to Lansdowne and Salisbury. They would not wreck his bill in the Lords if the Militia were excluded from his Territorial scheme. Haldane claimed that his concession entailed not an abandonment of principle but a tactical readjustment. Methuen then threatened to throw a spanner in the works when from sheer cussedness he deliberately sought to change the provision for cadet corps. An unpleasant constitutional incident was avoided when Esher drafted a clever compromise amendment. Thereafter, the bill was speedily ratified. Repington told Marker he had always anticipated victory by a large majority. But this was only a beginning and much remained to be done. He thoroughly approved the lines upon which the legislation had been laid out. Smugly he insisted he could now 'go touring . . . for nothing is left to discuss in London'.[45] His prediction, more confident than wise, was dictated by the belief Haldane had completed 'the more exacting part of his labours'. Repington wrote to Haldane's sister. He expressed the hope her brother would never again be 'such a prominent protagonist in the Westminster play.'[46] Despite the minister's robust constitution, he feared his health would be undermined by the relentless toil of office. His concern for Haldane's health was entirely genuine.[47] He was aware he had sometimes misjudged Haldane's methods and measures. Actually he had as often misunderstood them. But he had never doubted the minister's sincere intent to create a modern British army and acknowledged Haldane was the only Liberal politician capable of defining and executing a suitable programme of army reform.

9   Conscription

The National Service League was founded in 1902. Many considered its members mad militarists. Unlike the Navy League, it lacked real political influence until Lord Roberts became its president. Repington had ignored the NSL though he played a prominent part in the National Defence Association, founded in 1906. It sought to reconcile the NSL's programme with the beliefs of those who thought more might yet be achieved by voluntary effort. If conscription were ever achieved, Repington thought, it would be by stages. He would have preferred the association become a powerful pressure group to lobby for Haldane's Territorials. Later, they might raise the cry for conscription and perhaps develop an imperial dimension. He inveigled Roberts, the ideal popular talisman, into becoming the NDA's chairman, and among several other powerful publicists persuaded Northcliffe to join.

Repington insisted Roberts should say as little as possible otherwise he would 'talk for hours into space'.[1] Roberts realised he was being ignored and later resigned to concentrate his efforts on the fortunes of the NSL. Nor was he the only member of the association's original executive committee to leave. Those who viewed national service through the prism of their own prejudice found the association's declared aims too equivocal. Repington was convinced the theoretical case for conscription was unanswerable but acknowledged, for the moment, the public refused to accept it.[2]

The NDA helped to launch a campaign to secure the re-examination of the invasion issue. George Clarke was certain their real intention was to make compulsion acceptable. As Clarke suspected, recruitment for Haldane's Territorial Force was inextricably linked with conscription. Contrary to expectation, the 1908 invasion inquiry had concluded there was no need to increase military strength or to adopt conscription. Repington cursed the fact that in a world where force reigned supreme, British diplomacy had been left helpless. Then, on the opening day of the 1909 naval estimate debates, Asquith made a fatal admission: Britain could no longer guarantee to build capital ships more swiftly than the

Fig. 5 Field Marshal Lord 'Bobs' Roberts (1832–1914)

Germans. The consequent widespread public panic delighted the Fisherites as it prompted an irresistible demand for battleships. Repington assumed that even the most stubborn Blue Water advocate would have to admit Britain's naval supremacy was no longer guaranteed and the public would at last accept the need for national military training. But the public's mind remained stubbornly unchanged. For the moment he urged Roberts, in concert with Milner and Curzon, to promote yet another debate on conscription.[3] Repington was hopelessly depressed.

Optimism, he admitted to Roberts, was impossible when the prospect was so bleak. An immediate conflict with Germany was not an unlikely eventuality. Germany was strong by land and sea while Britain would have to fight with whatever organisation it possessed. Russia remained weak, France divided, and it was certain no country would contemplate alliance with Britain so long as her army remained weak. The Territorials were not even up to establishment. Unless supported by the Regulars, they were incapable of releasing the navy from its coastguard duties. His colleagues at *The Times* had 'joined the naval monomaniacs' and thought 'of nothing but Dreadnoughts'. Everywhere Blue Water supporters were in control and the lemming-like flight was not confined to PHS.[4]

In the spring of 1909 Thomas Kincaid-Smith, retired cavalry officer and Liberal MP for Stratford-upon-Avon, resigned his seat and stood for re-election on the single issue platform of national service. When Repington learned the Unionists in 'a miserable party move' had decided to oppose Kincaid-Smith, he despaired. Roberts promised he would bring a bill before the Lords demanding 'universal military training to provide Haldane with the required number of adequately trained men'.[5] He urged Balfour to 'speak out fearlessly', but the party leader's concern was with political practicalities. Whatever Unionists felt in their hearts, the national prejudice against conscription remained. To support a pro-conscription, Liberal candidate would be irresponsibly quixotic. It would certainly lose them votes in the next general election. For that reason, Central Office chose as their candidate P. S. Foster, an enthusiastic advocate of tariff reform who had publicly declined to promote the adoption of universal training.

The by-election deteriorated into farce. Kincaid-Smith was routed. Compulsionists' blushes were only spared because public attention was engaged by the furore Lloyd George's proposed budget measures generated. The Liberal press crowed delightedly at their opponents' disarray and what they described as 'the defeat of compulsion'. Repington was so thoroughly depressed he suggested subsidising the Legion of Frontiersmen, local rifle clubs and Baden-Powell's boy scouts to help provide 'a national army of second line in Great Britain'[6]. Jim Garvin described him as 'throwing himself into an absurd state of theatrical convulsions'.[7] Supposing once the Unionists regained power they would introduce national service, Garvin chose to ignore the confusion. Repington insisted Garvin could not have been more wrong. The Tories would not touch National Service with a barge pole.

Opposition spokesmen debating the army estimates taunted Haldane, insisting the failure of his Territorial scheme would make compulsory service inevitable. There was a sudden pause in the savage party-political battle occasioned by the king's demise. A party truce was mooted and Lloyd George prepared a memorandum 'on the formation of a Coalition', in which he sought to address those questions that might be solved only by combined party effort. Foremost among such questions was national defence. He proposed the introduction of compulsory military training but Haldane was one of the few ministers who reacted favourably.[8] Esher believed there was 'a strong party in the Cabinet ready to accept compulsion on certain conditions', but Repington 'did not give them credit for so much sense'.[9] He was right to be sceptical for within months the party truce had withered.

In the Lords, Esher bluntly rejected the government's claim the Territorials could be expanded, insisting that 'In London as elsewhere in the country, the limit has been reached.'[10] Repington, absent from town attending Territorial manoeuvres, was unable to respond until later. Then he wrote of his regret, 'less on account of what you said than the use to which it will be put by Mr H's destructive critics'. He believed that because Esher had been 'too absolute' in his opinions, there was a danger the Territorial babe would be thrown out with the bath water of failed recruitment figures. The London figures were bad, but why not circulate the COs of those corps that were below strength and ask them what might be done? He insisted the recruiting committee required immediate strengthening and it should be chaired by 'a good, live, modern man who is known to London'. He suggested Rosebery, a strange choice.

Outside London, the Territorials flourished and Repington had several practical suggestions to improve recruitment figures. They should acknowledge in the past there had been a lack of generosity and good sense. Territorial manoeuvres had been conducted too harshly. It would be best if Buckle wrote a brief warning in *The Times*. Repington thought it best not to make any fuss, but as a Regular in peacetime he had never been required to undergo such hardship as the Terriers had suffered. Staff officers, intent upon making an impression, had pushed the men too hard. They did not seem to realise that young troops needed handling as carefully as young horses. He was convinced a few Regular officers could make a considerable difference and Haig, never usually quick to say anything in Repington's favour, advised Esher, he ought to listen carefully to what the correspondent had to say.

Between June and August Repington, Esher and Haldane were taken to task. They were dismissed as busybodies by the *World* magazine, as amateurs who, to the nation's disadvantage, interfered in matters beyond their abilities. Esher and Haldane were the main targets, but Repington's constant visits to Whitehall Gardens to be briefed on the actions of the Defence Committee were also condemned as 'in the highest degree improper'. It was wrong that in return for official information improperly provided by Haldane, Repington should advertise and support the Secretary of State's schemes. There was more than a scintilla of truth in these charges. Esher was provoked to retort and in doing so upset Haldane. Repington was quite indifferent to the whole business, telling Esher that he had 'never read greater rot'. They should ignore the editor's drunken, libellous attacks.[11] Esher, however, refused to be placated and chose Maxse's *National Review* to publish a rejoinder.

Leo welcomed Esher's damning indictment that left readers with the inescapable impression there was no alternative but compulsory military service. Haldane accused Esher of betrayal. To provide a polemical counterblast he recruited Ian Hamilton who wrote a breezy memorandum attacking the critics of voluntarism, to which Haldane supplied a lengthy introduction insisting patriotism would ensure sufficient recruits. A volunteer army, the Liberal minister insisted, was an arrangement that suited both the British temperament and the nation's defensive needs. A review of *Compulsory Service* (1910) was solicited from Repington. His generous comments in *The Times*, despite the declared disapproval of Northcliffe, reflected not so much his thinking on the subject of compulsion as his hopes for the Territorials. Within four months *Fallacies and Facts*, the NSL's riposte to *Compulsory Service*, supposedly written by Roberts though largely the work of Leo Amery and Professor J. A. Cramb, appeared on the book stalls. In the subsequent debate neither literary effort secured many converts. Nevertheless, both sides claimed to be the victor.

In the autumn and early winter months of 1912 the *Daily Express, Pall Mall Gazette, Observer, Daily Mail, National Review* and rather more tardily Strachey's *Spectator*, mounted a prolonged and vitriolic attack upon Haldane and the inadequacies of his Territorial Force. Simultaneously they emphasised the absolute need for compulsory service. The surprising absentee from this group of Tory publications was *The Times*, although Northcliffe and Geoffrey Dawson[12] were known supporters of conscription. Fred Oliver, a particular friend of Dawson's, was deputed to try to find out why the editor was dragging his feet. Apparently Dawson had wanted to help but had been impressed by Repington's argument that neither the problem nor the solution was as simple and straightforward as was supposed.

Repington had very much approved the choice of Dawson to edit *The Times*, an appointment that signalled the waning influence of the 'Old Guard' of Buckle, Chirol and Bell at PHS. He found the younger man's thinking on many important issues congenial. On assuming the editorial chair, Dawson received an invitation from Repington to dine at Claridges.

The principal guests would be Sir John French and Kitchener.[13] Repington, fondly supposing the new editor would be amenable to his instruction, assured him the discussion could not fail to be of interest. To help with his initiation he provided his new editor with an analysis and critique of Roberts's latest series of public speeches on conscription that outlined the issue's convoluted background. The old warrior had coupled an overt warning about Germany's belligerent intent towards Britain and his familiar message demanding compulsory service for home defence with a critique of the Territorials' continuing inability to repel an invader. The Liberal press invariably condemned Roberts as a 'Jingo ... who interprets the life and interests of this nation and Empire by the crude lusts and fears that haunt his unimaginative soldier's brain'.[14] In their turn, the familiar cohort of Tory newspapers praised him. 'There is not a politician who does not know in his heart Lord Roberts speaks the truth.'[15] But not all the Tory press was uncritical and laudatory. The *Evening Standard* described Roberts as a 'wanton mischief maker'.[16] Much more politically significant, several Tory mandarins in letters to the press declared it was hopeless to seek compulsion so long as it was certain to lose votes. That was as useful as crying for the moon.[17] Repington had repeatedly warned Dawson it was hopeless to expect party magnates and organisers to support conscription so long as it remained a sure fire vote loser.

When Haldane created the Territorials, two conditions had been imposed by the government. First, the army's annual budget should not exceed 28 million pounds; second, recruitment should be voluntary. If the country required an army of a million men, it could readily be achieved. The government merely needed to state the number required and the War Office could then raise them. Roberts constantly grumbled and complained about others, but when he had been omnipotent in military affairs he had done nothing. The Volunteers then had been badly trained, ill-organised and lacking in both numbers and supplies. Despite great improvements in quality, recruitment figures stubbornly remained low. The military had always confidently expected the eventual introduction and acceptance of conscription. Few soldiers supported the NSL plan of conscription, seeing it as a temporary compromise. Ideally they wanted two years' compulsory service, sufficient to produce a large, well-trained, efficient force similar to the armies of other great European powers.

Repington had always thought the TF's numbers inadequate. To allow for effective home defence *and* intervention in Europe, they ought to have numbered 600,000. Only the Liberals could bring in such a force, for it would mean the complete democratisation of the army. The pill of compulsion would need to be gilded to appeal to the electorate.

Necessarily there would be a long period of transition when there would be weaknesses at home and abroad. Foreign garrisons and drafts, still less reliefs, were unlikely to be retained. Was there any sane minister who could accept that as tolerable? To put half a million troops into Europe, whenever they were required, would mean sacrificing the daily needs of the Empire. Also, to take the youth of the country away from its work for two years would necessarily entail great social upheaval. Across the whole empire there would need to be a careful calculation of profit and loss to establish whether the scheme was viable.

Having sketched out the difficulties the NSL and whole-hoggers like Henry Wilson always blithely ignored, Repington suggested an alternative. He reminded Dawson, the established conservative tradition was evolution not revolution. As naval expenditure was set to rise to dizzying heights, a limited amount of money only would be available to spend on defence. The existing system was inadequate to raise an Expeditionary Force of 200,000 men. The number of Territorials could be increased by fulfilling county quotas. Two weeks' training every year and musketry should be insisted upon, but unless they had a better alternative to offer constant, captious criticism was pointless. Criticism was easy, constructive army reform was not. Repington insisted *he* for one had 'no taste for destructive military criticism'. The critics of the TF were all alike. 'They cannot build, they cannot add one brick. Their tone will lead to steady depletion . . . by natural discouragement.'[18]

Dawson drew upon Repington's notes to write a leader that the correspondent described as 'admirably rigorous and brilliant', except that was, for the reference to the Territorials as a 'sham'. He sharply admonished Dawson's 'feather-headed observation that would only encourage the fatheads who know nothing of the TF'. What was worse, it would be remembered when the rest had been forgotten.[19] By return of post Dawson hastened to repent. The Territorial Force was no 'sham'; not an 'impediment to be swept away', but 'a first-class foundation to be built upon'. Repington cautioned Dawson. He should realise that to pin conscription to the Tories might 'keep them out of office for years'. The editor responded he was 'not in the least afraid of the word conscription, whatever its effect on the fortunes of the Unionist party may be'.[20] Repington had written he would like to see the Tories committed to opposition until they carried conscription to victory. They would 'always be beat on the bribery tack',[21] but might make a big appeal to national sentiment by championing national service as 'a big idea' and the 'noblest flag to fly.' Dawson's imagination was inspired with crusading notions. He talked of 'a mission to convince England's working class that universal national training is essentially democratic and an instrument of peace'.

Whatever reservations Repington had concerning Dawson's millenarian vision, he was certainly gratified the editor wanted *his* 'whole views in the paper all the time'. He reflected on how well he and Dawson worked together and told him of the difficulties he had experienced during the previous eight years working with Buckle, whom he unjustly characterised as 'not really interested in questions concerning the country's defences'. He realised what he had said was unfair but allowed his judgment to be coloured by recent heated exchanges over the navy. Buckle had often been generous, sometimes indulgent. Repington chose to forget the times he had been given his head despite the disagreement of other senior editorial staff.

Repington relished the prospect of a powerful and influential alliance with his new editor. He thought it might well afford the best opportunity yet to create a coherent defence policy for *The Times*. He pressed Dawson, 'You decide the policy then I will help you to suggest how a constructive military policy should match with it. Decide soon for we cannot keep out of the fray with credit much longer.'[22] He insisted, his part as the newspaper's military correspondent was to tell Dawson without fear or favour what he thought of ministerial decisions. Dawson's privilege as editor was to decide whether what he had written was appropriate or opportune to publish. When, in early November 1912, Dawson spiked a Repington article on the war in the Balkans, he accepted the decision without demur. A time would come when Repington would grimly resent what he would then condemn as editorial high-handedness.

Not everyone was pleased the military correspondent should be so close to the editor. Lovat Fraser, at Dawson's instruction had recently written a series of leaders on the Balkans. He grumbled about Dawson 'bowdlerizing Steed's telegrams' thus proving he was 'unduly influenced by Repington's theories. He was making *The Times* look silly'.[23] Was Fraser's criticism fair? A conversation Repington happened to overhear before a Cabinet meeting had prompted the thought the government might overreach itself in the Balkans. Repington's particular worry was Grey might bind himself more closely to the Radicals in the Cabinet. At the same time Churchill was talking as though an immediate naval confrontation with Germany offered England a better prospect of victory than in five years time. Repington disagreed.[24] It was in this context he had questioned *The Times*' pro-Balkan policy. He suggested to Dawson, 'A solid Balkan confederation would be a good thing for us.' He regretted, however, 'the total abandonment of the Turk ... I consider he is the shirt next to our skin in the Near East. We should identify him with our interests and not kick him when he is down.' He had earlier cautioned that Turkey's existence as an independent power was threatened just 'when we have an unequalled opportunity to bind Turkey to our interest by a firm conciliatory policy'. He urged Britain to take 'the long view'. He had no personal preference other than 'Britain's future security'.[25] Dawson's response was to say he was not prepared to write 'pro-Turk articles *now*', but he acknowledged Repington had 'furnished a strong argument against the case some are arguing'.[26]

During this period, in the Unionist press questions of foreign and defence policy were strongly influenced by protagonists' attitudes to the current, all-consuming question of domestic politics – whether they were pro or anti Tariff Reform. *The Times* under Dawson followed Northcliffe's *Daily Mail* and campaigned against 'stomach taxes'. Jim Garvin in the *Observer* abused the Northcliffe newspapers on behalf of the Astor group. Repington, together with Edward Grigg, consistently challenged Garvin's intemperate comments, something Dawson particularly valued. He frequently complained Garvin and the Astor press were violently 'vilifying and besmirching us in every possible way'[27] at a time when soothing the sensibilities of temperamental, senior colleagues absorbed much of Dawson's time and energy. The first diplomatic consequence of the Balkan League's attack on the Turks was a German press campaign designed to promote discontent between France and Britain. Wickham Steed, the difficult and prickly Vienna correspondent, seemed to think that France and Germany were drawing closer together. Dawson assumed Steed was questioning his editorial policy. He therefore dictated further editorials to Lovat Fraser and it was these that had prompted Fraser's charge that Dawson was 'bowdlerizing Steed's telegrams' because of Repington's 'undue influence'.

Dawson considered Steed's current advice on foreign affairs unduly elusive and complex. No editor previously had dared question Steed's work. He was not inclined to welcome criticism now. His extreme sensitivity, like his swiftly aroused and truly ferocious temper, was notorious. Editors had invariably handled him with kid gloves. Now Steed found himself accused by Dawson of needlessly dissipating the strength of his arguments; that his writing was 'not sufficiently short, simple and direct, the only way', so Dawson insisted, 'to guide a great body of lay opinion'.[28] Behind Dawson's advice the voice of Northcliffe could clearly be heard. Repington's writing though not always brief was invariably 'simple and direct'. It was for that reason Dawson listened to his views on foreign affairs more readily.

In late November 1912 Repington warned Haldane, efficiency had markedly deteriorated under the rule of his successor at the War Office. Seely had placidly accepted the anti-Territorial Force campaign inspired and engineered by Wilson. Everyone, not least Haldane, knew Repington had no good opinion of Wilson. Their antipathy was mutual. Somewhat despairingly Repington enquired whether Haldane had the measure of Wilson's innumerable weaknesses and inadequacies, particularly his 'hopelessly wrong appreciation of the situation in the Balkans'.[29] Couldn't the minister see what 'a serious danger' the man was? His constant intrigues were 'all part of his game to destroy the voluntary system'. They threatened the very existence of the Territorials. More immediately they could not fail 'to harm discipline, numbers and efficiency'. Wilson ought to be replaced as DMO by Robertson. An exasperated Repington, angrily expostulated, 'No other nation would permit what we allow.'[30]

From mid December, Repington and Dawson planned a series of articles on defence, the Territorials and compulsion. Lord Roberts would embark upon a further campaign on the NSL's behalf. There would be a Lords debate in February. Ostensibly it would be about the Territorials but in reality would be a plea for compulsion. Roberts did not intend to speak and disclaimed any intention to disparage the Territorials. By the end of January, in the final stages of preparing and correcting his proposed articles, Repington sent Dawson galley proofs for comment. He drew attention to the additions he had made, 'as you suggested', and the paragraphs 'to which you demurred' he had removed. As 'all [Dawson's] criticisms have been fully met' he hoped he would be 'quite satisfied'. He thanked Dawson for his 'valuable suggestions'. All too obviously Repington was minding his manners and watching his Ps and Qs. His campaign on Territorial enlistment was to be his litmus test for compulsion. He fully understood, if he were to succeed he *must* have his editor's support.

The first two articles were published on 6 and 7 February under the general title 'Military Policy' and caused something of a sensation. In six columns, with compelling force and clarity, he set out the principles of defence and their application to the army, navy and the Territorial Force. Dawson afforded vigorous support in his leaders. For the first time, without any equivocation it was stated in *The Times* the voluntary principle had failed. Only conscription would bring in sufficient recruits. The Territorials were 50,000 short and the present establishment required doubling to 600,000. The 1912 naval manoeuvres had revealed the figures set for the invasion inquiry had been woefully inadequate. He roused Wilson's ire by asserting the General Staff might want unlimited continental interference but it was out of the question. He claimed Britain's navy was worth 500,000 bayonets to the French. Wilson doubted it was worth a single bayonet.

Just when he needed to keep on side with Dawson, Repington needlessly caused offence by stupidly indulging a petty conceit. As one of the signatories to a memorial presented to the Prime Minister on the country's defences, he had been interviewed by the *Evening News*. He used the opportunity to emphasise the Territorials, in the absence of the Expeditionary Force, were not strong enough to provide an adequate defence against an invader. The single, obvious corrective, he bluntly asserted, was conscription. These comments were reported as by 'The Military Correspondent of *The Times*'. When Dawson saw the article and headlines, he was both horrified and deeply offended at this breach of *Times* tradition. He believed it 'seriously weakened the paper's authority if the names of the staff [were] used in this way'. Dawson blamed himself. He should have asked Repington not to sign 'the admirable memorandum to the PM'. The unfortunate episode would necessarily weaken the military correspondent's authority and influence.[31] Repington clearly was disappointed at Dawson's reaction to what he considered a trivial matter. Surely there could hardly be a person who was not aware that he was *The Times*' military correspondent? Rather than apologise to his editor and seek to calm his concern, he penned a hasty, self-righteous response.[32] Such an act was absurdly short-sighted. He risked damaging his valuable relationship with Dawson simply to satisfy his vanity.

At the beginning of March Northcliffe rebuked Dawson for *The Times* showing insufficient concern about Europe's growing military unrest and massive military preparations. At the same time, George Saunders, the newspaper's distinguished Paris correspondent, complained to Dawson of a recent undue preoccupation with military matters. He implied the French might interpret this as the British encouraging a more aggressive stance towards Germany. Dawson unapologetically rebuffed Northcliffe by referring him to Repington's recent contributions, but Saunders's complaint alarmed him. He had not given his support to conscription to place a British conscript army on the Belgian frontier but 'for Home Defence ... to release our Navy ... and, if necessary, our Expeditionary Force'.[33]

Repington hastened to reassure Dawson. He explained Saunders's fears as being inspired by a misunderstanding aggravated by his quarrel with André Tardieu, a popular journalist who wrote for *Le Temps*. Tardieu's uncertain patriotic loyalties were determined by the size of the bribes he currently received either from the French or the Germans to help pay the debts he had incurred entertaining his most recent mistress. Tardieu, when he was sharing the views of the French political right, wished to see the entente turned into an alliance to which British adoption of conscription he believed to be a necessary preliminary. Repington, always eager for an excuse to spend a few days in Paris, expenses paid, suggested he should speak with the French military authorities and tell them Britain had no intention of forcing the pace militarily. At the same time he might be able to help Saunders mend the broken relationship with Tardieu. Dawson agreed.

Upon his arrival at the Hôtel Majestic, Repington invited Saunders to join him. Saunders ought to dine and meet Tardieu, he suggested. It would be 'in the interests of the entente' to patch-up their quarrel. 'It is a journalistic handicap to both papers and a serious danger to our mutual interests in a large sphere.'[34] The invitation was declined. Repington had misunderstood the issue. What Saunders sought was to quit the Paris office. Repington had overreached and made something of a fool of himself. Only he might judge whether that was a suitable price to pay for his brief sojourn in Paris. His damnable complacency had once again betrayed him, though he invariably claimed the problem was other men were not as reasonable as was he. Dawson, who only the previous month had been in Paris, warned Repington he was unlikely to get any change out of Saunders. The editor had gone to France armed with 'several cuttings' furnished by Repington designed to demonstrate 'how much the Froggies had been pleased with my references to them'.[35] Lord Roberts had been in Paris at the same time. On the subject of conscription, the French government showed more interest in what the old field marshal had to say. However, de la Panouse, the French military attaché in London, doubted whether any of Bob's speeches would ever open 'les yeux à l'opinion anglaise sur la nécessité d'adopter le service universel'.[36]

In early February Seely made a statement to the Commons. This preceded a most acrimonious nine-hour debate in the Lords concerning the Territorials. Repington attended for *The Times* and on successive days wrote a detailed report and long commentary on the proceedings. He dismissed the government's 'policy of procrastination' as a 'blend of humbug, self-deception and obscurantism'. They had the effrontery to suppose their 'soothing syrup' would please those interested in the security of the state. Such was his anger and disappointment, he was sufficiently distracted to praise St John Brodrick (now the Earl of Midleton) for posing clearly and definitely the simple questions: 'In its present condition would the Territorial Force be capable of taking the field at once upon the despatch of the Expeditionary Force? Could it guarantee the safety of the country in case of invasion by 70,000 Continental troops?' The government had proffered no adequate reply. Instead its energies had been devoted 'to drawing a red herring across the trail to deflect the discussion'. In the face of the growing danger of Britain's weak military position facing the vast armaments of neighbouring powers, the government had proved 'incapable of meeting these difficulties. So far as army affairs are concerned its usefulness is exhausted'.

His slashing critique of the 'tomfool Government arguments in the Lords' had been entirely approved by Dawson, even though Repington had warned him it might lead to his exclusion from official help and information.[37] He had written to Seely to express his sincere regret that 'after all these years' he should find himself opposed to the Secretary of State and Haldane. It was his 'bad luck to find public duty conflicting with the claims of private friendship'. To Seely if not to Haldane, the correspondent's expressions of regret must have seemed somewhat mealy-mouthed. Repington could not have made more brutally plain, in private and public, how much he deplored 'the Government's lack of any serious plan for completing the TF'.[38]

A public announcement there would be a re-examination by the Defence Committee of the invasion issue was made on 12 February 1913. Repington should have been happy at the prospect. He had learned some months earlier from a junior minister the government felt hampered by the 1908 inquiry's conclusion concerning numbers. They had found it impossible to recruit enough Territorials to guarantee the defeat of a 70,000-strong invading force. Repington feared the government might simply lower that number and the 'lamentably weak General Staff', who thought only of their war on the Meuse, might well encourage them to do so. He was certain they would 'pass any folly'. Only the Radicals would gain from such a move. They would immediately claim the strength of the Territorials was of no consequence.[39] Repington hastened to impress Esher with his fears, making no mention of the Radicals but repeating his concern the General Staff was intent on abolishing the agreed number of 70,000.

What had prompted Asquith to set up another invasion inquiry? The initiative had most likely been inspired by Churchill.[40] After the disastrous 1912 naval manoeuvres, Winston had lobbied vigorously for a detailed re-examination of the invasion issue. He was no absolutist like his recent predecessors at the Admiralty. Early in 1912, Blue Water supporters were happily citing the recent Italian invasion of Tripoli as incontrovertible proof they and not the Bolt from the Blue advocates, knew best. Thirty-five thousand troops, though faced by inadequate opponents, had required almost three weeks to carry out their attack, so how long would it take 70,000 to succeed when faced by dangerous and determined opponents, even in the unlikely event that the greater part of the defending fleet was permanently absent? In the light of such calculations, it seemed British provision for home defence considerably exceeded actual needs. But the Bolt from the Blue school dismissed the argument as unfair and false. Tripoli was not an appropriate example and the naval manoeuvres provided a very pertinent contradiction. The attacking Red Fleet was adjudged to have landed 12,000 troops.

Churchill admitted to Asquith, there was no way of stopping a determined enemy from landing up to 10,000 soldiers. The threat could be obviated by the deployment of 'a compact force of Regulars with good artillery striking swiftly and vigorously at the detached heads of invasion destroying them before they could combine'.[41] This conclusion did not please the army. They wanted no Regulars shackled to home defence duties. Since the previous inquiry, the Admiralty and War Office positions had completely reversed. The Admiralty no longer claimed, as in 1908, serious invasion was complete nonsense, or that invasion concerned them alone. They wanted the army to increase its responsibility for home defence. To complete this picture of topsyturvydom, the army played down the threat of serious invasion, insisting the Territorials were more than adequate to see off any invader.

Politicians were filled with foreboding by the remarkably gloomy foreign and domestic political scenes. In Ireland the harmony and strength of the British Empire was seriously threatened. In south-eastern Europe the vassal Balkan states had turned upon their former suzerain and sought to free themselves from the Ottoman European Empire. The peace conference for this First Balkan War was not over when former allies turned against one another in a Second Balkan War. The Germans, previously amicably co-operative with Britain, suddenly seemed anxious to demonstrate their aggressive intent. They proposed to increase their army's peacetime strength to 850,000. Repington observed that this meant Germany would have 300,000 more men in arms than France, greatly outnumbering the advantage France had previously enjoyed. It was considered appropriate to compare the British and German fleets, so would it not be sensible similarly to compare the armies? He scorned the Radical call for armaments cuts and suggested it was a wiser measure of a potential enemy's military capabilities to adopt a comparison of the armies than to demand retrenchment every time Germany's ambassador delivered a friendly speech.

Between April and May Repington wrote and published in *The Times* no less than twelve major articles on invasion, repeatedly implying the inquiry was a Radical intrigue.[42] For the *National Review* he wrote a virulent article entitled 'A Marconi Enquiry on Invasion', asserting the majority of inquiry members were 'Radical politicians with no knowledge of strategy'. It was patent nonsense, quite unlike his usual, sceptical empiricism. Sectarian suspicion exaggerated by the bitter party divide over Ulster had quite vitiated his judgment. Nor was Repington the only offender. Esher, normally wary of such prejudices, was soon convinced the inquiry was the result of political intrigue. He could not say how matters might turn out but remained optimistic for he believed they had 'the brains of the committee' on their side.[43]

Repeating an unworthy private charge made by Bonar Law, Repington represented Balfour's membership of the committee, now he was no longer the Unionist leader, as 'an attempt to forestall the official Opposition'. To any non-partisan reader it would have seemed Repington had abandoned his frequently trumpeted independence and was now associating with extreme, ultra Tories. The price had been Law's private reassurance that he wholeheartedly supported conscription. That enthusiasm had, however, lasted only so long as his party leadership was insecure. Repington gave him a copy of the memorandum he, together with his 1908 inquiry associates Simon Lovat, Samuel Scott and Lord Roberts, had prepared for submission to the inquiry. He undoubtedly felt very pleased with himself supposing his alliance with Bonar Law would bring advantages to the conscriptionist cause. 'We have told him everything,' he enthusiastically burbled to Dawson.[44] On one occasion Law said he owed his conversion on conscription to the correspondent's arguments[45] and asked Repington to coach him for the defence debates. This might have accounted for the correspondent retaining his unduly optimistic expectations for so long.

In the spring of 1913, *mirabile dictu*, Wilson and Repington were briefly reconciled. Lovat was the matchmaker, insisting 'it was absolutely essential' the two men should meet to discuss the case then being prepared for presentation to the inquiry. Wilson initially refused to meet Repington but was persuaded to do so by Roberts.[46] In the company of others, the two long-term antagonists sat down to dine and were to meet for luncheon on several subsequent occasions. Their discussion was lively and free and at all times the civilities were observed – but not for amity's sake. Repington published a letter in *The Times* asking why Wilson, 'who as Director of Military Operations is best qualified to explain the military resources foreign countries possess for invading us', was not a member of the inquiry committee?[47] Wilson thought the letter 'excellent' though he was pleased not to be involved. He had no good opinion of CID subcommittee meetings. He saw little value in 'an immense amount of talk and nothing decided'. For Wilson the truth was always self-evident.[48] He had no interest in minutiae, the contradictions and the necessary compromises at the heart of the committee game. He more naturally pronounced his views and opinions as bold absolutes. He eschewed negotiable possibilities for his confident belief and expectation was that the patency of *his* logic and the potency of *his* brilliant advocacy would eventually win the day. The similarities to Repington's mode of thinking are striking, but their fatal division of purpose over the

Territorials and the Expeditionary Force would soon shatter their fragile reconciliation.

Jack Seely stated in the Commons the Expeditionary Force would go abroad confident the Territorials could cope with an invasion force of 70,000. Repington immediately wrote an article to challenge 'the opinion of the General Staff quoted by Seely'. All too obviously the minister had been coached by Wilson. 'We must fight this out,' Repington insisted to Dawson.[49] Once more the argument was about the figure 70,000, the maximum size of an invading force against which home defence should be planned. Repington challenged Haldane's claim the figure had been used for planning since 1902. On 30 March he submitted a memorandum designed to demonstrate that since 1908 the problem of invasion had changed. From evidence they had collected they were certain Germany would try to invade even without an assurance of success. 'The prize of victory would be greater than any attempted in the history of war.'[50] Both at sea and in the air, Britain could not guarantee invulnerability from invasion. The Territorials were wanting in training and tactics, their musketry ineffectual, and they were too scattered geographically for effective, large-scale, collective field training. Detailed, realistic analyses of the numbers available for home defence after the departure of the Expeditionary Force showed their nominal strength greatly exceeded the actual number of effectives. This in turn was much less than that required to face an invading enemy with confidence and the expectation of victory.[51] The memorandum elicited a sharp riposte from Esher. He bluntly asserted Repington and his associates had 'either never known or ha[d] altogether misunderstood' the 1908 inquiry's conclusions. They had assumed the Territorials could defend the country unaided. But what the 1908 inquiry had said was, after the outbreak of hostilities, two divisions of Regulars should be retained at home until the Territorials had been embodied and trained for six months.[52]

Esher was concerned that War Office and Admiralty delegates might well attempt to hijack meetings to promote narrow departmental interests. He had a series of sharp exchanges with Seely on this subject. The minister sought to dismiss his arguments as 'the counsel of despair'. Esher would have none of this. On the basis of his London experience he relentlessly listed the faults of the Territorials while insisting the main purpose of the present inquiry was to determine whether they were up to the task they had been assigned. He suggested to Asquith 'Send for the Roberts Group as soon as possible so that the case for invasion in its most aggressive form can be laid before the Committee ... instead of ... hypothetical cases framed ... in the interest of departmental proclivities'.[53] His suggestion was acted upon.

Repington thought the first two meeting 'most unsatisfactory'. Asquith had not allowed them to ask French their prepared questions that went 'to the root of the matter under investigation'. Their time had been entirely wasted. Asked to return the following week to listen to 'various generals spouting on what they think about the Territorials', he refused. 'I see no object ... unless we are permitted to ask the questions which we have handed in.'[54] At the second of the two meetings from which Repington absented himself, Roberts was at last given the opportunity to question French. The CIGS conceded that the Territorials could not defeat an invading force of 70,000, but backed Jack Seely's line that it was perfectly safe to despatch the whole Expeditionary Force abroad because invasion by an enemy 70,000 strong was impossible.

At the morning meeting of 17 July, Repington was asked to set out his views on the Territorials and the Special Reserve. This he did to some effect. When challenged by Asquith about the 'substantial sums' his proposed measures would cost, Repington boldly insisted, 'If you don't want a compulsory force then you have to pay for it. If you give us compulsion I dare say we shall get it very much cheaper ... It is either play up or pay up, Sir, one or the other.'[55] In his letter to the king's private secretary summarising the day's proceedings, Hankey noted how Repington's evidence had made a 'considerable impression' on the inquiry members.[56] In a further note he described Repington's contribution as 'brief and to the point ... making a number of very practical and useful suggestions of detail for improving the Territorial Force'.[57] Then, when compiling a draft report in October, he 'most particularly' drew War Office attention to 'Col. Repington's suggestions for improvement to the Territorial Force and Special Reserve'. Seely had thanked Repington profusely for his 'very valuable' evidence and asked that a copy be given to the War Office committee currently seeking ways to strengthen recruitment to the Special Reserve. Subsequently Repington claimed that his evidence was ignored because the October 1913 report made no mention of his recommendations.[58]

Lunching with Seely immediately after giving his evidence, Repington had been in high good humour. He told the minister he had 'come to plot with him the details of my next attack on the WO'.[59] Although recently the minister had taken a fearful mauling in the press and Parliament, he took the sally in good part. The invasion inquiry, adjourned after 17 July, was not reconvened until November when the annual naval manoeuvres provided much for thought and debate. On 9 July, a fortnight before the manoeuvres were due to begin, Repington revealed in *The Times* that as in the previous year the manoeuvres were intended to establish whether, in the face of full naval opposition, a hostile raiding party could land successfully. To make the exercise more realistic there would be an actual landing, although it would not be possible either to mobilise the Territorials or test the shore defences.

Long before official notice of the manoeuvres was given there was widespread unofficial briefing of selected journalists. The primary source of these leaks was the former First Sea Lord, Francis Bridgeman, forced out of office by ill-health and Churchill's desire to have Admiral Prince Louis Battenberg as his First Sea Lord. Bitter and revengeful, Bridgeman whispered in Jack Sandars's ear knowing him to be an efficient and profligate briefer of favoured journalists. Sandars effectively sustained an unofficial news agency to serve the interests of Central Office. It was hoped Churchill would be hung out to dry. No mean supplier himself of 'off the record' items, Winston shamelessly complained to the invasion inquiry about unofficial releases of information.[60]

During the manoeuvres Bridgeman sailed with the Red (German) fleet under the command of Vice Admiral John Jellicoe. On 28 July he informed Sandars the exercise had been stopped.[61] The Red fleet had enjoyed a complete success landing 60,000 men that could as well have been 100,000. They had seized docks, railway stations and junctions. Churchill had ordered the exercise stopped. When Jellicoe boarded *Enchantress*, Winston greeted him cheerily, 'Well you have made History. The PM will be frightened out of his life.'[62] Repington knew what had been said by the First Lord to the Admiral, but he was not sure whether his editor would allow him to tell their readers so that they might draw the appropriate conclusions.[63]

Repington had frequently and loudly complained about *The Times*' 'so-called naval experts', those 'rabid Fisherites' and 'Blue Water acolytes' who had enjoyed an excessive influence at PHS for far too long. He deplored the 'unduly optimistic rubbish' written by these 'profoundly mistaken naval fire-eaters' who talked about 'attacking the coasts of great Powers . . . There is no quicker way of losing an army to no purpose than this particular kind of tomfoolery'. Late in Buckle's reign, Repington had tackled his editor about the unjustified imbalance favouring the navy to the permanent disadvantage of the army. He was effectively excluded from making any comment upon naval matters because of the sensitivity and defensiveness of the paper's naval writers. His present complaint was his editor *ought* to listen to *his* 'expert' opinion. It was never the easiest of editorial tasks to manage opinionated, highly sensitive colleagues and avoid unnecessary altercations. On naval matters Buckle's general deference to the opinions of the newspaper's naval 'experts' would prompt Repington angrily to accuse him of lacking 'confidence in [him] as a naval critic . . . You regard war as something that can be divided into naval and military compartments whereas it is all one and so is the strategy of war by land and sea ... We should long ago have had meetings to thrash out these problems.'[64] The previous fortnight he had received advanced knowledge of senior staff changes at the Admiralty, material he had shown to Thursfield, who had failed to comprehend its importance. The matter was too important to be ignored. Failing Thursfield, he asked Buckle whether he should write. But even as he asked he knew perfectly well what he intended to do. He was going to 'turn on von D und B to make the points and insert them with a knife'.[65]

Repington created the fictitious German army officer, Colonel von Donner und Blitzen, specifically to smuggle into *The Times* a military view of naval affairs, and in particular to assess the Admiralty's strategic opinions. Repington in the persona of the colonel wrote to the editor of *The Times* a number of minatory letters. Their accurate accounts of the naval manoeuvres afforded the Admiralty much embarrassment. 'The protection your navy affords is not absolute,' the colonel insisted. 'As our wings have grown yours have been clipped by the cowardice of your rulers and the selfishness of your democracy ... Each of us, no doubt, will gain his deserts.'[66] Despite official silence, the colonel provided more than enough material to promote public concern. 'The Admiralty did not wish,' as Churchill later admitted, 'to create a situation that in certain quarters could have caused a panic in the country.'[67]

When the invasion inquiry was reconvened in November, Robertson, in his new guise as Director of Military Training, was the first to give evidence. His scheme was much the same as Repington's July proposal. When Asquith had read Repington's evidence on the Special Reserve, Robertson expressed his full agreement. Nicholson repeatedly pointed out the major issue was the complete reversal of naval opinion.[68] Repington told Hankey he wished to submit further evidence on recruitment to the regular army. He accounted for the fall in recruitment and demonstrated its deleterious consequences, listing, as in his earlier submission, a number of specific and carefully costed remedies.

Following the last meetings of 1913, Hankey prepared a draft report which when circulated prompted discussion. This revealed disagreement on a number of issues. A familiar bone of contention concerned the proportion of the Expeditionary Force to be retained at home to meet the threat of invasion. Haldane was at odds with Seely and French. The final report was not signed off until 15 April 1914. Such were the Territorials' poor standards of musketry and artillery and the general insufficiency of their training, especially of NCOs, it was agreed until such time as they were fit to take the field they required the support of two divisions of Regulars to secure the country against invasion or raids. More positively, it was thought the existing shortfall in recruits would be swiftly remedied on mobilisation. Territorial engineers together with their medical and supply services were almost up to Regular standards. A final decision on the Robertson–Repington proposal that Territorials should be allocated to garrison coastal defences was postponed and never subsequently taken. The inquiry report was approved by a full meeting of the CID on 14 May 1914.

Henry Wilson, beside himself with rage and frustration, dismissed the findings as 'rubbish'. He complained bitterly to Asquith. To retain two divisions of Regulars would 'entirely abolish the Exp[editionary] Force'. Why not send five divisions abroad and retain only one at home? Five would be more than enough and match existing mobilisation arrangements. Without any reference to the Defence Committee, there and then Asquith agreed five divisions should be released. 'This is good,' Wilson wrote in his diary.[69] What would Repington have thought? A few words from Henry Wilson to the Prime Minister achieved more than he had after a long and painstaking campaign.

Knowing nothing of Asquith's executive fiat, the opposition repeatedly demanded publication of the invasion inquiry findings. Asquith pledged a detailed statement and the opportunity for general debate. With Repington fully occupied by events in Ireland, there was scarcely time to consider the fate of the invasion inquiry report, recruitment or conscription. Seven weeks before the outbreak of war, Repington advised Dawson the Prime Minister was unlikely to make 'a splash with the Invasion Report ... I expect he will merely announce general principles'. At least the 70,000 men standard had been safeguarded. When the Unionists were returned to power they could 'fairly put in a claim for reconsideration of the whole question of defence. Everything should be made the subject of searching inquiries.'[70] Whatever he and Dawson expected to achieve when they began their joint campaign in 1913, had foundered on the shoals of political sectarianism.

To have had any hope of success before 1914–18, a pro-conscriptionist campaign needed to be part of the Unionist programme. Balfour rejected any such notion out of hand. He believed the strategic answer lay not in conscripted armies but in the strongest possible navy supported by better submarines and improved armaments. In pre-1914 Britain such was the prejudice against conscription that it was much too hot a political potato for any party to handle.

10 Northcliffe and *The Times*, Repington and the *Army Review*

In 1887 *The Times* suffered disastrous financial and reputational losses publishing the Parnell forgeries.[1] Three years later Arthur Walter, principal proprietor, appointed Bell as manager. Effectively Bell had charge of the newspaper. Eventually the constant need to find ways to supplement the newspaper's ailing finances sapped even his formidable energies. In July 1907 Walter put the newspaper up for sale but told neither Bell nor the editor, Buckle. Wishing to turn *The Times* into a limited liability company, Walter sought financial help from C. Arthur Pearson, proprietor of the *Daily Express* and the *Standard*.[2] The proprietor told Repington, who had long been his friend, what he planned. Repington told Esher who suggested it would be the ideal time to set up a *Times* Defence Committee. Though Walter approved of this idea, Repington feared Buckle might not. However, he hoped this might be one occasion when Walter, who rarely interfered with editorial decisions, would overrule Buckle. 'At a pinch Walter can and does control the policy of the paper.'[3]

Esher knew Jack Fisher was not impressed by Pearson. The admiral's anxiety was that under new management '*The Times* ... should take the right line about naval affairs'.[4] He suggested Northcliffe might buy the newspaper and make Garvin its editor, describing his proposal as 'Napoleonic in conception, Cromwellian in thoroughness.' He was confident a Garvin editorship would guarantee uncritical support for the navy and less consideration for the army.[5]

Northcliffe, who had long cherished ambitions to own *The Times*, kept careful watch as events unfolded. Staff members at Printing House Square did not want Northcliffe as their proprietor. They assumed his involvement would lead inevitably to *The Times* becoming an up-market, de luxe version of the *Daily Mail*. The suggested alternative, 'Hustler' Pearson, filled them with equal dread. Nobody wanted a national institution falling into the hands of any yellow journalist.

Bell was resolutely against any deal involving Pearson. There was something to be said for Northcliffe. He was an imperialist, known to distrust Germany and had retained the *Observer*'s historic cross-bench tradition under Garvin's editorship. It was entirely conceivable he might well make a more congenial business partner than Pearson. At a meeting with Bell arranged by an American intermediary, Northcliffe made clear his intention was to buy *The Times*. He could do it either with Bell's help or in spite of him. When Bell later met Walter, he did not mention Northcliffe's name. He assured him, however, what he was about to propose was in the best interests of *The Times*. If his anonymous principal's offer were accepted, then the newspaper's editorial integrity would be respected. Walter agreed.

On 17 March 1908 a cryptic notice announced a new company had been formed. Apart from a new board of directors, essentially *The Times* remained *The Times*. Northcliffe at his first meeting with editorial staff declared it was not his intention to be their 'Chief', as he was at the *Daily Mail*. Walter, Buckle and Bell, he insisted, understood how to run *The Times* better than he ever would.[6] Repington recognised, sooner and more readily than Walter and Buckle, Northcliffe had rescued the dignity of *The Times*. With its independence now ensured there would be no longer any need for the dubious financial and advertising expedients the newspaper had previously adopted to make ends meet. Repington, unlike some of his more senior colleagues, did not confuse his own *dignitas* with securing the dignity and influence of *The Times*. Nor was he so naive as to suppose Northcliffe would not wish to make changes at Printing House Square. From 1911 onwards the tempo of change would increase as 'Lord Vigour and Venom' sought to hustle PHS into the twentieth century.

Personally, Repington hoped Northcliffe's involvement with *The Times* might free him from unwelcome editorial and financial restraints. He knew Northcliffe distrusted Germany. A rumour had gone the rounds preceding his purchase of *The Times* that he had promised he would never interfere with editorial policy unless Buckle failed to warn readers of the threat Germany posed to Britain and the Empire. After exchanging numerous notes, Repington enquired of Northcliffe, would it not be better if they met? Then Northcliffe 'could learn at first-hand some of the difficulties I encounter and thus be in a position to help me'.[7] He wanted the new owner to appreciate he too suffered from the outdated prejudices of some senior staff whom Northcliffe scathingly referred to as 'The Black Friars', 'The Grey Beards' or 'The Old Guard'. Repington calculated Northcliffe would need loyal 'in-house' allies in his struggles with 'the barnacle-covered whale of Printing House Square'. He laid on with a trowel his appreciation of the new owner while advertising his own,

Fig. 6 Alfred Harmsworth, Viscount Northcliffe (1865–1922) (*The Times*)

necessarily more modest accomplishments. But for all his efforts, opportunities to beard the proprietor remained depressingly few and far between.
Finally he wrote, 'A short, fragmentary conversation with you in a damp
field on a cold day at Guildford has left in my mind a desire for a little
further talk so that I may become better aware of your opinions and ideas.'[8]
But the great man's customary mode of communication was by cryptically
brief, typed notes. He was not averse to a direct postal approach circum-
venting the editor or manager, but if what Repington wrote did not interest
him, he simply ignored it. Their relationship would prompt fewer signs of
strain than might have been anticipated; that is, until Repington became
editor of the *Army Review*. That did lead to tensions and concern.

In *Vestigia* Repington claimed the *Army Review* was largely his creation. He had talked with Esher about a journal designed to make General Staff doctrine more widely and better understood. When he raised the subject a second time his idea now embraced both services. 'The power and influence of the Defence Committee would be much enhanced,' he wrote, 'if they maintained general supervision and control over an official or semi-official organ which would appear, say once a month, and disseminate some notions or questions of Imperial Defence by land and sea.' Ewart's department for the army and the NID for the navy could supply 'heaps of interesting material'. The Defence Committee could 'supervise and coordinate' their contributions after approval by the War Office or Admiralty.[9]

F. J. Hudleston, the War Office librarian, insisted that Repington had '*absolutely nothing* to do with the *Review*. The original initiative was Col. A. L. Haldane's'.[10] He, with Hudleston's help, had developed what had originally been cyclostyled, typed book reviews into a printed quarterly, *Recent Publications of Military Interest*, published from April 1907, 'as a first step towards a General Staff journal'. When Haldane left the War Office in 1909, Hudleston continued to edit and compile this journal. He had assumed the editorship would be his by succession. When Repington was appointed editor Huddleston was understandably disappointed and angry, particularly as it had been given to someone no longer officially attached to the War Office. It was rumoured Repington's appointment was intended as a precursor to his permanent attachment.[11] Though technically not impossible, reinstatement was extremely difficult. In 1912 Repington confirmed it had been at the minister's personal insistence he had been made editor. He did not even hint, however, Haldane intended the editorship should secure his reinstatement. The rumours persisted because so many of his former colleagues believed his 'banishment' from the army unjust and disproportionate. Nicholson told Henry Wilson, Haldane wished Repington to edit the *Army Review* and was anxious matters were made as smooth as possible for him. Wilson unreservedly condemned the decision, insisting Repington was 'devoid of honour, a liar and absolutely untrustworthy'. If Haldane confirmed the appointment, the General Staff would 'without exception loath the idea'.[12]

Wilson generally affected indifference to anything Repington said or wrote, yet he talked 'a good deal' about him with Ferdinand Foch, the rising French military star. He put Foch on his guard against Repington and similarly forewarned Dawson. A recent article in *The Times* had condemned Wilson's poor staff work at manoeuvres. Repington certainly knew how to stick in pins where they hurt most. His criticism had been merited, not that it had stopped a wounded Wilson grumbling about the 'lying brute over-reaching himself'. When Robertson replaced Wilson as commandant at the Staff College, Repington made no secret of his pleasure. Wilson had educated 'sucking Napoleons', their young minds 'in cloud cuckoo land while the daily work of a staff officer in the field had been neglected'.

It had been in March 1911, during the troublesome and embarrassing annual renegotiation of his salary, when Repington first mentioned to Bell he had been chosen to edit a new War Office quarterly. Northcliffe claimed he knew nothing of this until late May and that another month elapsed before Repington explained the journal's purpose.[13] Northcliffe was not to be persuaded work for the War Office and *The Times* could be satisfactorily combined. He blamed the board for assenting to an unsuitable arrangement. Then he suggested menacingly that Buckle might consider employing a second military correspondent. How could Repington criticise the War Office when it was one of his paymasters? There was a further complication. Foreign readers might suppose the views expressed in *The Times* by the military correspondent were 'official'.[14] He correctly anticipated there would be questions in Parliament and the familiar calumnies broadcast by the German conservative press. In addition, there were the public and private imprecations of the kaiser, scarcely concealed threats from the *Wilhelmstrasse* and complaints by Metternich, Germany's ambassador to St James's.

Repington sent Northcliffe the first number of the *Army Review* seeking 'any suggestion your experience may dictate. Probably it is advantageous for *The Times* that its military correspondent should edit the *Review*.' He would know better 'in the light of experience in a year or so'.[15] A year later he admitted to Ian Hamilton, whatever was said to the contrary in Parliament, it was not as easy to ask for papers at the War Office now he was editing the *Army Review*.[16] He emphasised to Northcliffe his intention to secure for the *Review* authoritative articles by the 'leading men in the army [to] benefit not only the army but the public'.[17] Northcliffe thought the journal 'excellent' but continued to doubt whether Repington's status as an independent critic could be guaranteed. Repington responded, he needed to subsidise his work for *The Times* since they had unreasonably cut his expenses. Other than by editing the *Review*, how else could he 'retrieve the £500 a year by which expenses had been reduced that provided him with the sinews of war'? A room at the War Office and his 'semi-official position' he pointed out, afforded 'an excuse for some generals to grant me special favours'. At this point in his letter he paused and left a space before later adding, how much he would have preferred to concentrate exclusively on *The Times* but had chosen to accept the editorship of the *Review* 'simply for the money'. Whether he continued as editor, he told Northcliffe, was a

Fig. 7 George Earle Buckle (1854–1935) (*The Times*)

matter of indifference to him, but only he could have done the initial spadework. Having established the standard, inside a year he expected the thing would run itself. If the proprietor wanted him to give up the editorship he asked only to be given as much notice as possible, not for his own benefit but so as 'not to place Lord Haldane in any difficulty'.[18] Northcliffe, unfortunately, was not as impressed by this selfless avowal as Repington had hoped and intended.

In July 1911 Repington shamelessly puffed not only the contents of the *Review* but also his fitness to be its editor. He sharply disagreed with Buckle concerning the Moroccan diplomatic crisis triggered by the arrival of the German gunboat *Panther* at Agadir. Buckle steered an unruffled course of studious neutrality: Repington argued Britain should respond in kind and send a British warship to Agadir. He was considerably more excited by this second Moroccan crisis than he had been by the first. He believed this 'German act of brigandage' had been carefully planned in advance. He also warned, 'It would be as well to look after ourselves nearer home.' He had observed the British Home Fleet at Portland was taking no precautions. Hundreds of sailors had been released on furlough at a time of tension. He warned that a new spirit inspired German diplomacy. England might expect acts of vigour if German ambitions could not be satisfied by a French surrender over Agadir. Given the existing state of British military preparations, they had no right to run such risks. He offered his editor an article on the threat of invasion that Buckle turned down. He suspected, not without reason, Repington was sounding off again in his unending campaign for more recruits.[19]

Repington responded to Buckle's rebuff by complaining to Dawson. He hoped Dawson would remember what he had said when he succeeded as editor. His concern had been genuine. Different components of the British fleet had been scattered in a dozen ports in various states of unpreparedness when 'everything in Germany that can float and fight is now at sea'. It was 'perfectly damnable' that he could say nothing about the navy's 'hopeless, strategic disposition, because Buckle, Thursfield and company were alike ensnared by Blue Water mis-conceptions'. As for the Foreign Office, they never moved until too late. Germans now had an added incentive to serve France with an ultimatum because he saw no hope of any worthwhile initiative from the Admiralty. It was very much a case of Repington *contra mundum*.

His editor might have been excused for thinking Repington was being somewhat paranoid. He had stated, first in *The Times* and then the *Army Review*, the Anglo-French Entente ought to be converted into a precise naval and military alliance. He readily acknowledged to formalise the continental commitment, as he was suggesting, was to forfeit what euphemistically was referred to as 'Britain's free hand'. Alarm bells began to sound at Printing House Square. European correspondents, like George Saunders, feared a too intimate military commitment to a belligerent French government. Buckle responded by encouraging Thursfield to reject Repington's arguments, a commission the naval correspondent readily undertook. Repington's one concern, he insisted, had been to promote the importance of the army and the War Office. His hope was of course to undermine the Admiralty's strategic dominance. Repington angrily dismissed this as 'controversial nonsense' that could only do 'serious harm'. Did these Admiralty apologists suppose he was an unthinking agent of the General Staff? Constantly he emphasised the absolute need for a defence policy that was a *joint* enterprise embracing both armed services. Thursfield and the whole fleet of naval correspondents would have to wait while he first tackled the editor, who had infamously encouraged the naval correspondent to promote 'the Radical view that no military force should be sent to the Continent'. Buckle deserved to be admonished for publishing 'an argument ... that can only make England distrusted abroad and *The Times* ridiculous at home'. Buckle, not the least disconcerted by Repington's furious assault, stuck to his guns. Repington was obliged to beat a strategic retreat to the *Review*. He offered a reprise of his argument that there was need for an alliance, not only between England and France but also between Britain's two armed services.

The difference between Buckle and Repington was seemingly unbridgeable. The editor believed, in the event of war with Germany Britain's primary offensive and defensive force was the Royal Navy, not the army. Despite clear evidence supplied by Repington of naval unpreparedness at the beginning of the July crisis, his belief in the navy remained unshaken. He would not be persuaded to Repington's view that to despatch the Expeditionary Force to France was vital to Britain's national existence. Buckle saw only the insignificant size of the British army when compared with those of Germany and France. He did not believe it would be the end of the entente, as Repington insisted, if Britain sent no military force to France at the outbreak of hostilities. The editor was convinced, the military correspondent grossly exaggerated when he claimed, 'Every French statesman believes the only help of real service to them is the military force we can place in the line in fourteen days.'[20]

Repington had supplied Buckle with a long, detailed memorandum, 'Suggestions for the organisation of war news in case of war with Germany'. It set out the minimal preparations he considered *The Times* ought to make, at home and abroad, for agents, codes, wireless telegraphy and the organisation of a suitable headquarters to ensure an uninterrupted news service. He appeared to want to put Printing House Square on a state of alert prepared for the imminent outbreak of war. Three years earlier, when war had threatened in the Balkans, in a letter written to Bell he had prefigured this latest memorandum. He insisted the old methods and organisation were hopelessly outdated. No modern, sophisticated, belligerent power would allow correspondents access to important information. In wartime, if *The Times* wanted a constant supply of worthwhile information 'then it should resort to secret service employing a system which I have applied with success abroad'. Buckle wondered whether the correspondent was genuinely anxious or had his judgment been addled by the blare of his own belligerent trumpeting?

Pro-French sentiment at *The Times* was undoubtedly weakened by French truculence displayed in the latter stages of the second Moroccan incident. That was true of everyone except Repington. In October he attended the German army manoeuvres for what would be his last visit. His six detailed reports acknowledged certain German strengths, particularly the threatening firepower of their machine guns. He considered their troops well drilled and disciplined but thought they lacked the individuality, initiative and freshness of the French. They no longer warranted the formidable reputation they had once deserved. German artillery did not match the French and their cavalry would find the British Lancers more than they could comfortably handle. These comments he later admitted were avowedly propagandist. 'Opinion is everything in war,' he wrote. 'There was a danger the French and we might think the Germans invincible.'[21]

What he saw on the four days he attended the manoeuvres confirmed his earlier opinion; the Germans intended to repeat their favourite tactic, envelopment, ignoring the restriction imposed by the boundaries of neutral states. In January 1906, in a letter to Edward Grey, he had predicted a German violation of the Low Countries' borders. Then in a series of articles published 23 and 30 January and 6 and 20 February 1911, he had stated Germany would not respect the neutrality of small countries on or near the Franco-German border. Though afforded no editorial support, he went on to argue the future peace of Europe depended on Franco-British military and naval co-operation, the partners to determine immediately what part each would play in a war on land and sea against Germany. What followed – 'The Committee of Imperial Defence *must* have available a cut and dried solution' – should have been a familiar message to his readers. The kaiser, incandescent that a guest at *his* manoeuvres could have written as Repington had, insisted to the British military attaché in Berlin, 'the few divisions Britain could put into the field would make no appreciable difference'. Nevertheless, ignoring the All Highest's ire, Repington continued to emphasise, it was '*absolutely vital* we should be able and ready to send a thoroughly efficient force to aid France'.[22]

Buckle, most senior members of *The Times*' staff, the whole of the Admiralty, indeed the greater part of British opinion, would have agreed with the kaiser: the British army's contribution would be puny and unimportant in any continental struggle. Northcliffe, however, had been impressed by Repington's argument. So was Repington's friend, Sir Ian Hamilton, who wrote to congratulate him upon his fine series of articles. What he had written about German methods and intentions could only do much good for the thinking part of the British army. Most had no idea what German military writers thought, planned or discussed. The nationalist and militarist wing of the German press accused Repington of attempting to incite the French to resistance *à outrance* by holding out the prospect of military success. Referring to him as 'the crafty penman of Printing House Square', they accused him of attempting to arrest German naval expansion. He had the effrontery to attribute faults he pretended to find in the German army to excessive expenditure upon the Imperial navy.

The British military attaché in Berlin, Colonel A. V. F. Russell, was instructed by the War Office to establish whether official German circles supposed Repington's views were shared by the British General Staff. Russell's assurances it was not so did nothing to stop the German Chancellor and Foreign Secretary complaining separately to the British Ambassador about the damage the correspondent's pen had caused to good relations between their two countries. The British Ambassador thought German irritation 'justifiable' but pointed out Repington's writing was nothing like as irritating as 'the gross fabrications and abuse founded on them' by the German press. Alick Russell on three occasions complained of the 'mischievous consequences resulting from ... Col. à Court's articles'. Several times he had been harangued by the kaiser, who complained 'the Military Correspondent of *The Times* wrote the most horrible things about the German army causing untold mischief in America, France and other places by his writings on this subject'. Repington's comments had clearly done nothing to defuse the overheated emotions generated by the Agadir crisis.[23]

In February 1912 Repington's anomalous position as editor of the *Army Review* became a parliamentary issue. He published information in *The Times* abstracted from the army's 'General Annual Report'. It would have passed without comment had not several members of the Commons realised the 'Report' was not yet generally available to them. Immediately questions were tabled in the House. What exact status did Repington enjoy at the War Office? It was further discussed on another two occasions in March during the army estimates debate. Munro Ferguson described Repington as 'the first military writer in Europe'. Beresford insisted he was 'one of the cleverest men we have'. Despite the compliments it was nonetheless considered 'anomalous' and 'unbearable' he should write both for *The Times* and for the *Review*. The Germans were convinced he was not a journalist but must be a War Office official. 'Either he is one thing or the other.'

Repington's immediate reaction was to treat the incident as a joke. He dismissed the whole episode as a 'fine advert for the *Army Review*'.[24] He was stoutly defended from attacks from both sides of both Houses; by Haldane in the Lords and Seely in the Commons. But Arthur Lee, in a fine lather of righteous indignation, claimed Repington's appointment was not only 'incompatible with public interest', but 'an administrative

scandal, an extremely objectionable position'. Seely, all injured inno-
cence and the soul of reason, responded the appointment was 'a very
good arrangement . . . If you want to get the very best man . . . I do frankly
say I am convinced that Col. Repington is the very best man'. Haldane's
assertion that Repington did not have a room at the War Office prompted
incredulous guffaws. Seely did his best to make Haldane's claim sound
half credible. 'He never had a regular room', he suggested, 'but a kind of
corner'. Repington was greatly amused. He assured Dawson, from the
start of his editorship of the *Army Review* he had not changed his room
once. 'To read Seely I must have wandered around the War Office
looking for a desk.' It would make a fine April fool jape should Dawson
publish a short serial in *The Times*, 'From Lift to Lavatory' or 'How I
edited the *Army Review*'.[25]

Northcliffe was not amused. He asked for a meeting with Haldane and
insisted Repington's status was causing acute unpleasantness, prompting
odious suggestions among the chattering classes. He showed Haldane a
letter from Repington that had been addressed to him from the War
Office. It bore a particular room number, plainly engraved. For once in
his life Haldane was rendered speechless. Northcliffe reminded
Repington, he still thought it undesirable he should work for two masters
and that the present agreement had been made under sufferance. This
last Repington flatly denied. He was not anxious to abandon the *Review*
while his ambitious plans for its development remained unfulfilled. He
wanted it to reflect a joint approach to strategic thinking by both services,
a subject about which he had made his own thinking crystal clear to
Buckle in an admonitory letter written at the beginning of the year. It
had never been his idea, Repington insisted, that one service should boss
the other; 'both should be directed by *instructed* statesmanship . . . an
object gradually being obtained by the Defence Committee'. He had
discussed the whole matter with Haldane and Churchill some weeks
previously, but sadly there was still a tendency to dethrone the Defence
Committee from its proper place.[26]

Changes for the better had been made at the Admiralty under
Churchill's dynamic leadership. His promise to lay down two keels for
every German battleship built pleased Repington. There should be no
mistake: Britain was determined to maintain naval superiority over the
Germans. Repington congratulated Churchill on his 'masculine handling
of naval policy with which I am in complete accord. In naval affairs I am
what Palmerston used to call a fair foolometer', meaning someone who
shares the views of most right-thinking people. He admitted, however
'much anxiety [about] the actual numbers that make up a battle squadron
at sea'. A week later he forwarded to Churchill a sizeable memorandum

on the subject. A covering note requested 'some good naval opinions' that would be of greater assistance and more value 'if they disregard the personality of the author and deal only with his arguments'.[27]

Repington was all too aware he was not a popular man with the navy. Fisherites in particular were slow to forgive him for allying himself with Beresford. Fisher offered advice freely to an attentive Churchill and naturally assumed to do so was entirely acceptable; but that 'Cabinet Ministers should receive letters from a discredited soldier on how the Fleet ought to fight!' was 'absurd'.[28] Captain G. A. Ballard RN, after reading Repington's memorandum offered advice to Churchill that could as well have been written by Fisher. 'Knowledge of Admiralty policy ... should be confined to very few officers within the Admiralty ... It is highly undesirable that it should be communicated to any irresponsible person.' At considerably greater length, Hankey also advised Churchill to close the door of the Admiralty 'to this very clever journalist who lives by his cleverness'. He already acquires 'information denied other journalists' because of his 'privileged position at the War Office and his distinguished military career'. Given Repington's studies and his practical knowledge, Hankey judged it best he should not have the chance to find out 'what is in the mind of the Admiralty as regards the preparation for and conduct of war with Germany'.[29] Repington, unaware of how little information he was being vouchsafed by the Admiralty, told Churchill he could count upon the support of *The Times* for his 'proposal about the Dominions and the Navy'. Furthermore, Repington made it clear he was anxious 'to be in line with [Churchill's] policy. We must all pull together over defence questions if we can.'

The important burthen of Repington's memorandum was contained in its seemingly guileless coda: 'Possibly you have a paper on this subject you could give me in order to enable us to keep our place in the line?'[30] By hook or by crook Repington was determined to get the navy on board his *Army Review* and see it become the *Navy and Army Review*. In early July he told Esher how pleased he was at the quality of the writing in the *Review* and the huge increase in circulation. He blamed not the Admiralty but the Treasury, which was dragging its feet. 'I will write to Winston soon,' he informed Esher. If that proved unavailing then he would 'chuck the Editorship'.

He had remained editor as long as he had because of his affection for Haldane. So long as Haldane remained Secretary of State for War, Repington considered his own position tenable. But now Seely had replaced Haldane he could no longer contemplate with equanimity remaining editor. Despite the assurance he had given Northcliffe, when he took over the editorship he now adopted the contrary argument. If he was 'obliged to assail the War Office' then his position would be 'impossible'.[31] He scarcely knew what was going on at the War Office and would not support the minister until he was sure of the line he was taking.

Within the week Repington informed Northcliffe he had told the manager of *The Times* he was resigning the editorship of the *Army Review* and confidently expected Northcliffe would approve his decision, given the reservations he had previously expressed. 'At any moment I expect to have to attack the Administration. Many influential people have begged me to resign as my editorial duties are so onerous.'[32] Repington was told when he resigned as editor of the *Army Review* he would be paid an extra three hundred pounds annual salary for his 'exclusive services'.[33] It wasn't the five hundred he had hoped for, but it was better than nothing.

The following week a meeting with Seely led to impasse. 'He absolutely refused to accept my resignation [and] I absolutely refused to withdraw it,' he told Dawson. There was a problem. The former German foreign minister, Marschall von Bieberstein, was due to replace Metternich as ambassador to St James's. At the 1907 Hague Peace Conference he had made a name for himself as a skilled manipulator of the press. Consequently his arrival was awaited with trepidation. It was thought he would mount a formidable campaign against the Triple Entente. Seely informed Repington, at their first meeting the ambassador had first patronised him, then complained about Repington's assaults on the German army. Seely suggested should Repington resign from the *Review* immediately it would look like truckling to the Germans. Repington did not find this argument persuasive. He believed Seely's real priority was to keep him tied to the War Office 'unable to get off my chain to bite'. A number of War Office jobs were mentioned that might appeal to the correspondent. Money was also mentioned, but no specific sum. All the while Repington kept on insisting he was 'a free lance and preferred the life to official harness ... I would not look at anything under £2,000 a year [but] were it worth £4,000 a year I should not take it'. All this, but particularly the putative amounts of salary *promised*, he doubtless hoped Dawson would pass on to Northcliffe, the better to appreciate the value others placed upon his services. Eventually Seely had agreed he might leave 'after January 1st next'. The two men parted apparently reconciled. Repington had not changed his opinion of 'Galloping Jack'. Personally he liked him well enough, but as a minister he carried no guns. His promotion had brought about an undeniable and dramatic fall in the general efficiency of the War Office.[34]

Repington's relations with Northcliffe now settled into a much happier groove enhanced by a memorandum he sent on war with Germany. The king requested a copy to study and Northcliffe was told of the royal interest. Part of the memorandum was concerned with Churchill's proposal to reorganise the British fleets. To counteract the increased German naval building programme, the North Sea Fleet would be strengthened. Although this would involve weakening the Mediterranean Fleet, *The Times* approved. Repington told Northcliffe he was concerned and was speedily reassured, 'Nothing more of the kind will appear in the paper.'[35]

Repington immediately seized the opportunity offered to curry favour and score off members of *The Times* Blue Water Fish Pond. He hastened to send Northcliffe copies of his letters to Buckle complaining about 'the incurable habit ... of working in watertight compartments and not consulting me, or someone else who knows his business about strategical questions, before committing the paper to a policy'. He suggested, if in future *The Times* wished to appear less ridiculous on naval affairs, it might do worse than get him to approach 'Admiral Sir C. Ottley privately'. Ottley, the proprietor, was assured 'agreed on all essential points. He has little to do but draw £5,000 a year from Armstrongs', the shipbuilders and armament manufacturers. Repington proposed to appeal to him 'on patriotic grounds'.[36] Anxious to remain in Northcliffe's good books, he insisted it was 'all very well for Esher to ask [him] not to drop the Mediterranean', but he was unable to discuss the real problem. 'I did what I could in today's paper ... but the moral which I drew at the end was cut out of the article.'[37] There was no immediate reply from Northcliffe, but the following month he told Repington that he intended to make 'changes to *Times* naval matters' that Repington would approve. In anticipation Repington told Esher, 'We shall win. You had better warn Winston when he returns a storm is impending and opinion will not brook fooling.'[38] As Repington anticipated, in the face of such an extraordinary congeries of usually bitterly opposed interests, Churchill was obliged to give way on his Mediterranean idea.

For the last number of the *Review* he would edit, Repington planned to publish a contribution from Esher that proposed a *Combined Review* as the future organ of a real Imperial General Staff. To employ in tandem the full intellectual resources of both army and navy would be both splendid and desirable. Not blind to the difficulties that stood in the way, he warned, 'Never forget the General Staff's antipathy to the CID.' Changes were desirable but would have to be made very cautiously. Esher should also bear in mind the *Review* would 'always be very dependent on the General Staff for contributors.' Some of the best articles offered the *Review* as presently constituted had been 'rejected owing to the timidity and obstruction of a nincompoop DMO'. Esher ignored this thrust at Henry Wilson, but nonetheless appreciated the validity of the warning. Nothing came of the idea because neither Seely nor Sir John French would wear it; the minister, because he thought the *Review* had enough on its hands already; French, because he hated the idea of anything diminishing the influence of the General Staff. To Repington, 'the latent hostility or rather jealousy of the GS towards the Defence Committee' was scarcely surprising news. 'I dare say,' he told Esher, 'you have not been brought into contact with it before.' Esher's paper was returned to him. It would serve another day. [39]

While Repington remained editor there would be one more twist in the tale of the *Army Review*. He asked Kitchener to contribute an article for the first joint number. When he told former army colleagues they laughed and thought it 'too preposterous to suppose'. Nonetheless, the impossible had happened. The pity was the article was unsuitable. According to Repington, had it been published it would have prompted the German Ambassador to demand his passport. Kitchener's piece, entitled 'Am Tag', described 'the outbreak of an Anglo-German war and the defeat of the British Fleet! You may well say lawks', Repington observed, and promised to send Dawson the unique literary offering. Would *The Times* publish it? The only restraint upon publication was the author should remain anonymous. 'It is a baddish article,' Repington admitted, 'but it will be interesting someday perhaps as K's only contribution to journalism.'

This note had been written from Claridge's Hotel where Repington was temporarily staying. French and Kitchener had accepted invitations to dine with him. He hoped to discuss the article with them, but not once, during the course of two prolonged conversations with Kitchener, was the article mentioned. Instead they spoke 'partly about our military affairs here and partly about Egypt and Turkey ... the state of drift in home affairs, the want of big men [and] the Socialistic tendencies of the misguided masses'. When Dawson told him there was no place in *The Times* for Kitchener's story, Repington was not greatly surprised. [40]

Northcliffe's differences with Repington over the *Review* had been as nothing compared with the proprietor's struggle with Bell, Buckle, Chirol and other assorted lesser lights at Printing House Square. This had gone on almost continuously since his purchase of *The Times*. He was determined to reorganise his property thoroughly but it was taking much longer than he had originally planned. At a time of painful change Repington emerged relatively unscathed. It was some measure of how much his unique contribution to *The Times* was valued. Northcliffe recognised *The Times* possessed in Repington the best-known, most influential military correspondent writing for any British national daily newspaper. Financially Repington was better off under the new regime than he had been before and counted it a considerable advantage to have Dawson rather than Buckle as his editor. Sadly time would sow distrust and sour his present comparative content.

An exchange of letters between the proprietor and military correspondent in August 1913 clearly illustrated their different approaches to journalism. Northcliffe asserted he had been asked by a distinguished soldier why military news was always known in the clubs before it appeared in *The Times*. 'What I want,' the proprietor insisted, 'is a little of that pride of priority instilled into the paper by John Walter and Delane.'[41] Even from Northcliffe, Repington was not prepared to take a lesson in history or advice on how best to do *his* job. He rejoined, 'If all you want from me is a batch of indiscretions that can readily be satisfied.' They would be sent immediately to Printing House Square, but he warned, they were unlikely to do much good. His chief value to *The Times* was his 'expert criticism of home and foreign military affairs, not the divulgation of secrets which infuriate the authorities and especially the Crown'. He suggested both their interests would be better served if each stuck to what he knew best, and reminded Northcliffe, over all other military critics writing for the daily press he enjoyed a 'particularly privileged position. It is a question of confidence ... that confidence would not be *reposed in me were I to announce in The Times everything I hear*'. Perhaps Northcliffe might 'care to send [him] a line to say what you think after reading this'.[42] There was no answer: Repington's admonition of the great man had been accepted.

The Times needed to attract the attention of an ever-increasing readership. That commercial necessity was the imperative to which Northcliffe responded. Opinion making and winning were important to him so long as they improved circulation figures. Somewhat despairingly he declared, 'For six years I have thrown men, energy, ideas and fortune into *The Times* with negligible results.' When, in October 1913, he learned there had been a slight increase in sales, Dawson received his ironic congratulations. He raged and nagged to induce a degree of Carmelite House dash into Printing House Square, but his constant, irrational tantrums succeeded only in upsetting the staff. Repington he left relatively unmolested. As the instructor of a critical and intelligent readership, the correspondent deployed his specialist knowledge to examine and explain complex defence problems. This he saw as his awesome responsibility. He was convinced he had made *The Times* a watchtower to help secure and maintain Britain against the envious, ambitious Hun.

11 The Curragh incident

Repington particularly emphasised to the new Secretary of State how he met Haldane regularly, 'nearly every week to discuss measures before their adoption'. Clearly he hoped J. E. B. Seely would prove similarly accommodating.[1] Such an arrangement seemed more than likely given their earlier association so that Repington's already favoured position seemed about to be enhanced. But instead he was soon complaining Seely was idle, that he cut little ice with his permanent civil servants and that his undoubted 'amiability would never compensate for a lack of political acumen and foresight'. However, Seely's most damaging failing was he resented his predecessor's success. This, Repington believed, accounted for his failure to put down the conspiracy 'engineered by Wilson' against Haldane's Territorials. Repington had suggested Robertson might replace Wilson as DMO, but nothing had come of this, or his further proposal to publish an Army Order warning officers 'in very firm Wellingtonian terms' not to run down the armed forces in the press.[2] Reluctantly he concluded the time had come to impress a painful truth upon 'Galloping Jack': behind the quarrels about the Territorials lay a more significant difference – the unresolved Irish problem.

There had been no shortage of proposed solutions for Ireland's ills. The Liberals favoured Home Rule. Twice they had unsuccessfully attempted its introduction; first in the Commons in 1886, then the Lords in 1893. Their electoral victory in 1906 meant Home Rule would once more feature on the Westminster agenda. Probability became certainty when the Lords' veto was abolished by the 1911 Parliament Act. After two, closely fought general elections the Liberals remained in power but with their majority in the Commons so reduced they required the votes of Irish Nationalist and Labour MPs. The thought that John Redmond and his Irish Nationalist Party held the balance of political power at Westminster infuriated Unionists. They insisted, for Irish Nationalist votes to determine the future status of Britain and Ireland was unconstitutional. Unable to resolve their dilemma by conventional political means, some frustrated Unionists were prepared to countenance the possibility of mutiny in the army and armed insurrection in Ulster.

Balfour was convinced Home Rule could never resolve the Irish problem but unlike his successor as Unionist leader he refused to countenance unconstitutional measures to oppose the government's legislative programme. But in 1911 he was replaced as party leader by Andrew Bonar Law. Repington had never thought well of Balfour, particularly his failure to acknowledge the need for conscription. When Bonar Law privately professed he supported conscription, Repington declared him an admirable choice as party leader.

Home Rule was never intended formally to end the Union. The king would remain head of state in both countries and Irish MPs would still attend at Westminster. Ulstermen, however, were determined never to surrender to the embrace of a Dublin parliament dominated by Catholics and Nationalists. For them, Home Rule meant Rome Rule. In April 1912, two days before Asquith introduced the Home Rule Bill in Parliament, the Unionist leader, reviewing a military-style march past by 80,000 Ulstermen, described Home Rule as 'naked tyranny'. He pledged the support of *all* Unionists, those in Britain and the south of Ireland as well as Ulster, to defeat 'a treacherous conspiracy'.[3] Half a million men and women publicly declared their opposition to Home Rule and 28 September was designated Ulster Day. A binding covenant pledged they would 'employ all necessary means' to defeat Home Rule. Asquith and most Liberal ministers chose to ignore this intransigence. When the threat was repeated they still supposed once Home Rule was placed on the statute book Ulster would not resist. When, with all too obvious reluctance, Asquith at last seemed prepared to consider Ulster's concerns and take seriously the province's determination not to be included in an 'all Ireland' solution, his familiar mantra 'wait and see' neither endeared him to the impatient Unionists nor inspired confidence among Nationalists. All wondered whether he meant what he said.

There is no mention of Ulster's political and constitutional troubles until the penultimate page of Repington's pre-war memoirs. He notes how the danger of armed collision in Ireland had 'diverted attention from contemplation of the storm clouds piling up in Europe'. But in 1920, after five years of war, he supposed his readers might find it difficult to recapture their pre-war perspective on the international scene. In the final twelve months of peace, threats of civil disorder hid the true significance of events on the Continent from British eyes and minds. Repington had been in Ulster at the time, 'visiting the camps and parades'. He admitted 'a deep interest in the extraordinary movement which had all my sympathies'.[4] Although they disagreed as to what might constitute the best, most appropriate solution to Ulster's problems, Repington's affection and concern for the province was shared by *The Times'* proprietor and editor.[5]

Repington had first become involved as a player in Ulster's developing drama on 2 July 1913. A note from Dawson asked what might happen if the government thought to employ the army to coerce Ulster into accepting Home Rule? 'So far as one can see,' wrote Dawson, 'the Government is not sufficiently fatuous to allow the thing to come to actual fighting ... I hear already of officers preparing to go and fight for Ulster, and others preparing to send in their papers and get out of the whole business ... Others argue it is the business of a soldier to obey constituted authority, and that this is not the hundredth case when rebellion is justified ... What do you think?'[6] Repington never doubted many officers would *wish* to resign. *The Times* must strongly deprecate inconsiderate or hasty action. It should, however, sympathise with the dilemma officers faced and share their indignation. The troubles were entirely the government's responsibility. He concluded, 'Discipline is the first duty of the corps of officers ... We *dare not* admit politics to the army ... We must have no compromise with illegality on the part of the army. It might be the end of us.'[7] This response to Dawson's question was in full accord with the principle first formally enunciated by General Monck in 1660; the duty of the military is to obey the civil power. Yet Repington had associated himself with Bonar Law, who had implied, in circumstances that he would determine, he was prepared to use the army to defeat the government's Irish policy.

Repington was well aware his response to Dawson's inquiry could not be the end of the matter. In theory the army was apolitical, but he knew it to be thoroughly politicised. His response had concentrated exclusively on the army. Yet he perfectly well knew, the intentions of the political parties were central to the issue. The great majority of army officers instinctively sympathised with the Unionists and certain senior officers were actively and continuously involved with that party. Its increasingly extreme campaign was designed specifically to stop the Liberal government from coercing Ulster.

General French was plagued with thoughts of what might happen if the government employed the army to enforce Home Rule upon an Ulster armed and determined to resist. He asked Henry Wilson whether, in the event of civil war in Ireland, he would obey King's Orders. Wilson replied he could not promise to obey for it would mean firing on the North 'at the dictates of Redmond' when the great majority of Englishmen were against Home Rule. He could not bring himself to believe Asquith was mad enough to employ force. It would 'split army, country and the Empire'.[7] Wilson's logical and emotional confusion was shared by many retired as well as serving senior army officers. Nor was Repington immune. For some months, however, he was spared having to confront it as starkly as had Wilson. His time and energy was engaged upon other problems and issues.

In late February 1914 Repington had his first opportunity to pay a short visit to Northern Ireland to see just what had been going on there. The previous October, Dawson had sent Lovat Fraser on a fact-finding mission. What he saw and heard convinced him Ulster would resist any attempt at coercion. He had examined and assessed the Ulster Volunteers as best he might, but he was no military expert. Repington would now make a professional assessment.

The UVF was organised by county and district into regiments, battalions and companies. Volunteers were plentiful and enthusiastic. The Ulster Unionist Council had established a military committee to organise, arm and mobilise their force of 90,000 men. Their commander was Lieutenant General George Richardson. The threat of armed civil insurrection had long been part of Unionist rhetoric but not until now, under Carson's leadership, had serious military resistance been contemplated.[8] Did the UVF amount to more than an empty threat and rhetorical bluster, or was it a serious military force, an army, trained, armed and prepared to fight if the Liberal government dared to attempt to coerce Ulster? This was the question Repington set out to answer.

In a strenuous ten-day tour of the North he noted, UVF battalions were widely distributed across the province. Belfast possessed much the greatest concentration, 18 of the 65 organised and fully equipped battalions. Battalions varied in strength from 400 to 2,000. When he calculated the number of enrolled members Repington revised his earlier estimate upwards to approximately 110,000. Should the Liberal government attempt to coerce Ulster, numbers would be greatly increased 'by sympathisers in England, Scotland, the rest of Ireland and British possessions overseas ... who had made known their desire to help'. The one mounted regiment was the Enniskillen Horse, but each county division had a mounted section and cyclists besides. During his time in Belfast he had long, wide-ranging conversations with Ulster's political and military leaders including Carson and General Richardson. He questioned and examined everything; the number of recruits, their morale, training, organisation and plans for mobilisation. He listed specialist corps – signals, transport and engineers. It proved impossible to calculate an agreed figure for the number of rifles (80,000 with bayonets was his best estimate), but the number was growing each day. Ulster was 'full of arms'. He was convinced, if necessary, Ulster would fight and would make a formidable foe, efficient, disciplined and dedicated.[9]

On 4 March he sent the first of his UVF articles to Dawson. Much to the editor's annoyance, Repington had already despatched a rough proof together with a covering letter to Asquith. The correspondent acknowledged his editor's justified displeasure but thought 'the urgency of the case' excused his action. He had 'not heard from the PM yet', nor did he expect a reply for he had written 'nothing which could afford him pleasure or consolation'.[10] Repington had emphasised to Asquith 'the military value of the Ulstermen and the vulnerability of Gleichen's infantry brigade in Ulster'. His observations added little to the mass of evidence available to ministers provided by police spies. These included details of a raid, 'The No. 1 Scheme', planned by the UVF to assume by force the military control of Ulster. On 11 March the Cabinet appointed a special Ulster committee to examine all the disturbing evidence about which, as yet, nothing had been done. The committee was effectively run by the bristlingly self-assertive Churchill.

Lieutenant General Sir Arthur Paget, an old pal of Repington's, was Ireland's C-in-C. He was given verbal instructions but sadly no written orders. Precautionary troop movements were ordered to secure vulnerable, strategically important defensive sites. No one knew with absolute certainty what the UVF might do. Paget was a general of the old school. In uniquely difficult circumstances he was quite out of his depth, unable temperamentally or intellectually to discharge a task that required cool and sensitive handling. He flapped like a wet hen. Repington, well aware his friend was no intellectual, was angry that he should have been given a job for which he was both unsuited and ill-equipped. The poor man had been thoroughly confused; one moment battered by Churchill's aggressively specific invective, the next bemused by Seely's high-handed, vague generalities. General Gough later condemned Paget as ambitious, vain and stupid, but Gough's judgment was not entirely disinterested.

On 20 March Paget summoned Major General Sir Charles Fergusson, who commanded the Fifth Division, and Brigadier Gough, who was then commander of the Cavalry Brigade at the Curragh, to a conference in Dublin. During the course of a rambling, impassioned speech he implied it was likely the army would mount an immediate, extensive and aggressive operation against Ulster. Then foolishly and inexcusably he posed an hypothetical question. What would happen should any officer refuse to obey orders to march north? He stated that those whose homes were not in Ulster would be dismissed the service. Gough decided he would not go to the North and if ordered to do so would tender his resignation. He relayed his decision to his officers and sixty decided to follow his example. Though not a mutiny, their action constituted a collective act of protest against government policy. News of their decision spread rapidly. Gough,

Fig. 8 J. E. B. Seely (1868–1947)

described by Asquith as 'the hottest of Ulsterians',[11] had exploited Paget's weakness to cause the maximum embarrassment to the government. He was ordered to report immediately to the War Office.

At meetings on 22 and 23 March a truculent if understandably suspicious Gough was asked to treat the incident as a misunderstanding and return to duty as though nothing untoward had happened. He refused. Further, he insisted on being given a written pledge that neither he nor his fellow officers would ever be required to coerce Ulster into accepting Home Rule. Fearing the likelihood of the trouble spreading throughout the army, Seely and the Army Council gave way. They signed a text drafted by Spencer Ewart. It was subsequently altered in some details by Asquith before approval by the Cabinet. Gough remained dissatisfied and sought further, more specific assurances. Then Seely, without Cabinet sanction, added what Balfour would later describe as 'several peccant paragraphs'.[12] Gough, the bit now between his teeth, required and received a further pledge to which French agreed and signed. Later French admitted he would have signed almost anything so long as it served to get Gough and his officers back to duty.

Gough had behaved quite improperly. He deserved to be sacked or at least severely disciplined. Major General Sir Charles Fergusson's correct behaviour was ignored while Gough's ill-disciplined action was applauded by Unionists on both sides of the Irish Sea. He returned to Dublin bearing in triumph written affirmation the army would not be used to coerce Ulster to enforce Home Rule. Asquith discovered what had happened only when it was too late to recall the documents. Next day in the Commons, 25 March, the Prime Minister repudiated the unauthorised additions. That same day Seely admitted his mistake but sought to justify it. He seemed unable to realise it had been wrong to negotiate with Gough. He offered his resignation for there was no honourable alternative, but it was not accepted for a further five days. The Curragh incident had been short-lived, but its repercussions were long-lasting. This should have surprised no one for it is an accepted tradition of Irish politics that nothing is ever quite finished, nor anything entirely forgotten.

Repington's first article on the UVF appeared on 18 March. The figures he published on the number of Volunteers, arms and ammunition were the same as those contained in his letter to Asquith received on 4 March but not read to the Cabinet until 17 March, five days *after* the Cabinet subcommittee charged to examine the military situation in Ulster and to recommend military dispositions had been formed. The letter was never more than one among a number of factors that determined the subcommittee's recommendation to undertake certain precautionary troop movements in Ulster. Debates on the second reading of the Home Rule Bill in the Commons and Carson's dramatic departure for Ireland heightened political passions. Asquith alone among politicians appeared immune to the sense of imminent crisis. In Cabinet, Churchill spoke with characteristic belligerence. Even mild-mannered 'Radical John' Morley recalled how in 1893 the 'Govt. consulted Wolseley who counselled a swift descent on and coercion of Ireland'.[13]

Sir George Riddell in his diary for 25 April stated Repington's letter 'was the cause of the Government's proceedings' that prompted the Curragh incident. After receiving the letter, Asquith had 'called upon Seely to do what was necessary to protect the Government stores and ammunition'. According to Riddell, Lloyd George and C. F. G. Masterman, as well as General French, had confirmed the truth of his extraordinary claim.[14] The letter referred to in the diary entry has to be that of 4 March read to Cabinet on 17 March. It may well be that Riddell's Cabinet witnesses misunderstood or exaggerated the exact significance of the letter. Both were much preoccupied with problems other than the security of government installations in Ulster. Lloyd George was planning his imminent budget intended to boost Liberal electoral hopes by developing and supplementing the 1909 'People's Budget'. Masterman understandably was most concerned with his own parliamentary future. A statement made by Seely to Riddell seemed to confirm it had been 'Repington's letter that stimulated the Government to take action both military and naval.' Seely's words, however, must be discounted. They were inspired by his determination to demonstrate he had been unjustly victimised. His behaviour had been pusillanimous though he implied he alone among Cabinet members had been resolute. Subsequently, he blamed among others the Irish police, General Paget, Grey, Birrell, Aberdeen, even Asquith, for 'arranging things so badly'.

Riddell's diary entries encapsulated not a singular truth but the misapprehension of a newspaper man who supposed himself uniquely well informed on Cabinet matters. He supposed Repington *must* have been intimately involved in the Ulster crisis because for years he had been closely involved with anything and everything that determined the fortunes of the army. Riddell wrote up his diary entry *after* Liberal MP, Sir Harold Elverston had asked Seely whether Repington was still connected officially with the War Office, and whether he secretly communicated 'with certain persons who have organised forces in Ulster defying the mandate of the Commons'.[15] Speaker Lowther disallowed both questions. Repington was in no way implicated directly as a plotter or participant in the events at the Curragh. His significance in the whole affair, whatever others might have supposed, was limited to his interpretation of events. His, though not the only voice, was the most powerful and influential in the press arena. He wrote about a deliberate government 'plot' by force of arms to coerce Ulster into acceptance of Home Rule.

A second letter from Repington to the Prime Minister, received 22 March, did prompt Asquith to write to Churchill. Repington had censured Seely for high-handed and impolitic behaviour. He suggested as an immediate measure, Haldane return temporarily to the War Office to repair the damage a foolish and lazy minister had inflicted upon the army's morale. Asquith thought that there was much to be said for the wisdom of the Lord Chancellor, who was highly regarded by the army.[16] Repington, anticipating a change at the War Office and wishing to cover all possibilities, even the most unlikely, on 20 March had contacted the Colonial Secretary, the epicene Lewis Harcourt. A more improbable candidate for the post of War Minister is hard to imagine. The military correspondent wondered whether fate might make it incumbent upon him 'to take a deeper interest in your doings ... You can always count upon me as Lord Haldane did'. He suggested there was good reason to suppose 'Loulou' was about to take over Seely's responsibilities.[17] But a week later, when Seely left the War Office, the Prime Minister appointed not Harcourt but himself as War Minister.

An amused Asquith told Venetia Stanley, Churchill greeted the news with 'eyes blazing ... polysyllables rolling and the gestures of a man possessed'.[18] Asquith had hoped the hurt sensibilities of the army officer corps would be placated and to some extent his takeover did restore morale among army officers. Anyone taking over the War Office portfolio after Seely would have been seen as an improvement, Repington suggested. But within weeks he was complaining to Dawson the Prime Minister was 'rarely at the WO. He means to do nothing and is merely playing out time'.[19]

Repington demonstrated neither mercy nor compassion for Seely. In all his articles on the Curragh incident Seely's weakness in the face of Churchill's truculence was neither condoned not forgiven. On 27 March he had insisted the Prime Minister should accept Seely's proffered resignation. French and Ewart had sought to resign because Asquith had repudiated the wording of a document they had signed in good faith, believing it had Cabinet approval. They were told they must await a Cabinet meeting, but on 30 March, together with their two fellow members of the Army Council, they insisted on pressing their resignations. These were accepted. Repington's argument, demanding their dismissal was compounded of equal measures of xenophobia, political prejudice and sectarian bigotry. All had to go for fraudulently attempting to persuade the army 'into shooting down Protestants by the light of Mr Redmond's Roman candles'.[20] It was not one of his better, more enlightened or honest commentaries.

Two of Repington's articles about the UVF were published, but a third was permanently withheld by Dawson. The editor delayed the first two for a fortnight because he feared they 'might damage ... the Unionist cause. People would say, "They never meant to give the Government a hearing and their only answer to the Government's concessions is to parade their rebellious forces."' But the time would come when they would be 'extremely effective' and so he intended to 'get them all into type and have them ready'. Repington, however, believed delay would mean a loss of ground. There had been a hardening of Nationalist and Radical opinion due to articles in the Liberal Home Rule press. He judged a riposte was needed urgently. His articles offered a paean to the spirit that informed the Ulster Volunteers. 'Ulster Protestants come of fighting stock ... They *will* fight.'[21] The formidable Theresa, Dowager Marchioness of Londonderry, expressed her approval and invited him when next in Ulster to stay at Mount Stewart, the Londonderrys' fine house. He told her he planned a ten-day visit at Easter but his movements would rather depend upon what Carson and General Richardson wanted him to see. It would be the second week of April before Repington would be able to visit and 'talk of love and lotus with old Lady L.'.[22]

Repington was despatched by Dawson to Ulster on 22 or 23 March to investigate military and naval movements. All his writing about 'an episode without parallel in the history of the army' emphasised the culpability of the government, particularly Churchill and Seely. He found no fault with the army and praised Gough's initial act of insubordination. On 26 March, in his column flanked by colleagues' reports on 'The Plight of the Cabinet', 'Naval Plans' and 'Paget to Serve as Scapegoat', Repington analysed the White Paper that 'purported to represent correspondence relating to recent events in the Irish Command'. He condemned it outright as 'the most unsatisfactory document that can be imagined', instancing 'a series of significant omissions' before taking Churchill, French and Seely to task. Their 'hideous mismanagement' had been the direct consequence of 'arrogating to themselves rights which belonged to the Army Council'. Paget he exonerated. It was 'absurd to suppose that a man of his experience ... would have misunderstood and misrepresented his instructions'. He wrote this knowing full well it was exactly what Paget had done. The previous day, in a private letter to James Craig, Ulster Unionist leader, Repington had conceded Paget 'perhaps' conspired with Churchill, Lloyd George, Birrell, Seely and French to stage a coup d'état against Ulster, but 'accidentally let the cat out of the bag' with his wild speech to his Brigadiers. All the General Staff at the War Office solidly supported Ulster and declared had Paget set out 'he would now be languishing in a Belfast gaol'. The planned coup had been cooked up the previous week at the War Office. It read 'more like fiction concocted in a madhouse than fact, but Winston is capable of anything, Seely is a perfect ass ... French a mere tool. [They made] a pretty *junta* for making war on the peaceable inhabitants of the still United Kingdom!'[23]

Repington was deeply immersed in the paranoid environment surrounding meetings of the Ulster Unionist leadership. It did not make for objectivity. He became increasingly involved in their convoluted politics. In that rumour-filled atmosphere intrigue spawned, multiplied and flourished. He would have been better off spending more time at Mount Stewart with Lawson of the *Telegraph* and 'Taffy' Gwynne of the *Morning Post*. 'No one seems to know much more than we do in London',[24] he casually admitted. He had intended only to amuse, but unwittingly had revealed the truth about much reporting in Ulster: speculation often replaced fact while conjectures that were not immediately and convincingly rebutted became undeniable truths. A supposed plan Repington had at first described to Craig as 'so absurd as to be fictionally improbable', almost immediately transmogrified into a 'plot' for an intended 'coup'. Suborned by a madly bellicose Churchill, the Cabinet subcommittee planned to coerce Ulster's peaceful citizenry by bombarding them in their homes. At once, opposition spokesmen at Westminster confidently accused the government of a deliberate 'plot' to coerce Ulster.

To serve what were undeniably political ends, Repington was even prepared to sacrifice two very senior soldiers; French, the CIGS, and the Adjutant General, Ewart. He condemned them claiming they were associated with or sympathetic to the purposes of a Liberal government. Their political sympathies, he told Craig, made them 'the ready tools of Radical demagogues'. He liked and admired the cerebral Ewart; he knew what he had written about him was absurd yet disparaged him as a 'nice, old fat thing who didn't count anyway' and implied he had been no better than 'a time-server'. Spencer Ewart and French, he insisted, were 'completely disavowed and entirely discredited' for their actions. Warming to his sad task, Repington insisted he had suspected French for sometime as being 'guileless and susceptible to flattery and much too intimate with Winston and LG'. He went on, Churchill was fit only for impeachment, but his wicked scheme, thank God, had been foiled by 'gallant little Gough', but should he step out of line, even momentarily, the powers that be would have his blood. For that reason he had begged him 'to lie as still as a stone ... he has done his part ... I do not believe wild horses will drag the army into Ulster now. The feeling in the army against the Government is intense.'[25]

Dawson had every reason to be exasperated by Repington's blatant bias, the way he positively revelled in being *parti pris*. Editor peremptorily reminded correspondent he had been sent to Ulster to gather military information and in future should restrict himself to comment upon the

UVF. Nathaniel Hone would write on political subjects. Repington responded to this deserved wigging like a petulant child, gracelessly promising 'not to dabble in politics and the rest of the subjects which are woven into the UVF question', then insisting it was *impossible* to disassociate the Volunteers from all else that surrounded them. 'It is useless to write when one can say only a bit of what one thinks and knows.' But needs must and so he would attend 'drills and affairs that come along', and would go from Derry to see 'Carson's show at Limavady'.[26] But almost immediately, he sent Dawson a lengthy communication beginning with the injunction,'Must not appear in print in any form until Saturday morning.' Unequivocally it insisted, in just four days' time 'the whole evidence of the plot against Ulster' would be produced at a full meeting of the Unionist Council. They would probably demand a judicial inquiry. They intended to make 'the devil's own row in the House of Commons'. Feelings were bitter. They viewed the situation most seriously. So much was evident from 'the demeanour of the Volunteers who are working very hard'. Mass meetings were planned to begin 24 April. There might be collisions with the Nationalists, although every effort would be made to prevent them.

Repington judged the time appropriate for an attack in Parliament but remained concerned on two grounds. First, 'it would be *fatal* to abandon the Ulster catholic counties for the sake of compromise'. Second, there was so much talk of 'setting up the Provisional Government as soon as the Home Rule Bill received the Royal Assent ... The argument here is that the British voter will never believe in Ulster's determination until they perceive the Provisional Government in being.' He did not agree. He was convinced the British electorate 'would not understand Ulster's haste. Ulster has only to keep quiet ... Masterly inactivity on the political side and steady progress on the military side'. That to him seemed 'the right policy'.[27] If Home Rule were brought in, the law could not be easily enforced. 'Most assuredly the people here will fight like wildcats. I don't know who is to fight against them.' It was certain the army would not turn on the UVF.

What of the Nationalist Volunteers who were smaller but nevertheless formidable and whose cadres were drilling just as earnestly as the Ulster Volunteers? In Belfast the two forces frequently marched and counter-marched scarcely more than a stone's throw apart. There was a sense of anticipation, of barely restrained violence, as though the two groups were engaged in a ritualised exercise, a formal, stylised preliminary to licensed mayhem. He hoped to be back in London by 19 April after spending time with General Richardson following the Friday Council meeting. He also intended to talk with Brigadier Gleichen. Repington expected trouble to break out at any time but judged Londonderry not Belfast the more likely immediate danger point. It was a miracle peace had been maintained up to the present moment.

The Times reported on 17 April, 'Sir E. Carson's Charge'. Carson had spoken to the faithful declaring his absolute unwillingness to yield the smallest part of the rights of the constitution under which he had been born. No one would ever compel him 'to live under a Home Rule government governed by the Ancient Order of Hibernians'. He admitted, 'The full wickedness of the plot against Ulster's liberties has not yet been entirely unravelled', but they would, most certainly, unravel what was undoubtedly, 'a more wicked, more damnable plot against the liberties of a people than has ever been conceived'. Repington, mindful of Dawson's earlier strictures, confined his report of the Limavady review to a prolonged eulogy on the strengths of the Ulster Volunteers. 'No Compromise No Surrender' was the UVF's motto. Repington pronounced it as though it were a battle honour proudly stitched to a regimental colour, sanctified and laid up in some hallowed cathedral chancel.

In defiance of Dawson, Repington managed to sneak into his report a cut at 'those various party politicians at Westminster with their plans for carving up Ulster'. Their machinations he dismissed as 'futile'. The next day brought the Ulster Council's 'official statement giving the actual facts connected with the contemplated operations in Ulster'. He wrote, the effect of the 'Council's *communiqué* will probably be considerable. Ulster Protestants are firmly convinced they were the intended victims of a plot . . . The proofs now published will all the more firmly convince them they were right.'[28] Despite the masses of information elicited by questions and statements in the House and in two White Papers, a process to which ministers had submitted with varying degrees of candour and enthusiasm, key questions still remained unanswered. He would later accuse ministers – Asquith, Haldane, McKenna, and of course, Seely and Churchill – of 'evasions, contradictions, inaccurate and misleading assertions, humiliating withdrawals and qualifications'.[29] He quoted 'numerous examples of these unsuccessful devices of concealment'. Yet he *knew* it was still not established *beyond all possible doubt* that the government's intention had been to coerce Ulster. Repington seemed unwilling to admit this even to himself. His final column, published after his return to London, was a further paean to the many splendid fighting qualities of the UVF.[30]

Repington chose to closet himself for the better part of a week in his library at Maryon Hall in order to compose what he described as his 'complete analysis' of the Curragh affair. The article, published 27 April, covered two complete pages under the headline 'The Plot that Failed: The Attempt to Coerce Ulster'. To accompany the text a splendid sketch map illustrated 'the Government's plan of campaign and the forces to be employed by land and sea'. The tone of the text was considered and dispassionate. The first four sections set out the facts 'so far as they are known' in detail and chronological order beginning 5 December 1913. The fifth and longest section analysed and commented upon the government's supposed intentions for the period 11 to 22 March 1914. Repington concluded the government had been complicit in 'a calculated scheme for the investment of Ulster by land and sea that would have produced great bloodshed and precipitated civil war'. The major pieces of 'evidence' he cited to support this contention concentrated upon Churchill's words and actions, particularly his menacing orders to the Third Battle Squadron that left Arosa Bay on early 20 March to concentrate off the Isle of Arran at Lamlash. There was also the absurdly belligerent speech made by Churchill at Huddersfield on 14 March when he had pronounced that though bloodshed was lamentable, there were worse things than bloodshed 'even on an extensive scale'. That had been the occasion Winston had strongly hinted anti-Home Rule feeling in Ulster had 'a sinister and revolutionary purpose'. He had urged his audience to go forward together with him, 'and put these grave matters to the proof'.

The final section of Repington's exposé listed the 'Evasions of Ministers'. This demonstrated with chapter and verse how a variety of ministers, not excluding Asquith, had by their endless equivocation sought to hide, deny or confuse the truth that they and not the army had been responsible for the Curragh incident. It was, however, beyond even his powers convincingly to exonerate Paget, the perplexed and disconcerted General Officer Commanding for Ireland. He did convey a distinct impression Paget had been manipulated by Seely and Churchill and as a consequence had neither spoken nor acted wisely. Paget's words and deeds concerning the plan were made 'with the full cognizance of the First Lord of the Admiralty, the then Secretary for War and the Army Council'. That, Repington emphasised, was the essential point. 'The immediate object seems to have been to cow Ulster into submission by a display of force.'[31]

There still exists a degree of confusion and disagreement about the Curragh incident. People are unwilling to believe in 'bungling, amateurish incompetence', the alternative to conspiracy that Lord Blake canvassed in his biography of Andrew Bonar Law. Contemporary justifications for the failure of the government's action suggested everything from 'an untoward incalculable incident the result of a number of accidents' to the briefer 'faulty execution' and 'a blunder that revealed slack Cabinet methods'.[32] Plans were made badly and belatedly, the faults exaggerated by inept execution. But undeniably, as a consequence of the events at the Curragh, Repington was quick to realise, any threat by the government to impose Home Rule that employed military force was a dead duck. Asquith admitted to Venetia, 'if we were to order a march upon Ulster ... about half the officers in the army ... would strike'.[33] Six weeks later, Asquith stated unequivocally to the Cabinet, 'The army could not be used in or against Ulster'.[34]

As much had surely been apparent after the events of the night of 24/25 April when a full mobilisation of the Belfast UVF covered the successful landing at Larne from the *Mountjoy* of some 35,000 rifles, which were distributed throughout County Antrim. Repington, Dawson and Northcliffe did not blanch at this successful coup but rejoiced that the government's Irish policy was wrecked. 'No self-respecting Government could afford to be treated with such contumely.'[35] Repington had been in Northamptonshire when he received a telegram from General Richardson, the UVF commander, stating 'Night operations most successful: All through, no casualties.' In his memoirs Repington described the gun-running as 'a great moment, admirably organised and directed'.[36]

As late spring became high summer the talking continued. Schemes were designed to exclude Ulster temporarily or permanently, but nothing was resolved. As a response to Carson's private army in the north, the Nationalists had recruited their volunteers. Belfast boasted its own unit. In May 1,500 armed men paraded from the Falls to Hannahstown. They trained weekly with much ostentatious determination at Shaun's, now McRory Park, on the western edge of the city. Here too, the west Belfast unit of some sixty men were drilled thrice weekly by John Magee, formerly a colour sergeant in the Royal Irish Fusiliers.[37] Despite their demonstrable professionalism, *The Times* chose to pay the Irish Volunteers little or no attention. It had eyes only for the UVF.

Ominous news from Europe increasingly caught the attention of responsible men of affairs, but in *The Times* Irish news continued to take pride of place. Repington, as part of the vast caravanserai Northcliffe insisted was required to report adequately on events in Ireland, wanted to do something if he could for Paget, but was not sure whether a court of inquiry or resignation followed by a statement would best serve to clear his friend's name. Paget's position was difficult. But what most concerned Repington was not his friend's but the country's likely fate with Asquith in notional charge of the War Office intent on playing for time. He believed 'the whole question of defence in its widest aspect will have to be made the subject of searching inquiries'.[38] This was mid June 1914. Although no one seemed aware of it, time was fast running out. Repington's words scarcely suggest the apprehension one might have expected in an informed military critic when war with Germany was just six weeks away. The companies of armed men purposefully drilling in Ireland crowded out cognisance of the far greater threat in continental Europe as rank upon rank of conscripted troops readied for war. The nightmare the War Office contemplated was the British army deploying to support the civil power in Ireland. The possibility of imminent civil war gripped the minds and imaginations of men of affairs as firmly as ever. London, like Belfast, was replete that summer with rumours that Carson would declare a provisional government. The all-party conference summoned to Buckingham Palace, a last ditch, desperate initiative to mend what was beyond mending, broke down on 24 July. Even the murder of Franz Ferdinand and his wife at Sarajevo on 28 June had failed to push Irish affairs from the centre of the political stage. The Austro-Serbian declaration of war on 25 July at last alerted men to the imminence of a war that would not be limited to the Balkans but would embrace all the Great Powers. Now the question was, if Britain must play a part in this threatened European conflagration, were her army and navy sufficiently well prepared?

12   Are the army and navy prepared for war?

Repington declared his displeasure with the performance of the political heads of the War Office and Admiralty even though he knew a high price would have to be paid for causing offence to old friends. Nevertheless, as he acknowledged, the public excoriation of those who deserved to be reprimanded was a necessary part of his 'duty as a public watchdog on all things relating to peace'. Despite his supposed anonymity, everyone knew the identity of 'Our Military Correspondent'. Recently, the journal of the French General Staff had described him as the British public's 'veritable educateur militaire'. Undoubtedly, he was flattered to know his opinions were 'quoted and discussed in the world's press'.[1] His more uninhibited opinions, particularly those concerned with weaknesses he perceived at the Admiralty, he expressed in letters to *The Times* supposedly written by a Colonel von Donner und Blitzen, Repington's fictitious creation. The German right-wing nationalist press was furious. With characteristic humourlessness they vainly searched the *Rangsliste* for the colonel's name. They no more understood the joke than Fisher. When he read the colonel's uncompromisingly critical commentary on the disastrous 1912 and 1913 naval manoeuvres he was so anxious Balfour might find it persuasive he dismissed 'all manoeuvres [as] d—d rot. When you are not being fired at you behave quite differently from when you are!'[2]

   The poor staff work and hopeless strategic and tactical ideas of Admirals Fisher and Wilson frequently attracted Repington's censures. He was dismissive of 'Old Admirals who looked not much further than Duncan's tactics at Camperdown for their models'.[3] Fisher invariably dismissed such criticism as 'false physic administered by an unqualified quack', and urged his press acolytes to discharge a fusillade of derisive libels at the military correspondent. Repington paid no heed. Since Churchill had become First Lord, he acknowledged some changes for the better had been made at the Admiralty. Nevertheless, the navy remained what it had always been, 'the most glorious Service in the world that knows everything about fighting but nothing about war'.[4]

Churchill's proposed plans for the North Sea accentuated Repington's concerns about the Mediterranean. It remained 'the Achilles heel of the military position'. The need to diminish the Mediterranean fleet in order to increase that of the North Sea revealed the vulnerability as well as the interdependence of military and naval planning. Limits on naval building favoured Germany in the Mediterranean because no similar restraint was placed upon the navies of Germany's allies. The correspondent argued the reason naval superiority was required at all times in the North Sea was because England was 'unarmed at home. If we had a national army we could risk sending a larger detachment of ships from the North Sea, but . . . the knowledge of our military weakness at home will keep all our ships here in war time.' He warned, eventually the country would have to 'pay a frightful price for regarding the navy as a *bonne à tout faire*'.[5] Economic, naval and military strategy alike rested upon a dominant navy. The security of the world's sea lanes was a necessary condition for the government to suppose a policy of 'business as usual' might be followed in wartime.

Repington had been ahead of 'the old Admirals' on the subject of submarines and aircraft, certain that these were the weapons of the future, destined to change naval warfare entirely. The mine, improved torpedo, submarine, destroyer, airship, wireless telegraphy, long-range coastal ordnance, all would revolutionise the conditions of operations off an enemy's coast. When first he wrote of these matters, he had been savaged by so-called 'naval experts'. They derided his ideas and thought it a joke in the worst possible taste that *a soldier* should have the effrontery to suppose he had anything worthwhile to say on the subject of naval warfare. In 1914, when everything he had forecast proved to be true, he claimed not one of his critics had sufficient grace to apologise.[6] He believed the navy's most grievous failing was its lack of 'a War Staff and a serious thinking department'. This largely accounted for the disappointing wartime performance. When finally they began to address the problem it was too late to repair the neglect of the previous decade. Although an enthusiastic supporter of Churchill, Repington continued to criticise the First Lord whenever he thought it deserved. He had roundly censured Churchill's orders during the Ulster crisis as unduly belligerent and precipitate, but applauded the First Lord for despatching the Fleet to war stations and anticipating the outbreak of hostilities. Churchill likened dealing with Repington to a 'dog, fawning and licking your hand then suddenly giving you a most ferocious bite'.[7]

Repington had warned the Admiralty its preparations for war were inadequate, but had been ignored. The catalogue of disasters suffered in the first weeks of war underlined the validity of his claim. Three aged cruisers, *Cressy*, *Hogue* and *Aboukir*, the unwitting victims of one enterprising U-boat commander, were sunk with the loss of more than two-thirds of their companies. The principal war anchorages at Scapa, Rosyth and Invergordon were 'discovered' to be unsafe for they lacked anti-submarine defences. German mines rapidly accounted for a dreadnought battleship *Audacious*, a light cruiser *Amphion*, a gunboat, a submarine, seventeen fishing and thirteen merchant vessels.[8] Repington's prescience as a naval critic had been impressive. As early as 1903 he had stressed the importance of air superiority and pointed out the advantages of Scapa Flow as a safer anchorage for the fleet.

Fisher would never acknowledge that he and Repington might see eye to eye about anything concerning the navy. In a letter pouring opprobrium on the journalist's head, he advised Balfour, 'Submarines are the coming dreadnoughts and aviation will surely supplant cruisers' and insisted Balfour alone had the brains to grasp this future reality.[9] But three years earlier in two *Blackwood's* articles, Repington had made the identical claim.[10] In championing oil to replace coal to fuel the fleet, Fisher sought the help of Fleet Street acolytes such as Arnold White. It never occurred to him to recruit Repington, whom he thought of as an implacable and dangerous foe, 'a d—d War Office pimp . . . [who] writes a lot of d—d nonsense in private letters to Cabinet Ministers'.[11] But Repington gave his wholehearted support to the 1912 battleship programme that effected several revolutionary changes to the Fleet; most importantly, the adoption of a first division of 'Queen Elizabeth' class battleships. They outclassed the Germans in firepower with their 15-inch guns and had to be oil- rather than coal-fired to give them the required increased speed and greater radius of action for the weight of fuel carried. Not that Repington appreciated all the advantages these new battleships provided. He remained obsessed with numbers. Since Churchill had taken charge of the Admiralty, changes of material and personnel were 'satisfactory' but, he emphasised, the measure of the naval standard should not be the German fleet alone 'but the fleets of the Triple Alliance'.[12] He had no conception there were limits to the shipyards' capacity to armour an ever-increasing number of new ships built to ever higher specifications. He always suspected it was for political reasons they were asked to settle for two-thirds rather than the whole loaf.

Repington's desire to see more and better warships built for the navy was sincere. He also acknowledged the army would have to pay the price. 'We must do the best we can with what we have on land,' he told Esher, 'but we must have the deuce of a powerful navy.' This gave particular point to the as yet unresolved question whether the navy was capable of discharging all its tasks satisfactorily. 'I have recently been to Spithead', he wrote to Esher a year after the Agadir crisis. He was only 'fairly pleased' with the state of the Fleet's readiness and confessed, 'I should like our navy to have a trial gallop with Italy or some second rate naval power before they take on the North Sea crowd.'

Repington was not the creature of the War Office Fisher would have had everyone suppose. Six weeks before the outbreak of war he utterly condemned that department in a letter to his editor, but carefully stressed the incapacities of a 'moribund government' before those of the military members of the Army Council.[13] 'The trail of politics has been all over their recent decisions.' No significant change might be expected until the Tories came in. Asquith, both as Prime Minister and Secretary of State, 'meant to do nothing and was merely playing out time'.[14] This pessimistic assessment of the War Office dated back to when Seely replaced Haldane as Secretary of State. At the time Repington had complained to Esher, the new minister was 'incapable of administering even a small department, let alone a great one'. Seely was 'a lazy dog'. His expectations were very soon confirmed.[15]

Repington, always reluctant to criticise the military members in public, complained frequently to Esher. He regretted Nicholson's departure as CIGS as much as he did Archie Murray's. He believed their level-headed thinking would not readily be replaced. Not everyone would have agreed. French told his directors the army needed to get ready for war and Wilson estimated the whole time Nicholson had been CIGS 'he had done not a single thing to prepare the army for war'.[16] That was a typical Wilsonian exaggeration. The cultivated and intelligent Murray was not the 'complete non-entity'[17] Edmonds claimed, but the wound he had received in South Africa hopelessly compromised his fitness for campaigning. Nevertheless, it is probably fair to say that from 1906 to 1912 there had been a steady improvement in the practical work undertaken by the General Staff. However, Repington's greatest hope – an improvement in higher direction – was to be sadly disappointed, or as he would have said, 'betrayed'.

In the crucial final years before the outbreak of war, the General Staff was ill-led and served. After March 1914, when Seely and French were replaced by Asquith and Sir Charles Douglas, matters worsened disastrously. In the final crisis of late July and early August 1914, Asquith, as prime minister, had other, more immediately important, party-political issues on his mind than to give much thought to the General Staff. The new CIGS enjoyed such poor standing he was not even summoned to the initial meetings of the Committee of Imperial Defence.

If the General Staff were as weak in council as Repington claimed, how might they perform in war? The possibility of British involvement in a European war occupied many minds. The biggest peacetime exercise the British army ever held, the autumn 1912 manoeuvres, was designed to test its readiness for such an eventuality. It would afford Haig an opportunity to demonstrate his mettle. He had only recently returned from India to become General Officer Commanding Aldershot. Much was expected of him. French directed the exercise. Haig commanded the Red Force – two infantry divisions, a division of cavalry plus a Royal Flying Corps detachment (an airship and seven aeroplanes). They represented a hostile invading army that had landed in Norfolk and sought to advance upon London. Their opponents, Blue Force, were commanded by Lieutenant General Sir James Grierson, with one less cavalry brigade than Haig but otherwise equally matched. Haig, cautious and reluctant to make any offensive moves, was generally considered to have lost. French noted Haig had missed opportunities to defeat the Blue Force in detail.[18] Repington thought Haig had been completely outmanoeuvred, but the critical comment in his report was deliberately restrained. A private exchange with Ian Hamilton, however, allowed for more unguarded comment.[19] Sir Ian admitted, life was made difficult for critics, no matter how well-meaning or benign their intent, because 'British soldiers [were] utterly intolerant of criticism'. Hamilton was convinced the exercise would have served its purpose better had it not been prematurely stopped. 'RED [Haig] should have been told that whilst the issue of the actual battle was still uncertain, he had been so severely handled any advance on London would be inconceivable. Exactly a quarter of an hour should have been given him to get out his orders before "Commence Fire". Here would have been some real test of real leadership.' But the pivotal fault was not the incapacity of any force commander but of the chief umpires. 'They should have wider powers and should be the best men.'[20]

Haig's failure undoubtedly would be excused, but his performance at the concluding conference was disastrous. Before the assembled company of monarch, brass hats, civic and university dignitaries he abandoned his prepared script and extemporised. His rambling, ad-lib explanation was an unmitigated disaster, 'unintelligible and unbearably dull ... He alone seemed totally unconscious of his failure'.[21] Haig's inadequacies were made the more obvious by the consummate brilliance of Jimmy Grierson's account. In his concluding report for *The Times*, Repington noted but skated over Haig's abysmal performance.[22] His real reservations he stored away for another day.

The following year's manoeuvres, held during the third week in September, were intended to simulate the kind of combat in which the British Expeditionary Force might initially expect to be engaged. It would test the working of GHQ and Corps Headquarters during an encounter battle preceding an attack upon an entrenched position by two corps and a cavalry division under Allenby's command. Haig was one commander, the other was Paget. French directed the exercise and commanded the Brown Force with Grierson as his Chief of Staff. They were opposed by a skeleton formation, White Force, composed of Territorial and Yeomanry units commanded by Major General C. C. Monro. Subsequently there was much discussion and ill-tempered debate about which of the commanders had behaved least effectively. There was some disagreement about Haig's performance. Henry Wilson, now very close to French, accused Haig of disastrously disposing his troops with a three-mile gap in the centre. Haig blamed French's initial instructions. Grierson objected they were 'impractical'. He would pay a high price for his presumption; French replaced him as CGS with Murray. Henry Wilson thought French would have wanted him to have the post, but as a brigadier his rank was insufficiently senior.[23]

Repington's detailed analysis of the exercise was published in four articles appearing between 30 September and 16 October. Intended to be constructive as well as critical, most of his criticism concentrated on the performance of General Headquarters. This reflected not only his own observation and conclusions but also evidence and opinions provided in letters he had received from Haig, Forestier-Walker, Robertson, and the commanders of the 2nd and 3rd divisions, Lawson and Rawlinson. Before publishing his account, Repington showed a copy to his erstwhile friend French, who was not pleased. To Esher he later described Repington as being 'childish, *stupid* and inclined to be rancorous'.[24]

For Dawson, together with the corrected galleys of the third and most sharply critical article, Repington enclosed a letter he had received from French. 'You will see,' he warned, 'the Field Marshal is exceedingly angry with me and alleges all my facts are erroneous though he gives no reason to make me change my views.' Repington insisted that he was not disposed to withdraw anything he had said, 'even if the cost were to be the loss of a valued and old friendship'.[25] His words were published exactly as he had written them, but prefaced by the additional, damning observation that 'If the work of the General Headquarters ... were to be taken as a fair example of our General Staff practices we should have to sing very small'.[26] His criticisms were, in the circumstances, as mild as honesty would permit. He did not entirely exonerate the divisional commanders but the greatest burden of his criticism was directed at French. Repington knew many experienced military observers had been more critical than he. Robertson, for example, concluded that the duties of command were not properly or sufficiently understood. This perceived lack of command experience was addressed during the January 1914 Staff Officers' Conference. Brigadier John Gough presented a paper that asked and sought to answer the question whether more could be done to make officers competent commanders in war.[27]

Despite considerable reservations Repington felt about the readiness and fitness of the British army for war, particularly the want of sufficient recruits and properly trained staff officers, he felt constrained not to reveal the full measure of his concern to the public. German military ambitions needed to be thwarted but the time was not opportune for 'Ireland blocked the way'.[28] He therefore reserved the expression of his darkest thoughts to a colleague. 'I am not happy about the army just now.' He described the performance of GHQ at the recent manoeuvres as 'perfectly useless ... Our higher staff want a deuce of a lot more training'. They knew well enough all was not as it should be but had grown 'so despotic at the top they cry out if they receive anything but adulation and try to make out they are perfect. There is no progress to be achieved by such means.' The Army Council showed no sign of life. 'Nothing is done and things go from bad to worse.' He paused in his jeremiad. 'Thank God, we still have the finest corps of officers in the world. Maybe fate will throw up a leader one of these days.'[29] But even that optimistic claim was soon put seriously in doubt by events at the Curragh.

What happened in Ireland not only cast a disturbing and disconcerting pall over political life in Britain that boded ill for future civil–military relations, it also left a legacy of enduring ill-feeling and distrust within the officer corps. Deeply involved as he was with immediate events in Ulster, Repington at no point entirely cast aside his larger concern, which was the British army remained unfit to fulfil the European demands he was certain would soon be made upon it. Such a concern was neither unique, nor was his estimate unduly pessimistic. He complained how the Regulars had a deficit of 10,000, 'expected by the actuaries to amount to 18,000 by the end of 1914'.[30] A general air of pessimism clung about those who for more than a decade had struggled to improve British military readiness, so Repington was in no way unique in his concern. Paradoxically, even after the assassinations at Sarajevo on 28 June 1914, there was no real sense of urgency, no general awareness that little time was left before Europe would be plunged irrevocably into the maelstrom of war.

The German newspapers were filled with alarming news from Vienna, Budapest, Belgrade and Sarajevo, of rumours that the Serbs had been complicit in the assassination of Archduke Franz Ferdinand and his wife. The British press banished these stories hastily to the comparative anonymity of their inside pages. Of much more immediate interest to middle-class British newspaper readers than any Balkan imbroglio was the quarter of a million men under arms in Ireland and the implacable revolutionary ferment infecting the labouring classes that threatened the total disruption of British industry. If professional diplomats thought there were 'no very urgent and pressing questions to preoccupy us in Europe',[31] Repington could scarcely be considered purblind for engaging in a somewhat desultory exchange with Esher as late as the third week in July when they debated the need for more recruits and how they might be secured.

Among other issues, Repington touched upon the moral irresponsibility of the Defence Committee in its attitude towards recruitment, the inadequacies of the Adjutant General's department over the previous five years, and the hopelessness of a prime minister who, having taken charge of the War Office, seemed content to put aside all difficult questions until the Irish problem was solved. Esher wondered, except in times when trade was bad, would it ever be possible to obtain the old numbers of recruits? How were they to secure a supply of young officers? 'These questions are vital.'[32] Repington's response very properly elicited a stinging rebuff from Esher, who dismissed it as an 'attempt to hood wink the public ... It is no use to suggest half measures. If you mean to fight the Germans overseas then you must have a conscript army.' That was the core of the matter. Repington was all too well aware of this but showed a marked reluctance to admit what in his heart of hearts he knew was incontrovertible. The BEF, for all its many fine qualities, was fit only for a very limited confrontation with the mighty German armies; and then only as *an appendix*, no more, to the French armies, to hold *part* of the line for a *limited* time. In a word, the BEF was suited only for a *short* war, a war in which they might only *hope* to play a significant role. Still tinkering with what were peripheral issues, Repington suggested a pay rise might fill the ranks. Esher almost snorted his derision. 'No increase of the rates of pay within reason will get you the recruits you require. There are many reasons for this – social and economical – which you understand all about.' As for officers, Repington could 'add any number of West Points' but there would always be difficulties. He was deluding himself to suppose all would be resolved 'by substituting General Log for Field Marshal Stork ... for the causes of our difficulty lie deeper than the personnel of administration'.[33]

Repington had deserved the rebuff; he knew he ought to speak out, but it was a moral and practical imperative to which he found it impossible to respond. In the late summer of 1914 men interested in military matters seemed to think there was still plenty of time for debate and to beat about the bush. The Cabinet might well have supposed Esher's warning to them six months earlier was in reality an affirmation of the Liberal concept a British army was fit for purpose so long as it could fulfil garrison duties in the far-flung outposts of Empire, serve as imperial fire-fighters and always be ready as the navy's auxiliary. Nothing was said about a continental war where huge conscripted land forces would be engaged one with another.

It was the last week in July. A conversation with Ian Hamilton, recently returned from a tour of Australasia as Inspector General of Overseas Forces, left Repington in a happier frame of mind. He was 'glad' to be reassured the armed forces and government alike were aware of the current dangerous state of international affairs. 'It is so novel to learn that we are awake.' Shortly afterwards he was bearded by a friend from his days as military attaché to Holland and Belgium, Colonel von Leipzig of the German Gardes du Corps. In 1908 and again 1911, at moments of international crisis and tension, the colonel and his countess had appeared in London anxious to renew acquaintance with their old friend. Now they told Repington the kaiser was entirely opposed to the war about to break out between Austria-Hungary and Serbia. Germany denied any knowledge of the stiff ultimatum Austria had sent to Serbia on 23 July. Von Leipzig blamed Johann Graf von Forgách, an Austrian foreign ministry official. 'The style and tone' of the draft, Repington agreed, were certainly Forgách's.

How Repington loved to engage in such exchanges; explore the delicious diplomatic tittle-tattle that turned upon some foreign office or chancery minion's weakness or indiscretion. What he liked best was the feeling he was privy to information of which others were unaware. His failing was that invariably he would attach too much importance to the contribution made by someone he happened to know. On this occasion that person was Forgách whom he described as 'charming but vain and vindictive'. All too readily Repington visualised how he had 'seen his chance to score off Servia and ha[d] taken it'. Von Leipzig had 'expiated at length on the sin of England siding with the Slavs against the Teutons' and was 'very sarcastic' about the quality and value of France and particularly Russia as an ally. Germany had no need to fear them now or ten years hence, while 'their reservists will run away into the woods when called out ... the whole country is rotten'. All this Repington conveyed in his letter to Ian Hamilton suggesting he might like to pass it on to Churchill.[34] That same day Austria broke off diplomatic relations with Serbia. Repington on 27 July, writing in *The Times* assumed the Austrians were fully committed to fight Serbia whose one hope was 'to keep the field sufficiently long so as to enable Russia and possibly Rumania to intervene with effect'. He had been told by another long-standing friend, General Yermoloff, the Russian military attaché in London, that he expected the Austrians in Belgrade that day. What would follow, he thought, would very much 'depend on the phrasing of the Russian ultimatum'. Contrary to the tone of his article in *The*

Times, Repington told Yermoloff, he thought there was a faint hope that diplomacy might yet settle the quarrel.

There had been a distinct change in tone and content in Repington's writing for *The Times* during July 1914. He discussed failures in recruiting and divisional training at Aldershot in articles that appeared on 13 and 22 July. Then his article published 27 July outlined Austria's military plans in the Balkans. Increasingly his mind was exercised by thoughts of what he perceived would be the necessary military consequence of Austrian intransigence. From this would flow a great and terrible conflagration, he warned his readers, that must embrace nations large and small: 'a terrible automatic war ... as with a line of tin soldiers, if one is knocked over the rest fall down in turn ... We shall all support our friends and in a very short time it will be a miracle if all Europe is not aflame.' Was there a momentary nostalgic regret for the traditional independence of action Britain had forfeited when she became part of the entente system? Did he recall how, in January 1906, he had insisted to Esher that Britain should employ troops alongside the French if circumstances so dictated. Nevertheless, most men were opposed to participation in a land struggle on the Continent if it could be avoided.[35] The reason why the possibility of an alternative strategy had been forfeited was because the British had refused to become Haldane's nation-in-arms. 'As a consequence we are now dragged into quarrels which appear to be no direct concern of ours, in order to maintain our own security which depends on the maintenance of the balance of power.'[36] This was to repeat what he had pointed out in *The Times* in 1913. Politicians, like the public, had either failed or refused to acknowledge military reality. Instead they had chosen to procrastinate, never finally to determine if the primary purpose of the British army was to serve the defensive needs of the Empire or exclusively to engage in a European war. If it was to be the latter, then that necessarily implied combat against mass armies and the need to 'become an armed nation like the rest'. The basis of Britain's military power required broadening. This could be achieved 'only by the training in arms of a large number of the population'.[37]

On 29 July *The Times* in its first leader called for a closing of the ranks, a recommendation prompted by editorial concern about Ireland's stubbornly unresolved troubles. Only two days earlier, a leading article had spoken of 'confronting one of the greatest crises in the history of the British race'. That had followed the previous day's killing of three and the wounding of almost forty citizens by a detachment of British infantry at Bachelor's Walk, on the north Dublin quays.[38] But the suddenly worsening Balkan scene forced Dawson to realise political priorities had changed. Reluctantly he accepted, at such a dangerous moment, the nation could not afford 'to turn aside and engage in a General Election'.[39]

Ten days earlier, on 21 July, *The Times* in a leader, 'A Danger to Europe', had cautiously hinted at possible British involvement as a consequence of Austro-Hungarian action. Now it baldly asserted that England was 'bound by moral obligations' to stand by France and Russia. Not to do so would 'leave Britain alone to face a predominant Germany'. Up to this point Dawson had been holding in check what he described as 'volumes of incoherent Europeanism' promoted by Wickham Steed, aided and abetted by George Saunders.[40] Northcliffe had not been involved, utterly absorbed as he was in Ulster's problems. He had never grasped the full implications of the alliance and entente systems. He was frankly puzzled when *The Times* implied that an Austro-Serbian conflict could have serious implications for England's safety. What he did acknowledge was that Germany was not a power to be taken for granted. If they thought it to their advantage, Germany would unhesitatingly descend upon Britain's eastern seaboard. Now, as they had not even threatened to mobilise, Northcliffe believed a warning by Britain would be appropriate, perhaps a naval demonstration in the North Sea? He certainly would not countenance the despatch of British troops abroad.

The newspaper tycoon's instinctive circumspection prompted him to be mildly critical of Repington's article, 'Russian Mobilization and British Delay', 31 July 1914, the first of what was to become a series, 'The War Day by Day'. Northcliffe thought the admonitory opening paragraph 'a mistake. Coming from a soldier it is likely to be seized upon by the anti-war party only too prone to suggest military men are urging us to war.'[41] Repington had suggested a rapid assault through Belgium by the Germans could very well make them the masters of the North Sea. He wondered why that prospect did not strike consternation into more British minds and hearts.

The second article in the series, 'England's Duty', set out what Repington supposed were the appropriate actions to be taken by the government, press, private citizens and the army should 'efforts to prevent the outbreak of a devastating war' fail. The government should take 'common-sense measures commensurate with the great dangers which we may be about to incur'. They had already been given a full warning. Nothing would condone failure to issue the order to mobilise in time. To count such a measure 'provocative' could only be described as 'grotesque'. He focussed upon the absolute necessity for 'timely mobilisation and concentration of our land and sea forces'.[42] This was reflected not only in his writing for *The Times* but in his conversations. He praised the

Admiralty for taking advantage of naval exercises to move the Fleet from Portland, on 29 July, to a secret rendezvous and safe haven at Scapa Flow. However, the order for the mobilisation of the army was not given by Haldane to the Army Council until the morning of 3 August. This meant they were two days behind the French even though simultaneous action by both forces had been planned. Repington censured the delay. 'The French General Staff have counted during the last seven or eight years upon the support of our Expeditionary Force . . . If we fail to turn up on time to the place assigned to us, and as a consequence France is beaten, history will assign our cowardice as the cause.'[43]

As a 'simple, common-sense measure', Repington proposed the framing of 'a Press law that would absolutely prohibit under severe penalties any allusion to any British naval or military movement whatsoever . . . Not all the Press can be trusted'.[44] It is difficult to decide whether Repington's better sense had temporarily succumbed to an excess of patriotic zeal, or if he had forgotten he was a journalist and reverted to the traditional general prejudice and distrust most soldiers instinctively felt for journalists. From personal experience he knew of the frictions and difficulties that frequently arose between newspapers and the various departments of government. Early in the war a regulatory governmental agency, the Press Bureau, was set up to guide newspaper coverage of the war. Despite liberal and lenient intentions, it attracted many complaints. *The Times* felt 'oppressed by vigorous censorship and struggled with officials whose incompetence exceeded their common sense'.[45] Wartime censorship is a complex exercise and does not readily lend itself to regulation by simple, commonsensical laws. Within weeks of the outbreak of war Repington would complain of being 'muzzled' and express regret that the press was no longer free.[46] The last thing the country needed was a 'kept' press that on the spurious grounds of national security would suppress justified criticism or news of failures or defeats. Far from promoting national elan and inspiring confidence this would swiftly create suspicion in the public mind.

Altogether more far-sighted was his prophecy that at the outbreak of war 'thousands of volunteers' would flock to the Colours. What they needed was 'a steady and systematised supply of recruits for the Territorial Force'. Repington exhorted people to 'exercise calmness, patience and self-restraint'. Many men would be lost, and as well, ships and material resources of all kinds. If the public were selfish and showed a lack of balance, 'acts of indiscipline and panic would render it impossible for any Government to persevere'.[47] He assumed Britain would soon be at war with Germany, but it was not for him to determine the timetable. Throughout the Bank Holiday weekend the debate raged in Parliament and the press.

On 3 August he outlined Germany's strategic problem, having to wage war on two fronts. But a short prefatory paragraph insisting as 'indispensable' the 'nomination of a Secretary of State for War' drew much more attention. He insisted this 'onerous and important task' required 'not a politician but a soldier'. Kitchener 'would meet with warm public approval'.[48] He was well aware this suggestion dropped a rock rather than a pebble into the stream of opinion.

Repington had little to say in *The Times* for 4 August. His 'Summary of Reports' noted Belgium's 'worthy response' to the German ultimatum. 'King Albert's appeal to England ... would not fall on deaf ears.' The Dutch were paying more attention to their sea than their land frontier. This suggested to him they were more concerned that the Allies, rather than the Germans, might infringe their neutrality. An editorial insisted, 'It is no less our duty than our interest to protect Belgium.'[49] The next day Repington emphasised, 'It [would] take Germany nine more days to place upon the French frontier forces adequate to challenge the French masses. It will take the French about the same time to assemble.' He forecast, the first decisive battles of the war would take place between 16 and 22 August. 'Friends who are late at this rendezvous will be late for the fair.'[50]

A fortnight later, from Hythe where he had gone to take a short break, he wrote to Jack Sandars. In a week less than in 1870, the Germans had assembled four times as many troops. He warned, whatever might be claimed to the contrary, no one could foretell what would be the result of the impending shock in Belgium and on the Meuse. They were entering 'the region of the unknown. All hitherto ... has been according to programmes prepared laboriously in the long years of peace.'[51]

Part II

The war years, 1914–1918

13   The 1915 shells scandal

The outbreak of war for Repington meant not only the unremitting toil of compiling a daily column for *The Times*, but also dutifully inspecting new hospitals, monitoring the progress of troops in training and spending much time 'seeing important people'.[1] He claimed to have been the first journalist to propose Kitchener as War Minister, something later contradicted by Dawson who supposed it to have been no more than 'a sudden impulse'.[2] Kitchener's concern was that Repington had been prompted by party political considerations, but the correspondent insisted his initiative had been made 'in the public interest without prompting from anybody'.[3] Kitchener accepted the explanation but remained puzzled because he did not perceive the overwhelming political advantage his appointment afforded the Liberal administration. His presence in the Cabinet provided the necessary non-party element at a time when national unity was of paramount importance.

Northcliffe had lobbied for Kitchener's appointment, not because he wanted him in the government but rather, he wanted Haldane out. That was why he insisted *The Times* portray the Lord Chancellor as Germany's unwitting dupe who, if he should remain a member of the administration, would fatally injure the country's interests. *The Times* had reason to feel ashamed for promoting such a monstrous falsehood and acting as Northcliffe bid. That Repington did not dissociate himself from what he knew to be an unfounded attack was inexcusable. More than a year elapsed before he sought to make even partial amends to his friend. He feebly excused his disloyalty by claiming, to attempt to stop anti-Haldane talk was as hopeless as 'trying to dam Niagara with a toothbrush'. In July 1916, when Haldane was 'still being abominably treated', Repington at last publicly condemned the attacks as 'mean, cruel, and stupid'. No one had done more for the army than Haldane. Yet, 'like rooks, when one appears ill, the rest peck him to death'.[4]

At the war's outbreak Repington insisted he and Kitchener were 'on the best of terms'; good enough to persuade a phenomenally busy minister who distrusted journalists to talk to him freely about his war plans. In Repington's published *War Diaries* there are no daily entries before 29 September 1915 and the events of the war's first crowded year are summarised in a single chapter. This abridgement might explain, but does not excuse, his failure to comment upon Kitchener's plans, which differed so markedly from the previously accepted orthodoxy. As a rule, Kitchener never rushed important decisions. Therefore, we may deduce only after considerable thought had he predicted the war would last at least three years. Kitchener insisted, if Britain intended to play the part of a great imperial power, the existing military arrangements were woefully inadequate. To match other European armies, Britain should immediately recruit and train new troops. They would be late in the field but eventually would be sufficiently strong to deliver the *coup de grâce* to an exhausted enemy. Full British military involvement naturally would mean making peace on British terms. His plans were so radically different from anything pre-dating them, they amounted to a manifesto for a political as well as military revolution.

Previously it had been assumed the nation's major contribution in war would be naval, not military. In return for Treasury generosity the navy was expected to secure Britain from invasion, ensure the free passage of goods across the world's oceans, and to establish and enforce a blockade designed to dislocate, then throttle the enemy's economy, thus ensuring a swift end to hostilities. The navy's overwhelming strength was the keystone in the arch of traditional Liberal economic thinking. In war, as in peace, business would continue as usual. But to recruit and equip the new armies Kitchener proposed the nation's workforce would have to be displaced and redeployed. Repington immediately appreciated the revolutionary implications of this proposal but judged it wiser to say nothing. What he did acknowledge was that 'Kitchener alone possessed the immense prestige to ask the country for millions of volunteers.'[5] For years, Repington had unavailingly argued the British army was 'hopelessly inadequate to engage with the Germans in Europe'. If they did so, the 'inevitable fate of the BEF and the whole regular army would be annihilation'. His courage, however, had always failed him and at proof stage he would remove this shocking conclusion, excusing himself with the assertion, 'Such truths [were] suitable only for private conversations.'[6]

In August 1914 Repington's colleagues at PHS were shocked when he reported Kitchener's assertion of a prolonged war. One piece of evidence suggests Repington as early as 1907 had seriously considered such a possibility[7] but had said nothing at Printing House Square. Sir George Clarke now assured Dawson, Repington was hopelessly mistaken.[8] He insisted the war *might* last perhaps nine months but 'almost certainly' it would be less because 'the People would not stand the three years hinted at'.[9]

After Repington's report was published Kitchener refused to talk to him other than through intermediaries. In the face of his 'old Chief's' displeasure, Repington 'drifted away from him'. He grew increasingly angry that Kitchener should refuse to see him and turned instead to his contacts in France, claiming they told him 'everything'. He learned of the German armies' dispositions, in part from Colonel Dupont, a member of Joffre's staff, but his greatest debt was owed to General Macdonogh, head of Intelligence. It was he who provided Repington with his 'best journalistic coup at this time',[10] the exact location where the German army corps intended to concentrate. This graphically demonstrated their intention was to envelop the French army's left wing. Repington immediately urged a defensive strategy so the Germans might break their heads upon the Allies' prepared positions. But the French, as he had feared, were obsessed with notions of the offensive and ignoring the threat in the north they pursued previously prepared plans of attack further south. He claimed, had the French staff studied his map and drawn the *right* conclusions, then 'the great misfortunes of the opening of the war would have been avoided'. He was further 'persuaded had the French held their left defensively from Namur through Brussels to Antwerp . . . in cooperation with the British and Belgian armies, they would never have lost western Belgium, nine departments of France and the great harbour on the Scheldt'. The trouble was, Repington's scheme envisaged effective co-ordination and full co-operation between the Allies and there was none. So the French went ahead with their disastrous offensive while the BEF, expecting to fight the Germans in conjunction with the French Fifth Army, concentrated at Maubeuge.

Repington did not pay his first visit to the battlefields until November. His initial reaction was to claim it was too much for anyone to comprehend readily. 'It transcends all limits of thought, imagination and reason. We see . . . no more than a fraction of it . . . suspicion, prejudice, ignorance and optimism constantly obscure our vision.'[11] He was horrified to witness the mayhem and confusions of the battlefield. Once more he experienced a graphic demonstration of Clausewitz's distinction between war in reality and war on paper. It was a distinction he had emphasised frequently in recent months. The historian of *The Times* would later write, in war the newspaper's commentators 'could seldom be other than *laudatores temporis acti*' – praisers of what had happened, cheer leaders who eagerly sought to find any element of advantage in any stalemate and minimised or excused defeat. The *History of The Times* states, between the office and Repington there was constant disagreement about the content of his articles. However, throughout 1914 and 1915 what he wrote marched companionably with the editorials. His commentaries complemented Lovat Fraser's leaders. At this stage of the war he did not suffer undue editorial interference. *He*, after all, was the paper's acknowledged military expert. On the few occasions he was required to make changes, they were negotiated amicably. But government censorship proved an altogether different matter.

Repington was soon wrestling with a familiar problem. Kitchener had held back two regular infantry divisions as a safeguard against invasion. He believed the Territorials required stiffening with Regulars. More than a month elapsed before the sixth and last division was finally despatched to France. At the beginning of October, Churchill's personal 'side-show', designed to relieve Antwerp, denuded the country of regular troops. On 7 October the Cabinet was forced to consider home defence as 'a matter of urgency'. Ian Hamilton, C-in-C Home Forces, ever the 'happy warrior', declared his confidence at the prospect of deploying his Central Striking Force should the Germans be foolish enough to raid any part of the British coastline. Asquith, although no believer in invasion threats, was not entirely convinced by Hamilton's optimism. Privately he thought the force deficient in artillery and ammunition. With the army both at home and abroad at full stretch, Kitchener had good reason to feel uncomfortable. Rumours of invasion seemed well founded when, in early November, a lull in the fighting in France suggested a German raid was an immediate, real possibility. Fears were further excited by local intelligence reports of nervous fleet movements, preparations for the mining and blockading of harbours and the deployment of 300,000 half-trained troops along the east coast to repel a possible enemy invasion.

Repington's initial response was confined to his familiar, recently rehearsed tropes on invasion. When his readers suggested Roberts should be appointed C-in-C the British Isles, he reminded the octogenarian field marshal that he had predicted the public would ask for him 'directly things grew warm'. Some days earlier Roberts had unexpectedly visited him to talk of strategy, most particularly, his plan to land 150,000 men on the Belgian coast to outflank the German battle line. 'It must be done,' Roberts avowed, 'and I must go in command of it.' Repington later wrote a generous tribute to this, Roberts's last *beau geste*. 'He was prepared to risk his great fame, reputation and life to command an expedition attended with infinite risks and more suited to a man half his age.' There had been time to send Roberts one last letter with 'a few notes on home defence'. He had endeavoured to deal fully with the subject a few days earlier in *The Times*, but had been cut out by the Censor. 'I am muzzled and the Press is no longer free . . . Not the best way to create confidence in the direction of the war.'[12] He was not exaggerating because newspapers were expected not only to disseminate war news but to interpret and explain it.

The war immediately greatly enhanced Repington's status and influence. Especially in its early months, military 'experts' were treated with rather more respect than they deserved. Other than Kitchener and Churchill, no minister had any personal experience of war or the profession of arms. The third dominant political figure in determining war policy was Asquith – by virtue of being prime minister. This trio's dominance and the early, unquestioning deference to professional expertise were aspects of a larger problem: as yet no appropriate governmental machinery existed to determine strategy or co-ordinate and execute policies in co-operation with allies.

A particular dilemma arose when there was a difference of opinion, not so much between expert and expert as between expert and 'amateur'. Soldiers condescendingly referred to any politician as an 'amateur' who dared to have independent thoughts on strategy. This problem was not to be resolved either swiftly or satisfactorily. In October 1916, for example, the then CIGS, Sir William Robertson, wrote to Repington, 'There has been some discussion as to where the soldier ends and the politician begins. I hope you will be very careful how you deal with the subject.' Robertson believed the politician should back the soldier. What part a commentator might properly play, particularly an ex-staff officer like Repington, added an extra confusing dimension to an already vexatious conundrum. Repington's sympathies were usually entirely with the military. But where prejudice was fortified by a lack of mutual respect, solutions were unlikely to be arrived at painlessly. The lack of empathy between 'frocks' and 'brass hats' made co-operation extraordinarily difficult. Although its existence was denied there was another, more insidious source of difficulty. As the Liberal government struggled with its expert military advisers to determine what exactly Britain's best future strategy might be, Unionist politicians revealed increasing signs of discontent. The agreed facade of national unity in the face of the German peril began to wear thin. Journalists became the accomplices of those Unionist politicians uncertain what form political change should take. Should they seek coalition or a more aggressive, rejuvenated opposition? These were dangerous political waters for even a skilled politician to navigate successfully. Nonetheless, Repington was not averse to plunging in.

Despite his initial plea for censorship in the national interest, Repington was soon complaining to Churchill about the Censor's insensitive, often uninformed adjudications. The First Lord understood the correspondent's frustration. He invited Repington to 'talk things over' with him, but warned that difficulties in the way of repairing the system were 'almost insuperable'. Churchill had been sharply attacked by parts of the Unionist press for his Antwerp adventure. *The Times* and its military correspondent had not questioned whether the expedition should have been despatched, but had asked whether it had been Churchill's business to send it. Lord Selborne, a great imperialist and Tory grandee, wrote privately to Dawson, 'I do not understand how *The Times* or your Military Correspondent could take the line they do about the Antwerp blunder.'[13] What was never mentioned was many Unionists never forgave Churchill's 'disloyalty' in changing his party political allegiance. Haldane steadied him with the wise injunction, 'Do not pay the least attention to the fools who write & talk in the press.'[14]

Many soldiers, and even more politicians, found it impossible to ignore the press. They might hate it but nonetheless sued anxiously for its favours. So it was that even without Kitchener, Repington did not lack for reliable War Office information. As one door closed so another would open. When he told his friend Hamilton, Kitchener's rejection had been 'a merciful fate' for it absolved him from writing, the general knew him too well to be deceived. 'Writing is the salt of your existence. If you come here to see Ellison or me, you will get lots of stuff it is vital for you to possess.'[15] Censorship, however, remained a formidable hurdle to overcome so that Repington bewailed the 'ignorance of the people' who 'chloroformed by the Censorship believe the silliest stories'.[16]

Uncertainties and contradictions divided the government. A conference held at 10 Downing Street in April 1915 was attended by the editors of all the London newspapers with the exception of *The Times*. Responding to complaints about censorship, Asquith disclaimed any intention to interfere with criticism. Riddell, the newspaper magnate, had noted when Asquith made this claim, Churchill and Kitchener 'looked at each other in a very significant way. Evidently they did not approve.'[17] When the government refused to divulge information to the opposition leaders in the Lords, Repington responded with an article[18] warning 'the British Empire [was] in no temper to fight behind a veil of mystery'. Walter Long naturally approved and mentioned the article in a memorandum he sent to Bonar Law. Dawson was quick to point out to Repington the disadvantages as well as advantages of association with leading opposition politicians. He reminded Repington they were 'dealing with a secretive and rather hostile Government' but 'should not succumb to the still greater danger of identifying ourselves with any party'. With a certain asperity he noted, the last page of the article Repington had sent him 'read as though it came straight from the "shadow Cabinet"'. He should 'beware not to write as though you were the mouthpiece of the Opposition'.[19] This was the second time within a year Dawson had warned Repington of the dangers of too close an association with a group of political partisans. After Ulster, Repington could scarcely claim not to be *parti pris* with Law's Unionists. Repington's tangled web of informants went beyond the familiar embrace of Whitehall, Westminster and Fleet Street; it reached over the Channel to France, the Low Countries and British GHQ. He informed Walter Long he expected to be with French in a few days and Long straightway told Brinsley Fitzgerald how greatly he admired Repington for upholding 'the views you and I share'.[20]

The Chief of Staff to the BEF had made clear to Wigram, the king's assistant private secretary, he thought little of French as a commander and even less of his personal staff.[21] As French's friend and guest, Repington when visiting the front line enjoyed both privileges and considerable freedom to come and go and question as he wished. Commander and correspondent usually conversed at the beginning and end of each day. Repington enjoyed the use of a car to visit the French and Belgian fronts where he met and talked to the troops and their commanders. He enjoyed particularly friendly relations with the voluble Foch. He also visited La Panne and there engaged in lengthy military powwows with the king of the Belgians.

According to Repington, two issues particularly concerned Sir John. First, 'the supply of guns and shells'. All ranks were aware of the want of ammunition, but their concerns, like their complaints, were snuffed out by the Censor. The second issue touched closely upon French's personality. He was, not unnaturally, enraged by Kitchener's habitual interference with military operations. In his turn Kitchener had good cause to complain about French's behaviour. The insensitivity of the one exactly matched the excessive sensitivity of the other. Repington insisted he did his 'very best' to encourage French 'to remain on good terms with Lord K', if only for the sake of the cause they all shared. 'But each time I went out to France I found there had been more friction and that relations between the two men had become more strained.'[22]

Charles Callwell, upon his return to the War Office as DMO, had urged Kitchener to treat newspaper correspondents as responsible professionals, and also to acknowledge *The Times* was a special newspaper. Kitchener would have none of it. He had never liked or trusted the press and complained incessantly of inconsistencies. He called it 'newspaper embroidery'.[23] Dawson unavailingly urged Repington to try to capitalise on his former good relations with the war minister and 'make a special effort to see him',[24] but instead, Repington was pushed ever closer to French. Although C-in-C of the Expeditionary Force, French, uncertain about the tenure of his command, increasingly leaned towards his kitchen cabinet to bolster confidence in his qualities as a man and as a military leader. Billy Lambton, Brinsley Fitzgerald, Freddie Guest and

Fitzgerald Watt ran his errands and knew his secrets, but most significantly, fed his suspicions. Sir John was warned frequently and repeatedly that his close advisers did not serve him well. Repington was known to be a strong adherent and admirer of the Commander-in-Chief and became associated in people's minds with the activities of French's intimates.

The failure to break through the German's entrenched defences prompted considerable ministerial frustration. There was no shortage of suggested strategies designed to weaken Germany by attacking, severally or jointly, her Austro-Hungarian and Turkish imperial allies. Lloyd George advocated such a change. However it was the Admiralty and Churchill who proved to be the most fruitful source of ideas. Not in the least embarrassed by the failure of their Antwerp expedition, they suggested naval offensives and combined operations for Borkum, Heligoland, the Baltic, Zeebrugge, and finally, with various combinations of nationalities, naval and military forces, the Dardanelles. By a complex process, this last scheme emerged as the favoured option.

The possibility of an undesirable, new strategic initiative prompted Repington to warn French he feared 'a strong War Office party' favoured decisive action in some theatre of war *other* than France. In *The Times* he wrote about 'the damage of separating forces and seeking fresh theatres of operation'.[25] It was not a novel plea. He had long believed, 'The west is where decision of this war is to be sought ... I do not believe in the circular tour to Victory ... Study the practice of Napoleon. The shortest road to his enemy's capital was always the path that he preferred.'[26] For the moment they did not have sufficient military resources to win in both France and Constantinople at the same time. The most likely outcome of any such attempt would be failure in both theatres. It would be 'inconceivable folly', he told readers of *The Times*, to undertake an expedition that would 'postpone the hour of victory over our principal enemy'. Why change present strategy *on the eve of success* when 'scarcely an officer of experience with our armies in France does not consider it madness'? A single principle needed to be observed if the war with Germany was to be won: 'Every man and every shell to the decisive theatre.' After this clear statement he relapsed into silence, insisting he could no longer write freely about the Dardanelles since the Censor 'mangled the articles [he] drafted' on that subject. But he did not keep silent about the 'stupidity and obscurantism' of the censorship and warned that the 'feelings of animosity' aroused would inevitably be 'visited on the Government'.[27]

Knowing a substantial, joint, Franco-British offensive was planned to begin in the second week of May 1915, Repington made sure he was there in advance. Kitchener complained to French; the government did not permit war correspondents; he did not think it right the C-in-C should 'allow Repington to be out with the army'. French responded dismissively, Repington was an old, personal friend, staying with him for a day or two 'in an entirely private capacity'.[28] Sir Reginald Brade, concerned like Kitchener, had sought to suppress an earlier despatch that French had approved. Its author, Valentine Williams of the *Daily Mail*, had been staying with French at the time. Brade concluded French must be cultivating Northcliffe.

Repington had long shared French's concern at the 'lamentably short supply of high-explosive shells for field artillery, heavy guns of all calibres and all the necessary instruments and materials for trench warfare'. Unfairly and incorrectly he blamed Kitchener for this. He insisted, because Kitchener 'did not comprehend the importance of artillery he took no effective measures to increase supplies while concealing the truth from his Cabinet colleagues'. On each visit to France, Repington had been told the War Office had promised to make improvements. Then later he would discover no change had been made. Despite repeated representations British trenches continued to be 'plastered' by enemy shells while British guns were 'restricted to a few rounds per day'. Repington claimed that he tried on three occasions to see Kitchener to discuss the subject 'and three times I failed'. To see anyone else was 'useless'. When he attempted to allude to the problem in *The Times* he had been 'censored. Everything inconvenient to the Government is'.[29]

In the early hours of 9 May Repington had joined French to observe the beginning of the British attack on Aubers Ridge. Sir John confidently expected a victory followed by a major breakthrough. His optimistic prediction was based on the claimed success earned at Neuve Chapelle the previous month. What was more, he believed they had learned the lessons that battle had taught. Everything depended upon adequate supplies of ammunition for the guns. He was however, about to be betrayed by his over-sanguine temperament. Rather than suffer delay, he had reassured Kitchener the ammunition would 'be all right' though this was to contradict everything he had previously repeatedly said. Kitchener hastened to tell Asquith the welcome news and the Prime Minister used French's disclaimer in a fateful speech to munition workers at Newcastle in which he denied Repington's assertion the government had failed to supply enough ammunition to the troops.[30]

The British artillery's bombardment of the German position was spectacular but inadequate. The subsequent assault failed. French troops did rather better. Their preliminary bombardment lasted four hours and had employed high-explosive shells at a rate of 240 rounds a day per field gun. 'We could only afford forty minutes,' Repington bitterly observed. The

French had knocked the German trenches in front of them 'to bits' whereas the British had faced defences that were 'little injured, the wire uncut and very numerous machine guns'. What particularly enraged Repington had been the losses suffered by the men and officers of the 2nd Battalion of the Rifle Brigade. From a total strength of 1,090, at the end of their day's action only one of twenty-nine officers and 245 other ranks remained unscathed. They blamed their failure on insufficient shells, a verdict Repington repeated in the confidential letter he sent his editor as prologue to his telegraphed despatch the next day.

'The operations now going on will be scarcely comprehensible', he wrote to Dawson. 'The two Divisions that attacked did all men can be asked to do, but the German positions are three times stronger than they were at Neuve Chapelle ... This front is a devil and only heaps of high explosives can break it.' This letter, like his telegraphed despatch, gave a highly selective picture of the battle. He chose to skate lightly over the divisions between Haig and Smith-Dorrien and between French and Smith-Dorrien. The latter was made a scapegoat on the trumped-up charge of pessimism. He was removed from command on 30 April and replaced by Plumer. Repington had long admired and praised Smith-Dorrien for his qualities as 'a hard fighting General' but accepted his dismissal without mentioning the difficulties imposed upon his troops by the flat, water-logged terrain and the total lack of natural cover. He did not mention the strong German counter artillery bombardment, or the many British shells that fell short. Instead he concentrated his disgust and ire upon one issue. 'You will hardly believe,' he wrote, 'but on the first day of the offensive here, after we had hoarded shells like gold, we were ordered to send 25,000 rounds to the Dardanelles. Our protests have been of no avail.'[31]

Repington's letter encapsulated and juxtaposed two of his constant complaints: the lack of sufficient and suitable ammunition and the crassness of dividing the army's efforts. Repington knew his telegram would stir up a furious political row. In his published *War Diaries* he admitted he was 'determined to expose the truth to the public, no matter at what cost'. That was why he sent the telegram and why he did so 'without consulting anyone'. He insisted the key words – 'the want of an unlimited supply of high-explosive shells was a fatal bar to our success' – were his. They 'were not suggested by Sir John French'.

Because his telegram was sent from the front it had been subject to a two-tier censorship. First Macdonogh 'cut out all the allusions to the Rifle Brigade casualties [and] all remarks about the want of heavy guns, howitzers, trench mortars, maxims and rifle grenades'. Then the general had consulted Fitzgerald, who said that although French had not seen the despatch, he would approve. Written up for publication, the telegram went to the Press Bureau and finally the War Office where Charles Callwell adjudicated. He decided with one or two minor excisions it should be published 'in the national interest'. Sir Edward Cook, the Press Bureau's chief, afterwards concluded Callwell must have been 'confused'.[32] Although through and through a Kitchener man, Calwell thought publication of the truth about the shell shortage justified because he believed 'Labour had not yet fully risen to its responsibilities'. He hoped that when they had read the despatch the workers would at last 'realise the successful prosecution of the war depended to a great extent upon our factories'.[33] Repington had wanted to kick Kitchener and the War Office but Callwell thought the kicking better directed at insufficiently hard-working, unpatriotic munitions workers.

Repington's despatch, dated 12 May, strongly supported by a leading article, was published on Friday 14 May and headlined, 'A Lesson from France'. It named no individual soldier or politician but the message could not have been clearer. 'The attacks', which were French's responsibility, had been 'well planned'. They had failed for 'want of an unlimited supply of explosives'. That was the responsibility of Kitchener and the War Office. Although neither claim was strictly true, the article caused a sensation. Scarcely containing his anger, Kitchener observed to French, 'A good many remarks are being made about *The Times* correspondent.'[34] Some believed the despatch was really French's creation, intended to foment a campaign in his own interest. Others insisted Northcliffe, as Repington's paymaster, had reached an arrangement for joint action after Alick Murray, the Liberal chief whip, had acted as go-between.[35] The king's equerry told Haig, the general consensus of opinion was Northcliffe's newspapers conspired against Kitchener with the help of Sir John French's personal staff.[36]

Although Repington had made the biggest and loudest bang, he was only one among many. French had sent Guest and Fitzgerald to England with copies of the correspondence he had exchanged with the War Office complaining about the supplies of ammunition. He gave them specific instructions to lay 'these proofs' before Lloyd George, Balfour and Bonar Law. Sir John added a memorandum that explained why he needed the greater number of high-explosive shells. By the time Repington's despatch was published, the two emissaries had completed their task. French later sought to justify his action. It was 'to destroy the apathy of the Government', an intention he had confided to 'a friend, standing by my side on the church tower' before the first shot was fired at Aubers Ridge. The unnamed friend could only have been Repington. He had warned French the politicians would never forgive his act.[37] It would have been as well for Repington's future reputation had he given some thought to the possible dangers he faced. French's two personal emissaries had acted covertly. When the information they had provided was made public they had not wished it to be identified as supplied by them. Once Repington's despatch was published it not only did it make the lack of adequate ammunition supplies the subject of public debate but inextricably linked his name in the public's mind with that revelation.

Repington returned to London in the evening of 16 May. He was met at Victoria Station by Captain Arthur Stanley Wilson, MP. He had earlier recruited and briefed the King's Messenger to act as his temporary go-between with the Unionist hierarchy. The captain spoke to Bonar Law who asked to see the military correspondent at the earliest possible moment. The two men had gone immediately from Victoria to Law's house. There, after dinner, Repington regaled, among others, Curzon, Carson and F. E. Smith, with a detailed account of how matters stood concerning guns, shells and men in France. He 'neither minced [his] words nor concealed [his] feelings'. He did not hesitate to be closely identified with these opposition politicians because, he would have argued, his purpose had nothing to do with party politics. His one wish was to ensure in future there would be not only more munitions but a much higher proportion of high-explosive shells; more guns, better guns, heavier guns; and that extra troops should be made available for service on the western front. For him to have discounted the likely effect of his words on party politics at Westminster would have been naive beyond belief, and whatever else he might have been, Repington was not politically naive. He admitted in his *War Diaries*, if the achievement of the desired end involved the fall of the 'old Gladstonian Liberal party', he was not averse to that likelihood. They 'never understood foreign politics and had neither foreseen the war nor prepared for it'.[38]

In any political negotiation concerning the future of the Liberal government David Lloyd George would always be a key player. He had been angry with Asquith's Newcastle speech. He had thought it politically injudicious. Now he was furious the Prime Minister should, like him, have been deliberately misled on the matter of munitions by Kitchener's bland assurances. The despatch in *The Times*, he later told Repington, served as a 'train of gunpowder to which he applied the match'. He had immediately informed the Prime Minister 'he was unable to go on'. When it came to flattering an auditor, no one could tailor an account more adeptly than Lloyd George. He had known weeks earlier about disastrous ammunition shortages, especially high-explosive shells, and the 'damnable inaction' of the War Office compared with the French, who made the most of their facilities, 'turning out four times as many shells as us'.[39]

Now the public knew the truth, which was that the Liberal government had manufactured insufficient shells thus fatally impairing the army's progress at Festubert. The present administration was no longer viable. There would *have* to be a change. The opposition leaders had been briefed by Guest and Fitzgerald and after such revelations they would not for long be able to restrain the demands of their more awkward and impatient backbenchers. Defeat in the House could lead only to a general election. The Liberals would be reviled as an ineffectual war administration and as hopelessly divided on the issue of the war. Such conditions could only favour a huge Unionist triumph and the annihilation of the parliamentary Liberal Party, a prospect that appealed as little to Lloyd George as it did to Asquith.

On 17 May, after a bumptious Northcliffe had enjoyed an hour-long conclave with Lloyd George, the Chancellor asked to see Repington. Astonished that Lloyd George seemed to know so few of the facts, even though a member of two key committees dealing with munitions and war materials,[40] as soon as they parted Repington wrote him a hurried note listing the three key documents 'the Cabinet should extract from Lord K'. These were two reports French had sent to Kitchener on the subject of ammunition and more recently on guns. The third document was the Army Council letter of 14 May 'on the question of reinforcements'. Practically it said, the New Armies would no more be sent to France.[41]

There is no record of their conversation but the two letters Repington wrote to Lloyd George dated 17 and 20 May not surprisingly suggest their talk was largely if not exclusively about the want of ammunition, particularly high explosives, criticism of the number and type of guns, particularly the 4.7 heavy gun ('bad and nobody trusts it'), and the number of troops available to serve in France. This last would become Repington's next great public campaign in *The Times*, counterpointed by his descriptions and analyses of the German campaign in Russia that had begun on 1 May and that would continue until September. Repington wrote, 'I want to make the question of men for France clear to you. It is as serious if not more serious than, the question of high explosive.' For the moment, however, he wanted that subject kept secret.

Repington's necessarily abbreviated summary of a series of affairs, plots, rumours, meetings and negotiations preceding the making of the first coalition, much of which he would have learned about second hand and which previously would have been entirely unknown to the public, makes entirely credible his later unqualified assertion that the 'explosion' caused by the publication of his despatch had sent Asquith scurrying to shelter under the opposition umbrella, to accept the

Coalition Ministry that 'only the week before he had rejected with contumely'. Repington, it seemed, had not only brought down the Liberals by his revelation, but from that seismic political convulsion could be dated 'the general provision of an adequate supply of munitions of all descriptions'. He appeared to have rid the country of a Liberal administration that stood in the way of necessary administrative change, and as well was the *fons et origo*[42] of the Ministry of Munitions.

During Repington's lifetime it was generally accepted, the shell shortage had been caused by inefficiencies under Kitchener's supervision, and that subsequently these faults and deficiencies were remedied by Lloyd George and the newly created Ministry of Munitions. But the changes were evolutionary rather than revolutionary, though 'the speed of change from the middle of March 1915 almost warranted the more drastic description'.[43] The political crisis of May gave Lloyd George the opening to wrestle supremacy in the manufacture of munitions away from the War Office and Kitchener. This made possible the full wartime mobilisation of British industry. Repington's information confirmed Lloyd George's existing poor opinion of Kitchener and was the justification for the politician's denigration of the work undertaken by Kitchener and von Donop, Master General of the Ordnance. LG savagely criticised the prewar arrangements to supply munitions and ridiculed their dependence on a small number of approved manufacturers who had been scarcely able to meet the unexpected demand. Although output fell short of what the army required, munitions' production had increased impressively in the war's first year. The increases brought about by Lloyd George's ministry were achieved, as von Donop predicted, at a cost; a noticeable decline in quality. Llewellyn Smith, the senior civil servant crucial in wrestling control of munitions from the War Office, had been the first to recognise the shells scandal afforded Lloyd George the chance to effect 'a really comprehensive reform which even [the previous] week [had] seemed impossible'. So Repington could justifiably claim that he afforded Lloyd George the opportunity to begin to introduce what became a total war economy. That was a significantly greater change than Repington could possibly have initially envisaged or understood.[44]

Repington's abridged account in his *War Diaries* of the shell crisis and its aftermath understandably concentrated on his part in the events. He wrote only of 'a first-class political crisis at full blast' and made no mention of the publication, two days earlier, of extracts from the Bryce Report on German atrocities. This, together with the recent sinking of the *Lusitania*, the first use by the Germans of poisonous gas on the western front and the increasing intensity of Zeppelin raids, prompted among some sections of the public an unreasoning hatred of all things German. In some areas there was serious anti-German rioting and looting. At Westminster, opposition MPs grew increasingly convinced the government was neither sufficiently ruthless nor efficient in its conduct of the war. They demanded 'Prussianism' should be crushed.

The Liberal government desperately needed some good news to bolster its credibility. In France there was no sign of the army's frequently advertised 'early breakthrough'. The Aubers Ridge failure was simply the latest instalment in a sadly familiar story. On the eastern front the Germans had begun a hugely successful offensive at Russia's expense, prompting Kitchener to fear the Germans would soon be able to release troops from the east to supplement their forces on the western front. In the Dardanelles the joint Allied military and naval expedition recently launched against Turkey, instead of success offered the real probability of humiliating defeat and disaster. Ships had been sunk, disabled and withdrawn from hostilities and Hamilton's troops were corralled in two small bridgeheads on the Gallipoli peninsula. Asquith's administration was already under siege when a difference of opinion between Churchill and Fisher at the Admiralty over agreed additions to the naval reinforcements for the Dardanelles was used by the First Sea Lord as his excuse to resign for the ninth and last time.

Fisher's resignation on Saturday 15 May occurred the day after Repington's fatal despatch appeared in *The Times*. On Sunday 16 May Repington returned to London and spoke both to opposition leaders and Lloyd George. The next day, Monday 17 May, at Lloyd George's request he again saw and spoke with him. The new government, with Asquith still the prime minister, was announced on Wednesday 19 May. To the general public it seemed abundantly clear that the Liberals would not have agreed to coalition but for Repington's revelatory despatch, and so for a number of years it remained the generally accepted 'cause'. Ministers come and go frequently in the life of any ministry. A department's worth of senior and junior ministers may be swept into limbo by a prime minister and dismissed as no more than 'a little local difficulty'. But when a government engaged in a war of national survival, despite frequent requests and constant warnings fails to provide its army with enough or the right kind of ammunition and consequently a battle is lost, failure is bound to be deemed inexcusable. A change of administration in May 1915 was inevitable.

Bonar Law's friend, Max Aitken, in the first volume of his *Politicians and the War, 1914–1916*, wrote, 'The fall of the Liberal Government ... had nothing whatever to do with the shell scandal and was produced solely and entirely by the dissensions at the Admiralty ... which culminated in Fisher's resignation.' Aitken concluded, as much should be 'abundantly clear to anyone who impartially examines the evidence'.[45] But what was 'abundantly clear' to Aitken years after the event altogether escaped Stamfordham when he summarised the pertinent events for the king's benefit. He wrote his aide-mémoire after a conversation with the Prime Minister on the day the decision for coalition was made. Asquith had listed as 'the actual causes' which brought about his decision, 'Lord Fisher's resignation' and 'The Armament question raised by the recent letter from *The Times* special [*sic*] correspondent'. The conduct of the First Sea Lord and the unreasonableness of his demands had strongly suggested to Asquith 'signs of mental aberration!' He concluded Fisher was no longer fit to serve, which suggests his resignation merely antici-pated the inevitable. Concerning Repington's despatch, the Prime Minister asserted that 'the Opposition leaders were uneasy. The press had taken it up.' Typically, Asquith had implied he had for some time 'thought that the Government ought to be put on a broader base'.[46]

Whether the shell or Admiralty crisis is considered *a* cause or *the more important* cause that prompted coalition, or no more than the *occasion*, it is certain Repington never set out with the intention to change the govern-ment. His wish was to see Kitchener displaced. But when John Dillon, the Irish Nationalist MP, wrote to Augustine Birrell, Ireland's chief secretary, he insisted that because Repington's despatch had been 'enough to bring down a Government its publication *must* have had that object in view'.[47] The politician assumed a political purpose. Repington had not even envisaged it as a remote possibility but subsequently was happy to accept credit for it. He vehemently rejected those who accused him of intriguing against the government and equally vigorously denied those who sug-gested he had acted at Northcliffe's behest. It could not be an 'intrigue to endeavour to save an army from defeat by necessary public exposure when all official representations had hopelessly failed'.[48] His dismissal of any idea he was Northcliffe's stooge was equally peremptory, but whether it was persuasive requires further elucidation.

Northcliffe had been much upset by the recent death-in-action of his young nephew Lucas King. He held Kitchener directly responsible. As Kitchener was the minister ultimately responsible for the supply, quality, quantity and suitability of munitions, Northcliffe considered Repington's despatch to be primarily an attack on Kitchener's competence.[49] He implied the military correspondent's piece was one among a series of demands his newspapers had made over a period of months culminating in his personal attack on the minister in the *Daily Mail*, insisting Kitchener *must* leave the War Office. Yet despite the ministerial changes the formation of a coalition had made necessary, Kitchener remained unmoved and seemingly immovable.

Repington had thoroughly disapproved of Northcliffe's attack and characterised it as 'ill-judged'.[50] To denounce a man so incontinently when to most of the public he remained an untouchable talisman was likely to achieve precisely the opposite effect to that intended. The newspaper proprietor's too obvious contempt for Kitchener redounded to his grave disadvantage. Northcliffe suffered deserved personal opprobrium and a disastrous if temporary decline in the circulation of all his newspapers.[51] Kitchener was not only confirmed as a minister but awarded the Garter.

The shells scandal reinforced in many minds the idea of Repington as Northcliffe's accomplice. He was never seen as the initiator but always as a collaborator in his employer's scams. There is no evidence to prove, as has so often been alleged, they constantly plotted together. The letters they exchanged were very few and far between, brusque and not the least conspiratorial in tone. Repington insisted he never consulted with Northcliffe on the issue of armaments. Few, if any, believed him because they never chose to look beyond the looming figure of the proprietor. If a press intrigue *had* succeeded in pulling down the Liberal government, then it was too big, too significant a change in the nation's political life to be accredited to a mere journalist. It *must* have been the proprietor's doing. Northcliffe alone was big enough to precipitate a calamity on that scale.[52] After the dust of the shells scandal had settled, Fitzgerald, who had worked the press hard in the past months in French's interest, told Selborne, 'We have used Northcliffe and some of his men in order to force K's hand.'[53] Repington might strenuously deny such claims but few were inclined to listen and his warmly repeated assertions of independence were similarly ignored. As Northcliffe paid the piper, they reasoned, surely it was not unreasonable to suppose he also determined the tune? Repington was often seen in Fitzgerald's company when at French's GHQ. If, as many believed, French in attacking Kitchener was in cahoots with Northcliffe, then Repington was doubly involved and so doubly guilty. He was hopelessly and utterly compromised by his ready association with at one moment French, the next Bonar Law and the Unionists, then David Lloyd George. This last was an association that would grow in significance and importance in the coming months as the new minister for munitions moved ever closer to the centre of political power. At Westminster no one, certainly not John Dillon, doubted Repington's influence was enormously enhanced by these alliances.[54]

Esher was summoned by Kitchener. He wanted him to reassure French it had never been his intention to replace him as commander in the field and to tell the Field Marshal every available man and gun had been sent to Flanders.[55] French approved the message of reassurance Esher returned to Kitchener. At all times he might count upon French's loyalty, thus leaving him free to concentrate upon 'beating the Germans'. Esher suggested French might best ensure a trouble-free future by ridding himself of the worst of his unworthy companions. It was under this rubric that Repington was banned from visiting GHQ.

14 How do we secure the necessary troops?

At the height of the shell crisis, in mid May 1915, Repington told Lloyd George 'the question of men for France ... is more serious than the question of high explosive', but for the moment he wanted this divulged to no one. The British offensive in France had been undertaken in the belief that 'more troops would be available in the course of the present month'. It was for that reason 'British troops had taken over more of the French line'. The order had then been countermanded. Why? Some suggested a German invasion was feared; the extra troops would be required for home defence. The army laughed at such as implausible idea. Repington wondered whether Kitchener's jealousy of Sir John French might have something to do with it. Alternatively, perhaps Kitchener was unable to grasp the strain modern firepower imposed upon troops who could not stay long in the front line without becoming dead to the world. But that the extra troops had never been intended for France he deemed the most likely explanation. All along they had been destined for 'the Dardanelles sink'. If that were so, nothing could better signify the bankruptcy of the Cabinet's military policy. Without sufficient troops serious co-operation with the French was impossible. The Allies might have secured a great success, but how could French call for a mighty effort when the Cabinet closed the flow of reinforcements?[1]

Repington had opposed the Dardanelles adventure from the moment he learned it was no longer planned as a purely naval enterprise. It was a 'hopeless proceeding ... There were three times as many Turks ... as there were British. Sooner or later the Allies would have to meet army with army.' With the available forces divided the Allies would be too weak to achieve victory in either theatre. That was why at the beginning of April he had attacked the government for promoting and supporting secondary operations. They 'served only to postpone the hour of victory over our principal enemy. Every man, every shell, should be delivered to the decisive theatre.' Whether that one sure principle was observed or neglected would determine victory or defeat.[2] Critics argued Repington repeated this mantra simply to curry favour with the High Command, but he did so because he was convinced of its truth. Not all soldiers agreed with him. His friend, Sir Ian Hamilton, the chosen military commander for the Dardanelles expedition, characterised Repington's idea as 'jamming everything into the impasse of the French cockpit' and unfavourably compared it with Churchill's 'broad, strategic concept'. In *The Times*, Repington soon relapsed into silence about the Dardanelles operations. When his critical reports were mangled by the Censor, he abandoned the struggle as quite hopeless.

The campaign proved a dismal failure and a chastened Hamilton had been relieved of his command by Charles Monro. By mid October he was back in London. There, to his surprise and vexation, he found his conduct increasingly criticised. Clearly, responsibility for the failure of the Dardanelles venture was to be placed entirely at his front door. The Hamiltons even found themselves slighted by sections of Society. Sir Ian's final despatch, 7 January 1916, attracted much critical comment, not least from *The Times*. Repington was unaware it had been deliberately altered to conceal the fact British divisions had been 45,000 below establishment. From the beginning he had believed failure inevitable, but he found no fault in his friend's conduct of the campaign. Dining with the Hamiltons he learned the Gallipoli planning had been 'sketchy . . . exceedingly nebulous'.[3] But, he insisted, the inescapable flaw of all such 'sideshows' was they mitigated against the proper concentration of the British army's military effort against the Germans in France and Flanders.

Because his thoughts upon the Gallipoli operation were anathema to the Censor, for a time Repington's writing concentrated upon the issue of recruitment. Kitchener had foolishly ignored the ready-made organisation left by Haldane. Consequently the new armies lacked territorial connections for they possessed neither depots nor reserves. When the number of recruits began to fall, this was hidden from government and public. Kitchener seemed to think he could bluff everyone. Callwell thought it most unlikely he would be able to keep the truth from Repington for long. He *discovered* many things, supposedly safe from prying eyes, because of his numerous well-informed and reliable sources, Callwell told the editor 'Taffy' Gwynne. Callwell knew what he was talking about: he frequently provided Repington with extremely useful 'leaks'.

Despite desperate efforts to camouflage the truth about recruitment, the true figures were soon revealed in Parliament. A commanding officer complained of having to accept 'halt, lame and blind, men who cannot march, and even if carried to a trench cannot see to shoot'. Discharged they were promptly re-enlisted. After this fashion, in 1915 the army's nominal total had been swollen by 200,000 men who were absolutely useless for any conceivable military purpose. Parliamentary disclosure was privileged, but Repington's attempts to draw public attention to the problem immediately attracted the Censor's unfavourable notice. Repington said he would much like to talk with the new minister of munitions whenever he had 'a moment to spare', and when such a moment was found he particularly emphasised his *entire* sympathy with *everything* Lloyd George had said in his recent speeches. He was even prepared to assert LG had succeeded in pulling the country through the munitions crisis – a claim that was both premature and exaggerated but it made his further contention, that LG was the one man capable of 'pulling us through the crisis of numbers', more convincing. What he entirely failed to appreciate was the real reason LG wanted conscription. He was not concerned to meet the army's need for more recruits. What the minister wanted was to retain the necessary civilian workforce to produce extra munitions knowing that industrial conscription would be vigorously opposed by all Radical, Labour and Trade Union forces.

In the months that followed minister and correspondent frequently met for luncheon, either at the Carlton or at 11 Downing Street. On these occasions, as he smoked a large, post-luncheon cigar, LG's monologues would become increasingly expansive. He monopolised their conversations, even those concerned mainly with military matters. He discoursed at length on the Russian campaign, Salonika,[4] the Dardanelles and the faulty organisation he had discovered at Woolwich. He repeatedly emphasised Kitchener's many and serious failings. At some point in these *tours d'horizon* he would pause and ask Repington what *he* thought might be done for the best. To Repington's suggestions, Lloyd George would respond sympathetically but without commitment. Significantly he said nothing when hints were dropped about conscription. On that subject he believed it wiser 'not to hustle. It must come but is likely to come sooner if we do not raise too much Radical opposition'.[5] Lloyd George's attitude apparently differed little from that of most other Liberal politicians. He preferred prevarication and procrastination to action.

The *Manchester Guardian*, a newspaper known to be sympathetic to Lloyd George, declared 'there is no chance of conscription being adopted'. For months to come, 'the War Office will have more men than it can supply and send to the front'. So much was only to be expected from a Radical newspaper. Immediately Repington dashed off an angry note to Northcliffe admitting the claim was true. But it hid a more important truth. What had been said constituted a case not against conscription but against the War Office. It was perfectly shameful that men of the 4th and later New Armies who had been in training since September 1914, still had only eighty rifles for every battalion of 1,100 men. Third line Territorials were no better equipped. Northcliffe might easily establish this was so if he visited Salisbury Plain or the east coast.

The government shunned all enquiry while the General Staff were kept at arm's length lest the imposture be exposed. The Esher Committee had made the General Staff responsible for military policy, strategy, war organisation and operations, and yet their views on these subjects were never submitted to the Cabinet. The case for conscription would not, could not be made so long as those opinions remained unknown.[6] Northcliffe assured Repington he concurred and affirmed his belief that 'Conscription [would] come'. The response was polite but Repington recognised it for what it was, a brush-off. The great man made it abundantly clear to his hireling his immediate thoughts were occupied with what he supposed to be more important matters.

The Prime Minister was faced with the cumulative consequences of the heavy losses of the Battle of Loos, the obvious deadlock in the Dardanelles and of Bulgaria having joined the conflict as an ally of the Germans. In a last desperate attempt to save voluntary recruitment, Asquith told Derby, who only recently had been appointed Director of Recruiting, to employ the National Register to plan and direct a new recruiting drive. Those who attested were to be grouped by marital status, age and occupation. This was the so-called 'Derby Scheme'. Repington thought well of Derby, not least for his long adherence to conscription. He described him as 'Bluff, hearty and always smiling; not clever but very shrewd; a man of the world with very good sense ... popular with all classes, including labour and the army'. On 11 November, during a long conversation Repington learned that during the past month the number of recruits had considerably increased. Derby, who was convinced there could be an effective system of compulsion, instituted a system of local tribunals supervised by parliamentary committees. Repington would soon become directly involved as one of Hampstead's military representatives. The starring system, introduced to determine who might be enlisted or excused military service, was causing difficulties. Derby found Agriculture and the Home Office could be 'curiously obstructive'. Even a seemingly straightforward request could run into difficulties.[7]

Derby told Asquith on 20 December that 340,000 extra recruits were now available but that this was less than one-sixth of the potential number. Without revealing Derby's figures, Asquith asked Parliament to authorise an additional million men to serve in the army. British casualties on all fronts then stood at 512,420. Of these, a third was killed or missing. The 'wastage' rate of men at the front was 15 per cent per month. On Boxing Day, Repington bent his best efforts to 'make the Radical Press howl' and scatter the ill-favoured, defeatist forces of voluntarism.

Fig. 9 Lieutenant Colonel Charles à Court Repington, 1916 (aged 58)

He demonstrated with irrefutable logic, so he believed, if the army were given the men required, victory was assured. But if 'for reasons of trade' the men were kept back, 'then you don't get victory and eventually you get no trade. Victory gives all', he concluded, before adding with a flourish, '*QED*.'[8] How he wished the government had the courage of *his* principles.

On 5 January 1916 Asquith introduced a Military Service Bill. From 2 March all single males aged between 18 and 41, unless exempted, would be conscripted. Sir John Simon, Home Secretary, had been the only Cabinet casualty of this decision. He now led the parliamentary opposition to the conscription bill. Repington attended the House but was impressed neither by Asquith's 'lack of magnetism' nor Simon's 'unhappy speech'. The next day the bill was given a majority on its first reading of 298.

The previous day Repington had met Sir William Robertson, their first meeting since the general's appointment as CIGS. He told Repington, despite Simon's departure two other Cabinet members continued to cause trouble – the Chancellor, McKenna, and Walter Runciman, President of the Board of Trade. They insisted a sensible financial and trade policy required Britain to have a small army. McKenna was particularly alarmed. The financial cost of a bloated army would make it impossible to find the 600 million pounds loaned each year to Britain's Allies. Soldiers thought the minister unnecessarily concerned. Robertson reassured Repington, the Derby scheme's first tranche of 338,000 would, together with compulsion, provide enough men (that was to say 1.5 million) for the next nine months to bring the divisions up to war strength. The numbers, Repington contentedly observed, suggested ' Robertson [would] get the men he need[ed] for 1916'.[9]

On Wednesday 12 January Repington recorded in his diary the 'First meeting of the Hampstead Tribunal'. The chairman was the mayor, O'Bryen; the secretary, A. P. Johnson, the town clerk, 'and four or five others inclined to be Jacks-in-office'. Two of the three military representatives attended. There had been a dispute with some of the other representatives, who had questioned his and Colonel Sheffield's right to appear as they had failed to bring their credentials. Repington wanted members of the Military Advisory Committee 'to attend and listen and see how things were done and worked', but the chairman would have none of it. He refused for he did not want their help. His insistence puzzled Repington as it had been 'not at all to the point'. He admitted he had never before 'dealt with Municipal authorities' so it was scarcely surprising he should have been quite unaware of what he now called 'their idiosyncracies'. The chairman wanted the public excluded. The *Hampstead and Highgate Express* complained the tribunal had become a 'secret conclave'. When challenged, O'Bryen insisted he had an 'absolute discretion to conduct the Tribunal as [he] like[d]'. Once the novelty of their meetings had worn off, the local press chose 'not to devote much further space to them'.[10]

Lytton Strachey's appearance before the Hampstead Tribunal in mid March 1916 to plead exemption from service on grounds of his conscientious objection to war caused no great stir in the local press. Found to be unfit for any kind of service, he was granted exemption on medical and not, as he had hoped, moral grounds. Strachey's brother James had anticipated Repington would be the military representative, but possibly Lytton was interrogated by Sheffield. Military representatives generally had a bad name for bullying, browbeating and deliberately cheating. Repington took his responsibilities very seriously and concluded from what he witnessed at Hampstead and Finchley that the tribunals and advisory committees 'performed their work admirably'. He considered they conducted themselves with care, sympathy and believed their decisions were 'very just'. He did not deny there were difficulties. 'We have to create our own precedents, to act by the light of nature as in some cases our instructions do not help.' He was proud of the quiet efficiency with which the Hampstead Tribunal members operated. They 'worked like niggers, sat very steadily, showed excellent judgment and great patience'. The mayor for all his first-day idiosyncracies proved to be 'an excellent chairman. If only all Tribunals were as good',[11] Repington thought. He was conscious of the deserved criticisms being made by certain MPs, almost on a daily basis. On 22 March 1916 Philip Snowden in the Commons quoting from only 5 per cent of the cases that had been brought to his attention, cited more than fifty cases of injustice perpetrated by the tribunals.

Repington was convinced there was 'very little shirking among the people'; the problems were largely bureaucratic. Because 'the list of certified occupations [was] so long', the number of claimants for exemption became intolerable.[12] The CIGS seemed to know very little of how the tribunals worked. Repington told him how the absurd lists of reserved occupations were killing recruiting. Why was brewing designated a reserved occupation? Why were so many workers in the linoleum trade starred? Lloyd George should be made to reduce the number of men of military age engaged in the making of munitions. Similarly, when next he spoke to Derby, who angrily pronounced the results of recruiting under his scheme as 'appalling', he advised him, 'Produce a list of starred occupations and fling it at the Government.'[13] Derby was not in the best of moods, having been pilloried in the Northcliffe press as the progenitor of the 'Bachelor's Bill compromise'.

The final months of winter and the early spring of 1916 proved difficult and sobering for Repington. Unremittingly mired by his intractable financial problems, he was genuinely stricken at the end of February by the death of his much loved mother. He experienced a rare trough in his spirits. He was haunted by thoughts of the pathetic men that came before the tribunal. He found 'very interesting' the insight tribunal members were afforded 'into the home life and the circumstances of numerous people and classes one never mixes with ... there are many cases in which it is a great hardship for a man to go and I get a very clear impression of the social upheaval caused by compulsion in any form'.[14] Of the thirty-eight meetings of the Hampstead Tribunal up to 20 May 1916,[15] Repington recorded attending six, the first on 12 January and the last in May. He found the work 'fascinating' and undoubtedly took it very seriously. He attended no meetings in April because that month he paid two visits to France. The tribunal dealt with 1,164 cases. Where a final decision was reached, forty-eight men were given an absolute exemption but of these seventeen were classified as medically unfit. Of the forty-three cases concerning conscientious objectors, one only was given absolute exemption, but twenty were granted exemption from combatant service. By the following summer Repington noted all their 'clients [were] oldish men in low medical categories quite unsuitable to become infantry'. They were 'getting down to bedrock'. As a military representative he was permitted to wear uniform and despite a serious shortage of funds he nonetheless ordered a new one which he wore on every possible appropriate occasion.[16]

On Thursday 23 March he lunched with Lloyd George at 11 Downing Street. The minister, who had come straight from a meeting of the War Committee, was more than usually forthcoming. He blurted out, 'I cannot see the way to victory in 1916.' Asked what he thought, Repington could only concur. He noted Lloyd George's 'particular gloom about numbers'. There would simply not be enough men in 1916.[17] It might have been that the Welshman's less than sanguine mood prompted Repington to spend the weekend before his scheduled visit to France 'looking into affairs', tabulating the figures on manpower, guns and money. Various political contacts had recently given him statistics that were 'all quite unknown to the public'. They confirmed LG's gloomy prognosis. Britain and Germany together with their allies deployed approximately 6 million men in the chief war theatres. They enjoyed a rough equality in troop numbers. Equal armies suggested drawn battles. Robertson had very properly not placed a figure upon the numbers Britain might have to find to win the war. Based on past experience, Repington calculated, if they could work up to sixty-two divisions serving abroad, they would need a monthly draft of 123,000. It was the sort of figure that might be realised without causing industrial disaster.

Repington's base for his French visit was the Hôtel Ritz.[18] Always keen on his creature comforts, the Ritz never failed to offer the best available food and wine. While in Paris he grabbed the opportunity for a conversation with Robertson, who was attending an Allied conference. He wanted to discuss those points he intended to raise with the various French commanders he hoped to meet the following week. He expected the supply of troops to be high on the agenda, but the supply of ammunition was Robertson's foremost concern. He had already lost his struggle with Joffre over troops. The Frenchman had proved intransigent, refusing to send any French soldiers from Salonika to the western front. Repington thought the French would eventually give way, but by then it would be too late. Robertson complained the trouble was British ministers refused to take the lead in the debates with their French counterparts. Because only Kitchener spoke French, they had to rely upon the translator that Lloyd George had acquired. He would listen for as much as a quarter of an hour without interruption and then give a fluent translation that sounded infinitely better than the original. 'The whole thing', Robertson concluded, 'was babble.'

Before meeting Joffre in the late afternoon of the Saturday, Repington had made a brisk inspection of Verdun and then walked a section of the front line trenches held by the French Fourth Army. The previous day he had much enjoyed a prolonged chinwag with Pétain. He had been greatly impressed. He had also taken the opportunity to sample French army opinion by talking to the charming and gallant Général Gouraud, commander of the Fourth Army, still obviously seriously incommoded by the severe wounds he had suffered during the Dardanelles campaign. Finally he met Joffre and as their conversation progressed so Joffre visibly relaxed. Repington initiated their discussion about troop numbers. He asked, 'How many British divisions have you been promised?' Joffre responded, 'Nothing in writing merely general indications.' Naturally he wanted 'as many troops as could be spared'. More importantly, he wanted British 'troop numbers in France to be kept up to strength'. When Repington suggested the British in France were 'short by forty thousand, Joffre replied emphatically, "More"'. A recent request he had made of Haig had been refused 'for want of men'. 'There are a million men at home, 200,000 in Egypt and an Army in Salonika', Repington insisted. He would do his 'best to get them hurried out' to France. Quite how he intended to perform this miracle he did not say. The two men parted 'on cordial terms'.

After Joffre, Sir Francis Bertie seemed very small beer. The British Ambassador, an unfailingly brilliant and amusing raconteur of ancient scandals, was not really interested in the current political scene. Haig had asked Esher to act as his ambassador because Bertie never told him anything of what the French government intended. The newly appointed French war minister, Berthelot of the Foreign Office, shared Repington's poor opinion of Kitchener as did Aristide Briand, France's leading Socialist and eleven times premier. Neither the politicians, nor even his old friends the queen and king of Belgium, made half the impression on Repington that Joffre had. The king told Repington, Belgium lacked for only one thing – men! Recruitment to their field army was hampered by a constitutional law of 1832. Repington again promised the impossible; he would somehow or other 'find some way of seeing that the effectives [were] put right'.

On Sunday 9 April Robertson visited Maryon Hall, all too eager to talk about recruiting. The present position was 'impossible'. Something had to be done. Quite what exactly, he was less certain. He hoped the Prime Minister would have his hand forced by Parliament. Matters might well come to a crisis that very week. What did Repington advise? The correspondent, who never wittingly understated his influence, was always delighted to proffer advice. His idea bore more than a passing resemblance to the bill the Prime Minister presented to the House three weeks later, on 2 May 1916.

A secret session of the House savagely rejected Asquith's earlier attempt to achieve compromise and forced his hand.[19] The soldiers were given what they had long demanded. For this they took all the credit, boasting they had 'proved too much for the Cabinet'. Robertson exulted to Murray, 'I think we shall now get the men we want ... it takes many months to put the men into the field ... in another two months time the whole show will be going much better.'[20] Repington gave all the credit to Robertson, who had remained 'very firm dragging K and the Army Council with him'. Robertson had insisted it was the government's business to secure the men required. He complained of the endless trouble attending meetings of the Army Council. They had occupied so much time he had been unable 'to concentrate on the strategy of the war'. Repington, a few unimportant reservations aside, declared he was satisfied.[21] Now conscription was finally achieved the long, eagerly anticipated 'big push' could take advantage of a German army exhausted by its endeavours before Verdun.

On Wednesday 17 May Maxine Elliot called to take Repington to Hartsbourne Manor, her fine country house. An invitation from Maxine was always prized. She possessed unrivalled talents as a hostess and invariably attracted the prettiest women to her house parties. A fellow guest, F. E. Smith, advised Repington his recent article, urging Allied prudence before they launched another attack, had created a great impression with the Cabinet. He attempted unsuccessfully to persuade Repington to repeat it. The Attorney estimated an offensive would probably cost 300,000 men and would do no good. According to F. E., everyone had got everything wrong about the war; the soldiers, who had been running the war for the last six months, as much as the financiers and politicians. Repington had heard all this before. The previous month, on his return from the trenches, Churchill had insisted Haig was 'not strong enough yet to attack. We will not be able to do a big thing until next year'. A little later French told Repington he did not think 'even an archangel could attack under present conditions. It was so frightfully expensive of men'.[22] This rather gloomy mood was widespread. When Repington bumped into de la Panouse at the Army and Navy club, the French military attaché enquired anxiously what resources would be made available for recruiting by the new Military Service Act. A short exchange on the war's strategy made clear he was 'very keen that our armies should do something'.[23]

Repington was due to visit France once more before his planned trip to Italy. He wanted to see Robertson and find out what he thought the chances were of a large-scale attack by the Allies given 'the ministerial pose' was 'the whole war was being run by soldiers'. Robertson, not his usual confident self, seemed to suggest the idea of an offensive might be ruled out. Yet Repington was left with the unmistakeable impression there might well be an offensive sooner rather than later. Consequently he drafted an article 'gently hinting' at a possible Allied attack. 'Whether an attack materialised depended upon very complex considerations'! When he visited Robertson on 12 June, the CIGS was much more his usual confident and assertive self. He expressed the hope that 'all our troops in France will attack and not only one army, with the French on our right with as many men as they can spare from Verdun'.[24] Who now would doubt the big attack was imminent?

Repington returned to Paris from the Italian front on 1 July to be told by Esher the Battle of the Somme was well begun. On a front of twenty miles they had taken the first-line German trenches. According to Esher's son, Maurice, the French had been successful south of the river. Hopes were high that weekend, but on Monday 3 July came news that perhaps the British offensive was not going quite as well as previously thought. The artillery had 'failed to overwhelm sufficiently certain defended villages'. Lieutenant Pernot had brought Repington this news together with an invitation to visit GQG at Chantilly and Foch's HQ at Dury, south of Amiens. Pernot, echoing the estimate Joffre had given Haig, did not doubt, the battle would be *durée prolongée* – long drawn-out.

15   Changing the old guard

While Repington was closely and personally involved in the May 1915 shell crisis and thereafter the continuing campaign to secure more troops, his attention and loyalties were also engaged in the changing fortunes of Britain's two most senior military figures. In December 1915 Sir John French was replaced as C-in-C of the British Expeditionary Force by Sir Douglas Haig. In June 1916 the great Kitchener, since 7 August 1914 Britain's Secretary of State for War, was drowned at sea. In very different ways the fortunes of war dramatically determined the fates of both men.

At the beginning of the battle for Loos, French would not have supposed, even in his wildest imaginings, it would drag on until early November, cost the British almost 50,000 casualties and him his command. Loos was intended as a subsidiary assault. In Champagne, four French armies would make the main thrust while the British, attached to a fifth French army commanded by Foch, would assault Arras across the plain of Loos. Kitchener would have preferred the proposed British action postponed for another year, but the French strongly hinted if denied their battle, they might abandon the struggle and seek an independent, negotiated peace. Kitchener thought the French plan unlikely to succeed. However, a failed offensive seemed to him a better diplomatic and political prospect than the fatal rupture of Anglo-French relations. Even if it meant suffering heavy losses, the British were instructed to do everything they possibly could to help the French.[1]

Joffre had recommended Loos as 'particularly favourable ground for attack'. Sir John never favoured it unconditionally but as the time for battle approached grew ever more optimistic. He discounted the strong German defences although he could not altogether ignore the formidable obstacles his infantry would have to face. Yet it was anxiety about retaining his command that weighed most in French's scale of priorities. His insecurity was fuelled by a paranoid distrust of Kitchener. Haig could scarcely believe French feared K's presence might undermine his own position.[2] French's kitchen cabinet fed his fears, warning him a growing number of influential critics were losing faith in him. They instanced a recent investiture at which the king had been overheard to condemn French for his 'most unsoldier-like dealings with *The Times*, Repington and Northcliffe'. Clearly the king had 'lost confidence in the Field Marshal'.[3]

Loos had seemed to afford Sir John another opportunity to rehabilitate himself after his most recent debacle. Despite the presence of accredited war correspondents, the public had not been informed French's army had suffered twice as many casualties as the Germans.[4] Repington professed himself perplexed by the 'unbelievable ignorance of the people'. He cited an 'intelligent man of good class' who believed the Serbians would beat the Germans, Allied troops would be in Constantinople in ten days, and on the western front supposed nothing stood between the British army and Germany. Repington angrily insisted 'the country had been chloroformed by the Censorship'.[5] Accurate reports that would have provided the public with better, more honest assessments were silenced. Silence would have been an appropriate fate for the work of some correspondents, he admitted. Hilaire Belloc he considered a particularly insidious false prophet whose wild optimism in *Land and Water* regularly misled the country.[6]

Haig frequently complained about journalists and chose to deride *The Times* Military Correspondent in particular. Repington, he professed, 'deduced his military lessons from gossip'. It was true Repington positively encouraged others to tell him what they thought about the war. Leading British and French politicians, War Office officials and high-ranking officers in both services shared their secrets with him. One might say, these men more than most were privy to the war's progress and were acutely aware of the urgent need to improve the Allied performance. Such opinions were worth sounding, often worth reiterating. While he certainly valued such informants, the choice of what he might use or ignore was his. Haig would soon discover he might despise Repington, deride his military opinions and judgments to others, but he could not afford to ignore, be without or disregard his support.

Haig told his friend Rothschild, his ideal war correspondent would be 'the Bennet Burleigh type', a writer of highly coloured descriptions of no real military value, that would please ''arriet and sell the newspapers'.[7] He employed the same condescending tone to address official war correspondents at GHQ before the Battle of the Somme. Philip Gibbs, customarily never disobliging, found it difficult to swallow the C-in-C's insistence that *he* knew what was wanted; 'little stories on heroism and so forth to write up in a bright way for Mary Anne in the kitchen and the man in the street'. Not that Haig had any cause to grumble about the copy the official war correspondents forwarded to their various newspapers. Vividly written, their reports were generally based upon the experiences of individual soldiers. Invariably optimistic, there would be frequent references to an 'imminent breakthrough'. The cheerful optimism matched the assessments and prognoses issued by Haig's own staff. Correspondents never admitted to being dispirited. The unspoken rule was, whatever the outcome of any battle, never criticise the commander.

Nothing Repington ever wrote in *The Times* seemed to satisfy Haig. He complained, the wretched correspondent wrote as though he knew all there was to know about war. What Repington made abundantly clear was, he had a mind and will of his own and therefore saw no reason why he should be the kind of press poodle Haig wanted. The commander was interested only in a writer who never criticised or judged adversely because he thought it not 'within his liberty or duty when with the Armies in the Field'.[8] Repington readily recognised there was one absolute limitation upon his freedom. Any opinion he expressed should never threaten the army's safety or cause it to suffer any avoidable or unnecessary disadvantage. It was on just such an issue – the alleged consequence of a report by Repington during the Battle of Festubert – Haig would accuse and condemn him.

Accompanied by a member of French's staff, Repington had turned up at Haig's headquarters six hours after the failure of the initial infantry attack on 9 May. He asked if he might see the commander. When told neither the general nor his staff was available, Repington did not argue. He left immediately. It was twelve days later when Haig noted in his *Diary*, the previous day, an observation post at La Couture had suffered a heavy shelling. He blamed Repington for this German success. He had written in *The Times* of his 'excellent view from La Couture of the German position which we attacked'. To assume, as Haig did, a causal connection between Repington's account and the successful German bombardment was absurd. It was prompted by Haig's engrained prejudice against journalists in general but most particularly by his dislike of Repington. No correspondent, he insisted, should ever again be allowed so close to the front during active operations. When a *Daily Telegraph* special correspondent expressed the hope the rule would be relaxed, Haig repeated, 'Repington's article about our gun positions at La Couture' was sufficient reason for introducing the prohibition.[9] In Haig's mind, though in no one else's, the incident had become a stick with which to threaten the press but particularly to belabour Repington. Twice after his accreditation as a war correspondent, William Beach Thomas was reminded of Repington's article, and on both occasions Haig repeated his unfounded allegation. Beach Thomas, more familiar with writing bucolic rhapsodies than reporting wars, wrote that 'a soldier technically skilled in warfare was more likely to give away secrets' than someone like himself, who was 'not interested in the technique of war'.[10] Haig agreed. This Alice in Wonderland logic implied a correspondent with any knowledge of warfare ought never to write on the subject as he might otherwise reveal military secrets.

In October 1916 Dawson would question Haig about Repington's alleged 'give-away of a battery position'. Had he used the episode 'deliberately to hamper' the military correspondent? Haig replied, 'At the time I had not the faintest notion who had written the despatch. I acted on the urgent representation of my gunners.'[11] When it suited, Sir Douglas possessed a truly amazing capacity to dissimulate.

Who should be blamed, who held responsible for the failure at Loos, and what were the likely consequences for British High Command? These questions prompted much speculation and gossip although few knew what really had gone on behind the scenes. There were some spectacular spats that October and November in the House of Lords. French was accused of mishandling his reserves, being idle and incompetent, indulging in late-night bridge parties and entertaining ladies at GHQ. Repington paid these slanders little attention for he knew most were without any foundation, the usual noises off stage. But he acknowledged that French was all too obviously under serious siege. Not without good reason, he presumed it must be Haig who orchestrated these moves.[12] What he did not suspect was Robertson had been assigned a key part as link between Haig, the king and Stamfordham. Robertson fortunately had no need for Repington's services. The last thing he wanted him to know was that he and Haig were in cahoots. Archie Murray was equally keen to let no cats out of bags in the correspondent's presence. Then early in November he dropped a strong hint French would not remain in his command much longer. He *supposed* Sir John would be replaced by Haig. All the while Haig insisted he 'had been more than loyal to French'. What was more, he had done his best 'to stop all criticism of him and his methods'. Most reluctantly, eventually he had been persuaded it would 'not be fair to the Empire to retain French in command'. These weasel words concerning Haig's sentiments and actions could not have been more palpably false. It had been he who led the conspiracy against French, openly discussing with his subordinate commanders Sir John's supposed incompetence. Scarcely surprisingly, soon there was not a corps commander who retained any confidence in French's military abilities. Robertson told Haig he agreed with his judgment and knew what he had to do now.[13] These words particularly pleased Haig. They would help to ensure his hands would appear unsoiled by any hint of him plotting against French.

206 The war years, 1914–1918

Repington realised there was little he could do to save Sir John's command but perhaps he might queer Haig's pitch. Commenting on 'the rumours of impending change in the command of our armies in France', he insisted to Bonar Law, 'It is not in the public interest to appoint Haig as C-in-C. He is a staff officer and is not and never will be a commander.' Haig had anticipated this criticism.[14] Repington assured the Unionist leader, his judgment was not hasty, but based upon years of careful observation in peace and war. The one incontrovertible truth was, 'Haig possesses no talent for command.' Repington borrowed and elaborated Paget's earlier assertion there were too many cavalry generals in a war which 'mainly concerned other arms'. But Haig was not simply another cavalry officer, he was 'the one to whom the losses and disappointments of Neuve Chapelle, Festubert and Loos were owed'. This last, most damaging assertion was made as boldly as if it were a notorious commonplace. Until this point in Haig's career, his generalship had been subject to scarcely any serious scrutiny or criticism. Repington's criticism did not lack substance, nor was he wide of the mark. But at this stage nothing could have sunk or weakened Haig's claim to succeed to French's command. Politically his position was absolutely watertight.[15]

Haig lacks 'the great qualities of character needed in a Commander in Chief', Repington insisted, but had to admit that among the likely contenders 'the Wellington type' was impossible to find. Allenby came nearest, 'but he too is from the cavalry'. Smith-Dorrien undoubtedly possessed the character for high command, but falling foul of French's jealousy had been replaced for no good reason by Plumer. He said no more of Plumer, his silence eloquent testimony to his poor opinion of 'Plum's' fitness. Of the younger cohort, Cavan and Gough were the best. That left Robertson and Murray, whom he 'admired and trusted greatly' but both were 'best kept in their present positions'. That brought him back to French. 'I know of no one who excels him in the qualities of character needed in high command.'[16] From the beginning he had known he was almost certainly pleading a hopeless cause. Bonar Law had advertised previously how little he admired Sir John's military qualities. Repington could read as well as any other man what was so plainly written on the wall, yet clung as long as he decently might to the hope that something would yet turn up to save his friend. Three days later, after a conversation with Archie Murray, he wrote, 'Apparently the fate of Sir John still hangs in the balance.' He was whistling in the dark. The best hope remaining was not that French might retain his command, but that Robertson would succeed him as C-in-C.[17]

The news Haig would replace French was not made public until 17 December. For the better part of a month Repington, fearing the worst, had no idea of the real march of events concerning French's fate. Haig had thoroughly outmanoeuvred him. For someone normally so well informed, it is difficult to believe Repington was kept in total ignorance. Callwell made it abundantly clear, most of the soldiers involved were neither discreet nor secretive.[18] A number of other perplexing issues troubled Repington, most particularly the Balkans and the Middle East. Probably he felt it best to keep his powder dry rather than waste any more upon what by then was clearly a lost cause.

On 23 November Esher had been summoned by Asquith to deliver the ukase to the notoriously irascible French. He would be told to tender his resignation 'on the grounds of his age and fatigue'. French took the news better than Esher had expected. However, his initial sweet reasonableness belied his later attempts to avoid becoming 'Lord Sent-Homer', to name his successor as C-in-C, and mortally wound Kitchener. In these endeavours he failed but succeeded in making his dismissal embarrassing and disagreeable rather than dignified, as Asquith had intended.[19] French's fate cut Repington deeply. His angry despair was made replete by Cecil Bingham's description of the farewell the 19th Hussars gave French at Boulogne. When Sir John finally shook hands with him, Bingham had been too overcome to say anything.[20]

The next day Repington visited Sir John at 94 Lancaster Gate to hear French relate his version of what had happened. He described a series of good-humoured meetings, first with Esher, then Asquith. The Prime Minister made apparent his wish he should take command at home, where he could sort out the present state of chaos and more conveniently afford the Cabinet the benefit of his military advice. At this moment Kitchener made a most unwelcome intrusion upon the scene. His return from his Eastern peregrination was quite unexpected. Sir John insisted, it had been at this juncture Walter Long advised him, were he to resign at that precise moment it would be the greatest help to the Prime Minister. This, French claimed, had been the overwhelming consideration that had prompted his action. Asquith *really* wanted him to sort out home defence. Yet Repington could not help noticing, French seemed uncertain about some aspects of the job he was due to start in just two days. Repington had pointed out to his readers in mid December that home defence was 'a real job'. It included not only the defence of London but the whole of England from aerial attack. Other duties included organising the nation's defences to withstand German invasion. Long overdue, the appointment would be no sinecure although, so long as the British army remained undefeated in France, French took the threat of invasion rather less seriously than Repington.

Six weeks elapsed before Repington again called by Horse Guards. Sir John was about to metamorphose into Viscount French of Ypres. He occupied the same set of rooms as when he was Inspector General. The feeling of déjà vu was inescapable. French looked 'uncommonly well', altogether better than a month earlier when life had been difficult. He cursed London's 'damnable atmosphere', polluted as it was by 'perpetual political intrigues, lies and squabbles'. He longed to hear again the sound of the guns. He admitted to Repington he had toyed momentarily with the notion it might have been better had he put an end to his life while still in France. But now, he was getting on with the work of reorganisation. Asquith was 'most kind' to him but other influences – he named no names – were 'very hostile'. His time was taken up, 'not with fighting the Germans so much as the Home Office, Treasury and the War Office Finance Branch'.[21]

French never spoke to Repington of Haig, but Kitchener featured frequently. Lord K had been in France for four days, although he could not imagine why K should go there. He complained of the inaccurate figures of troop numbers Kitchener supplied – a 50 per cent overestimate of the number fit to fight.[22] Nothing Kitchener did pleased French.

When Repington met Churchill, Churchill confirmed how well Robertson was doing but spoke without enthusiasm about Haig. Repington did not disagree; he merely wondered 'whether [they] would find anyone better'. When it came to 'the sacred fire of leadership', both concurred, 'French was unsurpassed as a commander'. Haig's proper place would have been as French's chief staff officer. The soldiers in France had not forgotten their lost leader, but 'Lord French of Wipers' was inescapably yesterday's man.

Two months before French's fate had been settled, Cabinet members agreed, Kitchener's departure from the War Office was an urgent priority. He could not avoid responsibility for his part in the disastrous battle of Loos, for it was he who had sanctioned the British army's involvement. The heavy losses once more concentrated minds upon conscription, the most contentious issue dividing the political parties. Because of his colossal influence with the public, pro-conscription Unionists looked to Kitchener to support them in their demands. He, however, remained loyal to Asquith, who supposed the demand premature. The wrath engendered by Unionist frustration fell upon Kitchener, who made matters more difficult with his aloof, unnecessarily secretive behaviour. Those who had initially most enthusiastically advocated he be made Secretary of State for War now made no secret of their disillusion and disappointment. He had taken on much too great a burden and seemed unable to comprehend the impossibility of doing everything himself. His failures emphasised his inability to delegate. An autocrat, he reduced the General Staff to nonentities, their only function to rubber stamp with obsequious regularity his inscrutable and increasingly capricious decisions. As for his Cabinet colleagues, he never found them congenial companions and considered it 'repugnant to reveal military secrets to twenty-three gentlemen with whom I am barely acquainted'.[23]

To avoid an unseemly contretemps, Asquith suggested Kitchener decamp to the Near East as C-in-C of all British land forces other than those in France. He refused. Nor would he accept the alternatives suggested by Lloyd George: to be Indian Viceroy (since 1910, Hardinge's appointment), C-in-C Home Forces (soon to be French's new appointment), or, finally, C-in-C in France (then French's but soon to be Haig's post). Kitchener insisted he remain the Secretary of State for War. It took the wily Asquith to persuade him to visit the Dardanelles to report upon that desperately problematic campaign. It was a clever ploy to get him out of the way that would please everyone yet not displease Kitchener himself who would retained the War Office. Asquith acknowledged, he had 'avoided the supersession of K as War Minister but attained the same result'.[24]

Kitchener had scarcely left England on his way to the Dardanelles when Repington made the first of frequent references to him in his *Diary*. He seemed to know an endless series of contacts all eager to impart relevant information concerning the 'banished' warlord. He had only to lunch at Prince's with a former mistress and she would happen to have met a member of the Egyptian Service who not only could reveal all Indian troops in France, other than the cavalry, were off to Mesopotamia the following week, but also that Kitchener had set out for the Eastern Mediterranean the previous Thursday, probably would winter in Cairo and remain there. Three days later Repington met Arthur Lee at the Ministry of Munitions. They got on well with one another for they shared as many friends as prejudices. Of particular and immediate relevance was their conviction that the Salonika and Dardanelles campaigns were disasters. Lee thought Asquith had been 'very astute the way he had unloaded Kitchener'. He doubted whether he would ever return to the War Office. Lee was 'contemptuous' of the way Kitchener had administered or rather failed to administer that department.[25]

Assessing the likelihood of Kitchener's return, Repington noted Lee had seemed uncommonly well informed. He had insisted the War Office was deeply relieved at K's absence. Kitchener knew he had failed. Another failure in the Mediterranean would see him try to get India. Repington immediately recognised this last assertion as no more than a hunch. 'Who really knew what the Sphinx thought or meant?' Only this much was certain. If the Cabinet had its way, Kitchener's return would be prevented if at all possible. He reflected upon the 'astonishing' difference between the general public's assessment of Kitchener and that of 'those behind the scenes'. It would be as well to remember Derby's reservation that it would be a 'most terrible mistake' not to acknowledge the influence and prestige Kitchener's name continued to inspire. Derby had been more critical of Lord K than Repington had expected, although he appreciated Derby aspired to the War Office, an aspiration Repington doubted would ever be fulfilled. Derby's independence and frankness was disliked by too many ministers. If Lloyd George did not want the post he could think of no one better to replace Kitchener than Derby, but it would not be wise to advocate his appointment. He thought to himself, far better to see how things worked out without any interference from the Fourth Estate. It remained as uncertain as ever just how the conundrum of K's future would be resolved.

A visit to Northcliffe occasioned an unexpected chat with Churchill, who was about to depart for France and his brigade. He avowed he was glad to shed his political burden. He was not just critical of Kitchener; he was 'disposed to put down most of the misfortunes of the war to him'. When it came to his own reputation, Churchill was neither careless nor uncomplaining. While he was absent from Parliament he desired Northcliffe's newspapers should 'treat him in a gentlemanly way'. Repington saw no reason why that wish would not be fulfilled. Churchill then talked about the Dardanelles and urged operations there should continue. Repington thought he discerned 'less conviction in his voice than formerly'. Could it be that now he was no longer a member of the War Council, Winston accepted his less fortunate colleagues would be in a mess when the Salonika adventure ended in grief?[26]

A few days later, a dinner party at the Beresfords afforded Repington the ideal opportunity to talk with Carson, and more particularly Bonar Law, about personalities and the conduct of the war. Both politicians were 'very critical of K'.[27] Subsequently Repington expanded his ideas on Kitchener in a considered letter to the Conservative leader. He wrote that he had learned of some 'mad schemes'. He knew Kitchener of old and warned, 'I tell you frankly you must control him.' He should be given 'explicit instructions', a good staff with naval and Allied representation and 'ordered to work through his staff, all orders written and copies kept'. Kitchener would hate these restrictions and would not obey them unless told he must. Anyone could be chosen to undertake the fighting so long as it was not Kitchener. Instead, after wintering at the Cairo Agency, he should 'spin his webs all over the Middle East ... he knows the country like the palm of his hand ... in general he will make things warm for the

Turks and be in his element'.[28] Repington's letter identified many of the great man's faults but did not hide his admiration of K's heroic stature, his influence and prestige with the public, his independence, honesty and dominance over strategic thinking, so obviously demonstrated in July 1915 at Calais. Initially Kitchener had argued for a standstill in the west while a breakthrough was sought in the Dardanelles. Joffre had ignored this agreement and continued to plan his offensive in Champagne. In August Kitchener visited Joffre. The lack of progress in Gallipoli and German success in Poland persuaded Kitchener to change his strategic priorities, even though in doing so he alienated the affections of Lloyd George and Churchill. They thought he had deferred to Joffre. He contemptuously rebutted their simplistic hypothesis by reminding them of a great and unavoidable truth: 'Unfortunately we have to make war as we must and not as we would like.'

Repington had sought a meeting with Kitchener's old enemy Curzon. He had hoped to learn if the absent war minister would remain in the Mediterranean or return to London. Instead, he learned something entirely unexpected. In order to secure his tenancy of the War Office and thwart any aspirant to his portfolio, Kitchener had absconded with the seals of his office.[29] Curzon, always more interested in his own prospects than those of others, declared, a posting to either the Foreign or War Office would not come amiss. Either would suit his particular administrative gifts better than his present employment as Lord Privy Seal. He acknowledged Asquith was more likely to reward a political friend. Should Kitchener go, he thought Lloyd George his most likely replacement. But within days the focus of speculation changed.

Kitchener was known to be on his way back to London and Repington wondered how he might react when he discovered his department had been cut to bits in his absence. He anticipated a 'great row'. Even the Army Council had thought the changes 'were made in a rather shabby manner behind Lord K's back'.[30] But in this instance, the correspondent was well behind events, the consequence of overindulgent socialising when staying with his cousin, Reggie Pembroke, home for a long weekend from the front. Kitchener returned on 30 November to learn the Cabinet had transferred most of the functions of the Master General of Ordnance to Lloyd George's ministry. His immediate response was to resign. Asquith refused to accept and managed to persuade Kitchener, if he resigned it would be a betrayal of his duty to the king, army and people.[31] He knew Kitchener could not refuse such an appeal. Kitchener duly agreed to remain.

Repington, attempting to establish what exactly had been Kitchener's fate, was – unusually for him – obliged to resort to nods, winks and such rumours as he could elicit at the War Office. His main sources were Hamilton and Derby. Sir Ian, smiling but still all too obviously exhausted by his Gallipoli experiences, was not an unbiased witness. He resented the way he had been treated by Kitchener. Getting troops out of him had been 'as hard as getting butter out of a dog's mouth'. Usually the soul of good humour, Hamilton had no kind words for K's lack of skill in the general management of the war. So far as he was concerned, the great warlord could go hang! Derby was all for freeing Kitchener of all War Office administration, but Repington discounted Derby's view for his vision was clouded by his ambition. Wanting the War Office as his own fief, he suggested Kitchener should be made Commander-in-Chief, and while they were doing so why not also make him head of the General Staff? 'That would not do at all', Repington insisted. 'He would never allow it to represent its views freely in Parliament.' Such thoughts, however, were no more than idle speculation. It was increasingly evident to him that 'Lord K was comfortably installed at the War Office and did not look like moving.'[32]

The man with whom Repington urgently needed to talk was Robertson. Unfortunately there had been no opportunity to discuss these matters before preparing his pre-Christmas summary for his editor. The key issue for all soldiers was control of the war's strategy. Until May 1915 strategy had been determined by Asquith, Kitchener and Churchill. From May until December there had been an indeterminate dispute between Churchill, Kitchener and Lloyd George while Asquith held the ring between the disputants. But when Haig replaced French as C-in-C in France and Robertson replaced Murray as CIGS, the army, enjoying the support of Asquith, had become the undisputed dictators of strategy. The emphasis then clearly focussed upon the western front and 'side-shows', so beloved of politicians, were disregarded. It had been unfair to tarnish Kitchener's name and reputation with the claim he had thoughtlessly and constantly frustrated the best strategic interests of the army in the name of loyalty either to the Anglo-French relationship or to Asquith. More often than not his natural inclination had been to side with the military. Repington thought it could no longer be doubted that a major preoccupation of Lloyd George, Derby and Robertson would be the 'steady and intentional undermining of Lord K's position'. The great warlord seemed destined to 'sink back tamely into the position of a civilian Secretary of State'. All his Cabinet colleagues had really wanted 'to get rid of him but no one could quite bell the cat'.[33] A conversation with Robertson early in 1916 confirmed Kitchener's powers as War Minister had been curbed and considerably hedged about, although Robertson had been obliged to moderate his first aspiration, that as CIGS he would be entirely independent. Instead, what he now preferred to do was 'range up along-side Lord K and to act with him', and to this Kitchener had agreed.

When Robertson and Repington next met, in the course of a long conversation Robertson declared he was 'fairly satisfied'. He hoped the politicians would in future leave him alone. He did not want to take part in any political moves against Kitchener, with whom he got on well. Repington said nothing.

In the months that followed Kitchener's name, which once had dominated the pages of Repington's *War Diary*, merited scarcely a single entry. At the beginning of June Repington met with Churchill at a weekend house party at Maxine Elliott's. Both men eagerly seized the opportunity to spend a wet Sunday morning dissecting the Dardanelles story. According to Winston's tale, the entire Cabinet and Balfour appeared 'to be implicated in the scheme of attack'. Inevitably Kitchener shared in the blame for the decisions. His letter of instructions to Hamilton had been 'infantile'. It seemed the warlord possessed no redeeming feature. It was then that they received the telegraphed news of Kitchener's drowning, the loss of all his entourage and almost everyone else on board the cruiser *Hampshire*. He had been on his way to meet the tsar – a tough, demanding mission he had anticipated with pleasure. His unescorted cruiser, as it scythed through mountainous seas to the west of the Orkneys, had struck a mine, foundered and almost instantly sunk. Kitchener's body would never be found. The news had not reached London until the following day, 6 June 1916.

It was three days before Repington allowed himself to make two references in his *Diary* that reflected his personal sense of loss. He attempted no formal eulogy. He recorded that Kitchener's preference had always been to work independently and this had not 'consorted with the needs of the huge syndicalism of modern war'. Kitchener had 'made many mistakes' and was notoriously not a good Cabinet man. 'His methods were not suited to democracy.' Esteemed for his courageous services to Crown and Empire, he had proved impatient, insensitive and untutored, languishing in the toils of democratic politics. Repington did not ignore entirely what had made Kitchener unique among contemporary political and military leaders. They had lost not a man but a national icon. 'A great figure, he had towered above all others in character as in inches, a firm rock amidst the raging tempest.' Those services he had rendered in the early days of the war ought not to be forgotten for they 'transcended those of all the lesser men who were his colleagues most of whom envied his popularity'.[34]

16 The Somme

Initially, Lloyd George wondered whether he should accept the War Office. Under Kitchener some of the minister's power had been ceded. He did not hesitate for long since he shared the general assumption he would enjoy 'a greater influence on the war's conduct as the Secretary of State than any other member of the Cabinet'.[1] It soon became apparent that his ministerial powers had been circumscribed. He had wanted Arthur Lee to be his Under Secretary of State, but the appointment went instead to Derby, the candidate the soldiers favoured.[2]

Repington was anxious to discover what the War Office thought of their new minister. Apparently, he was inclined 'to consult subordinates instead of the heads of departments'. That would never do. Robertson insisted strategy was his responsibility; the minister's independent views were undoubtedly a cause for concern. A particularly disconcerting rumour was that Lloyd George intended to replace Jack Cowans as QMG with Eric Geddes, a leading businessman and railway management expert. In his former ministry LG had appointed experienced, energetic businessmen to provide increased vitality and improve management skills. As this initiative had proved startlingly effective there was every reason to expect he would repeat it in his new ministry. A growing national war effort implied the increased integration of civil and military. Repington shared the soldiers' dislike of civilian infringement upon their powers. He feared for his friend's future, especially as Jack was mired in his usual trouble – 'his susceptibility to "ladies"'.[3] Repington sought an informal chat with Derby. Unlike Lloyd George, he 'knew the ways of soldiers',[4] and would understand why Cowans was irreplaceable.

Robertson had insisted he was 'in exactly the same position with LG as he had been to Lord K'.[5] The minister confirmed as much when they lunched together at the Carlton, insisting he and Robertson were getting on 'capitally'. It was particularly pleasing, the new minister averred, to have 'some good men under [him] at the War Office'. Repington advised him, 'Work through the soldiers.' Consult with them as Haldane had. They would soon eat out of his hand, but not if they were treated as one might civil servants in other departments of state. Soldiers were 'kittle cattle' – difficult, sensitive creatures – and if he did not carry them with him, he would certainly be beaten.

Repington did not presume to suggest to Lloyd George, as he had to Jack Seely, that he should run *all* his ideas past him. Instead, he advised the new minister, 'Do nothing for three months until you get to understand the machinery.' He implied there was more than sufficient time to get to know individual soldiers. But Lloyd George would soon discover the soldiers created a barrier of professional exclusiveness that shut him out. For that reason, he never managed to overthrow or weaken Robertson's power. Had he established personal links with soldiers, it would have helped him to get to know the army better.[6] Robertson would later quite incorrectly claim, as Secretary of State Lloyd George was connected 'with no measure that had any special influence on the course of the war'.[7] But the translation of Eric Geddes from business life to the service of the army in France was both significant and important.

Was the army making the best use of highly qualified civilians? This question had prompted a lively exchange between Repington and his Hampstead neighbour and friend, H. G. Wells. Repington was clear: jobs previously undertaken by soldiers ought to be retained by them rather than surrendered to so-called civilian 'experts'. Since August 1914 the army had greatly increased both in size and complexity. Never had civilian expertise been required so much as now. Repington acknowledged it would be absurd to suppose, given such an 'extraordinary improvisation, everything can go on oiled wheels or that mistakes are not made'. When men distinguished in other walks of life joined the new armies, naturally 'they expected to find places equal to those they held in their former employments'. He assured Wells, the intellectual ability that had come into the army *was* being used. That civilians *should be* employed was a large admission for Repington to make. It revealed how much and how relatively quickly he had modified his former intransigent viewpoint. He instanced no less than ten brigade commands in France that were held by non-regulars. Similarly, a large number of brigade majors at the front were non-regulars. He cited with apparent approval the names of Eric Geddes and his brother A. C. Geddes, until recently the Professor of Anatomy at Toronto University, now a Brigadier General and Director of Recruiting. He also mentioned Sir William Garnet and Sir Sam Fay, who, like Eric Geddes, were railwaymen destined between 1917 and 1919 to become Directors General of Movements and Railways. But soldiering was a hard profession; he emphasised it required a long apprenticeship. The professionals could hardly be blamed for showing a certain reluctance 'to confide the lives of their men to those who are not fully qualified to lead ... In a war like this it takes time to get the best men to the right places and much forgetfulness of one's own opinion of oneself has to be contributed to the common good.'[8] Wells valued Repington's military knowledge and sound common sense. It had obviously been a struggle before he had managed to come to terms with what was inevitable. Churchill would frequently complain of the way in which the 'old Regular army officers still have all the higher commands even when all the intelligence of the country is now in the army'. To this assertion Repington invariably would respond, 'In no profession would apprentices be at the top after two years.'[9]

During the course of his first luncheon with Repington after he became minister for war, Lloyd George had admitted he did not look forward to defending the Mesopotamian campaign.[10] Robertson, four days earlier, had let slip the campaign was 'an awful mess they could not get right'.[11] He distinguished two problem areas: logistics and relations with the Indian army. It was 'difficult to say who was responsible for the muddle', but it soon became clear that the chosen 'fall-guy' was Beauchamp Duff, since March 1914 India's C-in-C. In October Charles Monro succeeded Duff in the Indian command. His subsequent success in that command was crucial to Britain's war effort, for Indian troops constituted the Empire's principal strategic reserve. The increased power and efficiency of the Indian army enabled it to make the major contribution to General Sir Frederick Maude's successful campaign in Mesopotamia. Repington advised Lloyd George that Monro was a general with 'a good head and very dependable'. He further advised the minister to leave questions about the Indian army alone, implying it was a mystery understood best by military experts, 'full of pitfalls' for the unsuspecting civilian. This ancient military 'wisdom', by constant repetition would become very familiar to LG.

The logistical problem remained unresolved. Cowans was the one member of the General Staff capable of finding a satisfactory solution. Since becoming QMG in 1912 he had demonstrated exceptional capacity and ability as an administrator. His talents exactly fitted the particular requirements of his office. In an army and a department that traditionally thought small-scale, he had the capacity to think big. Without fuss he had rapidly expanded services ranging from food to transport and buildings. The minister readily appreciated his unique skills, and the king and a host of other influential figures found 'Jolly Jack' irresistibly likeable. His romantic adventures afforded them a never-ending source of delight. When told of Jack's latest romance, the king roared with laughter. 'They tell me he is fond of the ladies', he chortled. Lloyd George rejoined, 'I believe the

Fig. 10 Lieutenant General Sir John Cowans (1862–1921)

ladies are very fond of him.'[12] But Jack's relationship with Mrs Cornwallis-West was about to change the picture. The backbench Liberal MP and friend of Lloyd George, Sir Arthur Markham, took up the case of Sergeant Patrick Barrett, for whom, it was alleged, Cowans had improperly arranged a commission. At the behest of his elderly aristocratic would-be patron and mistress, Mrs Cornwallis-West, Barrett had been despatched to France. Markham insisted there would have to be an inquiry to determine the exact facts of the affair. Provided that he did not raise the matter in the Commons, Lloyd George guaranteed Sir Arthur should have his inquiry.

Cowans was undoubtedly shaken to learn there would be a court of inquiry. Repington raged that his friend's 'time for the next three months would be wasted over a trivial and idiotic case'. He contrasted this with the enormous demands imposed upon 'the man responsible for feeding and supplying 3,400,000 men'.[13] When Markham suddenly died it was suggested the inquiry might conveniently be dropped, but Lloyd George felt in honour bound to keep his promise. As the inquiry would be chaired by the former CIGS, Field Marshal Lord Nicholson, and one of the three other members was an army man, it was thought this might favour Cowans. F. E. Smith, however, feared the inquiry might well find against Jack. He thought 'Old Nick' showed every sign of being thoroughly contumacious.[14] The inquiry sat in private and delivered its finding to the Army Council in November. While not entirely damning, the verdict was undoubtedly damaging. Cowans was found to have behaved indiscreetly and without a proper measure of propriety. Particular exception had been taken to what he had written in some private letters. The irony was that he had voluntarily surrendered the letters so that it might not be said he had anything to conceal. Repington thought the inquiry's use of the letters grossly offensive. They had been wantonly misused. Nor was he alone in his feelings of outrage.[15]

Robertson had hinted to Repington the inquiry report might not favour Cowans. Thoroughly disquieted, Repington was already uneasy about his friend's prospects. So far as he could judge, at the War Office there seemed to be 'a regular set against Jack'. What exactly inspired this prejudice was difficult to determine. Absurdly, he began to wonder whether the aim all along had been to use the Cowans case 'to get rid of all soldiers in the QMG branch and on the Army Council and to substitute civilians'.[16] It was a measure of how worried Repington was that he should indulge in such paranoid fantasies. He finally learned what his friend's fate would be. Lloyd George angrily declared he had no alternative but to sack Cowans because the king had written to him supporting the QMG. It was not the king's business, Lloyd George angrily insisted. It had been very wrong of the king to attempt to use his influence. It left him with no alternative; the QMG would *have* to go. But as Lloyd George reflected, there was a positive aspect. It would undoubtedly make the military more wary of him and demonstrate he not only possessed the powers, if necessary he would use them to enforce his will.[17]

When all looked black for Cowans, Derby successfully stepped in to plead he should be let off with a reprimand and reduced to QMG in France alone. Derby further proposed that his other duties could be carried out by some 'great civilian'. Cowans had been told that he was being demoted because Lloyd George 'could not defend him in Parliament for having written "indiscreet private letters"'. Repington justifiably observed that in their time they had all written such letters, 'including LG and all his friends'. The official explanation was patently absurd. Repington's ubiquitous, all-knowing, 'well-placed friend' in the

War House, within twenty-four hours had quashed any idea that any 'great civilian' would materialise to undertake Jack's duties. Now that Derby was Secretary of State for War he clearly intended to be master in his own house. Derby decreed Cowans effectively would suffer no punishment.

With his career and reputation once more secured, the QMG was able to address and solve the logistical problems that had previously plagued the Mesopotamian campaign. Repington half suspected there was an intrigue and that 'political hangers-on' were still intent 'to fix their claws in the branch'. He remained fretting and fuming late into December. Perhaps it might help, he thought, if he wrote something about the QMG's work for *The Times*. He would emphasise Jack's indispensability. He also had Freddy Clayton's fate on his mind. As he had feared might be the case, he had been sacrificed.[18] Such treatment, Repington considered 'disgraceful'. Returning home Clayton sought to appeal to the king. That had been more than a month earlier but his letter was still held up at GHQ; it had not even arrived at the War Office. Repington suspected the explanation was unwonted political interference, and this strengthened his belief there must be a widespread intrigue. It did not seem to occur to him that he was allowing his imagination to run riot.

A regular village to house a thousand clerks had been built for Geddes's new branch at Montreuil. The troops called it Geddesburg. Repington made no effort to hide his contempt. He more than distrusted, he feared this civilian empire growing at the nerve centre of a great military enterprise. What exactly might it portend for the army he had known, the small, tightly knit family of regiments that had nurtured his generation of soldiers? What did it portend for a friend like Stuart Wortley?[19] He was almost certainly going to be sacked and Jack might well suffer the same fate, even though the QMG's work had been admirably done without hitch or complaint. Didn't the minister understand? Delicate machinery was 'liable to be thrown out of gear if a pack of civilians without knowledge of military affairs was dumped down to run it'.[20] Several months earlier, in one of his lunchtime conversations with Lloyd George at the Carlton, Repington had stated his objections to the replacement of soldiers by civilians. He had chosen quite the wrong moment and LG, unhappy with the military, made 'very uncomplimentary remarks about several of them'. He refused to recognise any difference between soldiers and civilians and was determined to take the best man wherever he found him.[21] Before this storm Repington judged it wisest to beat a hasty, tactical retreat.

His 'article on Cowans' great work' was published but its head and tail had been removed. Thus truncated, Repington thought it failed to serve as a warning that the efficiency of the QMG's department was threatened. Whether the cuts had been made by the Censor or in-house, he could not tell. A few days later, although he was reassured by Derby there was no longer any danger Cowans would be moved from his post, Repington continued to grumble. Soldiers had every right to look askance at the 'dispossession of some of their important functions'. He hoped his censures had caused Derby a degree of anxiety.[22] To the end of the war he would, if at all possible, resist any attempt to 'civilianise' the military, his opposition the more exaggerated because the Prime Minister so clearly had lost faith in his generals. It seemed businessmen were much more Lloyd George's cup of tea than soldiers.

It was entirely understandable that Repington should have followed the fortunes of a close colleague and friend whose military career, not for professional incompetence or failure but for indiscrete behaviour, had been placed in jeopardy. He could not have failed but be aware of the parallels as much as the disparities between the prolonged and careful inquiry into Jack's indiscretion, and his own, earlier cursory examination by Roberts and Kelly-Kenny. The most obvious difference between the two cases was the very different professional consequences suffered by the accused. He had been required to resign his commission; Jack suffered no professional penalty other than a reprimand. He was not in any way resentful but asked himself why, when his friend's offence had been so much more serious than his transgression, had Jack got away with it?

In part the question answered itself. Undoubtedly Cowans avoided the consequences of his folly because he was fortunate in his political friends. Almost scuppered by the king's well-intentioned interference, he was rescued by Derby.[23] It was also Cowans's good fortune that the last stages of the Court of Inquiry happened to coincide with the heightened political machinations and manoeuvrings over the premiership. Naturally, Lloyd George's immediate personal political prospects and the fate of the coalition government had been at the forefront of his thinking, and not what might be the appropriate disciplinary measure for Cowans. But what had counted most in his favour was that he was uniquely gifted at his job; he was virtually indispensible. To ensure and maintain adequate and speedy supplies for British forces on all fronts was a task that had grown increasingly demanding in scale, complexity and urgency. It was not a sensible time to contemplate making disturbing changes.

The proposals made by the military commanders at Chantilly in December 1915 and endorsed by their political leader shaped the intended Allied strategic pattern for 1916. The major British contribution would be the Somme offensive. The consequent evacuation of Gallipoli and concentration of effort on the western front pleased British High

Command. What it did not do was resolve a fatal irresolution at the heart of military planning. Was the offensive intended to force a breakthrough, or was it only one of a series of offensives designed to grind down the German forces? The debate remained unresolved when the Germans pre-empted everything by attacking Verdun on 21 February 1916. In the months that followed a remorseless battle of attrition developed. The French paid a fearful cost in casualties for their stubborn resistance. That June, as had been agreed earlier, the Russians began what initially appeared to be a very successful offensive against the Austrians in Galicia. The Italians, meanwhile, were once again fighting hard if inconclusively in the Trentino. All this military activity suggested, sooner rather than later, the British army would begin an offensive against the Germans.

As early as April, Haig had accepted he would need to help relieve the pressure on the French. He had argued for a small-scale offensive because the forces available to him were comparatively weak. By June, as his supplies improved, he was persuaded a large-scale effort was required provided he was given sufficient artillery and munitions to sustain it and could be certain that his troops were properly prepared. This suggested August as a possible starting date. Joffre, however, was adamant he could not wait so long. Such a delay would mean that the French army would cease to exist. The offensive should begin not later than July. The defence of Verdun had made such demands upon available French manpower they now could supply only sixteen divisions, much less than half the forty previously promised. Joffre insisted the attack should not be in Flanders, Haig's preferred choice, but north and south of the Somme.

As he had been unable to choose either the time or the place of his first major offensive as Commander-in-Chief, Haig was extraordinarily sanguine about the battle's likely outcome. For a time he sustained his familiar, deluded belief that a breakthrough was a real possibility; that the enemy would crack under pressure and he would secure a decisive victory. On the basis of Haig's previous unsuccessful promises of 'breakthrough', unsurprisingly Lloyd George was not convinced. Haig meanwhile was forced to adopt the opinion that Robertson and Joffre had shared from the beginning: essentially, the Somme would be a battle of attrition. On the first day the British sustained almost 60,000 casualties, dead, wounded and missing. This figure constituted 14 per cent of the total losses suffered in the 140 days the battle lasted. The brunt of these losses was borne by Kitchener's volunteer divisions. The seemingly endless flow of blood from both sides – the German losses were equally heavy – was finally staunched only by the mud and relentless autumnal rain.

The Somme had been in progress almost three weeks when Lloyd George met Repington at the Carlton. That day Repington had been greatly surprised the first of the articles he had written about the Somme had been returned unaltered by the GHQ censor. Naturally, their conversation largely concerned the fighting. Lloyd George was persuaded the very heavy casualties already suffered by the army meant they could not hope to be successful. He feared the Germans were likely to bring more guns and troops from the north and Verdun to the battle. Repington was obliged to admit that he shared LG's pessimism. There would be no great change until all British armies were equipped with sufficient heavy guns. He then told Lloyd George exactly what he had learned from Foch two weeks earlier.[24]

Foch attributed his success to the way he had deployed his artillery. He had used his 500 heavy guns in co-operation with field guns and trench mortars to mangle and smash to smithereens the villages of Dompierre, Fay and Estrées, which were part of the German defensive line. He had ordered his guns to fire at nothing but the first line. If he were asked to attack a position, he would no longer ask how many divisions he was to be given but only how many heavy guns. He considered each Army Corps of two divisions should have 100 heavy guns over and above the normal field guns and howitzers. The British artillery preparations had been ineffective because they were dispersed and not concentrated upon the enemy's first line. This more than any other reason accounted for the excessive losses the British had suffered. Foch had afforded Repington the opportunity to examine the German trenches recently taken by the French. Trench mortars had been used to wreck the German wire and the heavies had pounded the rest. Seventy-fives had set up a barrage to keep back reinforcements while long-range guns had counter-battered the German artillery. The devastation, Repington recorded, was 'very complete'. On an eight-mile front Foch had as many heavy guns as Luigi Cadorna, the Italian C-in-C, had for one four hundred miles long.

Lloyd George and Repington agreed, the Germans would not be beaten before 1918. So much for Haig's idea that a swift and decisive breakthrough could be achieved in 1916. The Germans were not ready to surrender so soon. Hard battles would succeed each other until eventually, their men and material wasted and exhausted, German resistance would finally be worn down. Lloyd George was convinced the grinding would proceed even better if there were not only more guns but also if Germany were compelled simultaneously to defend more areas. It was clear to Repington, this last was why the minister favoured the Salonika offensive. LG agreed with him that nothing could be done there this year 'unless Romania joined in. Then we would have to keep the Bulgars employed'. Thus, Haig's first offensive as C-in-C, the Somme, had been in progress less than three weeks when Lloyd George betrayed he was already considering other possibilities. He asked Repington, 'If there were to be a change of commander in France who would [he] choose?' Repington proposed Allenby. Lloyd George said he 'did not remember him'.[25]

Some of Foch's comments about artillery could not have failed to remind Repington of a conversation with Haig shortly after his appointment as Commander of the First Army in January 1915. At the time Repington supposed the German front was impregnable and had expressed considerable doubts over whether there was one British general sufficiently fearless or uncaring of public opinion, prepared to suffer the inevitable heavy losses if an attempt were made to breach the enemy line. Modern weapons gave an undue advantage to defences and enormous casualty lists were inevitable. Repington was convinced the public would not tolerate such losses. Haig, however, responded that given the appropriate guns, ample ammunition and high explosive he did not doubt they could easily walk through the German defences in several places.[26] Haig avoided the obvious implication of Repington's question by claiming he could find a way through without his troops having to suffer huge losses. But instead of developing his argument and pressing Haig, Repington allowed himself instead to be tempted to injure Henry Wilson. He drew attention to efforts to have Wilson appointed CIGS in Murray's place. Haig, pretending an innocent naivety in such matters, later wrote in his diary in his best maiden-aunt tones, 'Such an intrigue greatly surprised me.' His claim was nonsensical. Repington's words had reminded him Wilson possessed an unmatched capacity for intrigue. But playing the sneak also reminded Haig that Repington and Wilson were birds of a feather, the one as bad as the other.[27] Repington would have done better to have pursued his original argument and let Wilson go hang.

Foch argued that Haig had failed because unlike the French he had sought to conquer ground with his infantry, not his guns. On Saturday 8 July Repington had gone by invitation to British GHQ, north of Amiens, to meet and talk with Douglas Haig. It would be their first meeting since his appointment as Commander-in-Chief. The correspondent had hoped he might discover whether British artillery tactics were as hidebound as Foch had implied. Haig attempted to snub Repington but was thwarted. It was pointed out to him that the military correspondent of *The Times* enjoyed a political importance he could not afford to ignore. That consideration was particularly pertinent given the scale of the casualties suffered in the offensive's first week. Politicians and public alike had every right to be given an explanation by the C-in-C for these losses. Haig unwillingly and reluctantly deferred.[28] As was inevitable, the exercise was conducted in a frigid, guarded fashion. Kiggell, who since

December 1915 had been Haig's Chief of Staff, attempted to lighten the gloomy atmosphere. Occasionally he would shoot furtive smiles towards his old friend but dared to say or do very little beside. Repington was well primed for his meeting. He had spent the previous two days talking to, among others, Castelnau, Foch, Charteris, Rawlinson, who was now commanding the new Fourth Army, and a particular old Ulster friend of his, 'Putty' Pulteney.

Haig prefaced his account of their meeting in his diary with the general observation that while 'Correspondents [were] given a free pass to go anywhere and could write what they liked they should not divulge anything of value to the Enemy.' According to Repington, Haig had referred directly to 'an old telegram of mine from France of which he thought he had cause to complain'. Repington reminded Haig, his telegram had been cleared by the Censor. To judge by Kiggell's reaction, this was news to him. Haig gave a brief exposition of how the battle had progressed so far – effectively saying nothing – before announcing he would welcome criticisms. But when Repington suggested the artillery could possibly have been deployed more effectively on the first day of the offensive, Haig bluntly denied there could be any truth in the suggestion. The manner of his response, indeed, his whole defensive demeanour, clearly demonstrated how much he resented the least criticism. Repington did not pursue the matter for Haig was clearly unprepared to talk about any substantive issue of real interest. Repington was left 'with the strong feeling that the tactics of July 1 had been bad'. At the end of their meeting he wrote, 'I don't know which of us was more glad to be rid of the other.' Mutual antipathy was probably the only sentiment both men shared. Repington bumped into Esher as he left GHQ. He refused to say what he thought about his briefing with Haig. He wanted to see the rest of the front for himself and gather more information. That task occupied him for the next two days. What he saw and what he was told served to confirm the opinions he already held.

Before a luncheon conversation with Lloyd George on 19 September, Repington spoke to French twice and also to Robertson. Apparently 'Wully' was 'pretty happy' with the way things were progressing on the Somme. Repington noted how Robertson seemed inclined to skate swiftly over negative but nonetheless significant issues. They had suffered a third more casualties than the Germans. They had insufficient heavy guns, although Robertson said he was certain there would be enough by November. The numbers for drafts were standing up well; 58,000 trained men had been sent out and 15,000 were standing by. He saw Haig every two or three weeks; not that he interfered, but it afforded an opportunity to discuss broader issues. Robertson thought the war would continue well into 1917, but insisted the British army and their Allies were doing well. Repington spoke of the failed attacks by VII, VIII and X Corps on the first day of the Somme, but was careful to describe them as 'a very glorious failure'. He judged that the generals had done their best. He would deplore it if it were thought fit to punish them. His conversations with French served only to reveal the former C-in-C's increasingly pessimistic outlook. He told Repington they had just learned from the War Office that the losses by Saturday 15 July had exceeded 100,000. Did Repington think the game any longer worth the candle? He compared losses and gains with those at Loos to the Somme's considerable disadvantage. At this rate, he concluded, he did not think they could win. Repington agreed. French pressed him to speak with Lloyd George.[29] But after their 19 July meeting it was another three months before Repington and Lloyd George met again for an extended post-luncheon conversation about the war. Then the Somme was about to reach its inconclusive, temporary ending, the taking of the Redan Heights on 19 November. In the intervening weeks much happened to shape the future relationship of Lloyd George and Haig. Then, in the first week of December, the Secretary of State for War replaced Asquith as Prime Minister.

On 29 July Robertson had sent a note to Haig pointing out that the 'Powers that be' were growing increasingly restless. If the loss of 300,000 men could not guarantee really great results, ought they not to be satisfied with something less? If the primary object of the exercise had been the relief of pressure on Verdun, was that not already achieved? In the course of his long reply justifying himself and his strategy, Haig insisted that they must continue to maintain their offensive. His defiant explanation and rationale was that losses were not significantly greater than if there had been no offensive. He calculated that July's fighting had cost *only* 120,000 extra losses and repeatedly insisted the rising casualty count alone could not be 'regarded as sufficient to justify any anxiety as to our ability to continue the offensive'.[30]

Churchill for one was not impressed by this argument. Recently Repington had seen much of him. Churchill had always been against the Somme offensive; had pronounced from the first day it 'would come to no good'. He claimed to know exactly what was going on and why the British army had suffered such heavy losses – a pretty big claim even by Churchillian standards. At the next vote of credit he intended to comment on how the war was being conducted. He wished to consult with Repington beforehand. When the military correspondent attended the Commons on 1 August, Churchill showed him the memorandum. It would be fathered by F. E. Smith. Well written and highly critical,

Repington observed, there was nothing in it to which he took exception. However, he failed to see what useful purpose it would serve.

Next day Repington dined with French. Sir John was 'in his best bantam-cock form' and apparently intent upon striking at Robertson. Repington pleaded with the Field Marshal to acknowledge Robertson had a difficult hand to play. So long as Haig remained C-in-C, he was obliged to support him. It was not in the country's interest for the C-in-C and the CIGS to quarrel. '"Ah!" said French, "you used to say the same thing to me about Kitchener when I did not get on with him."' It was one of those occasions when Repington was only too glad of Brinsley Fitzgerald's presence to help him calm the hopelessly irascible Field Marshal. Repington admired French, as he did Churchill. Boldness, dash, indomitability and magnanimity of spirit more than compensated for their undoubted faults. Repington found himself persuaded by Robertson's assertion there were 'a great too many people buzzing about trying to interfere with and run the war . . . We were under a mutual obligation to go on; we could not tell Paris we have had enough and meant to stop . . . The best thing to do was not to give way to the busy bodies.' Repington considered Robertson's opinion 'very sound'. For that reason, he told him, although the recent corrections made to his article on the Somme by the Censor at GHQ were 'dishonest', the war was 'too big for [him] to trouble about such trifles at present'. Robertson merely repeated his earlier assertion: 'The great thing is to win the war; nothing else matters.'[31]

Northcliffe, in the *Daily Mail*, 'in a vein of awe-struck reverence',[32] had claimed, 'The doings of the army are put before the world each day with the frankness that is part of Sir Douglas Haig's own character. He is opposed to secrecy.'[33] This monumentally absurd claim was soon contradicted by Northcliffe's brother, Rothermere. Dining with Lloyd George the evening after the Cabinet had seen Churchill's damning memorandum, he insisted that the Somme offensive was a failure, a simple, dreadful truth withheld to delude the public and mislead his host. Rothermere insisted the communiqués he received were 'full of lies, lies, lies!'[34]

The following week Lloyd George paid a lightning two-day visit to France. He scarcely found a moment for Haig. Fred Maurice, who had accompanied him, told Repington all about it when, a few days later, they met to dine at the Savoy. Maurice had been greatly amused by Lloyd George's enthusiastic description to the House of his first visit to the front. From his account it might have been supposed 'he had been everywhere and seen everything'. He had certainly left a favourable and optimistic impression with the soldiers. What truly surprised Charteris, who had anxiously monitored the Welshman's progress, was his apparent lack of concern about the casualty figures.[35] Had this, he wondered, truly reflected the minister's frame of mind?

As Repington discovered when he called at Horse Guards, one man who was not prepared to change his mind was French. The Field Marshal believed the army had by now lost more than 200,000 men. Facing ruin, it had failed to gain any compensatory advantage.[36] Visiting the War Office on 6 September, Repington hoped to see Lloyd George but instead learned the minister had left for Paris two days before insisting that the Somme offensive was all wrong and that more troops should instead be sent to Salonika. Repington saw no reason why there should be any change of plan at this late date. Admittedly Haig's tactics had at first been not only bad, but expensive. They had, however, improved. There was no real alternative now but to go on and no point in sending more men to Salonika when 'they could only come from France and the Somme'. If Sarrail could do nothing with 400,000 men, why give him more? Repington bewailed 'a tomfool expedition that had cost so many lives uselessly'.[37] He had learned from two old school friends, 'Fatty' Wilson and 'Bockus' Nicol, more than half their strength was down with dysentery and malaria. It would be fair to say that matters turned out very much as Repington had forecast from the beginning.

Meanwhile, on his second, extended tour to France, the series of questions Lloyd George asked Foch really set the cat among the pigeons. He had clearly not forgotten his earlier conversation with Repington, who had emphasised the superiority of Foch's tactics over those of Haig. LG knew that he could not hope to get a detailed response either from Haig or any of his commanders. As Secretary of State he was their nominal head, but they, like the CIGS, were more Haig's men than his. In the circumstances Lloyd George thought it not unreasonable to question an Allied general who had enjoyed success on that disastrous first day of the Somme when the British had suffered so many casualties. He wanted to know why the British had taken fewer prisoners and why they had occupied less ground and at a much higher cost in killed and wounded than the French. As the responsible British minister surely he had a right to be told the truth? Lloyd George was about to learn an important and significant lesson: professional loyalty among soldiers extended to allies. Foch, sensing that Haig could find himself in trouble, had instinctively returned cagey responses to the politician's eager interrogatories. He insisted he did not know the answer. He reminded the Secretary of State the British troops were green and untried whereas his had been veterans. These had not been the answers Lloyd George wanted to hear.

Next day, at Lee's suggestion, he posed the same questions to Henry Wilson. Though the most political of the British generals, as a soldier he instinctively felt a loyalty to fellow senior officers. He returned the same answers as had Foch – that the British 'troops and artillery were new to the game'.[38] Soldiers were never more aware of their brotherhood-in-arms than when threatened by politicians. Haig wrote in his diary, 'I would not have believed that a British Minister could have been so ungentlemanly as to go to a foreigner and put such questions regarding his subordinates.'[39] The CIGS said he would confront Lloyd George but Haig advised him to let the matter drop. Nevertheless, he made it his business to see news of the politician's faux pas was widely publicised. As a result, Gwynne's *Morning Post* threatened Lloyd George. Should he ever repeat his gaffe, the *Post* would reveal exactly what had happened. Lloyd George responded by praising the British army and its generals and denying he had done anything that exceeded his legitimate sphere of activity.[40] Politician, editor and generals were all behaving in character.

Scarcely contained, anger bubbled beneath the masks of friendship and camaraderie so readily assumed for the public stage. In private they did not seek to disguise their differences. Robertson told Repington in confidence, he was expected to give so much time to Lloyd George he found it increasingly difficult to give his whole mind to his key task, defeating Hindenburg. Could they not 'all be pals and work together'? That, Robertson acknowledged, was a pious, unrealisable hope considering the personalities, the stubborn determination, the self-righteousness of the characters involved. He vowed he would try to 'go on quietly in his own way, stick to his own job and brook no interference in his sphere'. But, he admitted, Lloyd George had tested that resolve more than once. 'I am a poor man,' he told Repington, 'but that makes me no less determined to resign if my advice is not followed.' And there was reason for hope and optimism, Robertson admitted. 'On compulsion, LG had been splendid. He fought like a tiger, even for compulsion in Ireland.'[41]

When Repington next enjoyed a long conversation with Lloyd George, he noted the politician was in good form. But frustration with the military lay not far below the surface and soon would be revealed dramatically. LG proudly told his mistress, he had 'triumphed over the soldiers' at the previous day's meeting of the War Committee. An earlier decision had been reversed and two divisions would now be sent to Romania. The lesson he drew from this was that 'Soldiers respect nothing so much as power. This [would] considerably strengthen his influence and his prestige among them.'[42] Yet, he admitted to Repington, he was more dissatisfied than for a long time with the general state of affairs. What did Repington think? Did he see a way to winning the war? How would he propose to achieve it? The correspondent was not the least disobliged to be questioned thus. His immediate response was to pose a question of his own: 'What exactly did Lloyd George mean by "winning the war"?'

Soldiers and politicians notoriously offered very different answers to that seemingly innocuous question. The antipathy both groups felt for each other undoubtedly coloured their exchanges, but the real stumbling block was when either party spoke of 'winning the war'. Identical words concealed real differences, ambiguities, confusions. Lloyd George unhesitatingly asserted the war would be won if the Germans were thrust out of France and Belgium. Repington's response was that to win any war, as Hindenburg had said, was 'a question of the strongest will-power ... in the language of the Prize Ring, to keep on punching'. Even to '*win the war in the ordinary way*' (my emphasis) would require 'a very much greater superiority of force than we possess'. At present, enjoying a numerical advantage of perhaps six to five in the west, they needed to be stronger '*to annihilate the enemy*' (my emphasis). For soldiers, the enemy was Germany and the western front the only place where the war could and would be settled. The fundamental strategic aim therefore, in France and Flanders, was to inflict a crushing defeat upon German arms so great that the Germans would never again attempt to seek a position of world dominance. The inevitable consequence was a war of attrition. The German army would be brought to its knees by inflicting more losses upon it than it could inflict upon the Allies. Robertson had adopted this strategy reluctantly and with no great certainty. He had grave reservations about the dependability of France and Russia as allies. But, he confessed, he could see nothing better. He stuck to it instinctively rather than for any convincing reason in its favour.[43] Haig had arrived at the same conclusion more by accident than design. He was slowly obliged to admit (despite the advantage of inspiration courtesy of Napoleon and his dead brother Geordie, kindly supplied in the letters of his sister Henrietta), that the way to victory would inevitably be paved by hecatombs of dead and mutilated infantry. That was the sufficient, awful, human sacrifice and the necessary consequence of his strategic planning. Initially this was hidden from him by his lack of imagination and his unrealistic optimism.

Lloyd George complained to Repington it was his experience that commanders 'only concerned themselves with their special fronts. They were unable to take broad views.' He expressed considerable doubts whether they could continue to 'get sufficient men to carry on'. Repington admitted it was 'not very encouraging'. At this point in their conversation the minister suddenly and vehemently declared it simply was not good enough that everyone should be 'asked to keep silent and bow the knee to the military Moloch'. He was not prepared to remain perpetually quiescent. He was the Secretary of State for War. His was the responsibility. He would have to accept the blame. Therefore, 'He meant to have his own way.'[44]

Repington appeared shocked by this outburst, although why he should have been is difficult to understand. Earlier, warned by Robertson of the latent antagonism between Lloyd George and the High Command, Repington noted it was 'even deeper than R suspected'. How could he have forgotten that exactly the same issue had been rehearsed only a fortnight earlier?[45] Robertson had asked Repington what he thought of a letter of resignation he had drafted as CIGS. He was no longer prepared to have his military opinions constantly opposed at the War Committee. Lloyd George, who had long wanted to exploit the Salonika front, had argued that a small extra effort there compared with the vast expenditure of men and munitions on the Somme would reap the considerable dividend of a victory over the Bulgars and turn events to Allied advantage in Romania. Lloyd George made it clear to Robertson, he, like any other member of the War Committee, was free to take his own line on strategic thinking. He would not be a dummy, 'a part for which I am not in the least suited'. He was not prepared 'merely to advocate the opinions of my military advisers'. Robertson and LG knew very well their argument was not about strategic choice so much as about their relative powers as Secretary of State for War and CIGS. Robertson's authority was entrenched by an Order in Council. That considerably out-trumped Lloyd George. The minister could be as sarcastic as he liked, but the CIGS won hands down.[46] The Chancellor of the Exchequer, Reggie McKenna, no friend of Lloyd George, claimed 'LG was silenced and overshadowed by Robertson who was the real Minister of War.' LG was 'effectively an extinct volcano'. Repington did not believe that, even for a moment.[47] He neverthess valued McKenna, who was generally a reliable and generous source.

LG, with a fine show of simulated self-righteousness, accused Robertson of divulging secrets to the press. He knew the general regularly spoke to Repington, but the military correspondent was usually careful not to divulge in *The Times*, 'anything that any competent observer could not have reconstructed from conversations in clubs and current rumours'.[48] The responses to Lloyd George's views on strategy that he recorded in his *War Diaries* are much more muted, even open-minded than those he had published in *The Times*. He admitted there was 'a need to discard all the baggage of our earlier learning and teach ourselves anew in the light of our new experiences. We should not allow ourselves to be hampered by anything.' He even went so far as to agree heartily with Lloyd George's criticism that 'the soldiers should have made better plans when Romania entered the war'. But in *The Times*, for months he had disdainfully dismissed all politicians' strategic choices as inept. He had slammed the way politicians harassed, hampered and interfered with military matters. 'Their common denominator is a complete ignorance of the principles of strategy.'[49] Seeking to please, he had told Northcliffe of one piece of presumption perpetrated by the Secretary of State. This had prompted the proprietor to storm down to the minister's office and leave a message warning Lloyd George, if he continued to interfere with strategy then he, Northcliffe, would 'expose it both in the House of Lords and in his own newspapers'.[50]

From time to time all parties to the debate had behaved badly, but no episode was worse than when Lloyd George, in early October, sent Field Marshal Lord French to question the French high command about their artillery techniques. On his return French was to report directly to Lloyd George and not to the CIGS. Le Roy Lewis, the British military attaché to the Paris embassy, informed Repington, French's commission was not intended to be complimentary or helpful to Haig. Repington said and wrote nothing. He was never more eloquent than when he chose to keep silent. He knew Johnny French's trip on Lloyd George's behalf did no favours for anyone. Lloyd George achieved nothing other than create more frustration.

In effect, the Secretary of State for War had despatched the former British C-in-C to provide him with the means 'to tell tales against Haig and his command'.[51] Even to a Field Marshal, Foch refused to provide the required evidence to compromise the British high command. This distrust and duplicity were never admitted in the public record. Instead, Derby told the Lords in late November (an ironic if not farcical prelude to Lloyd George's removal to 10 Downing Street), 'We have a combination which cannot be equalled much less improved.'[52] It did not matter the claim was nonsense or that it was 'the opposite of what Lloyd George believed'.[53] He thought Haig neither a competent strategist nor a big man, though he was prepared to admit he was a good fighter. If possible he thought even less of Robertson. Derby's claim did reflect a greater truth; that LG, despite his most strenuous efforts to resist, had been bested by the military, and it was they who determined Britain's military effort should remain concentrated on the western front.

The Battle of the Ancre, the last futile stage of the Somme offensive, was largely a knock-down battle of wills, a consequence of the mutual mistrust and ill-feeling between the frocks and the brass hats. Repington acknowledged that Haig decided to have 'one more smack at the Germans' because he supposed 'LG was still such a dangerous factor'.[54] There is scarcely anything in the *Diaries* about the bloody confrontation on the Ancre. He did note, almost off-handedly, 'We had more guns with Gough's attack than on the whole Somme front on July 1', and that 'Gough accounted for 20,000 to 30,000 Germans'.[55] Between 13 and 18 November, at a cost of more than 20,000 casualties, Gough's Fifth Army, before they were bogged down in mud and slime, secured the ruins of Beaumont Hamel and Beaucourt, villages originally planned to be secured on the first day of the Somme. This victory – an 'advance' of 2 kilometres – was achieved four and a half months later than originally planned. It assured Haig would get his way at the Chantilly Anglo-French conference. There, all the military leaders concurred that 'The old strategy should be continued'. Repington judged it 'the best conference yet . . . We shall press on in the west after a delay for training and repairs'.[56]

Long before Beaumont Hamel and Beaucourt, Repington had been concentrating upon the question Haig had chosen to beg in their January 1915 meeting, as had Lloyd George in their meeting of July 1916. How were sufficient men to be recruited and trained[57] to fill the drafts until Germany was finally wasted, exhausted and beaten? Matters grew worse, not better when Asquith's intended National Service Bill for men from 16 to 60 years of age was cut short by Lloyd George's assumption of the purple. Any measure Lloyd George could bring in would not begin to produce trained men until June or July at the earliest. Repington was planning a whole series of articles on the subject for *The Times*. Not cheered by his early experience of the mercurial Welsh prime minister, Robertson provided Repington with a very gloomy picture. All LG wanted, apparently, was 'a quick victory, a victory while you wait. He does not care where so long as opinion will be impressed.' Robertson suggested Beersheba might be a better bet than Damascus. LG did not think that Beersheba would catch on, but Jerusalem might. Repington sardonically summed up the whole issue in his diary: 'So this is War Cabinet strategy at the close of 1916. If we can win on it we can win on anything.'[58]

1 7   Repington leaves *The Times*

In October 1916 Repington prepared a long memorandum. It recorded his
'real opinion of the war'. He claimed that during Dawson's absence the
assistant editor 'prevented him expressing it in *The Times*'.[1] It analysed the
Somme offensive, then in its fourth month, and the campaigns in Russia,
Romania, Bulgaria, Salonika, Egypt and Mesopotamia. Repington
favoured 'continuing the offensive in the West throughout the winter.
Any spare resources should be employed to help Russia. The strict mini-
mum of troops required to hold the enemy should be maintained in Egypt,
Mesopotamia and Salonika. More men, guns and shells would be needed.
The Man-Power Board and the Tribunals should be supported and Ireland
forced to keep up the Irish divisions.'[2]

He next addressed a message to Northcliffe that censured Lloyd
George's strategic ideas. The 'Welsh mystic' appeared to suppose he
was 'Heaven sent to win the war'.[3] Repington repeated the generals'
insistent demands for ever more men as the only way to assure victory.
For such advocacy he would subsequently be accused of inhumanity, a
lack of imagination and heartlessness. Lloyd George had vehemently
insisted he was 'not prepared to accept the position of a butcher's boy
driving cattle to slaughter'. Repington's response had been to insist, any
organisation and any strategy to ensure military success depended upon a
rationally calculated, reliable supply of manpower. It was the government's task to decide the number of men, whether as many as
2,000,000 or as few as 200,000. Then the commanders would know the
amount of cloth from which they might cut their coat. Repington had
written an article, 'The maximum effort'. It explained the new German
formations, the need for a reply, and the implication in terms of recruitment. The Censor had refused publication and had similarly treated a
contribution on Salonika. 'I am muzzled', a frustrated Repington
recorded. What could he do when the public was denied information on
'the two most critical questions of the hour'?[4]

Repington was anxious to be closer to Northcliffe particularly because
he was convinced Dawson was being 'inspired' from a source outside

Printing House Square. Northdiffe, wooed and won to the cause of the generals, three weeks after the start of the Somme offensive announced he must be told if anything in *The Times* ever displeased Haig.[5] Repington meanwhile had written to tell Northcliffe he intended to support the government provided 'they play the game by the soldiers'. So long as the government guaranteed 'munitions, compulsion and the direction of operations by the General Staff', they deserved support. His words had not been chosen at random; he intentionally echoed the headlines in that day's *Daily Mail*, Northcliffe's favoured megaphone when addressing the general populace. The article 'Hands off the Army' had bluntly warned Lloyd George he was not to interfere with strategy for that was not his concern, and to cease requesting troops be sent from France on 'mad, wild expeditions in distant places'. Repington greatly approved. He suggested the best way to ensure the government remained on the right track would be for Northcliffe to 'join the Government and hold a watching brief for us all'.[6]

Northcliffe assured Repington he was keeping a very close watch upon the government, but insisted, a newspaper owner would never be tolerated. Having first flattered Northcliffe, Repington now complained he no longer enjoyed the 'scope in *The Times*' that once had been his.[7] He knew Northcliffe was wilful, opinionated, obstinate, and never easy to influence consistently. Nevertheless he persevered. He told him he had been looking into the manpower question and promised to send him a written report. There was much for them to talk about, but this plea fell upon deaf ears. There would be no conversations with Northcliffe whose favoured form of communication with employees, save for a favoured few, had become the peremptory dictated injunction. Repington's typed note from Northcliffe bluntly urged, 'More "combing out".'[8] Repington attempted to persuade his lordship to consider 'the *whole* question of Man-Power ... I would value your remarks', but this failed to elicit any response. Northcliffe, accompanied by his younger brother Leicester, paid a visit to Maryon Hall early one Thursday morning in March 1917. His express intention was to discuss the manpower issue, but most of their time was spent discussing a civilian Army Council. A frustrated Repington scornfully dismissed the exercise as 'a complete waste of time'. Leicester Harmsworth disliked Repington and accused him of being 'desirous at all times of currying favour with the heads of the army'. He thought Repington was 'undoubtedly clever' but 'spiteful, vindictive' and resentful whenever he was overborne by Northcliffe.[9]

In April 1917, while on a tour of the western front, Repington dined with Haig. It could not have been easy for Haig to play the suppliant and seek Repington's support. Nor was it an easy pledge for Repington to make although he responded readily enough. Haig had frequently made obvious his personal antipathy for Repington. On numerous occasions he had falsely accused him to others of compromising the safety of British troops in the face of the enemy. These slanders were neither forgiven nor forgotten, yet Repington agreed he would explain the connection between Somme and Arras and why it was necessary to wear out the German armies in the field before doing anything else.[10] Four days after this meeting Repington wrote to Northcliffe from France to repeat his mantra that the one and dominating issue was manpower. 'Everyone on our staff implores us to push it ... My views formed in England are more than borne out by information here. I have been told everything. The one pressing need is men. There are more German Divisions than we have and miracles must not be expected ... We have no right to expect a decision until the folk at home do better.'[11] He then made one more attempt to arrange a conversation with Northcliffe, but failed.

Haig's next conversation with Repington was on Sunday 24 June. In his diary he briefly recorded that he had asked the correspondent 'to continue to insist in *The Times* on men being provided'. He then asserted he hated having to see 'such a dishonest individual' and did so 'only out of my sense of duty to the army', for had he not agreed to see the correspondent, then Repington would have been an 'unfriendly critic'! The claim was as undeserved as the misrepresentation was infamous. Haig's selfish and spiteful mendacity compares sadly with Repington's account of their meeting, which was generous to a fault, even praising Haig's compassion for 'hating the idea of thrusting the army into such a daedalus of mud and water'. Haig had made the highly dubious claim, had he been given the men he had been promised, the mud could have been avoided and he would have pushed the enemy back to the Meuse. He seemed unconscious of the difficulties his troops would necessarily experience if, as he proposed, they fought over sodden ground. *He* was not concerned about Flanders mud. His concern was if possible to thwart Lloyd George. He asked Repington what he thought was going on in London and what explained Lloyd George's attitude to men and strategy? Repington responded by unreservedly condemning Lloyd George's ideas. He declared them 'inexplicable' and avowed he would do everything he could to help Haig.

Newspapers and journals other than Northcliffe's properties welcomed Repington's reflections on the war. One such was the extraordinary *National News*, to which he contributed regularly for some months in 1917–18. This extra work was, for the most part, dictated by his increasingly desperate need for funds. Notionally Liberal, the one-penny Sunday attracted the strangest *galère* of disparate contributors.[12] The newspaper was edited by the formerly Dutch now naturalised Briton, A. de Beck. Encouraged by the *Observer*'s owner, Waldorf Astor, Garvin sought to get the *National News* suppressed on the entirely spurious grounds that it 'attacked the British Government in ambiguous circumstances that would not be tolerated in any other belligerent country'.[13] Repington's pseudonymous contributions, highly critical of the government, were the main source of the government's discontent. In November 1917 de Beck was hauled up before a tribunal and threatened with prison unless he disclosed the name of the troublesome correspondent who wrote on army matters. Fortunately for Repington, de Beck proved to be a doughty defender of the rights of a beleaguered free press in time of war, and Repington's anonymity remained the editor's undisclosed secret.

Repington had first made it his business to get to know Garvin in 1908, but their relationship had always been rather fractious. By December 1917 both men had grown far apart; while Repington was the General Staff's passionate advocate, Garvin was committed to Lloyd George and Milner.[14] As journalists, neither ever despised the strength or professional ability of the other. Before their differences had become insupportable, whenever he could Repington would eagerly grasp any opportunity to contribute to the *Observer*, and not simply for the money. With its vastly increased circulation of approximately 200,000, the paper enjoyed a considerable and deserved influence. A loyal readership had been created, then sustained and maintained by 'Garve's' passionate and intelligent editorship. His eloquent leaders provided informed commentaries upon the war and the domestic political scene. Reading what Garvin had to say each Sunday became something of a national institution.

When his beloved only son Gerard was killed on the Somme, Garvin was so debilitated by grief that for weeks he was unable to contemplate writing his trademark long leader.[15] At Garvin's personal request Repington agreed to take over from Sunday 22 October and for the subsequent three weeks. In his diary he observed what a pleasure it was 'to have such scope after the shabby manner in which I have been treated by *The Times* of late'. The required 5,000 words – 'rather a lot, but there is a lot to say' – when revised and set in type made almost six columns. He thought it the best summary of the war he had written. A delighted Garvin expressed his gratitude fulsomely. Repington wondered why *The Times*, not even occasionally, found time to praise.[16] He was sore with Northcliffe and increasingly concerned about his editor's loyalties. At the beginning of November he asked Dawson to meet him at The Travellers, but the opportunity to quiz his editor was lost when their talk became sidetracked. In 1917 differences between Repington and Dawson were destined to fester and grow until finally they would lead to irrevocable rupture.

Fig. 11 Geoffrey 'Robin' Dawson (1868–1947) (*The Times*)

H. W. Steed, who succeeded Dawson as editor of *The Times*, thought his predecessor 'centralised the business of the office too much and insisted upon keeping all the threads in his own hands'. His assertion 'Milner was really the editor of *The Times* throughout the Dawson period', was largely accurate. During the war, while Steed dealt with foreign politics, Dawson covered military and home affairs. In 1950 Steed recalled a quarrel he witnessed between Repington and Dawson. The military correspondent accused the editor of 'destroying his reputation by suppressing his work'. Dawson dramatically pointed to a drawer that supposedly contained the military correspondent's unpublished articles, declaring, 'There's your reputation, Repington.'[17] Repington was not unaware that from time to time his 'opinion pieces', dashed off in passionate haste, were not always worthy of publication. Dawson was never heedlessly brutal or cavalier in his employment of the editorial blue pencil. At first he edited Repington not by diktat or spiking but by an exchange of opinion as between equals. Then with time Repington's suspicion hardened to certainty that many of his contributions were being deliberately delayed, mangled or excluded to please the editor's particular political friend, Milner.

Alfred Milner had many and powerful Fleet Street friends but counted Geoffrey Dawson his most trusted and valuable. Dawson had been Milner's disciple since the turn of the century when he had edited the *Johannesburg Star*. A leading member of the proconsul's *Kindergarten*, since his appointment in 1912 as editor of *The Times*, Dawson had commanded 'the most influential position of any journalist in the Empire'.[18] Milner had been anxious his protégé should command *The Times*, but the gift had been Northcliffe's and not his to bestow. Buckle, Dawson's vastly experienced, long-serving predecessor as editor, always insisted the basis of the newspaper's authority was its independence. Yet, from the beginning Dawson had 'routinely acquiesced in Northcliffe's views and prejudices',[19] while never abandoning his earlier loyalty to his old mentor, consulting him on most substantive issues. When Lloyd George became Prime Minister in December 1916, Milner became one of the five members of the War Cabinet. He ensured that as many of his friends as possible occupied positions of power and influence. This 'new bureaucracy', according to Massingham of the *Nation*, employed not only Lloyd George's ideas but those of Lord Milner.[20]

On 20 August 1917 Repington had dined with Robertson. Among other subjects they had discussed manpower. Less than two-thirds of the 500,000 men required that month had been obtained. Milner, who with Jan Smuts formed a subcommittee of the War Cabinet concerned with manpower, claimed 80,000 men were essential for agriculture. Robertson acknowledged the War Cabinet's difficulties but argued the country could find more men. Whatever the difficulties, it remained an unalterable, indisputable fact that battles could not be won without men. Repington spoke to his colleague Lovat Fraser, who was due to go to France. He wanted him to 'look carefully into the question of men'. *The Times* then, if necessary 'might commit a calculated indiscretion'. He had in mind the furore and political upset that had followed upon his revelation of a shortage of shells. When Dawson joined in the discussion, Repington rudely interjected, 'People doubt whether you will help' because you are '*too close to Milner*' (my emphasis). If Dawson responded and sought to rebut Repington, it is not recorded. It never seemed to occur to Repington, if Dawson were guilty as he charged, he was even more obviously open to the charge of being too close to the generals, most particularly Robertson. Eventually it was agreed Fraser would find out all he could in France and on his return see Milner. 'We shall see', a sceptical Repington wrote in his diary. 'I do not much care for parleying with the War Cabinet when we may have to attack them.'[21]

When Milner first joined the War Cabinet he publicly promised Robertson 'all the help [he] possibly could'. He looked to 'the wisdom, experience and judgment' of the generals 'to show us the right way'.[22] Robertson doubted the minister's sincerity. The previous day, in a great rant to Repington, he had torn a strip off the War Cabinet for criticising Haig. Apparently ministers doubted the spirit of the troops, 'had no clear idea about anything' and took up Wully's time but never his advice. Instead they spent their time pouring over military plans. That was not their concern but his. In France and in England, 'A little body of politicians, quite ignorant of war and all its needs, are trying to run the war themselves.' Robertson prefaced his tirade with a sharp commentary on individual Cabinet members. Milner, he judged to have been 'so long away from affairs that he is little help'.

For all their talk the War Cabinet had done nothing to secure sufficient men. Upon this, 'all our best soldiers are agreed', wrote an exasperated Repington, 'yet the politicians will not accept their opinion'. He telephoned Dawson to relate his concern. The editor promised to do what he could to help. In an attempt to reassure Repington he told him he had very recently dined with Milner. The minister had impressed upon him the Cabinet were not against the General Staff. But next day *The Times* still said 'nothing to help'. Dawson's leader was useless. He had disappeared to Yorkshire as he always did when you needed him most.[23] Northcliffe was in France. Should Repington try Balfour or perhaps Marlowe, the editor of the *Daily Mail*? He decided Marlowe was the better bet. They met at the Automobile Club for luncheon. Marlowe promised a leader in the *Daily Mail* the next day. It duly appeared and although it was not as strong as Repington would have wished, it was, he thought, 'quite useful'.

Lloyd George desired the Allies to adopt the defensive in the west. It made no sense placating the General Staff. Their sole intent was to lock up massive forces in France and he was utterly convinced their strategy was no longer valid. A series of murderous frontal assaults and four months of attrition designed to wear down the Germans had temporarily secured a small, slimy, indefensible salient surrounded on three sides by German artillery. The price paid in blood was almost 400,000 killed and wounded. That was enough to convince Milner that Haig and those who shared his strategic thinking would have to change 'or suffer the consequences for their defiance of the Government'.[24]

The Prime Minister was delighted to have secured Milner as his ally. However, Derby, Secretary of State for War, did not share Lloyd George's pleasure. He told Repington, if the CIGS had to go then so would he. Repington assured him, if he stuck to his guns he could not fail to make a great name for himself.[25] Derby showed no sign of reneging on his pledge but was profoundly unhappy. Lloyd George was 'the *only* possible PM', but Milner he found 'intolerable'. He 'sneered at soldiers as though they were all damned fools'. Milner together with Henry Wilson, the British military representative, had gone to Versailles to attend the meeting of the newfangled Supreme War Council. 'I very much distrust that combination', observed Derby.[26] Repington had even less faith in the duo.

The Supreme War Council first met officially on 1 December 1917 at the Hôtel Trianon. Haig's attack at Cambrai had begun well in November, but by December it was clear it would not be the promised, significant victory. Allenby, fighting the Turks in the Holy Land, had won a string of victories. The capture of Jerusalem became more than a powerful morale booster; it provided a persuasive case for 'side-shows'. On 16 December Russia signed an armistice with the Central Powers at Brest-Litovsk. German divisions were now free to fight on the western front, a prospect scarcely counterbalanced for the Allies by the promise of a growing number of American troops. In the nine months since joining the Allied cause, the United States had despatched just four divisions to fight in France. At the year's end Henry Wilson was summoned to London to tell Lloyd George what he thought were the Allied military prospects for 1918. Wilson's mission did not please Haig. The government apparently preferred to listen to the 'Versailles gentleman' rather than to him. He noted incredulously that Wilson had reached his conclusions 'as the result of a War Game'. If it were not for their serious position, Haig thought, the whole matter would have been laughable.[27]

Repington had followed the events of the past two months with a growing sense of despair. Initially he had expressed reservations about Haig's line of attack in Flanders. His warnings about the viability of the chosen ground for an offensive proved justified. 'The troops in parts were literally flooded out. Perhaps', he suggested in weary irony, 'no one had listened to him because [he] had been military attaché in the Low Countries and happened to know the district!'[28] A week later, dining at Claridges with the DMO, Major General Maurice, Repington was told all was going well. They hoped to take the Passchendaele Ridge and the next ridge on the way to Roulers. Repington was not too convinced. He hoped it would materialise but it all seemed a trifle petty. 'One can only approve because it entails killing Germans all the time.'[29] However, he and Maurice could agree unequivocally it was the politicians who posed the greatest problem by their persistent interference. Repington estimated soldiers spent 50 per cent of their time and energy fighting politicians. Maurice thought that figure too low.

In October, while visiting the western front, Repington had spoken in turn to Foch, Joffre, Painlevé, Clemenceau and finally Pétain. The French, respected Haig's tenacity and the achievements of his troops, but did not think the Flanders attack a particularly good strategy. What did Repington think? He replied he would have kept out of the Low Countries, 'because one could fight anywhere except in water and mud'. Pétain suggested the problem was that Charteris was providing Haig with falsely optimistic figures for the number of Germans he was killing, thereby 'egging Haig on to believe he is winning the war'. Repington next talked with General Pershing and his staff. Then, before reaching advanced GHQ he spoke with Charteris. He was 'strongly set upon continuing the Flanders offensive next year and most optimistic as usual'. A later conversation with Plumer confirmed that he too was 'heart and soul for the Flanders offensive',[30] while a meeting with Haig on Monday 15 October found him 'as firmly set upon the Flanders offensive as possible'.[31] Despite the reservations he had previously expressed, his pledge to Haig determined that in public at least, he must, he would support the Flanders offensive. Eventually he would find himself desperately justifying Third Ypres to Pétain on the grounds of the number of Germans killed, all other strategic aims having been abandoned. Pétain thought Haig's tenacity was admirable but wondered whether it was because 'he ran in blinkers'. Perhaps, he suggested, the strategy had been imposed by the Admiralty.[32]

Returning to England, Repington met his editor at the Travellers. They posted each other up on what had happened at home and abroad. Dawson wanted Repington to persuade Robertson to be more amenable to the idea of a War Council. Milner, as a kind of *quid pro quo*, intended to make sure Lloyd George would in future be less rude to Robertson. But when Repington met 'Wully' he seemed to think the soldiers and the War Cabinet were getting on 'very fairly'.[33] This news was unexpected because Repington had heard from a number of different sources, a dead set was being made against Robertson and the General Staff in the press, inspired by Downing Street. He wrote a general article on the military situation and enclosed a letter to Dawson stating his fears for the General Staff. *The Times* must no longer allow the matter to go by default. Unless they supported him, Robertson's days were numbered. Should he fall, most serious consequences would follow. The CIGS was 'trusted by the Army, by our commanders, by the public and by our allies'. The man most likely to replace him, Henry Wilson, 'distrusted by the chief men in our Army, was *brûlé*[34] with the French ... and a political general of the most dangerous type ... He will do anything that the politicians tell him'. The crisis, however, afforded Dawson an unique opportunity. How he responded 'could very well determine Robertson's fate'. If Robertson went then Derby would go too and probably the Army Council, 'just the result which the gang around LG desire. They will then fill it with their creatures.' Knowing how close and important a colleague Milner was to Lloyd George, and how Dawson constantly consulted with and leaned on his mentor, Repington was effectively issuing a challenge to his editor. Where exactly did his loyalties lie? Could Dawson bring himself to follow his advice and support the General Staff against the government? Surely he would wish to discuss these matters with him, in which case he had only to telephone him at home.

When he heard nothing from Dawson, Repington rapidly developed his ideas into an article for *The Times*. An accompanying letter declared Dawson's latest leading article was 'useful', but he wished the editor had 'done justice to Robertson by acknowledging his great services ... He weighs most in the war councils of the Allies'. Dawson had been right to say 'co-operation is very important' but he saw no reason to expect any good would arise from an inter-Allied Staff. He particularly emphasised, it would 'have made no difference on the Italian front'.[35]

Once more, Dawson neither responded nor published Repington's article. His silent rebuff spoke volumes. The next day Repington lunched with his friend Cowans and they bearded Sutherland, Lloyd George's private secretary and principal press officer. Repington attacked Sutherland for 'the beastly things being said about the General Staff', before telling him 'the Army was greatly under establishment [and] that the Allied War Council was eyewash'. One thing only mattered, 'to raise fresh divisions and make up the deficit in our ranks'. LG's minion affected surprise and declared he knew nothing. The next day, a friend of Repington's at the Foreign Office declared he too was surprised to learn the army was under establishment. To Repington it was obvious the public needed to know the War Cabinet was refusing to acknowledge there was a desperate need to provide sufficient troops. But whenever he 'put down his ideas for *The Times*, Dawson had not published them'.[36]

When Repington discovered Churchill was as much for the inter-Allied Staff as he was against it he refused to be too downcast. It did not alter the fact that without exception, 'leading soldiers home from France' shared his aversion to it. 'They all hate it like the devil.' A conversation with Robertson upon his return from Italy confirmed he too shared Repington's contempt for the concept 'of making war by committee'.

Haig thought likewise. Repington could not wait to get to Printing House Square. He had not yet entirely given up on Dawson. He impressed upon his editor and several other *Times'* worthies, his 'grave objections to the Paris Military Committee'. He took up the cudgels again the next day. Dawson must be made fully aware the Allied Advisory Committee was nothing but a '*moyen détourné* to give LG control of strategy'. That day's leader in *The Times* was slightly better and he thought Dawson might be 'wobbling'. The next day he was again at Printing House Square seeking to impress Dawson with his views. Although Haig and Robertson had not yet resigned, he informed his editor, all Haig's generals were furious about the Rapallo agreement of 7 November and the decision to go ahead with the Supreme War Council. They riddled the notion with criticisms.[37]

Repington was not the least bit surprised to learn from Cowans, 'the Government [were] rabid with [him] for supporting the General Staff'.[38] Doubtless, Dawson had been telling tales out of school. But given the general atmosphere of doom and gloom, he was much cheered by the early news of Cambrai. A victory was the most suitable riposte to Lloyd George's constant sarcastic references to Allied efforts on the western front. He had to make the most of that first day's triumph because two-thirds of the ground gained was subsequently lost, together with 111 guns. In total 35,000 troops were either killed, wounded or made prisoner. Over-optimistic arithmetical calculations put German losses at twice that number of men and a third more guns. It did not alter Lloyd George's conviction the western front was a hopeless stalemate. Repington resolutely continued to believe winning against the Hun was not a matter of deploying forces elsewhere, but of making more men available in France. To win elsewhere but to lose in the primary theatre was 'sheer fatuity'. The Prime Minister and his War Cabinet did not think so because they refused to listen to those schooled in the arts of war. Repington refused to acknowledge that the losses of Third Ypres had diminished trust in Haig's plans. It was no longer sufficient to repeat the best soldiers were unanimously agreed victory was achievable provided the full available manpower was sensibly deployed. At the moment, approximately one-third of the men were engaged in Egypt, Salonika and Mesopotamia while in France the British army was short by 114,000 troops. Next year's natural wastage (the unfortunate, officially favoured euphemism employed instead of dead, wounded, deserted or lost) was expected to be more than 50,000 a month. The Germans were now free to release an increasing number of divisions from the eastern front to augment their forces in the west. It was clear to Repington, Lloyd George's real problem was he had never told the British people the truth about the military situation. Had he done so, surely they would have responded generously? When friends asked Repington why he did not advertise these facts he would answer, 'I am unable to get the support from the editor of *The Times* necessary to rouse the country', a state of affairs he thought impossible to tolerate much longer.[39]

Five days later, a leader in *The Times* suggested that there should be an inquiry into the setback at Cambrai. Repington was furious. He was certain from its 'inflated and pontifical style' the editorial had been 'officially inspired'. While it stopped short of demanding Haig's head, it rebuked him for too often publishing 'fatuous messages from France of German losses of men and morale' and for remaining loyal to inadequate subordinates like Charteris whom he had defended and retained in the face of Derby's most recent 'hint' that the War Cabinet wanted him out. Charteris was clearly one intended victim of the proposed searching inquiry. But as Northcliffe bluntly emphasised, if that sacrifice were not forthcoming, Haig's own head was in jeopardy. A furious Repington wrote to his editor with every expectation of being published. His letter explained in some detail why he disagreed entirely with his newspaper's demand for an inquiry. Dawson neither published the letter nor confirmed the military correspondent's assertion that the leader had been inspired.[40] On reflection Repington thought it not worth pursuing the matter. 'As the inquiry will be at GHQ in France', he supposed it could now do no harm. It was a matter of little regret to Repington when, two days later, Charteris had gone.

Confined to his house with a cold, Repington wrote an article on the *Généralissimé* contesting the French idea of a commander-in-chief. It appeared in *The Times* on Monday 17 December and though much bowdlerised the main argument remained. Esher wrote from Paris to inform Hankey what view the French took of Repington's article. Hankey passed it on to Lloyd George 'for information'. Esher supposed it had affected no change in French thinking but 'between the lines it has been read as a condemnation of Versailles as well as the *Généralissimé*'. Much more shocking, at least to 'every Englishman', had been Northcliffe's attack on GHQ. 'Everyone thought certain changes highly desirable but this plan of open attack was universally condemned.'[41] Northcliffe had changed sides with a vengeance. Now he was anxious to achieve high ministerial office.

A seasonal snowfall and the usual quiet of Christmas week combined to dampen Repington's sense of angry dissatisfaction and displeasure. He concluded his summary of 'a dramatic year' with the reflection Britain faced a great threat because it lacked 'the courage to face the music of facts'.[42] Northcliffe's latest step in the peerage to viscount was generally regarded the price Lloyd George had been persuaded to pay for the newspaper proprietor's support. 'I almost alone,' Repington wryly reflected 'am left to fight the case of the Army for men.' It was a public misfortune the Northcliffe press had chosen not to support him.[43]

On leave in England and now field marshal, Haig invited Repington to meet him for a talk. His immediate complaint was the failure to maintain numbers. The need not merely to maintain but to increase the numbers of British infantrymen in France ought to have been painfully obvious to anyone. Throughout 1917 there had not been a month when he had not been short of fighting men. Now lacking 114,000, he was as much as a sixth short of his full rifle strength. The figures rehearsed were all too familiar. But to campaign in the press, as Haig obviously wished, was easier said than done. Repington's arguments, for all their eloquence, passion and persistence would be based upon statistics that bore the imprimatur of the High Command, and probably, almost as certainly, as often before, they would be spiked or laundered by his editor.

Repington was left feeling more miserable than at any time since the beginning of the war. He had learned, *inter alia*, that the War Office had been compelled to reduce all divisions in France from twelve to nine battalions of infantry. The source of all the trouble was 'the shameful poltroonery and the strategic incompetence of the War Cabinet'. Why had Northcliffe chosen this of all times to tie himself to Lloyd George's chariot wheels? 'The Northcliffe Press', he concluded, was 'playing a despicable role'. If *The Times* did not demonstrate its customary independence and act as the public watchdog, he would wash his hands of it. His mood grew harsher. Formerly sacrosanct, he now pronounced Derby and the Army Council 'no good'. 'They should have resigned rather than see all their warnings disregarded and criminal follies perpetrated.'[44]

On Friday 11 January the military correspondent received a note from Dawson. Returning after an absence of several days, he had published the first of Repington's recently written articles. There was neither excision nor any alteration, but their author's response was not as generous or as welcoming as Dawson might have expected. He told Dawson he resented them no longer meeting regularly to discuss army issues. He enquired petulantly, how much did Dawson know of present affairs? All Repington could tell his editor was how matters stood according to the information *he* possessed. The army was 130,000 men in deficit. The Army Council had asked for 616,000 men. The War Cabinet offered 100,000 general service men and the boys of 18 of the yearly class. If matters were not changed, the war would 'unquestionably be lost. The strength of our infantry is permanently diminished by one quarter.' The War Cabinet should do its duty and tell the country frankly how bad matters were. He had heard the Versailles soldiers recommended remaining on the defensive in the west while taking the offensive in Palestine and Mesopotamia. These schemes were 'so mad' he doubted whether they would be pursued. Meanwhile the Germans were massing in the west. Soon they would be ready to mount an offensive. One chance remained. 'You', he told Dawson, 'must attack the War Cabinet without mercy' while he *must* be afforded 'a free hand to stop these mad eastern schemes. *The Times* simply is not fulfilling its duty towards the country. The gravest responsibility now rests on you, graver than has ever rested on any Editor of *The Times*. I beg that you will be equal to the occasion and only have the public good in your mind.' He had been loyal to editorial opinion in the past but recently he had been obliged to express his dissent openly. He had to reconsider his position. He hoped Dawson would allow him in future 'to express [his] opinions without editorial bowdlerizing'. But should *The Times* have abandoned its position as an independent public watchdog, then he neither wished nor intended to carry on at Printing House Square.[45] He knew his message was forthright to the point of being damnably rude. His intention could not have been expressed more clearly. He had thrown down his gage. It was for Dawson to decide whether to pick it up.

The following working week Repington ostentatiously occupied the days gathering routine information. Whatever the cost he was intent to avoid Printing House Square. That Sunday, Dawson carefully composed a detailed, judicious and generous response to Repington's captious challenge. After it had been typed the editor added a further, handwritten paragraph pointing out in measured terms the central problem. 'If the Man-Power plans are bad, or if the Cabinet fail to carry them out, I am quite ready for a vigorous campaign – with or without your help. I hope *with* it.' He did not mince his words. Like Robertson, Repington had adopted the same 'absurd assumption as the *Morning Post*', that antagonism between soldiers and politicians was a necessary condition. Soldiers seemed to think 'they need only indent for unlimited men without assuming any responsibility either for getting them or cutting their coat according to their cloth ... *You* fall into exactly the same attitude when you call for thirty or sixty fresh divisions without even suggesting how they are to be found.' He challenged Repington. 'What exactly is your planned solution?" Did he propose to get men from the mines, the munitions factories, agriculture, that Geddes had rejected? Was he in favour of a 'clean out'? The only suggestion the military correspondent had made was to repeat 'the old antithesis between "Victory" and "Trade", never very convincing ... This is not a simple question to be solved by catchwords.' That was fair comment, as had been his characterisation of the way both Robertson and Repington had framed their demands for troops.

Dawson observed, whereas the Prime Minister could 'generally be convinced by those who took the trouble to convince him', Robertson treated all members of the Cabinet as his enemies. He insisted he realised the seriousness of the situation just as much as Repington. However, it would have been 'infinitely more serious if *The Times* had lent itself to the kind of raging, tearing quarrel between the Cabinet and the General Staff which you have frequently tried to foment'. That box about the ears from his editor was deserved, but Dawson somewhat softened his censures with a parenthetical afterthought. He was sure the military correspondent had always been motivated by 'the best intentions'. This letter, with its well thought-out challenges and reasoned admonitions, was not the response Repington had expected. He chose not to respond.[46]

The final breach was initiated by the treatment *The Times* chose to give the words of the recently elected Unionist MP for Basingstoke, Sir Auckland Geddes. His speech to the Commons had provided its members with a comprehensive review of official thinking on the allocation of manpower for civil and military purposes. The British army in France would be reinforced by the youngest men available to be taken from non-essential industries. It was made clear that the Committee on Man-Power afforded greater priority to ship-building, repairs and aeroplane construction than to the reinforcement of troops in France. In the course of his speech Geddes deprecated 'the thoughtless waste of lives' occasioned by British military planning.[47] It was this last comment by Geddes that particularly infuriated Repington. His response was to wonder whether Britain had gone mad. Geddes's speech had been both misleading and incorrect.

At least to Repington's satisfaction, his judgment was confirmed the very next day. A 'well-informed friend' thought the present deficit of 136,000 men, including the 86,000 infantry short in France, under the new provisions, would not have diminished by April. These 'well-informed friends' so often conveniently turn up to confirm facts or concur with Repington's judgments it might well seem more than a little suspicious. But in this case, a letter from Esher to Haig demonstrated Repington had good reason for complaint. Although *The Times* had professed to report Geddes's speech verbatim, passages had been deliberately omitted that made his meaning misleading. And in a letter to Robertson, Esher wrote of the editorial 'distortions, the tergiversations and the concealments'.[48] Repington had thought the initial editorial response by *The Times* to Geddes's speech 'pathetic' and 'silly'. These faults were compounded the following day by a leading article that further misrepresented the facts. This was too much for Repington to stomach. 'If I remained with these imbeciles any longer I should deserve to be hanged as a Boche agent.' The response may seem unduly melodramatic but it was not wildly ill-considered. His words were weighed and expressed exactly the anger and frustration he felt.[49]

Some time afterwards, when immediate passion had cooled a little, Dawson began his more detailed retellings of the breach with Repington.[50] Starting with the military correspondent's letter of 11 January, he asserted that for him to pick a quarrel with *The Times* on the subject of manpower was 'quite unjustifiable'. The manpower question had not been the correspondent's real reason for seeking a quarrel. His attack had not been principled but fuelled by vanity and greed. He suspected the whole altercation had been prompted 'for commercial reasons'. This had been confirmed – at least to Dawson's satisfaction – when, a few days later, articles written by Repington appeared 'in a whole syndicate of papers', both in Britain and the United States. The whole fandango, he concluded, *must* have been a put-up job. Strip out Repington's outrageous vanity, his inordinate sensitivity about his contributions to *The Times* being 'mutilated', not forgetting his constant desire for more money, then his only substantive complaint concerned the newspaper's 'alleged apathy' over the manpower question. As for that, Geddes's recent speech 'completely knocked the bottom out of the War Office theory England was crawling with "slackers"'. The editor knew that was a misrepresentation; he could not have honestly believed he had *convincingly* dismissed Repington's complaint. Then he conceived what seemed a more plausible *raison d'être* for the correspondent's conduct. For years Repington had refused to say anything to Henry Wilson's advantage. Dawson suggested Wilson's promotion to CIGS and his refusal to countenance criticism of Wilson in *The Times*, had 'more to do with Repington's resignation than anything else'.

Repington described the interview with Dawson as 'stormy'. Being kept outside the editor's door for so long kicking his heels had done nothing for his good humour. In the course of a tirade he accused Dawson of writing 'mendacious leaders', 'subservience to the War Cabinet', 'misleading the country' and 'endangering our army'. Although he had 'constantly exposed the War Cabinet's failure to provide men', *The Times* had said nothing. Neither the interests of the country nor those of the army were safe in Dawson's hands. Thus, he had been left with no alternative but resignation. When later he reflected on that final falling-out with Dawson, he decided it had been 'a good day's work'. If he had any regret, it was that he had 'delayed the step so long'.[51] A short note to Northcliffe expressed his sorrow at having to end his fifteen-year association with *The Times*.[52] A formal letter of resignation to Howard Corbett requested Northcliffe should be assured, it had been his conviction he could no longer usefully serve the interests of the country and the army by continuing to work for *The Times* that had compelled him to sever their long association.[53]

In his pocket diary Dawson recorded that Repington tried to pick their quarrel on patriotic grounds. 'I told him not to violate his conscience by remaining another day.'[54] The next day there is no mention of Repington but a tangible sense of his troublesome presence remains. Dawson lunched with Northcliffe 'as of old', walked to Milner's house, thence to Fred Oliver's and finally to the Saville. There he met Spenser Wilkinson to whom he proposed 'a loose Military Correspondent-ship'.[55] It was an unintended but nice paradox that Dawson should have approached as a possible stop-gap replacement for Repington, a former, distinguished contributor on military and imperial politics to the *Morning Post*, the very newspaper his unlamented but irreplaceable military correspondent was about to join.

18   At odds with DORA

Two days after Repington's breach with *The Times*, he learned the current weekly summary of statistics the War Office compiled for the Prime Minister revealed German strength had recently increased. 'A nice moment', he observed 'to reduce our infantry in France by a quarter in order to go prancing off to the Holy Land.' The War Office had failed to save the government from its folly. To avert otherwise inevitable defeat 'he and some honest editor must speak out'.[1] Free to work for the *Morning Post*, he informed Gwynne his first article would be ready in two days. It would be written, not as formerly by 'an independent critic, but by an overt protagonist of the General Staff'. They had urged him to 'Begin by exposing the man-power struggle.' Through the *Morning Post* he hoped he might achieve 'what he had brought to pass through *The Times* in 1915'. He could certainly promise, what he had to say would not be ignored.[2]

The news Repington had permanently quit Printing House Square for 346 The Strand, had raced like wildfire through Westminster and Whitehall, the clubs of Pall Mall and the editorial offices and taverns of Fleet Street. Dawson had hastened to tell Milner, who in turn informed Lloyd George. He predicted his news that *The Times'* military correspondent had been shown the door by the editor would neither unduly surprise nor disappoint the Prime Minister. He warned LG, the man who had 'run the extreme military view that everything the army did was right and had claimed a *fainéant* Government had refused to take the necessary steps to provide sufficient "cannon-fodder"', sooner rather than later, 'would doubtless be up to some devilry in other quarters'.[3]

Recently Repington had not approved the line taken by Northcliffe's newspapers, particularly the *Daily Mail*. But he knew that all employees on the *Daily Mail*, including the editor Marlowe, did exactly as their proprietor told them. Northcliffe's diktat did not apply in the same absolute way at PHS and for that reason Repington held Dawson entirely responsible for *The Times'* increasing subservience to War Cabinet decisions. The editor had followed not Northcliffe's but Milner's instructions.

He had supported every hare-brained War Cabinet scheme, effectively approving its vendetta with the General Staff.

Repington insisted Dawson had been the reason why he had left *The Times*. Nonetheless, it was generally assumed the architect of his downfall had been Northcliffe. H. A. Gwynne supposed, although Northcliffe had agreed with Repington, manpower was *the* issue. 'When it came to forcing the Government to deal with it, his moral courage had failed him and he began to follow Lloyd Georgian tactics.' It was then, the dissatisfied, military correspondent finally abandoned the newspaper.[4] Gwynne was not the only editor who was convinced Repington's departure had been intended to serve the proprietor's personal political ambitions.

Among those who commiserated with Repington was the *Spectator*'s owner editor, John St Loe Strachey. He congratulated him upon his 'most public spirited action', then blamed 'Northcliffe and his entourage' for Repington's departure. It had been part of their campaign to make their 'Chief' prime minister. 'That he performed the *nolo episcopari* stunt' convinced Strachey 'he desires to be Prime Minister'.[5] Strachey returned to this theme in a long postscript in which he condemned Northcliffe but also found reason to censure Lloyd George. 'We must be rid of LG,' he enjoined Repington, 'or at any rate get rid of him from the seat of supreme power. He is fit only to be Public Orator and Spell-binder to the nation. He should be told to go to – Aleppo!' Repington admitted he had no direct evidence to suggest Northcliffe aspired to 10 Downing Street, but agreed both men were 'a curse on the country directing this odious campaign against the High Command'. The Army Council ought to have had both men shot. Generals in France wrote to tell him, if the present state of affairs were allowed to continue then the army's discipline would certainly be ruined.[6]

Politicians as much as journalists anxiously debated who exactly had been responsible for Repington's sudden departure from Printing House Square. Austen Chamberlain warned, now that Repington was writing for the *Morning Post* he would 'undoubtedly be briefed by the entourage of the CIGS and Haig'. He would ask questions 'the answers to which could not be given without injuring the public interest'. Chamberlain did not for a moment think Repington was acting disinterestedly. He had been prompted by a desire to avenge 'his personal quarrel with Henry Wilson who had turned him out of the War Office'.[7] Many of the political and social establishment seemed determined to believe likewise. Thereby, a magnanimous sacrifice, designed to serve the national interest, was reduced to a selfish act inspired by a desire for personal vengeance. What was more, by damning Repington's intent, effectively they discredited his message.

Apparently, Esher's concern was the corrupting influence he supposed the press increasingly exercised over Westminster.[8] He wrote to warn Stamfordham of an approaching crisis. The press had been allowed to usurp political authority just as the Inquisition had in the sixteenth century. Northcliffe would surely reach 'a dizzier height before his ducal head rolls'. Loss of confidence in the General Staff, the falsification of manpower figures given to Parliament by Auckland Geddes, the resignation of Carson from the government and Repington's departure from *The Times*; all these, he suggested, might be explained as the consequence of actions taken by the press and all too often initiated by Northcliffe. The next month he would add to his charge sheet against the proprietor insisting it was Northcliffe who 'instigated the prosecution of Gwynne and Repington'.[9]

Esher's opinions, though not directly mentioned, nonetheless formed the agenda for a conversation on 22 January between the king's private secretary and the Prime Minister. Repington's recent 'retirement' was the first subject upon which the Premier, in his own words, 'opened up his heart'. Lloyd George insisted Repington 'left *The Times* because he was against the Allied General Staff at Versailles', a judgment motivated solely by 'his personal dislike of Sir Henry Wilson'. LG claimed he disregarded what Repington said for, like his 'expert' opinions, they were determined by a profound, personal prejudice, jealousy and hatred.

The competing explanations for his sudden departure from *The Times* could have been rapidly resolved by a simple statement of the actual circumstances by the two parties most directly and immediately involved. But neither Repington nor Dawson agreed either about what had happened or why. Notice of the military correspondent's resignation from *The Times* had appeared in the *Morning Post* and *Daily Mirror* on 21 January eliciting a hail of congratulations and requests for interviews. In the days that followed Repington received several unsolicited offers of employment, all exceedingly well paid, from, among others, Beaverbrook's *Daily Express* and the *Philadelphia Ledger*. Being the kind of man he was, despite all Dawson's mean-minded aspersions to the contrary, Repington when he contemplated resignation had not concerned himself unduly or for long with thoughts about the practical and particularly the financial consequences of quitting *The Times*. The way Fleet Street and the United States press reacted to the news of his resignation made clear the high esteem he enjoyed as a military commentator.[10]

Repington completed his first article for the *Post* on Sunday 20 January 1918. It explained why the army was in need of men on the western front. When an increasingly strong German force was likely at any moment to mount an offensive, British troops were being withdrawn for service in secondary theatres of war. This decision and consequent crisis he blamed on the cowardice and procrastination of the War Cabinet. He confidently expected his words would create a sensation. He explained he chose not to mince his words for what he wrote about was whether Britain would win or lose the struggle with Germany. He explained to Gwynne, he had deliberately presented the statistics as though they were conjectural so they might more readily and successfully pass the censors. 'Actually they are those of the AG except that I have budgeted on French advice for increased losses for 1918.' He assured Gwynne that the article *would* safely pass the censors because either 'Maurice or Macdonogh will see it gets through'.[11]

Meanwhile, there was a sharp exchange with Dawson. A reporter from the *Star* had interviewed Repington on Monday 21 January, the same day as notice of his resignation appeared in the *Daily Mirror* and *Morning Post*. Gleefully Repington told Gwynne, 'The Lord alone knows what he will say, but I refused to speak about *The Times*.' Gwynne agreed with what he had said and was glad Repington had spoken out.[12] The *Star* report had particularly upset Dawson. He claimed it implied the military correspondent had left *The Times* because of some *intrigue* that was being pursued against Sir Douglas Haig and Sir William Robertson, 'a suggestion for which there is not the slightest foundation in fact'. This was to repeat the charge made in a paragraph printed that same day in *The Times*.[13] Repington had wanted *The Times* to publish the letter he had written to Corbett on 16 January, the day of his resignation. Dawson refused. He insisted that morning's paragraph provided 'an accurate account of your reasons for resignation as you had previously conveyed them to the Editor'. Dawson clearly was not inclined to budge, certain his was an accurate recollection of what had been said. Repington was just as certain his letter to Corbett reproduced exactly what he had long thought and felt. After discontentedly chewing the issue over with a number of friends, Repington had to settle for publication in the *Morning Post* alone. In his diary he wrote, 'everyone who cares for truth and straightforward dealing will see the mendacious character of *The Times*'s explanation'.[14]

Gwynne published Repington's article on 24 January.[15] It had not been sent to the Censor. 'I hope that [Gwynne's] courage and public spirit will be gratefully remembered', wrote Repington. Editor, like contributor, wondered whether this first article in the *Morning Post* might lead to their imprisonment. Repington wrote of this jokingly to Ian Hamilton. He promised 'to make the fur fly soon'. If as a result he was 'clapped in the Tower' he hoped Hamilton would bring with him 'some Dardanelle heroes and get me out'.[16] Lloyd George earnestly urged upon his Cabinet colleagues the imprisonment of editor and correspondent but after much argument he was dissuaded from such a course. He complained to Derby, Repington *must* have been supplied 'by someone who had access to the highly confidential material of the General Staff ... intelligence as to enemy numbers and also to our reserves'. To publish them had been 'a gross breach of Army Regulations'. If there were any repetition then he intended to seek the sternest remedy. 'The publication of confidential information for the benefit of the enemy [was] an act of treason.' In his own mind, the Prime Minister was convinced that the culprit who had given Repington the classified information could only have been Robertson. He would dearly have liked, there and then, to have sued the CIGS. However, he was obliged to urge Derby to discover by legitimate process the culprit who had leaked these secret documents.[17] Derby's tardy reply, after he had considered all the available evidence, including an article published that day by the *Morning Post*, concluded the journalist might well have gathered the statistics he quoted 'in the course of his constant communication with Clemenceau and other authorities'. The French, as all Englishmen knew, were notoriously leaky. Derby decided to submit the offending article to the Director of Public Prosecutions. He thought a prosecution would offer 'the best opportunity of finding out all there is to know about the sources of his inspiration'.[18]

Lloyd George desperately hoped Derby's move might yield the means both to silence the troublesome *Morning Post* and bear down upon Robertson. He wanted him removed as CIGS to be replaced by someone more biddable, less blindly loyal to Haig, and most importantly, sympathetic to his views and his way of thinking. Lloyd George wanted to have complete control over strategic planning. Before his departure from Printing House Square, Repington had warned the War Cabinet they risked upsetting everyone and everything if they contemplated sweeping changes to the Higher Command. He had been thinking primarily of Robertson's vulnerability. What he had not perceived was that Lloyd George also wanted Haig removed. When it became obvious Haig was too tough a nut to crack, LG was obliged to make a virtue of necessity. He then learned, much to his surprise, that Haig would not stand in the way of his colleague's replacement as CIGS. Robertson's earlier confident response to Repington's anxious query whether he and Haig were as one proved worthless.

Lloyd George's initial attempt to limit Robertson's powers by establishing a Supreme War Council at Versailles had failed. The CIGS's simple but very effective response had been to refuse to co-operate. However, in early February 1918 the proposal to establish an executive war board to take control of the general reserve forced Robertson out of cover. The creation of the SWC was in many ways desirable: an important and necessary advance towards co-ordinated Allied decision making. Potentially it offered a considerable improvement on the previous hapha-zard arrangements, but inevitably it aroused the opposition of the British General Staff for it trespassed on questions of 'personal ambition and professional *amour propre*'.[19] Robertson was incensed Foch had been appointed chairman of what he referred to dismissively as 'the Versailles Soviet'. Effectively that made Foch the Allied *Generalissimo*. Robertson insisted this would confuse British troops. Who exactly would be their commander, Haig or Foch? What sort of prime minister was Lloyd George that he was prepared to see 'the fine British army placed at the mercy of irresponsible people – some of them foreigners'? The soldiers were always being told to stand up to the politicians. Well he had stood up. What Robertson wanted to know now was, what did the country propose to do?[20]

Repington had been invited by Clemenceau to pay a short visit to France. From his favourite Parisian watering hole, the Ritz in the Place Vendôme where he had been ensconced for the previous four days, he informed Gwynne he had 'thought it best to avoid the members of our recent mission here'.[21] He had crossed the Channel and arrived at the Ritz before dawn on Friday 1 February. General Maurice had come over to Paris five days earlier to meet Robertson prior to the Versailles SWC meeting. Repington had not breakfasted when Maurice called to provide him with a full account of what had transpired up to that date. During the course of the day he received further reports upon the progress of the council and more particularly, the temper of various political and military protagonists. From some unspecified source Repington learned the British General Staff had been utterly defeated. He, the more stubbornly, clung to his own impression that the council's conclusions were 'lame and impotent'.

On the Sunday he met Painlevé, with whom he enjoyed a long, ani-mated conversation. However, it was Georges Clemenceau, the 76-year-old French prime minister, who proved to be his most important source of information. Most cordially he told him the whole history of the War Council. That devious politician, 'masterful, dangerous and capable of anything' had his own reservations about the Versailles compromise. He favoured Pétain rather than Foch and so all the more willingly provided Repington with the very information Lloyd George had decreed should be kept strictly secret. The French tiger was convinced he had bested the Welsh dragon in debate. He openly supported Robertson's 'brilliant and emphatic speech' opposing the proposed Salonika expedition.

When he discovered the 'Versailles soldiers, one from each of the four nations with Foch as President, [would] have control of the reserves', Repington was 'cast down'. He realised this decision virtually stripped

Haig and Robertson of responsibility and could 'see no ray of light in this dismal gloom', graphically describing the outcome as 'a disunity of command with three Richmonds in the field'.[22] Repington had also spoken at length with the former wartime French premier and leading 'Easterner', the 'brilliant but luxurious' Aristide Briand, who had little to contribute about the War Council exchanges but did share Repington's disapproval of the new scheme for the reserves. This was strange, given he had so recently at Rapallo agreed with Lloyd George on the SWC's creation.

The other person who might have given Repington illicit information and with whom he enjoyed several illuminating chats about diplomatic comings and goings was Colonel Herman Le Roy-Lewis. Since 1915 he had been the British military attaché in Paris. An able man, he had nothing but contempt for his ambassador, Bertie. He was, however, close to Esher, who thought him the only man at the Embassy who knew exactly what was going on.

Repington moved from one appointment to another, mixing pleasure with business.[23] Perhaps he was not always as circumspect as he ought to have been. His supposed words to two young and 'notorious' ladies over dinner prompted Dame Ethel Smyth to write an extraordinary letter to Gwynne accusing the correspondent of being 'a *défaitiste*', demonstrating 'a lack of moral worth and straightness succumbing to the charms' of the young women. Gwynne absolutely rejected the idea Repington could be a *défaitiste*. Perhaps wisely, he had nothing to say on the subject of the correspondent's resistance to feminine charms. A former *Times* colleague, Leo Amery, was also keeping a careful eye on Repington. On 3 February he warned the Prime Minister Repington was in Paris. 'You must be prepared for a raging, tearing press attack on your decisions over here beginning at once.' He emphasised that the effectiveness of the attack would depend upon the co-operation of the War Office. Lloyd George should '*lose no time ... do it now*' – put the War Office under 'proper control'. Derby ought to be replaced as war minister by 'someone who knows his own mind'. Of course, Amery meant Milner, whom he was certain would not hesitate either to 'bring Wully and Co. into line or sack them as he thought best'.[24]

The letter Repington sent Gwynne to provide background and guidance contained secret information to which Repington ought not to have had access. The measured calm of its opening was soon abandoned. He made no attempt to hide his indignation that British High Command would be deprived of all responsibility for the conduct of operations. The arrangement was absurd and must be opposed strenuously and vehemently. 'The French now practically have their *Generalissimo*', he grumbled. Everyone knew modern battles were decided by the use of reserves, yet their deployment was now in the hands of 'a committee of four made up of mainly foreign generals. Our man [Wilson] is in a minority of one and is not trusted by our commanders. I do not and cannot approve of this grotesque decision that may be fatal.'[25] On 8 February but under the date line 'Versailles 5 February', in defiance of the government's ruling forbidding publication of the SWC's decisions, a telegram from the newspaper's 'Military Correspondent in Paris' was published in the *Morning Post*. It described 'the strange character of the decision of a recent Inter-Allied War Council concerning the control of British troops in the field'. Parliament should immediately examine it 'in the light of the opinions of our General Staff'.[26]

Lloyd George claimed Repington initially hid his identity as the author of the telegram because he 'was intriguing with all the discontented elements in politics to overthrow the Government'. That same day, the *Globe* reprinted what they described as Repington's 'disquieting telegram'. Milner told Lloyd George, 'This kind of thing cannot be allowed to go on.' The *Globe*'s involvement LG supposed was but one more indication of a powerful conspiracy against the government. Incensed with Repington, he was equally furious with Robertson because he assumed 'Wully' was the source of the confidential information upon which the telegram had been based.

Lloyd George was now utterly convinced, a cabal was about to make a determined attempt to overthrow him and the Cabinet. It might seem strange that such a consummate political creature as Lloyd George should have had such an exaggerated and constant dread of plots and threats. However, the very existence of his administration depended upon a coalition of parties as he had usurped power from Asquith and joined with the Tories. Therefore it was natural he should maintain a wary eye and suspicious concern for potential revolt or opposition *within* the coalition. Wherever he looked, he saw possible rivals and scheming enemies. Many men had good reason to do him political harm if they could. The nature of coalition government meant there had been compromises on matters of political principle and this suggested to his enemies Lloyd George either had no principles or was an unduly devious, selfish and unscrupulous pragmatist. Absorbed in a struggle with senior generals who refused to see any alternative to their preferred strategy, he supposed the military and its supporters within Tory and Liberal ranks would seek to oust him and his Cabinet, and to replace them with an administration that would be in thrall to the military. German intelligence supposed this to be a possibility, acknowledging the existence of an 'English military party' whose members 'loathed Lloyd George heartily'.[27] German hopes and Lloyd George's conspiracy theories were alike fantastic, but that someone as judicious as Hankey could share their suspicions provides some measure of the paranoid, delusional thinking swirling within not only the Prime Minister's head but also in the heads of all those about him. It is true there were a number of different groups and individuals who, for a variety of reasons, sought Lloyd George's scalp. They, however, were disparate and antagonistic in their loyalties and philosophies and possessed nothing in common save their dislike and distrust of the Premier. As a coalition leader, he had constantly to be on the *qui vive*, aware of the possibility of realignments, betrayals, revolts. To judge by his *War Memoirs*, Lloyd George entertained such notions in their most exaggerated form up to and immediately after the Maurice Debate.

What did constitute an appropriate relationship between politicians and the military? That was the crucial question. Long before, Repington had decided what he thought on that particular subject. In the month before and then immediately after the publication of General Maurice's notorious letter and the subsequent debate in the House, Repington twice affirmed that after experiencing Kitchener at the War Office it was clear to him soldiers had no part to play in cabinets.[28] In October 1916 at a luncheon *à deux* with Robertson, the two men had thoroughly discussed the subject. The crux of the issue was 'politicians and soldiers should keep within their respective spheres',[29] a concept to which Repington happily subscribed. He had abandoned any idea of entering the House himself and when approached to stand as a candidate for a division of Manchester, he refused.[30]

On his return from France the military correspondent had met his editor at the Bath Club to compare notes on recent events. Repington agreed to 'write and expose the Paris proceedings', but when submitted to the Press Bureau his article was returned stamped, 'Not to be published'. Gwynne then made certain changes to the text. Rather than diminish they considerably increased the coverage and detail of those subjects about which the Censor had complained. Gwynne supported the offending piece with a powerful editorial. 'There are times', it declared, 'when we must take our courage in both hands and risk the consequences.' The particular time and event both Gwynne and Repington had in mind was the debate due on 12 February to discuss the Versailles decisions. Lloyd George, Repington fiercely asserted, had 'ignored the advice of his legitimate military advisers'. He had starved the army of men, advocated wild adventures and deprived the commanders of their full and necessary powers. He had 'clearly and finally proved his incapacity to govern the country in a great war'. Parliament was challenged to clear up the mess 'in such manner as you think best'. He implied there was only one sensible course to be taken; immediately to rid themselves of an incompetent, interfering prime minister.[31]

Repington's powerful rhetoric would have surprised no one. What threatened to embarrass the Prime Minister politically, was the revelation he had reneged on an assurance he had made to Parliament only a matter of months earlier. Then he had stated the Versailles soldiers would have advisory powers only. Now he could do nothing but fume at what he was pleased to describe as Repington's 'extraordinary effusion'. Almost two decades later, Lloyd George's considered verdict in his *War Memoirs* was that a 'sordid' and 'treacherous' journalist had not only chosen to 'incite the Army Council to an act of insubordination against the Government', but had 'disclosed to the enemy the complete Allied plan of campaign for the year'. He professed to know 'nothing to compare in the whole of our history' with this 'perfidious and treasonable act of betrayal that might and ought to have decided the war'.[32] LG was frequently accused of being 'a bigger liar than Ananias'. This claim concerning Repington was undeniably absurd, a farrago of magniloquent falsehoods.

When the War Cabinet met, Repington's article prompted 'considerable agitation' among their company.[33] Well aware that the contents would be exploited by other newspapers, Lloyd George raged he wanted both the author of the 'malignant and treasonable' article and the editor of the newspaper that had published it arraigned for high treason. He was clearly much perturbed and very angry. According to Esher, the War Cabinet spent the whole of that day 'discussing the seizure of the *Morning Post* machinery'.[34] The opinion of the Solicitor General was sought. After conferring with the Director of Public Prosecutions, Sir Gordon Hewart advised the Prime Minister 'that part of Colonel Repington's article ... constitutes both on the part of the writer and on the part of the editor an offence under Regulation 18 ... Proceedings may be taken by way of prosecution under Regulation 18 or by way of seizure under Regulation 51.' The Solicitor General advised that Repington had published information and plans likely to be of use to the enemy. However, Macdonogh, the DMI, said that he would find it difficult to testify what had been published was likely to have been any great use to the enemy. If it were decided to proceed against Repington and Gwynne, Hewart advised, 'the case should be tried in a hurry'.[35] After a second meeting of the Cabinet Sir George Cave, a Conservative Chancery lawyer recently appointed Home Secretary, in his usual quiet, unemotional but persuasive way outlined certain legal obstacles that made seizure unacceptable. Even more persuasively he pointed out that were Lloyd George to insist on seizure, he would be defeated in the Commons. Reluctantly, Lloyd George deferred to this advice.[36] Instead Gwynne and Repington would be tried before the Bow Street Magistrates on the lesser charge of a technical breach of DORA.

Repington wrote a detailed account in his *War Diaries* both of the trial and of his attitude to the prospect of a trial. He describes someone untroubled, confident and truculent enough to tell his solicitor that he would 'as well be hanged for a sheep as a lamb' for he intended the country should 'learn the whole truth' even if he were to be convicted. Yet he was no fool. Though he did not mention it, there had been the recent, disconcerting example of his friend, the distinguished portrait painter de László, who had been arrested, interrogated by the Special Branch and then imprisoned for a small infraction of DORA's draconian provisions. Even more immediately, he would have remembered how, on the day his first article appeared in the *Morning Post*, Mr Justice Darling, senior Puisne Judge, invited him to dine at the Inner Temple. There he had been advised if 'he got into trouble and was imprisoned with the intention of silencing him, he was to apply for a writ of *Habeas Corpus*'. If the writ were refused, then he should apply to other judges until successful.[37] Imprisonment for an indefinite term was not a pleasing although quite likely possibility he had to face. Apparently undeterred, Repington had written, in his own words, several 'slashing attacks' on the War Cabinet. Many, even among his friends, thought his latest articles 'most reckless'. Everyone was left wondering what step the government might take. Colonel Cole, a particular admirer of Repington, supposed that his recklessness for his own neck suggested Repington 'must have gone mad'.[38]

Late in the afternoon of 12 February two Scotland Yard officers called at Maryon Hall. The following day Repington was served with a summons. Together with Gwynne he was charged with having 'published information regarding "plans and conduct of military operations and military dispositions"'. The trial was due to begin on Saturday morning. Carson had been approached to act for the defence but had declined, much to Lady Carson's disappointment for she was quite sure 'her Edward would make mincemeat of them'.[39] Carson had suggested Repington should defend himself. 'I should prefer to do so' was the correspondent's bold but foolhardy response. But Gwynne, not normally timorous in such matters, begged him to leave their defence in the hands of their counsel, Mr Tindal Atkinson KC. To this appeal Repington 'reluctantly agreed'.[40]

An altogether different picture of the bold and careless colonel from that of the *War Diaries* emerges from Jean Hamilton's diary. On Wednesday 13 February she wrote, the Repingtons were to lunch with them. The two men from Scotland Yard had left Maryon Hall when 'The Col. and Molly arrived, both very white and shaken.' Molly had thought 'her beloved Charlie was about to be dragged off to prison at once'. He telephoned Gwynne. Their exchange took so long the other guests 'went down to lunch without him'. When eventually he joined them at the table, 'he looked terribly upset and talked wildly about the possibility of being shot'. The luncheon, Lady Hamilton admitted, was 'very awkward and uncomfortable'. Repington after his initial outburst had become unusually taciturn and 'very careful about what he said'. Sir Ian, trying as any good host should to lighten the prevailing atmosphere, declared his wife thought Rasputin and Bolo the two greatest villains of the war. Repington immediately responded by asking, 'Who will be the English villain?' Everyone round the table without exception thought 'You', but dared not say so aloud. In the ensuing embarrassed silence, sensing what they must be thinking, he attempted to hide his discomfort by volunteering the name of Horatio Bottomley. He was all too well aware that colourful tales about his past, many invented and none to his advantage, were at that moment the meat and drink of a thousand fashionable dinner tables. It was for once a relief to leave the Hamiltons.

Later that same day Bonar Law announced to a sparsely attended Commons that Repington and Gwynne would be 'prosecuted under the Defence of the Realm Act Regulations with all despatch'. Scarcely a backbencher sought to question the Chancellor, but there was a brief, interesting exchange between him and Percy Harris. When asked whether he was aware Repington had 'written for the first three and half years of the war in *The Times*' and at no time had action been taken against him, Law responded, 'Every criminal lives a long time before he is convicted.'[41] No one seemed the least surprised or disconcerted by the Tory leader's scarcely relevant or judicious assertion. In Society, Cynthia Asquith recorded in her diary, 'Everybody [was] very full of Repington's arrest.' Few, however, troubled to make sure that their facts were accurate.[42]

In all the eager speculation Gwynne scarcely merited a mention. Everyone anticipated scandalously fascinating legal proceedings and it was this that prompted Dawson to suggest '*The Times* ought to have someone in court with a watching brief.' He thought it likely Repington might try to malign them.[43] The last two days before the trial the defendants spent locked in discussion with their solicitor and counsel wrangling over what might or might not be said. A friend who treated Repington to luncheon urged him to defend himself 'and take the big line of the freedom of political criticism'. But his own lawyers suggested the odds on him winning were no better than even money. He did not feel particularly sanguine and this dark mood was reinforced by the news that his great friend Locket Agnew had that morning suffered a fatal heart attack. The two had lunched together only three days previously, when Locket had promised to bail him out if he were arrested and to arrange his defence. It was not the most propitious omen.[44]

At 11:30 a.m on Saturday 16 February, the day of the trial, correspondent and editor set out together for the Bow Street Magistrates Court. A great throng crowded the streets. 'No such crowd at Bow Street since Crippen!' wrote young Lieutenant Guthrie to his mother. This observation by a friend's son Repington happily recorded for posterity in his *Diaries*, adding for good measure the exclamation mark. Now the day had come, he determined to make the most of the occasion. Notables and their ladies filled all the available seating for spectators while fifty shorthand reporters and sundry officials crowded the well of the court. Repington looked remarkably svelte in his newly tailored uniform. It enhanced the appearance of calm nonchalance he affected. The initial hearing lasted little more than the hour before it was adjourned until the following Thursday. During that time Sir Gordon Hewart, with moderation and courtesy, presented the case for the prosecution. The only person to give evidence was Sir Edward Cook, Director of the Press Bureau. The day concluded with a suitably dramatic flourish – a prolonged air raid.

Before the trial recommenced, on 18 February, Bonar Law announced to the Commons that Robertson had accepted a home command. Despite his earlier insistence he had not resigned, he had been stymied.[45] Repington might have been expected to have been upset, but he told Jean Hamilton he thought Robertson had played the patriot. All things considered, Repington seemed remarkably cheerful. The many letters of sympathy, congratulations and approval he received by every post helped. The promised 'big row' in Parliament was no longer a likely contingency, but he saw no reason why he should abandon his criticism. He thought the Prime Minister's explanation of the Versailles plans offered an opening and a fine opportunity to wound him at a later date.[46] The article he wrote, 'with a stiff criticism of LG's explanation', greatly pleased Gwynne but attracted the unfavourable attention of the Censor who desired the political criticism excised. Gwynne objected strongly but to no avail.

The trial proceedings recommenced on Thursday 21 February but finished shortly before luncheon. Unlike his fellow defendant, at the trial's approach Gwynne had grown more confident, expecting the case against them to be dismissed. Their counsel made what Repington described as 'an effective speech … showing clearly that we had not contravened the regulations'. Nonetheless the magistrates found them guilty 'of the technical offence of disobeying the Censorship'. Each was fined £100 and costs. The decision was flawed, the prosecution blatantly political. Hewart had argued, under Regulation 18, the defendants were unable to claim the information published was, for whatever reason, not directly or indirectly useful to the enemy. That was absurd. It meant even

Fig. 12 Field Marshal Sir William 'Wully' Robertson (1859–1933)

an official communiqué could be a breach of the regulations.[47] Repington thought the decision nonsensical. He had written nothing that had not appeared previously in the German press and had the satisfaction of knowing most of the national press thought likewise. If offence it were, the press condoned it and congratulated the *Morning Post*. Every day brought him 'shoals of letters all approving our action, several offering to pay our fines ... and not one word of hostile comment'. General Maurice wrote to say, although he had been told not to talk to Repington, nonetheless he must tell him how greatly he admired his 'courage and determination'. He had not thought it possible in England but it was quite clear to him now that the correspondent had been the victim of a political prosecution. Repington replied with unwonted if understandable braggadocio, 'If they want to shut my mouth they will have to lock me up. I propose to continue my criticisms without allowing myself to be deterred by political prosecution.'[48] There was a letter too from Robertson. 'Like you I did what I thought was best in the general interests of the Country ... I am in no way surprised at the turn events have taken ... Your sacrifice has been great. You have a difficult time ahead of you but the great thing is to keep on a straight course.' Repington had fought hard and long for Robertson and thoroughly earned the general's commendation. Not had he needed reminding that there would be difficult times ahead. If Lloyd George continued to do as he was doing, he would lose the war for the Allies. Repington certainly was not 'complacent'. Nor did he believe, as Lord Blake suggests, 'the sympathy of the fashionable world and an agreeable sense of political martyrdom' amounted to 'ample compensation' for the fine and costs he suffered.[49] A letter Repington received from Allenby touched on what was, for him, the real priority. 'The Bull' clearly acknowledged 'the west was the essential battle-ground where victory would be decisive. Make sure of victory there',Allenby had written.[50] Repington had always found this view of strategic priorities compelling. So long as he remained convinced it was the necessary and sufficient condition of any Allied final victory, then he had no intention of abandoning his own crusade.

19 Repington discredited

When Robertson replaced Archie Murray as CIGS and Haig usurped French as C-in-C, Repington had not been impressed for he thought such changes no more than 'throwing dust in the eyes of the public'. Much more effective would have been to change the politicians. What had pleased him was that in future, orders concerned with strategy and operations would be issued in the name of the CIGS.[1] As prime minister, Lloyd George found it increasingly difficult to accept advice that differed from his own very definite views. He was not sympathetic to the generals' strategic opinions, most particularly their relentless concentration upon the German army and the western front. The way they continued to sacrifice men and treasure demonstrated a complete indifference to political imperatives. Robertson was never persuaded LG's ideas were sound. He utterly opposed what he denigrated as 'amateur schemes' or 'side-shows' and, like Haig, condemned them as a waste of time and effort. When LG proposed they refer their differences to the military representatives of the Supreme War Council at Versailles, the generals were shocked. It seemed that because the Prime Minister did not like their advice, he was prepared to look for more congenial counsel elsewhere.[2]

In the prolonged struggle with Lloyd George, Robertson was loyally supported by his imperturbable, clear-thinking friend, Major General F. B. Maurice. As DMO, he deservedly enjoyed a formidable reputation for his efficiency. In mid February 1918 Henry Wilson, altogether more amenable to the Prime Minister's notions than Robertson, replaced 'Wully' as CIGS. Maurice was convinced the thinking of the Prime Minister and the new CIGS was so fundamentally flawed it would lead to disaster. They chose to ignore the compelling evidence he had carefully elicited of an imminent and massive German attack in the west.

On Thursday 21 March 1918 Maurice informed Wilson the battle he had long forecast had begun opposite the British Third and Fifth Armies. Wilson chose to report to the War Cabinet the Germans had launched 'no more than a big raid'.[3] Repington at once feared the worst and declared only the valour of British soldiers could atone for the War Cabinet's blind folly. The true reality of the danger the German offensive posed was soon apparent to Lloyd George. He warned the country, defeat would be avoided only if the 'extra men needed to maintain our armies in the field' were forthcoming. Although he insisted this claim had never been challenged, scarcely a fortnight earlier Bonar Law had claimed the Germans on the western front enjoyed no dangerous superiority of numbers and it was for that reason he remained 'a little sceptical' about the threatened German offensive. Law's 'scepticism' had prompted a slashing retort from Repington in the *Morning Post*. He had condemned Law for his lack of any 'sense of the realities of war, of its mechanics, of the way Germans fought, or the advantages of the initiative'. He prophesied, the follies and blindness of the War Cabinet would bring forth bitter fruit.[4] The Cabinet, he claimed, was in a state of confusion, the Premier sunk in the depths of despair. The country awaited Cabinet orders, but in vain. When the king had visited Flanders his troops had called-out, 'For God's sake send us men.' But still the lies, the hypocrisy continued. Repington noted how, like the politicians, the *Daily Mail* never mentioned their earlier support for the War Cabinet's criminal dilatoriness. Suddenly they had all discovered, 'the men should have been sent earlier'.[5]

His *War Diaries* do not reveal how hard Repington worked at this time. He gathered facts and elicited opinion from many disparate sources. Despite his work being circumscribed and frustrated by the Censor, he wrote on half a dozen different subjects in as many days. It grew increasingly plain, the censorship was politically inspired. For the second time an article critical of Lloyd George had been heavily censored. Certainly he had intended to offend Lloyd George, but he had written 'nothing that could have given the slightest information to the enemy'.[6] For the second consecutive week Gwynne apologised to him that his work had been 'butchered for purely political reasons'.[7]

Not so immediately worrying had been a number of attacks made upon Repington in the foreign press. In *Az Est*, a front-page article set in large type reported, 'Colonel Repington wants peace with the Dual Monarchy.' The *Corriere della Sera*, the source of the story, had revealed Repington was 'Achilleris', a regular contributor to the *National News*. 'I saw the *Corriere* attack', Repington told Gwynne. He professed to be very fond of 'our dear, pleasant, inefficient, Italian friends. When the Italian Army performs creditable actions I shall be the first to applaud them.' But he did not choose to have his military views dreamed up for him by the Italian Information Bureau. He had written a sharp letter telling them to mind their own business. It would have been wiser had he bluntly denied what were claimed to be his opinions.[8]

He wondered whether the source of these 'foreign' stories might not lie nearer home – perhaps as close as Lloyd George's 'Garden suburb' where so many members of Milner's *Kindergarten* were employed.[9] He referred, somewhat elliptically, to this possibility in a diary entry. On the night of 7/8 March he had watched from an upstairs window of his Hampstead home an air-raid by German bombers. A misdirected anti-aircraft shell had exploded close by, scattering shrapnel that lodged all round the window where, moments earlier, he had been standing. Friends suggested, only half-jokingly, the shell must have been fired by the *Kindergarten*; Milner's disciples were now shooting at him from St James's Park. He observed laconically, how fortunate 'they could never hit anything they aimed at'. He thought he might ask the nearby anti-aircraft gun emplacement at The Spaniards 'to shoot back at No. 10'.[10] At the time he was more concerned about Haig's future than any supposed danger to himself. He warned Gwynne, it seemed to him that Lloyd George, determined 'to cut the painter of his responsibilities', might well choose 'to sacrifice Haig ... kick[ing] him out if anything went wrong'. LG was capable of sacrificing anyone and anything to save himself. He reminded Gwynne, responsibility for their present troubles in France was 'the Government's entirely. They alone failed to maintain and reinforce our Armies in France.'[11]

On Thursday evening, 4 April, Repington dined with Robertson at York House. It was their first opportunity in a long while for an extended leisurely conversation, or as they called it, 'a good growl'. They did not differ in their estimate of the renewed German attack. Enemy troops were only 10 miles from Amiens and 30 from Abbeville. The key would be whether they could hold on to Amiens. At the very end of their conversation they momentarily broached the subject of the Prime Minister's obsessive concern, shared by some of his closest political friends, that some soldiers were intent upon interfering with civil government. LG's misapprehension amused more than concerned them. Didn't he realise, soldiers had no wish to interfere with the government's concerns? They had enough on their hands already; all they wanted was to be allowed to get on with their own business. Some politicians were unable to appreciate the difference between peace and war. Endlessly, inexhaustibly, they sought to interfere in matters about which they knew nothing. They were the real source of the trouble.

On Sunday 10 April Gough, until recently commander of the Fifth Army, telephoned Repington and arranged to meet him that night and dine at Maryon Hall. Repington assumed that the War Cabinet had sent Gough home because they were looking for military scapegoats to deflect criticism from themselves. That evening, Gough gave his version of the first week of the battle and the fate of the Fifth Army. His front, he explained, extended for 42 miles and was too thinly held. He had no more available reserves. Those troops he did have, New Army volunteers and second-line Territorials, were inexperienced or insufficiently trained. Reorganisation from twelve to nine battalions in every division had reduced his infantry strength and thoroughly unsettled the men. The German attack had been anticipated for more than a month.[12] His instructions had been to lose ground rather than men, but in the first eight days of fighting up to 29 March, he had lost 60 per cent of his strength together with some 600 guns. Yet at no time was the army broken, nor had it lost alignment. Repington concluded, after four great holes had been punched in Gough's battle line at Tergnier, Essignol-le-Grand, Massemy and Hargicourt, retreat had been inevitable. On the basis of Gough's briefing, the next day he wrote an article 'defending the 5th Army from their traducers'. When its return from the Press Bureau was delayed, he assumed it was because the Prime Minister, due to make a speech that day to Parliament, intended to blame the soldiers. The last thing Lloyd George would want was for the other side to be given a fair hearing before he had manufactured opinion in his favour.[13]

The significant section in Lloyd George's speech was his unqualified assertion, the army in France had been '*considerably stronger*' on 1 January 1918 than on the previous New Year's Day. The country, Repington believed, like Parliament was 'so utterly ignorant of military affairs and so entirely misled by LG's accounts of the situation', whatever explanation he offered the House would be believed. He bitterly regretted there was 'not one man in Parliament with the knowledge and courage to denounce and expose' the Prime Minister for the charlatan he was. The few critics outside Parliament would be 'muzzled by the Censor'. This final, pessimistic premonition seemed fulfilled when his own 'strong condemnation and refutation of LG's excuses', which should have appeared in the *Morning Post*, languished instead in the Censor's office. However, two days later, on Wednesday 17 April, to his surprise and to the considerable anger of Lloyd George, the article appeared. Even Repington admitted his criticisms were 'pretty severe. I am told it cuts like a knife', he recorded with all too evident satisfaction.[14]

A luncheon with Robertson provided the opportunity for an exchange on how they thought events in France might develop. That day the army lost Neuve Chapelle and the Germans took Wytschaete and Bailleul. Accounts coming out of GHQ in France indicated the troops were 'dog-tired after 26 days of continuous fighting'. It was next day before Brigadier General Joe Laycock, brought more cheering news. He agreed that the men were 'pretty worn [but] the Boches suffered a lot'. The

Brigadier had been with Gough's Fifth Army during the retreat. The officers and men had told him how pleased they were with what Repington had written in their defence. He had 'told the truth where the politicians had lied'.

At a luncheon party Cambon likened Repington to Clemenceau: 'a polemical journalist ... aggressive and fond of the offensive ... who cannot resist the temptation to score off people.' Repington was, as intended, duly flattered. But Cambon sought also gently to warn his English friend that hubris must inevitably lead to nemesis. Clemenceau as his country's premier was much more than a mere journalist. For that reason he might be excused conduct or opinions that if indulged in too often by Repington would cost him dear. Cambon's observation had been prompted by the ministerial changes announced at the end of the previous week, most particularly Derby's appointment as Ambassador to France. Cambon made it all too obvious that he was not impressed. Repington had written an article ostensibly about Derby, but which was actually much more about Milner, the 'King of Lancashire's' replacement as the Secretary of State for War. In the same piece Repington had also criticised Lloyd George's 'latest fatuous excuses to the House'. He had said as much and as roughly on many previous occasions and so had no reason to suppose his words would soon bring a storm of unparalleled ferocity about his ears. He happily accepted McKenna's smiling reassurance that his articles were among 'the best things in the press ... most terrible and ruining LG'.[15]

The words of a soldier critic of the Prime Minister now almost, if not entirely, stole the limelight from Repington. Might he reasonably have anticipated that a letter written by Maurice questioning Lloyd George's veracity would be supposed to have had something to do with him? He had neither seen nor communicated with Maurice for more than three months,[16] yet their enemies accused them of conspiring together.[17] The two men were not friends but acquaintances rarely in one another's company. They had first met eight months after Maurice became DMO. On that occasion they had dined at Claridges. Maurice had been Repington's guest. On this, as on future occasions, Maurice pursued his own clearly defined agenda.[18]

For some time Maurice had reflected upon the speech Lloyd George had made to the Commons on 9 April. His first thought had been to wonder whether the Prime Minister had 'as usual [been] working secretly against Haig'. Although a most unlikely interpretation, the Prime Minister might have made his mistake innocently. Much more likely and to a less fair-minded person than Maurice, the obvious design had been to allot to Haig and Gough the entire blame for the reverses the army suffered. Indeed, it is difficult to see why this explanation was not *immediately* apparent to Maurice. He did not choose to comment on the way Lloyd George had heaped praise upon Henry Wilson's inaccurate forecast of the attack yet made no mention of his own more accurate forecasts made throughout the previous two months. Not until he paid a brief visit to France, a week after Lloyd George's speech, and spoke to a variety of senior officers, had Maurice realised how greatly the army resented the Prime Minister's unequivocal assertion that they had been stronger in 1918 than in 1917. That claim implied the Fifth Army's retreat was due either to the inadequacy of its commanders, or of its troops. Only then had he promised to scrutinise the statistics upon which Lloyd George's claim had been based.[19]

He discovered the increase of 325,000 men in France was almost entirely accounted for by British and coloured labour. The most scrupulous of men, he still hesitated. It was *just about within the realms of possibility* the Prime Minister's mistake had been unintended. But Bonar Law's assertion, on 23 April, the decision to extend the British line had *not* been contrary to the wishes of Haig and Robertson but agreed between the British and French military authorities,[20] put the matter beyond any remaining doubt. Maurice was now certain the government *was* pursuing a policy based upon a false and dangerous strategy, contrary to the repeated advice of the British high command. Not the soldiers but the politicians had been responsible for the disaster the Fifth Army suffered.

It had been a genuine surprise for Repington and Gwynne when, on Monday 6 May, Maurice paid them a visit. As they had not the least idea of what he planned, they were amazed to learn he intended to publish a letter in several newspapers, including their own, that would contradict the claims made to the Commons by the Prime Minister and the Leader of the House.[21] Repington immediately realised, Maurice's proposal amounted to professional suicide. Robertson insisted Maurice chose to act as he did of his own free will. He felt no one else could do it. This duty he owed to his country.[22] When Jean Hamilton visited Maryon Hall the following week, the first thing she asked Repington was had he anything to do with the Maurice letter. He replied, 'Nothing,' but then added, as Maurice had so much to lose he had begged him not to submit the letter. 'Allow me to do it in your stead,' he had pleaded. Jean Hamilton immediately appreciated that this would be construed as evidence of a coup planned by the two men. Repington's action, she thought, was prompted entirely by his vanity. She always found it difficult to credit him with any noble or charitable sentiment. On this occasion, the balance of evidence suggests Repington *had* been moved to protect Maurice for selfless reasons. He certainly admired Maurice's nobility of purpose.[23]

The letter's publication caused a political sensation. To Lloyd George and his colleagues it afforded positive proof of the military cabal they had long supposed conspired against them. If Maurice's charges were true, then nothing could save the government. That, however, was for the Commons to determine. Asquith demanded a select committee of the House; Bonar Law, a judicial inquiry as a more appropriate instrument to examine an issue that affected the honour of ministers. Lloyd George *insisted* upon a vote of confidence, confident he could satisfactorily respond to all Maurice's claims. His was a high risk strategy and if it failed, none better than he knew his administration *must* fall.

Bonar Law could only defer to the Prime Minister. Was Lloyd George being too clever, too confident? A conversation with Carson soon convinced Repington the Prime Minister knew exactly what he was doing; that there was no danger of him losing. On the day of the debate Repington published a stirling defence of Maurice in the *Morning Post*, but the parliamentary set-piece, as he had anticipated, proved most disappointing. Asquith was hopeless. He utterly failed to make any sort of case to discredit the Prime Minister, whereas Lloyd George was at his brilliant best. No one in the House possessed the knowledge to refute him. His rhetoric blew away every shred of effective opposition. He not only secured the confidence of the House, but triumphed in the lobbies with a majority of 187.

Lloyd George refuted Maurice's figures by quoting from the War Office Weekly Summary. He had never placed much trust in the accuracy of these figures, supposing them to be cooked up by the military to suit the interests of the War Office. Hence his amazement, then fury when the first Weekly Summary produced under Milner converted the previous 'Allied superiority of 86,000 rifles into a German superiority of 330,000'. The Premier was 'staggered' by this seemingly 'inexplicable exaggeration'.[24] If the new figures were accepted as true then his recent, successful defence was obviously scuppered. How could Milner, as Secretary of State, have allowed such politically damaging figures to emerge? LG demanded a thorough investigation. Milner was unable to respond satisfactorily and chose, as the wiser part, to remain silent. In that moment the very special relationship he had enjoyed as Lloyd George's colleague and valued adviser was, if not sundered, fatally weakened.[25]

Repington, after examining Hansard, had determined he must answer the Prime Minister. Whether lies or damned lies, statistics most certainly lay at the heart of this debate. To rebut Lloyd George most effectively he would need his own *reliable* figures. He thought he knew where he could get them. He should have anticipated, as he was very soon to discover, that doors previously open were now firmly barred. Only the previous month he had sought fruitlessly to secure reliable official information from Auckland Geddes. Repington could not know, though he must surely have suspected, Geddes had passed his request on to the Prime Minister. 'I know he has been a very hostile critic,' Geddes wrote, 'so I should not like to see him without your knowledge and acquiescence ... Do you desire me not to see him, or shall I see him and give him such information as it would be advantageous to make known to him?' LG's response had been instant and angry. Whatever others might think, he *knew* Repington was 'a very dangerous man'. That he should 'demand' military information was nothing less than 'sheer impertinence on his part ... What does he want it for? Sheer mischief – I would not trust the man with any information.'[26]

It would not have surprised Lloyd George to learn that on the day following the Maurice debate Repington dined with the Robertsons and that Maurice accompanied by his wife completed the party. The Prime Minister's sensitive political instincts had increasingly induced in him, if not paranoia then something closely resembling it. He suspected he was surrounded by men who caballed and plotted to his disadvantage. In his overheated imagination he created an alliance of soldiers and politicians plotting to take over the levers of civil government, eager to replace him and the War Cabinet with their own nominees. In particular, he had long suspected Robertson, Maurice and Repington. His recent, brilliant parliamentary triumph based upon a conjuring of statistics had successfully thwarted his critics' immediate purpose. But if he was not mistaken, they would soon be plotting further mischief against him. Had he been present at their meeting, their obvious depression could only have pleased him. They agreed that 'M[aurice]'s action had undoubtedly done harm'; sadly, not to Lloyd George's fortunes, but to Maurice's. Maurice spent the next morning with Repington and that same evening dined at Maryon Hall. There was very little that could usefully be said. He confirmed he had 'received his blue pill ... for his breach of King's Regulations'. Knowing that Maurice was not a rich man and would miss his full salary, Repington was delighted to learn he had accepted a handsome offer to write for the *Daily Chronicle*. At least he would be 'financially *à l'abri*'.[27]

When Milner was appointed Secretary of State for War, a leader in the *Morning Post* had declared the War Office had been doubly fortunate in gaining him and losing Derby. Gwynne had always looked upon Milner with particular favour. A member of Lloyd George's War Cabinet from its formation in December 1916, he was the Prime Minister's very close and influential associate. Yet scarcely one week later Repington chose to describe the new Secretary of State not as Lloyd George's 'associate' but as his 'henchman'. The single cause of the present crisis, Repington insisted, was 'the ignorance and contempt the War Cabinet show for the best military advice'. Milner, just as much as Lloyd George, deserved to be arraigned for the 'culpable misconduct of the higher direction of the war'. It was 'astonishing' Milner should have been given charge of the army when his decisions had 'brought the army into its present deadly peril'.[28] An impenitent Repington seemed uncaring of any injury his words might inflict. When Charlie Beresford over luncheon happened to enquire whether Repington was alarmed by the present military situation, he responded, 'Only when I see the War Cabinet is sitting.' As an afterthought he added, 'But when I learn they are sitting continuously then I'm frightened to death.' Charlie B could scarcely suppress his delighted guffaws.

Milner took himself far too seriously to appreciate any quip made at his expense. He never ignored what he considered were undeserved private slanders, so it was not likely he would disregard Repington's recent outburst. He never understood why uncomplaining acceptance of ill-informed criticism should be the necessary price a minister was expected to pay for doing his public duty. He disapproved of a constitution that in the name of parliamentary democracy made the executive answerable to the majority in a legislature whose authority rested upon the approval of an ill-informed electorate, more often than not misled by a venal press. He had never readily tolerated anyone with whom he disagreed. No man in public life can expect total immunity from critics any more than he can expect to avoid an occasional painful or embarrassing shellacking from opponents in the press. But the new Secretary of State's friends seemed to think that he ought to be the exception to that rule and remain inviolable. In particular, they thought it outrageous he should be the subject of Repington's invective.

That weekend Milner carefully considered the whole matter and manner of the attacks upon him and how best they might be answered. His peremptory admonishment by Lloyd George, as though he were no more than some lowly clerk, had made him feel particularly vulnerable and sore. The clear if painful implication was the Prime Minister no longer considered him his most trusted and highly valued adviser. Consequently he was less inclined than ever to ignore Repington's gratuitous insults. Months earlier he had successfully 'suggested' to Dawson that the doors of Printing House Square ought to be barred to that same pestilential busybody for his constant assaults upon the War Cabinet in general and the Prime Minister in particular. Though stripped of the influence he had previously enjoyed as *The Times* military correspondent, it appeared

Fig. 13 James Louis 'Jim' Garvin (1868–1947)

Repington had not learned his lesson. Milner determined this time the wretched fellow should have no opportunity to forget. He would not only see him stripped of what influence he might still retain as a military pundit, but ensure his public humiliation. Accordingly, on Monday 29 April he instructed Waldorf Astor, 'See to it that Repington's conduct does not go unpunished.'

Astor had achieved his place among Milner's most intimate counsellors because he owned the *Observer*. Milner had never doubted the power and influence of the press to shape and create opinion. Astor's *Observer* did not possess anything like the prestige and influence of

Northcliffe's *Times*, where Geoffrey Dawson kept watch in Milner's interest. Nevertheless, in J. L. Garvin the *Observer* possessed an editor of genius who, in terms of political influence, punched well above his weight.

Milner did not wish it to be known generally that he was in any way involved in the planned humiliation of Repington. It served his purpose ideally that Astor should be his agent. Astor in his turn chose Garvin to be their proxy assassin in the *Observer*. He was instructed to expose Repington 'thoroughly and ruthlessly'.[29] Garvin did not flinch from the task. He seemed more than happy to play the character assassin, to destroy his fellow journalist's reputation even though, on several occasions, privately and publicly, Repington had most generously acknowledged Garvin's outstanding gifts as a prolific and innovative journalist and editor. Their occasional differences of opinion in the past had been borne well enough without any particular rancour.[30] He had thought enough of Repington's abilities to ask him to take over his trademark *Observer* editorial for weeks when the burden of mourning his son's death had become too much to bear. He had freely and generously acknowledged Repington had discharged that onerous task brilliantly, to his entire satisfaction. But Garvin was the prisoner of his passionate, mercurial temperament. In a moment it could hurl him into the depths of misery and self-pity. In such a mood, his violent temper was readily roused. He was beset with acute, seemingly intractable financial problems that despite his constant and frantic endeavours by the early months of 1918 obliged him to consider whether he had any future at all as editor of the *Observer*. Perhaps this explains his willingness to carry out his proprietor's instruction, but it does not excuse either the violence or the dishonesty of his tirade.

In his 'Exposure', Garvin insisted that Repington's character and temperament alike were 'defective', 'weak', pusillanimous', 'unstable' and 'hysterical'.[31] A 'devious trouble-maker', he was 'irresponsible and inconsistent', his judgment 'disfigured by passion and disordered by private enmities'. His articles 'slanderous, malicious misrepresentations', were full of 'falsely, fraudulent charges' and stuffed with 'jeremiads, panegyrics, Jobations and imprecations'. He had 'encouraged and delighted the enemy', 'sown dissension among Allies', 'bred distrust between the Army and the War Office', 'distorted American opinion', 'struck at the foundations of both army discipline and stable government' and 'weakened the public's faith and cohesion in the hour of crisis'. What could account for this impossibly long catalogue of alleged wickednesses and betrayals? Garvin insisted it was motivated by Repington's 'long-standing, private vendetta against the most searching professional mind in the British army', Henry Wilson.[32] However, the climax of Repington's most recent 'disreputable and miserable crusade' had been his 'disgraceful attacks upon the Government'. Repington was 'a mutinous nuisance, a cancer on public life that ought not to be tolerated any longer'. Garvin's style had always been somewhat flamboyant, but even his biographer had to admit on this occasion his brutal assault upon Repington 'from beginning to end stuttered with bad taste'.[33]

After this opening tirade Garvin impertinently claimed he had no wish to take issue with Repington on personal grounds! His arguments would be 'impersonal, objective, thorough, detailed and rational'. This was an absurd claim for his personal insults were more appropriate to a Punch and Judy show than the calm, forensic study he had promised. His hectic diatribe successively insulted, maligned and defamed Repington, addressing him one moment as 'the Duke of Yellington' and next as 'a mad-mænaed in uniform disordered by passion and private enmity'. 'Who was Col. Repington?' was no honest interrogatory but a device to demonstrate 'a once distinguished soldier' had forgotten to honour 'the hope so recently expressed by the Bow Street magistrate, that in future he would remember to be a good citizen' and not write 'notorious articles helpful to the enemy'. Those were not the magistrate's exact words but it scarcely mattered for their incorrect remembrance served as preface to a series of false characterisations of Repington. He was 'one of the worst enemies of his country', 'more mischievous than any Bolo', 'a self-hypnotised impressionist with a shallow-shifting mind incapable of thinking any hard problem clean out', someone who, when 'fairly stung by Io's gadfly, rushes amok and abroad without any sense of direction'. He was 'a criminal mischief-maker', and much else besides. All this, Garvin concluded, served to demonstrate Repington deserved to be 'squelched without remorse'.

Intent to reveal the supposed inconsistencies and contradictions in Repington's thinking, Garvin claimed to quote 'chapter and verse' from the military correspondent's own articles. The problem was that frequently the quotations he employed lacked the original vital caveats and qualifications. Their absence entirely alienated the original meaning. Similarly, words shorn of their former context sometimes conveyed quite the opposite of what had been intended. From the pastiche of Garvin's making, it might reasonably have been concluded that during the course of the war, in his contributions to *The Times*, *Morning Post* and *National News*, Repington not only frequently contradicted himself, he had done so knowingly and intentionally. Upon the basis of Garvin's 'evidence', a historian would later conclude that 'it was as though [Repington] had tried to walk down both sides of the same street at the same time in opposite directions'.[34]

The 'quotations' Garvin had purloined were a few from the familiar daily *Morning Post* and the rest from the much less well-known *National News*. According to Garvin, 'Everyone knew' Repington had once been capable of brilliant work, but 'profound weaknesses of character ha[d] always marred [his] versatile ability and thwarted his career'. He was prone to make 'wretched gaffes' and 'fatuous prophecies'. At *The Times* he had been 'restrained' by his editors and proprietors. Even so, he perpetrated an occasional example of 'unwonted levity'. One such had been his forecast, made at the end of August 1914, 'that the Russian steam-roller ought to reach Berlin in two months'.[35] Garvin, with bold effrontery, claimed, 'the exposure of this fantastic delusion caused Repington to jump the other way and become the blindest of extreme Westerners'. Confidently Garvin asserted there had been other examples of the military correspondent's 'unexampled ill-judgment', but failed to provide any.

Since Repington's 'dismissal' from *The Times*, his 'hysterical instability' had enjoyed an exceedingly free range until eventually he was sufficiently deluded as to persuade himself it was possible 'to write both for the *Morning Post*, a reactionary but ultra-patriotic organ, and the *Naturalised News* which professed to be of an extreme democratic tendency'. Garvin, who knew perfectly well what he was doing, persistently referred to the *National* as the *Naturalised News*, a pathetic schoolboy pun intended to appeal to the confused xenophobic prejudices of his readers. For the same reason he repeatedly emphasised the paper was edited by a former Austrian and financed by a former Dutchman. Though a respectable, Liberal, Sunday newspaper, he insisted it was 'politically well to the Left'.

On Irish conscription, Garvin accused Repington of 'hedging' and 'sentimentalising'. This he sought to prove with twenty words extracted from a contribution to the issue for 14 April. Had he quoted the entire sentence, no one could have thought that the author advocated 'leaving Ireland out of the account'. There was no difference and so no inconsistency between what Repington wrote in the *Post* and what he subsequently advocated in the *National News*. And despite Garvin's disparaging remarks, the wartime loyalties of the *National News* were unimpeachable, as reflected in its motto, 'Country before Party'. This, however, did not stop Garvin shamelessly savaging the paper, falsely accusing it of being 'unpatriotic and an enemy of the Government'. What peeved him, and similarly his proprietor Astor, was the *National* still sold for a penny whereas the *Observer* had recently raised its price to tuppence. This explains why he insisted it was 'carried on at a heavy loss for no intelligible reason'. Also, why he added the spiteful false innuendo,

'perhaps it was to attack the British Government in ambiguous circumstances such as are not tolerated in any other belligerent country'. What
he did not choose to disclose was he and Astor had laboured unsuccessfully to have the *National News* suppressed. In condemning as disloyal and
unpatriotic a thoroughly respectable newspaper, his biographer admits,
he 'came close to denying the freedom of the press in time of war'.[36]

Garvin's attack, devised at Milner's behest, had been born of intrigue.
Scarcely surprisingly, therefore, it was permeated with notions and pre-
monitions of secret plots. The better to incriminate Repington, Garvin
affected to give substance to the paranoid delusion haunting Lloyd
George's waking hours – that there was a conspiracy to replace his
administration with, if not exactly a military junta, then a government
entirely in thrall to the army. Garvin now suggested Generals Robertson
and Maurice had been involved in such a conspiracy. They had chosen to
conspire to replace Lloyd George's administration because Repington had
mesmerised them into doing as he wished. He had been their Svengali. The
entirely spurious status Garvin afforded Repington in this make-believe
conspiracy explained why he treated Maurice as though he was no more
than a mere 'cipher', a tool used to serve Repington's purpose. He did not,
however, go as far as Lloyd George, who later would suggest that Maurice
was not only 'subservient' but 'unbalanced'.[37] Garvin avowed Repington
had exploited Robertson. With 'melodramatic absurdity and false pathos'
he had portrayed the former CIGS as 'a blunt, rugged, unbending soldier
wantonly overthrown by crafty and cruel politicians'. Garvin insisted that
Robertson had not been a significant conspirator whereas other newspapers recently had linked Robertson's name with those of Asquith,
Jellicoe and Trenchard.[38]

Garvin's many absurd allegations continued in relentless spate. He
insisted, 'the tragic events at St Quentin were the direct result of the
fatal dualism that sophists like Repington tried to preserve'. But now
the correspondent's campaign of 'demoralisation and calumny' had
been exposed. 'Under the Prime Minister, Lord Milner and with men
like General Sir Henry Wilson ... we have by far the most efficient and
modern system of war-direction and army-management at the British
War Office since this struggle began.' For 'the sake of the Allies, the
people and the British Army' there should be 'an end to vendetta and
claque'. Garvin confidently asserted Lloyd George and Milner would 'cut
out this malignancy of public life'.

According to Professor Gollin, Garvin's exposé 'thoroughly smashed
Repington'.[39] Milner, supposing enough was enough, piously told
Robertson he now intended 'to do all I possibly can to put a stop to all
poisonous controversy ... With the enemy at our gates we simply must

close our ranks and put an end to internal discord.'[40] He sent a copy of this letter to Lloyd George and with it included Robertson's letter in which he had denied the rumours that with others he had been involved in a political plot. The pathetic, apologetic tones showed that 'Wully' desperately wanted to make his peace with the government. In the circumstances, Milner thought it was probably 'better to help him to get out of a false position'. Robertson had not been 'the principal intriguer but [had] got in with bad company'. Repington and the *Morning Post* crowd were 'really the devils of the piece'. Their plot had failed. 'The sooner we get him out of the way of temptation the better.'[41]

The bounds of the anti-Repington campaign had been set wider than the confines of the *Observer*'s circulation. Astor asked Buchan to ensure Garvin's exposé received the widest possible publicity. Buchan promised the article would be cabled to America. The Milnerites particularly wanted Repington damned in the eyes of American readers for his writing on the war was popular there. Garvin had written how much he 'regretted Repington's wretched campaigns of intrigue, blind favouritism and vendetta' should have been read in America. He quoted with relish M. André Cheradame in the current issue of the *National Review*,[42] who had 'felt duty bound to call the attention of the Allies to the immense amount of harm done by Colonel Repington'. He 'has been instrumental in leading the Allies to commit errors in strategy which have cost millions of men and endangered the issue of the war'. Cheradame's nonsensical farrago about 'the Repington peril' duly appeared in the pages of *Atlantic Monthly*.

Austin Harrison, editor and owner of the *English Review*, a literary and political monthly, mistakenly believed Garvin's attack owed its genesis not to Astor but André Cheradame. Considering French journalism 'the most corrupt in Europe', he warned Gwynne of a number 'of exceedingly violent attacks recently made on Colonel Repington in several Parisian newspapers'. He desired such attacks stopped, 'in the name of honest and impersonal journalism, the common cause of the Allies and public morality'. He wished Gwynne to publish his letter in the *Morning Post* but the editor refused.[43] He was more concerned to avoid controversy with the French press than to protect Repington. The French press needed no lessons about corruption read them by 'an English press as corrupt as those who govern us'.[44]

Gwynne attempted to explain to Lady Bathurst why Repington had been attacked so sharply. The *Observer* had been 'wickedly unfair'. Somehow, Gwynne had managed to convince himself that Garvin's polemic had been directed as much against the *Morning Post* as the reputation of its military correspondent. 'Do not be concerned about

Repington', he told Lady Bathurst. 'The army is with him to a man. Haig agrees with everything he has written.' On reflection he thought perhaps it might have been better had Repington written only on military subjects. In future he intended to keep him strictly to that. '*My* mistake was to rope him in for my polemic against LG.' When fighting on his own ground he thought Repington 'supreme'. But when it came to political comment, he was 'too nervy and unbalanced'.[45] Gwynne always appeared anxious to give Lady Bathurst the impression Repington was his creature. 'He is a pawn in our game, a salient in the enemy's position which he assails vigorously . . . He is not allowed in the *MP* to air his personal animosities and our enemies know this.'[46]

From the beginning of the military correspondent's association with the *Morning Post* the editor had emphasised all important initiatives were his alone, although this was far from the truth. After Repington's articles on the manpower muddle – the major cause of his quarrel with Dawson and eventual departure from PHS – Gwynne claimed to General Rawlinson it had been '*his* disclosures on the man-power question [that] put the Government in a most frightfully difficult position'. In similar vein he wrote, '*I* still have a lot up *my* sleeve for the Government and *I* will force them, sooner or later to face this man-power question. *My* articles have had a great effect already'.[47] What part of any campaign was Repington's and what Gwynne's became increasingly difficult to distinguish.

It was no intrigue to criticise the government's policies openly, exactly what Repington had striven to do in *The Times* and in the *Morning Post*. Even by the furthest stretch of imagination, that did not constitute a conspiracy against the government. So long as Repington was confident he was behaving in a manner consistent with the best traditions of journalism and was sincerely intent not to damage his country's best interests, it was no less than his duty to point out faults he discerned and suggest how errors might be ameliorated. But the government, because it resented the message, dishonestly defamed the messenger and effectively accused Repington, the most patriotic of men, with treason.

Garvin insisted, 'The *Morning Post* ruined or injured every person and every cause it supported.' The editor, H. A. Gwynne, possessed an inexhaustible capacity for suspicion and hostility together with an insatiable appetite for conspiracy. There would come a time when there would scarcely be a person in British public life against whom 'Taffy' Gwynne had not intrigued.[48] But they were uniquely Gwynne's intrigues. Repington's misfortune was, after a year working for the *Morning Post* with Gwynne, many wrongly supposed him to be inextricably part of all his editor's plots and conspiracies.

Repington was the hapless victim of 'the perfect Establishment "job"'.[49] What astonished him was that Garvin should have been the assassin. Hamilton and his wife readily discerned the influence either of Milner or of his disciples. Sir Ian could not bring himself to believe Milner was the instigator. Instead, he suggested it might well have been dictated by F. S. Oliver – 'so typical of his nasty, mean way of lying low and instigating others – following the methods of his friend Harry Wilson'. Jean Hamilton supposed Garvin had acted as Fred Oliver's tool. 'Blinded by hate and the evil passions of war; the knife he thrust into Repington's back was envenomed with spite.'[50] Astor was delighted that they had so successfully 'ambushed' Repington. He was convinced the military correspondent's reputation had been utterly destroyed. 'Garvin's article has finished him', he chortled. All Milnerites shared their mentor's belief.[51]

20   A consummation devoutly to be wished

From 1917 onwards, the two questions that dominated Allied thinking were: how many troops would the Americans send?; and, when would they arrive? In October 1917 Repington had been mistaken by a French shopkeeper for an American. 'Vous venez nombreux, Monsieur?' the shopkeeper had anxiously enquired. He had cheerfully replied 'Quelques millions, Monsieur', and had never seen a man look happier.[1] Britain and France had hoped the United States would encourage multitudes of Americans to enlist to fill the depleted Allied ranks. Alas, their initial military co-operation was a single division.[2] Because they incorrectly supposed the French had borne almost all the Allied military effort on the western front, the division was sent to serve on the French sector of the line. They continued preparations to despatch a much larger force, but to their allies their build-up seemed excessively slow. Robertson supposed them unlikely to undertake any serious military operation in the near future. He was quite indifferent as to whether the Americans decided to be independent of French or British commands. 'We want to beat the German Armies,' he said, 'and America will not help us much in that respect.'[3] Repington disageed. He was convinced the presence of the American Expeditionary Force was essential. Material help was all very well, but what really mattered was more men.

The French mission to the AEF was large and led by a general; the British relied upon a single officer, Colonel Cyril Wagstaff. He was popular with the American officers, who referred to him frequently for advice. Repington was convinced, American 'keenness, intelligence and zealousness' would soon overcome any difficulties born of inexperience. Time was short, but he considered it correct to wait. Then, instead of feeling dislike and jealousy, the Americans would begin to realise 'our people feel a deep and semi-paternal pride in them and a longing to help'. The British, not wishing to appear condescending, deemed it wiser to take no initiative.

The day of his arrival in October 1917, Pershing was made a full general. When visiting the AEF, Repington stayed with Pershing as his

guest. Initially he thought 'Black Jack's' staff impressive, but later modified his view. A million and a half men were in training in the United
States, but the general did not expect to have 'a serious army for offensive
operations' before the autumn of 1918. Consequently he would 'not be
able to undertake anything big before 1919'. By that stage, he thought,
the French might well be so reduced as to be incapable of a great offensive. Consequently, the burden would fall upon the British and American
armies. It was particularly important their two forces should co-operate
readily. Repington discovered 'strong approval' for this among the troops
and 'a steady increase in pro-English sentiment'. Nonetheless, 'surtout
point de zèle', he cautioned, was for the moment the best and most
appropriate maxim.[4]

Repington had 'complete confidence' in Pershing. He was 'frank, clear-
headed, wise, uncommonly determined and intent not to be rushed into
any folly by anybody'. Repington was flattered to learn the general had
said more and spoken more freely to him than with anyone else. The
military correspondent spent three days with the American forces, questioning and examining everything from staff organisation to troop equipment. He thought the troops looked 'really good, a nice lot of keen,
upstanding young men, all very serious and determined to do a big
thing'. They deserved to be allowed sufficient time for much was needed
before the AEF would be fit for offensive action. However, given 'the
enthusiasm, virility and competence of all ranks and the vast forces
behind them, both moral and material, they must overcome all difficulties'. He wrote this in the autumn of 1917 fully expecting that by spring
1918 he would see an immense improvement.[5]

Haig, in January 1918, was anxious to use American recruits to make
good British deficits. Repington urged him to be cautious. Should anything go wrong, it might well prompt the old American antagonism
against England. The difficult decision to preserve American independence of command had been Secretary Baker's, to which President
Wilson had given his approval. The Americans did not publish the numbers of their casualties in the British press. For this reason Repington
supposed the scale of the American sacrifice was insufficiently acknowledged. He thought this a real pity. By early July the news from America
was most cheering. 'That great country is doing fine and is enthusiastic
about the war', Repington purred like a cat that had all the cream.

He was in almost constant contact with various US political, military
and naval representatives. During a fascinating weekend at Coombe he
talked with, among others, Paul Cravath, head of the American Financial
Commission, Colonel Griscom, formerly US Ambassador to Rome, acting liaison officer between Pershing and the War Cabinet, and Major

Robert Bacon, formerly Ambassador to Paris, a former Secretary of State who acted as a general factotum on Pershing's staff and now liaised with British GHQ. All four travelled back to town together and that evening met again when Repington dined with the American mission. A wide-ranging conversation with Vice Admiral W. S. Sims USN preceded an exchange with Bacon, who showed him the figures for past and future American arrivals. With thirty complete divisions promised in France by 1 September, Bacon did not doubt the Americans would wish to unite their troops in one portion of the line, preferably on the British right. Repington realised that might cause difficulties because it ran counter to all French thinking.

The Americans rapidly made a name for themselves as effective and fierce fighters. It amused Repington that the Australians, formerly credited with being the roughest, toughest operators, now awarded that accolade to the US troops. The compliment, paid by such notoriously rugged troops, was accepted with delight. On Sunday 8 September 1918, while travelling in 'a train full of Americans' from Paris to Chaumont, Repington discussed with Wagstaff how the troops might best be employed. They were now a truly formidable force – 1,050,000 fighting men armed with 13,000 machine guns, 1,300 field guns and 200 heavy guns. Thirteen divisions with two in reserve had been charged with pinching out the St Mihiel salient. The American QMG, General Moseley, agreed with Repington, the management of long lines of communication stretching across France presented great difficulties. However, he thought they could improve efficiency at least 80 per cent if they had sole charge. Repington privately dismissed Moseley's claim, but did not allow this to diminish his pleasure one iota. It was enough to be in the company of such 'a capital set of fellows'. They still had something to learn from their British instructors but would clearly soon 'get rid of all French and British, create their own tactics and run their own show'. He judged them capable of fighting alone. They would be better for it. 'They are proud and as keen as mustard.' He generously embraced the US military effort and described the troops as 'Crusaders'. 'They have their troubles', he admitted, hastening to add, 'just like the rest of us. They think that they are winning the war; but then, so do all the rest of us. History,' he concluded, 'will probably assign to no army the most conspicuous share in a victory gained by the common effort of all.'[6]

Repington watched the I, IV and V American Corps from Pershing's GHQ at Ligny en Barrois undertake their first serious engagement. He thought their complete success convincingly answered any question about whether they were capable of conducting a great operation on their own account. Admittedly there were still some unresolved concerns about the quality of the staff work but, he and Wagstaff agreed, 'Yankees learn fast. They would soon learn you couldn't wander about in the narrow country lanes of France as though they were at home on the prairie!' Repington had absolutely no reservations about the infantry; they were excellent. He wrote up his experiences a few days later when he had returned to Paris.[7] Some ill-informed voices continued to claim that the Americans had been reluctant to provide troops for the Allied cause. With figures provided by Colonel L. C. Griscom, Repington gave the lie to that particular calumny. *Morning Post* readers learned that on 1 February 1918 there had been six divisions of US troops in France of which one division was in the line. By 1 August that number had risen to thirty-two divisions of which ten were in the line and five in an active sector. A further ten divisions were held in reserve.

In an attack between the Argonne and the Meuse in early October the Americans suffered heavy losses. The figure might have been as high as 100,000, but no one could say for certain because they kept the figure secret[8]. Foch did not think they were ready to fight as an independent army. It would be better if they were distributed instead among the French. Repington insisted they would soon be all right. He reminded Foch, 'All armies get knocks at times. We have all had to buy our experience in this war.'[9]

Despite the Allied successes, Repington's commentaries retained their sombre tone. Robertson was no longer CIGS but languished in Eastern Command, effectively 'reduced to a spectator, a watcher in the war's wings'. This new perspective did not please him.[10] In late July Robertson and his wife had been fellow guests with Repington at Mrs Greville's house at Polesden-Lacey. Robertson ruefully confessed, nowadays he was never told anything, a complaint he repeated next time he met Repington. But once his sad admission was made, he seemed quite happy to chew over recent events. They 'were, as usual agreed'.[11] Now Robertson was no longer at the centre of events Repington had lost his most important contact at the War Office, the *authoritative* voice and his most invaluable source of news.

In early September Repington visited Foch's headquarters, a splendid chateau at Bombon, an hour and a half's drive from Paris. General Mangin's troops were engaged north-west of Soissons at the time. 'A warm corner', Foch admitted before typically insisting that 'Everybody was getting on well.' 'He is an invincible optimist', Repington admiringly observed. 'I have discovered that all the chief actors in a war are always optimists. The chief spectators are the reverse.' What then did this make him who necessarily was the perpetual spectator of events and decisions about which he could do nothing? He said not a word.

Foch's thinking now effectively determined Repington's estimate of the likely outcome to the 1918 campaign in the west. The Frenchman remained utterly convinced; 1919 was the earliest conceivable date for victory. He planned to make his big effort on 1 April that year. 'The infantry need guns, tanks and aeroplanes, but these do not win battles', Foch insisted. 'They are only accessories. It is the infantry that wins battles.' By 1919, the Allies were expected to enjoy a technical and numerical advantage. Foch believed it was unfortunate but such thinking inspired amateurs not professionals. He pressed Repington to propagate his views. Nothing could have been easier for Repington concurred with him entirely. Foch seemed to think the British War Cabinet was 'ruled by amateurs'. That undoubtedly explained the previous spring's defeats. Like Foch, Repington supposed key British ministers were 'unconsciously defeatist'. But next spring would be different. Foch would be ready then.[12]

The next day Repington motored to Provins to talk and lunch with Pétain. After the ever ebullient Foch, Pétain seemed forbiddingly formal. The two commanders shared one overwhelming priority, the absolute need for more troops. Pétain, despite his formality, was surprisingly kindly, believing Repington had been ill-served by the British government. It had been wrong to have him put on trial and fined. He had given much distinguished service in the past and now had an opportunity to do so again. He must insist the number of effectives should be considerably increased.[13] Foch had earlier told Repington he would warn Lord Reading, if Britain did not keep up her numbers of infantry, then he would refuse to be responsible for the British army. When asked, Reading protested Foch had said nothing of the sort to him. This, to Repington, clearly demonstrated the difference between the two marshals; Pétain would not have hesitated to tell Reading 'in set terms' what needed to be done.

Repington complained that because his editor wanted him to write every day he had no time to think. For want of time for reflection, he felt his comments had lost something of their acuity. He could scarcely admit that his refusal to write on a Sunday was because it ruined any Saturday to Monday stay in the country, 'having to come up in the middle part of the day and go down again after doing my scribbling'.[14] It was not that he had suddenly become a reluctant writer. He was acutely aware, in addition to his regular contributions to the *Morning Post*, the more he wrote for other newspapers and journals the better. His purse remained yawningly empty. The threat of imminent penury was a powerful inducement to prolixity. The prospect of him expressing his views on the conduct and progress of the war even more frequently was not pleasing to everyone. The steady demand from the United States for 'opinion pieces' from Repington infuriated Lloyd George. Reading reminded the Premier, anything Repington published in the United States was regarded as 'authoritative' and 'semi-official'.[15] His most recent contribution in the *New York World* had prompted considerable concern. He had 'called upon the British Government to emulate France and America and speed up their efforts for victory', but sadly had not been able to discern any evidence of such effort. 'The sooner our Government state their intention to do so the sooner will our Allies believe our War Cabinet are playing the game.' Reading thought it 'very unfortunate that such a view should be published in America when a minority there were always ready to decry British effort'.[16] Meanwhile, Repington was nursing a big scheme he hoped would at least restore the income he had previously earned from the *National News*. However, he could not get started until there was some relief from his present grind. He planned to go abroad 'for three weeks or so'.[17] Gwynne knew about and approved the plan.

Lord Reading continued to fret. How had Repington's *New York World* article managed to avoid the British authorities? He could only assume the British Censor had been by-passed and the cable sent directly from France. To suffer from the Censor's blue pencil once in a while was part of the game. What caused Repington to complain was that 'The Censor's masters' (by which he meant Lloyd George and his Cabinet colleagues) were 'behaving like tyrants'. He felt his anger was entirely justified. There was no good reason why he should 'not have alluded to facts stated by Col. Fabry and Monsieur Bidou in Paris newspapers or made fair comment on those facts. Why will they not let me give the credit due to Pétain for this French counter-stroke which has been so effective? All the folk in Paris know that it is Pétain's plan and execution. *Débats* had openly stated it.'[18] His complaint was entirely justified, but he had sufficiently recovered his equilibrium the following day to admit, whosoever gained credit for beating the Germans was 'a small matter so long as they were defeated'.[19]

Contretemps with the censors were frequent and painful. They generally ended with an angry Repington having to concede defeat. It was some small satisfaction to learn almost anything he wrote induced a high state of concern among his tormentors. A stand-in officer in the Censor's office had let that cat out of the bag. He had admitted, whenever one of Repington's *Morning Post* articles turned up, panic invariably ensued. They arrived 'usually when everyone wanted to get off for dinner' and had to be forwarded to the DMI, or the Secretary of State, or to Number 10. It was pleasing to think what he wrote induced dyspepsia in the Prime Minister.

One question constantly troubled Repington: how many British troops were there in France? The War Cabinet told Haig he must reduce his divisions to forty-five. Repington in a leader for the *Morning Post* acknowledged the Allied offensive was proceeding well but warned, it was vital strengths were maintained. He feared Lloyd George would covertly reduce the numbers. Where were the drafts to come from – the 18½-year-olds and the recovered wounded? Would he be reassured when he visited GHQ at Roulers? It was so much easier and better that he should assess matters on the ground himself rather than have to rely on the impressions of others. He realised the debt he owed Gwynne for sticking by him in a hostile world, yet he would be glad to be free of the omnipresent, ever opinionated editor. His private correspondence home to Molly indicated he was altogether happier and more animated than he had been for sometime. Then, late in his visit, he was laid up for a few days in the Ritz in Paris. Enforced idleness made him realise how much he was missing his English friends.

He had been wounded 'by French war-bread', he told Gwynne, 'the worst projectile of the war. [He had] been able to write only footle'.[20] He enclosed a poem of six eight-line stanzas entitled 'The Drafted Man', inspired by an US infantryman killed on the field of St Mihiel after the first battle fought by American troops in France on 12/13 September 1918. Repington, who had experienced many a stricken field, made light of his poetic effusion but undoubtedly he had been much moved. He was familiar with war's brutality but had been impressed by the raw courage and selfless determination the conscripted US infantry had demonstrated. He had noted the formidable strength of the German position; the 'long glacis, several forward trenches, much barbed and coiled wire, a concreted main position ... good dug-outs and bomb-proofs and a daedalus of trenches'. He said nothing of the German dead, but noted the US dead still 'lay where they fell, with all their arms and equipment on them'.

The body of a drafted man of the 366th infantry, Roy Bassett, had been the first fallen American he came upon that day at St Mihiel. For a single, abstracted moment he concentrated upon not an army but one private soldier. He identified Bassett by his name tag. Not an acquaintance or someone distinguished who had held a position of command, but a private soldier, a doughboy whose only distinction was his lack of distinction; a conscript, one among the many who had died fighting for the Allies far, far away from his homeland. Repington's poem was unique in his record of the war. Much earlier, Lloyd George had told him how he refused, unlike the generals, to be a butcher's boy, driving men to slaughter as though they were cattle. Repington had condemned these words as sentimental, unaffordable in the mouth of a national leader engaged in a fight for national survival. One fact, he insisted, needed to be remembered; no general could hope to succeed without adequate manpower to repair the inevitable wastage. On this occasion, if only momentarily, he acknowledged the individual sacrifice. Customarily, he employed the accepted euphemism and wrote of 'losses' or 'wastage', never of 'dead' or 'death'. It was not that he was callous, indifferent, uncaring or unaware of suffering humanity. As an old soldier, as a professional military correspondent, necessarily his talk of war was served by a particular mental and emotional faculty that left no room for ordinary sentiment.

He spent the first three weeks of September in France followed by two weeks in Italy, then a few more days in France before returning to London on 10 October. The trip had more or less begun and ended with conversations at GHQ, particularly with Lawrence, who had replaced Kiggell as Haig's Chief of Staff, and with Birch RA, the artillery specialist. As late as 9 October, based upon what GHQ had been told by the War Cabinet, they were 'still very anxious about strengths'. They had been told, in 1919 sixty divisions were to be reduced to forty-three. It was nothing short of an outrage. 'Today, 1 September 1918', Repington recorded, they were 'down to 47,000 infantry, but the depots and men *en route* reduce it to 31,000'.

From the artillery came a different, happier story. Birch could not have been more pleased and confident.[21] They were throwing 12,500 tons of shells a day at the Germans. That still left Repington wanting to know why enemy guns, though of similar calibre, regularly outranged those of the Allies. Birch explained, technically enemy arms were more efficient. They had not increased the charges; to have done so would have worn their guns out more swiftly. Instead, they had streamlined their shells. The British were firing three to four times more weight of shells than the Germans, and Churchill as Munitions Minister deserved to be thanked for helping to make this possible.[22] Repington remained far from satisfied. He constantly complained about the failure to keep up strengths. When 'ragged' by a female acquaintance that the frequency of his complaints could only be accounted for by his dislike of the Cabinet, or more likely of its leader, in a rare display of anger he 'spoke his mind about something [he] felt very strongly ... There was no question of hostility to the Government or personal feeling against any member of it. The point was the War Cabinet was not playing the game by the army.'[23] Repington was convinced that 'just about as much as could be had been extracted from the army'. They could give no more.[24]

He was back in London by Friday 11 October. It had proved a fascinating few weeks but, for the moment, he had had enough of travel. He agreed with a fellow passenger's observation that those who enjoyed wartime travel would surely 'travel to hell for a pastime'. The faces of everyone in London showed just how glad they were to at last be approaching the war's end. Yet many difficulties remained unresolved and these he discussed at length in an article for the *Morning Post*. Carson, whom he had met with Gwynne, said he entirely approved of the line Repington took. It appeared to be the case that nothing could be decided politically until the exchange of letters with President Wilson was concluded. However, the successes gained by the Allies in the field more than compensated for the delays. 'The Boches were in retreat in most parts' and from Russia came news that German troops had 'shot their officers and hoisted the red flag'.

With an almost paternal anxiety, Repington continued to monitor the progress of the American divisions. In the last three weeks they had suffered more than 150,000 casualties. 'I fear they have suffered much owing to the weather, few roads and strong opposition.' Turning his mind to the approaching peace, he wrote about ensuring security against the Germans. They simply could not be trusted. His thoughts proved an apposite prologue to the American president's uncompromising reply to the Germans, described by Repington with evident approval as 'an extremely harsh document. No nation has been addressed in such severe terms since the time of Napoleon. The Boches can take it or leave it.' Informed opinion in London was much divided as to what exactly the Germans would do.

His spirits were lifted when that last Friday in October he lunched with Robertson and his wife at York House. Sir William provided a downbeat opening with his now familiar assertion that he had 'practically no troops for home defence'. The War Cabinet accepted responsibility for they believed, not unreasonably, 'the enemy had no troops to spare to invade Britain'. Presumably they were not too concerned at the navy's official declaration they could not 'guarantee to stop a landing'. Repington retailed his recent experiences abroad to Robertson before they fell to discussing 'the happy change in the fortune of war and its cause'. Although they both agreed, they wondered whether the public or even history would understand 'the real cause of the Allied recovery was the arrival of over 2,000,000 fresh Allied troops in France between March and October'.[25] Undoubtedly the best feature of the war on the western front was that at last 'the War Cabinet had practically nothing to do with it'. Yet Cabinet members supposed they had cause to complain because they were not given advance notice of even the great battles. 'Why should they be told?' Repington wondered. When they had been told, 'They only ran about and prattled.'[26] An undisturbed Saturday to Monday at

Polesden-Lacey, a cheerful house party, a wonderful spell of weather and the continuing good war news from all fronts, served to keep Repington cheerful. He was amused to be told by Emilie Grigsby, his former American mistress, she had been defending him against the 'Georgian Press confraternity'. Gwynne described them as 'George's myrmidons'. 'I expect I need it', Repington happily admitted. He found himself 'having constantly to take up the cudgels' on Pershing's behalf. The general was frequently the subject of what he considered unjust and ignorant criticism. On the afternoon of Friday 1 November, Repington attended his last tribunal as a National Service Representative. There was no ringing of bells, no waving of flags for the recent victories. He acknowledged 'An implacable feeling of seeing the thing through … as we approach the end of this bloody, prolonged and horrible war. *Væ Victis!*'[27]

Now the war was almost over men asked, 'By what name should it be known?' That question had been posed much earlier by the editor of *Burke's Landed Gentry* in a letter to the editor of *The Times* on behalf of 'those who have to record such matters'. 'General opinion' pointed to the clearly inaccurate 'European War'. A reader immediately responded, 'No better name could be found … than the "Great War"'.[28] Both titles, 'European War' and 'Great War', continued to be used indiscriminately. In September 1918 a Professor Johnstone of Harvard, who planned to write an official history of the war for the American government, called to discuss with Repington what should be 'the right name of the war'. They considered some alternative titles. 'Finally we mutually agreed to call it *The First World War* in order to prevent the millennium folk from forgetting that the history of the world was the history of war.'[29] The name stuck as it was both short and accurate.

An hour before midday on the eleventh day of November 1918 the maroons sounded to signal the end of conflict. In London, as in most of the country, the day was miserably wet and foggy, yet the joyful spirit of the celebrating multitudes thronging the streets refused to be dampened. They were determined their long-awaited celebrations should not be delayed for a moment longer than was necessary.

Part III

After the war, 1918–1925

21   Peace poses its own problems, 1918–1920

In stern, retributive mood, Parliament had listened as the Prime Minister read out the terms of the Armistice. Repington noted with satisfaction that though not without fault, they were 'severe'. However, German demobilisation should have been insisted upon. Kaiser and Crown Prince had decamped to Holland, deserting throne, army and nation. The lesser kings and princes of the German Empire hesitated before they too, like Humpty Dumpty, toppled to destruction. In the *Morning Post* Repington wrote, 'The sins of a whole people cannot be extirpated by the abdication of the Kaiser and his heirs ... All Germans are associated with the initial, odious treachery of their government. They should not be allowed to escape the consequences of their shameful acts.'[1] He would repeatedly affirm only a harsh peace would be a sufficient response by the Allies. It was not enough to punish Germany, she deserved to be humiliated.

At Westminster, anticipating the general election, the politicians lost no time making their arrangements. The Prime Minister intended to maintain the political status quo. Apparently his assurances had been sufficient to satisfy Unionists and Coalition Liberals, but not the Labour parliamentary party. A remarkably resigned Repington did not even baulk at the Prime Minister's political friends recommending themselves to the electorate as 'the party that won the war' when for more than two years he had persistently maintained the opposite, insisting *everything* was owed to the soldiers. 'No one but a perfect fool could lose a campaign with a British army to back him.' He repeated the same sentiment four months later conversing with Robertson, who was about to assume his new command, the Army of the Rhine. Robertson spoke of how nearly the war had been lost because politicians 'had spared no effort to distort and conceal how critical affairs had been'. Repington, improving the moment, insisted politicians did 'what we told them to do, but nine months too late and after being kicked hard by the Boche. Our men fighting against odds saved our bacon'.[2] That was scarcely what Lloyd George and his friends thought. The war had hardly ceased and already very different explanations of why, how and to whom the Allies owed their success were being offered by some of the principals.

Before the Peace Conference had assembled for its first informal meeting there was unrest among some British troops in France caused by a two-month delay in their demobilisation. Repington initially had dismissed the trouble as 'the result of reaction after strain'. By February 1919 he took a more critical view when labour disputes became widespread. The soldiers declared 'the demobilisation plans foolish'. Repington agreed and thought the considerable sympathy shown by the public for the men was justified. Indiscipline, however, had to be stopped.[3] Democracy voted and the Lloyd George coalition secured the 'huge majority' it had anticipated. All who during the war had argued 'against national sentiment or were even sup-posed to have been remiss had been thrown out'.[4]

The war had ended with an unexpected abruptness. Equally sudden were the changes in Repington's professional life. Domestic problems for the first time seriously impinged upon his work. It became increas-ingly difficult to concentrate upon his daily journalism when he was constantly pestered by the importunate pleas of duns who refused to be ignored any longer. Long-overdue accounts demanded immediate satis-faction, new debts multiplied, secured funds dwindled alarmingly and familiar sources of credit ceased to exist. Yet he refused to consider the obvious solution for his chronic financial problems – the sale of his Hampstead home, Maryon Hall. He thought he could secure his future by writing a best-selling book. To ensure its financial success he would eschew the discretion he had shown in his recently published memoirs, *Vestigia*. He intended to tell his story of the war years in diary form; a combination of personal and public intelligence set out in strict chro-nological order. As little would be excluded as the law allowed.

Despite all the self-imposed pressures from his other writing tasks, he met all Gwynne's demands punctiliously. To explain daily to his *Morning Post* readers the difficult and complex questions surrounding the peace terms was exhausting and often a severe test of his imaginative powers. He had given a short address to the 1900 Club on the Versailles negotiations and afterwards had been 'asked a heap of questions'. What he described as 'a good yap' with his audience had helped to 'show [him] how minds were working'. Once the Peace had been signed, typically he insisted, the priority was to 'get the Government to declare their military policy'. He was concerned with 'matters relating to the re-Insurance Treaty[5] between us, the French and the Yankees ... which must affect very considerably our military policy'. When next in France he proposed to get Foch to tell him 'what he wants from us and the Yanks and how soon'.[6]

Staying in Paris at the Ritz, previously an entirely pleasurable experience, was no longer so. First he was buffeted by influenza, then suffered severe abdominal pain. While the cause of the pain remained undiagnosed, he feared it might be cancer. He was also plagued by violent bouts of indigestion. There were other lesser but no less uncomfortable inconveniences that added to the misery. None of 'Chantilly's beastly hotels' offered a hot bath, a necessary comfort he was unwilling to abandon. Thus, he was obliged to undertake a train journey each day from Paris. He found the shortage of suitable company particularly trying. By late July 1919 the British delegation had been considerably reduced. Scarcely any personal friends were left in town. He particularly missed Le-Roy and Esher. 'Most of the ladies had gone home or off to the watering places at the coast.' He petulantly observed how even the Ritz now seemed to him to be 'enervating'. Finally, he had been put on a diet by his physician!

As the *Post*'s military correspondent and occasional leader writer, he had nothing new to add to the debates on peacemaking. His invariable emphasis was upon the need to secure Britain's and her empire's safety. Delegates, he insisted, should never forget 'the fate of nations is determined and only determined by military strength'. Talk of leagues and covenants was fundamentally mistaken. The only league worth considering was 'that great *de facto* League of Nations cemented by blood, sacrifice and heroic endurance through the long dark nights of trial that led to victory'.[7]

His mood was not improved when from London came a highly displeasing item of news. There had been a 'wholly laughable, mutual admiration society dinner given for Harry Wilson'. To make him Field Marshal, 'especially to do so before Allenby, Robertson and all the army commanders [was] an outrage'. To Repington it was an obvious case of Lloyd George 'rewarding his obedient tool'.[8] A chance meeting a few weeks earlier and a comment by his friend David Henderson must also have raised rather bitter-sweet thoughts about what might have been. Henderson had been covering Colonel Le-Roy Lewis's duties as military attaché. He said his replacement in Paris 'should be a gentleman, a trained soldier and a French linguist'. The British army possessed many who could meet two of those requirements, but few who could answer all three.[9]

That summer, every moment he could spare Repington reordered, edited and revised materials for his new book. The division into chapters was sometimes difficult, the material proving more intractable than he had anticipated and his publishers more cautious and careful than he would have wished. Four letters he wrote in July and August 1919 trace the book's progress. After talks with Constable's solicitors, Meredith & Kyllman, he accepted their advice and 'cut out *all* home

Fig. 14 Field Marshal Sir Henry Hughes Wilson (1864–1922)

talk of Maryon lest my enemy critics seize upon it and exploit it'. When Mary asked him why it was acceptable to talk of the many ladies with whom he was acquainted and yet not of her, the woman with whom he lived, his *de facto* if not *de jure* wife, he gave no answer but promised, 'when the polemics aroused by the first edition are at an end' then the next edition would be illustrated and would 'contain all'. The conference arranged with Constable the following week raised considerable concerns; about 'revealing private conversations ... the Official Secrets Act and Robertson's confidences'. Remove these and Repington feared the book's value would be lost. The following week he met counsel in an attempt to sort out some of the problems. He avowed he had done his best to follow the directions but found them 'too general to be a clear guide'. They only made revision more difficult. On 26 August he finally relinquished the corrected galleys into Constable's care, leaving his publisher to have the final say. Too long he had been 'fearfully busy' with the book. Now 'I must', he told Mary, 'turn back to the *Morning Post* again.'[10]

He had told Constable he was seeking Gwynne's advice. He suggested Gwynne might wish 'to publish extracts' in the *Morning Post*. They 'need not touch upon the social side of the diaries'. He said he would welcome a general critique but the letters' postscript revealed what was his real interest. 'I am told that the *Daily Telegraph* gave John French £5,000 for the right to publish his recollections before the book comes out.'[11] Gwynne did not respond to this or to several more obvious promptings. Repington, seeking to reignite interest in his project, suggested what he had previously sent the editor bore little likeness to the book. 'It has been severely revised on the advice of counsel for legal points and that of the Ribblesdales and my hostess here [Lady Downshire] on other points. I hope when you see it again that it will suit even your exacting taste!' Gwynne declared he was pleased to hear Repington had revised the diary; 'it wanted rather severe editing'. It scarcely inspired confidence the *Post* would pay him a fortune for serialisation rights.[12]

Although counsel's opinion and Repington's specific responses no longer exist, he undoubtedly took the task of revision very seriously. This may be elicited from his response to Ribblesdale's suggested emendations[13] as reflected in the final published text. Repington was not cavalier or uncaring about the advice given him by those he asked to read his galley proofs. He generally accepted suggestions and criticisms. He had warned Ribblesdale that in the final version some of the text would be much changed[14] to meet possible difficulties caused by the Official Secrets Act. Ribblesdale hoped this would not mean too many changes. 'Your conversations with military and civil personages at home and abroad will be read with great interest.' No one, in his opinion, could doubt the independent value of much of what Repington had written. No one was better qualified than Repington to tell how the cards had been played 'by those who were responsible for the control of the war both in this country and abroad', though some of the conversations, he suggested, might be somewhat condensed; readers might then more readily understand the conclusion that should be drawn. His wife wished Repington not to 'deprive his readers of stories and *mots* which he had said were enjoyed but had not treated them to in the text'. There were 'too many of these "tantalizers"' but in the second volume 'too many stories told pretty fully required sifting'. They both hoped he 'would not cut down what Lady R styled "the highter [*sic*] spots of social intercourse"'. Some sentences 'of a personal and hard hitting quality' wanted to be toned down, but he urged the diarist, 'do not mitigate and do not, in Arthur Balfour's phrase, "Labour to be fair"'. He should not be 'nervous about indiscretion'. Pages 'that teemed with Xs and Ys were a mistake; where you cannot satisfy you must not whet!' He questioned the value of reproducing long letters *in extenso*, unless possessed of 'a particular military or political value. In an original diary "thrown into print",' Ribblesdale observed, 'there is certain to be a good deal of surplusage.' He had not failed to spot the padding but did not doubt Repington's intention 'to reduce considerably the citation of those you met'. The relentless name-dropping had been purposely designed by Repington to attract the attention of Society. But a familiar ploy to persuade otherwise reluctant purchasers to part with their money in the end would serve only to impoverish and compromise his name and reputation.

The diary's final chapter, 'The Peace Conference, 1919', reflected Repington's impatience and frustration at the way events refused to be resolved as swiftly as he, like more or less everyone, had expected. It was damnably difficult to think high thoughts on universal themes of peace, disarmament, arbitration or security, when thoughts of his need to finish his book and so ease his chronic indebtedness persistently impinged. What was more, try as he might he could find precious little to report from Paris that was fresh and novel. Much of the time he was left to hem and haw or guess. Only occasionally would the diplomatic entourage surrounding the Versailles circus provide him with worthwhile information and repeatable anecdotes. Of these bearers of tales none excelled Harold Nicolson. He insisted the conference could be run one of two ways; by a process of empiricism and improvisation or by trusting the experts. The British would try the one and then the other and often found that their experimental processes were unworkable so that then they would have to start all over again. Nicolson's thoughts certainly coloured Repington's published opinions but the two men differed markedly in their appreciation of Lloyd George. Nicolson admired the Welshman, most particularly his support for the Greeks. But Nicolson admitted, on many subjects the British Prime Minister had not the faintest idea what he was talking about yet infuriatingly always seemed to get his way.

Repington asked Foch what had happened to 'the tiger'. Foch insisted Clemenceau's nickname was no more than make-believe. More often than not he rolled over and gave in to Lloyd George or Wilson. Foch complained, he could not have his Rhine frontier because it was against Wilson's *fine* principles. 'When war comes we shall have fine principles in place of a natural frontier.'[15] When André Tardieu asked Clemenceau why he gave in to Wilson and Lloyd George, he replied, 'Mais, que voulez vous que je fasse entre deux hommes dont un se croit Napoléon et l'autre

Jésus-Christ.' Repington noted all the best stories that in the past had concerned Talleyrand, were now attributed to Clemenceau.[16]

Pershing shared Nicolson's hopes for the League of Nations but was convinced, the future of civilisation rested upon the co-operation of England and America. That idea particularly appealed to Repington. Invariably, his interest was always more engaged with the practical problems of military security than with the abstract principles of peace. The attitude he adopted to the process of making and securing peace resembled that of a vengeful Jehovah. He showed little of the gentle, forgiving spirit that informs the Beatitudes. In France he would spend as much time as possible talking with Foch and Pétain, previously having run an expert eye and rule over the British army on the Rhine. Foch shared Repington's opinion that the Peace Conference had become a bore. Peace ought to have been achieved months before. Like Pétain he was thoroughly out of sympathy with Clemenceau. Politicians were dissipating the fruits of the armies' victories with their endless and needless hesitations, tergiversations and delays.

There seemed no end to the diplomatic procrastination. Repington was furious, frustrated, principally because he could not write *Finis* beneath the diaries he had now convinced himself would generate his financial renaissance. His commentaries in the *Post* on the 'Big Four', Lloyd George, Wilson, Clemenceau and Orlando, almost implied they were deliberately delaying their decision simply to hinder him. He was not alone in his impatience. 'The unspoken question in everyone's mind was not "How much longer?" but, "Who is to blame for the unconscionable delay?"' Countess Benckendorff blamed Lloyd George. Repington quoted her judgment without comment. She was certain the deliberations would take nine months, 'puisque le plus célèbre accoucheur anglais y est.' At last, on 28 June 1919, Repington, with much relief, recorded 'This day the Treaty of Peace with Germany was signed at Versailles.'

Warned in advance by Tyrrell, all that week Repington had waited in a fever of impatience for the announcement. He wrote to tell Gwynne, once the Germans had signed, he hoped he could be unmuzzled. He 'had a few things he had on his mind to say', but would wait to see what political line Gwynne adopted. What was this, waiting upon his editor's nod to say where he may or may not trespass? He might wish to ignore or contradict what Gwynne thought but could not, for his only guarantee of a long-term future was with the *Morning Post*. Given the perilous state of his finances, he could not afford to put in jeopardy his regular salary cheque. Where now were his frequent, former, proud boasts of independence? Careless of the possible financial consequences, he had broken the shackles that had bound him unwillingly to Dawson and *The Times* but now he could not begin to contemplate an overt disagreement with Gwynne lest it lead to his having to leave the *Morning Post*.

He told Gwynne that he was 'very full of work', not only for the *Post* but also 'correcting the proofs' of his diary while 'awaiting your opinion with great interest'. He was genuinely grateful Gwynne had not asked him to review French's *1914*. The editor had asked Callwell to undertake it instead. Gwynne acknowledged, while no one could have done it better, as French's friend Repington would have found it difficult and very awkward to speak freely about the Field Marshal's indescretions.[17] He had dined with Haldane and both regretted they had not been asked to edit the advance instalments published in the *Daily Telegraph*. French's reputation had been enormously damaged, 'when a few excisions would have made things alright without spoiling a fascinating story'.[18]

In the months between the Armistice and the Peace Treaty Repington had been forcibly reminded more than a war, an era had come to an end, a conclusion most painfully marked by the sudden and unexpected deaths of Ladies Paget and Londonderry, two true friends who had been blessed with 'entirely unique personalities'.[19] Earlier that same week he had attended the memorial service for F. E. Mackenzie, former correspondent and leader writer of *The Times*. He met John and Godfrey Walter and noted Geoffrey Dawson among the congregation, but not the new editor Wickham Steed. 'Fleet Street wonders', Repington cheekily recorded, 'whether the policy of *The Times* will now be Croatian, Serbian or Slovene.'[20] 'The biter is bit' was how he delightedly recorded *The Times* not printing Dawson's letter of resignation, the same treatment he had been afforded. Northcliffe's constant interference had left Dawson feeling 'like a dog with a tin pot tied to his tail'. Repington respected Dawson's motives for resigning but he was glad he was out. 'He was not big enough and I can never forget or forgive that he failed us at the crisis of the war.'[21]

After the signing of the Peace Treaty at Versailles the *Morning Post*'s Military Correspondent, just like many another veteran, was most anxious to revisit old campaigns – but this time with the immeasurable benefit of hindsight. This pleasing exercise became part of his analysis and criticism of the war's sudden efflorescence of memoirs and histories. Meanwhile, with much relief he had despatched his diary galleys to the publisher. When he was not lecturing on the war and the peace settlement to audiences all over England and Wales, there was much else to occupy his time and thoughts.

By the autumn of 1919 the weight of his debts had become so intolerable he at last agreed or rather was reluctantly forced to sell his much loved Maryon Hall. The price realised at auction was considerably better than he had anticipated. It would have been an opportunity entirely wasted, he believed, to employ this unexpected and pleasingly large sum to service or pay off all his old debts when there were so many more gratifying ways in which it might be employed. A portion was set aside to satisfy his more demanding creditors but the greater part he retained for his own use. To add to those original debts that remained unpaid there swiftly accrued a mountain of new liabilities. Respite from the urgent demands of creditors, old and new, proved short-lived and at every turn he was once more harassed by imposts and exactions, a fate he considered 'unjust and entirely undeserved'. Molly unconvincingly excused his chronic indebtedness in a letter to Jean Hamilton as 'the sad, inevitable consequence of Charlie's artistic temperament'. He continued to behave in a thoroughly indulgent manner, intending to do so for as long as he could get away with it. He freely acknowledged his financial immolation was self-inflicted and so continued his heroic if doomed efforts to extricate himself from the toils of debt. He was as relentlessly optimistic as he was determinedly and furiously industrious, but all would be in vain.

Meanwhile work continued remorselessly at the *Morning Post* as he abridged and adapted those books for which Gwynne had secured the rights to serialise. Among the first was von Falkenhayn's *General Headquarters 1914–1916 and its Critical Decisions* (1919), covering German military operations from the war's outbreak to Falkenhayn's resignation as Chief of the German General Staff in August 1916. Repington thought the book an 'engaging contribution on the high conduct of war', but that did not make the task of selecting material for the required six instalments any easier, or the writing of the necessary accompanying commentaries. The task was finally completed in early November 1919 when Repington delivered his last commentary accompanied by a leader. 'It may seem a trifle long,' he wrote to Gwynne, 'but as you do not wish for military criticism of the book I feel bound to forestall some of the expert criticism which the book will certainly arouse.' By way of an apology for the article's length he added the further, interesting and revealing explanation: 'I am rather of old Blowitz's opinion that in journalism facts do not matter a hang, but comments do!'[22] Gwynne valued Repington because he was so much more than an outstanding military correspondent. He was a first-class journalist who unfailingly produced his copy on time and to order. It came, therefore as both a painful and unexpected blow for Repington when in December 1919 he received a handwritten note from Gwynne that bore unwelcome news. 'The powers that be *malgré moi* have decided that our military correspondent is too great a luxury. I am frankly not of their opinion and I want you to believe that I have fought hard for you but without success. I am very sorry but there it is – I can't help myself.'[23]

The parting was as amicable as such events ever can be. In the following months Repington continued to contribute leaders as well as articles on military subjects and international relations. His most important contribution was a series of long, analytical reviews of a variety of histories and biographical studies of the late war. Reviewing Sir George Arthur's *Life of Lord Kitchener* (1920), Repington managed to be fair to Kitchener without damaging the reputations of either French or Ian Hamilton. He had made 'a damning statement about Lloyd George's desire to transfer our army in France to the Balkans'. Sir George told Repington he had 'LG's papers on the subject locked up at his bank'. Gwynne hoped that were Repington to be challenged by the Prime Minister, Sir George would 'have the pluck to produce the original documents'.[24] Gwynne and Repington were as one in agreeing the military deserved considerate treatment. Politicians were another matter altogether.

22   Last post, 1920–1925

Freelance journalism was not without its attractions but Repington acknowledged he needed to secure regular employment as a salaried member of staff. Now was not a good time to have to seek employment in Fleet Street with fewer titles concentrated in fewer hands. The survivors engaged in a constant struggle to secure a larger, more profitable share of the mass-circulation market. A war of attrition, relentless and destructive, embraced much of the press.

Repington wrote to Northcliffe to ask him what he thought about the idea of him writing for one of his newspapers once again. Not *The Times* of course – at least, not straightaway. He had left Printing House Square in 1918 but not because there had been any difference between them. *They* had *always* seen eye to eye on all important issues. His quarrel had been with his editor. Now Dawson was no longer editor, surely there was no obstacle in the way of him returning? He was filled with regret 'to see how my many years of hard work on the paper have been thrown away'. It was time 'this sad state of affairs was rectified and our defence affairs properly presented and put in order'. Others had been misled but he and Northcliffe had both seen through Lloyd George. 'It was time he was put out in the street.' The tone of his letter suggested Northcliffe would eagerly welcome him back into the fold, but it came as no surprise to Repington when his letter elicited a curt, dismissive reply. 'I have made enquiries', Northcliffe condescendingly dictated. 'There are no vacancies at Printing House Square. We have men whom we do not know what to do with.'

That was that then. Would it have been more prudent had Repington sounded a little less smug, less presumptuous, had sung a little lower about future prospects of worthwhile employment when all was so uncertain? The truth was he had been whistling in the dark to keep up his spirits. He had known this and so too had Molly. She had never seen him so low. She described his mood to a friend as 'utterly discouraged, defeated and depressed. In the gambler's life he has led for so long, his greatest, his one sure asset, has always been himself, his conquering personality, his faith in his own star and his luck. Every time I see him he is sadder and more hopeless about the future.'[1] Repington knew the employment he sought was as rare as hen's teeth. For the foreseeable future he knew it was unlikely he would receive even a half-suitable offer. All seemed irretrievably doomed. Then salvation arrived courtesy of Lord Burnham, principal proprietor and editorial director of the *Daily Telegraph*. With as much relief as alacrity Repington accepted the post of military correspondent that Burnham offered. In the immediate post-war period the *Telegraph* was the only newspaper that retained a military correspondent.

His initial contribution to the *Daily Telegraph* in January 1921 was a series of six articles not about defence but diplomacy. They culminated with a detailed historical analysis of England's foreign policy.[2] He wrote a number of measured pieces on international relations, literature and sixteenth-century history. This did not mean the familiar Repington was entirely extinguished. He warned the Allies' political leaders, they needed to maintain careful watch to prevent Germany rearming.[3]

Soon Repington was fully engaged discharging the demanding task Burnham had set him: to travel the length and breadth of Europe, meeting and talking with the new political leaders who had inherited an unfamiliar world created out of the havoc of war. The endless round of introductions, interviews and conversations with politicians, statesmen and monarchs required frequent, lengthy, uncomfortable train journeys. He was twice robbed while upon these exhausting excursions. The two months he was back home scarcely afforded sufficient time to write up his experiences before he embarked for America on the *Adriatic*. He was to cover the Washington Conference on the Limitation of Naval Armaments. His impressions of Europe and North America were grist to his literary mill. Published in a single volume, *After the War: A Diary* (1922) was clearly intended to be a sequel to his wartime experiences. Sadly, and it has to be said deservedly, it enjoyed nothing like the same acclaim. His American reviewers universally noted with regret there were 'less [*sic*] indiscretions than before'. What he had not forgotten was how to stir up controversy. Only he would have told a reporter, New York was 'amazing and gargantuan but I cannot imagine anyone wanting to live here'.[4] His impressions of America were unmistakeably superficial. The book was rushed, its structure disorderly. The signs of impatience and fatigue were all too apparent.

Disarmament allowed him to lobby for the solution he had consistently promoted since he attended the First Peace Conference at The Hague almost a quarter of a century earlier. In the *Atlantic Monthly* he combined disarmament with the need for stable exchanges and sound money. He insisted, 'Cure this disease and armaments will cure themselves.'[5] Those who knew of the state to which he had reduced his own finances must have wondered at his effrontery, offering advice on international finance! His American readers were particularly interested in his thoughts on American foreign policy. He feared the nation's relapse into post-war isolationism doomed the League of Nations and any realistic long-term hope for peace. He blamed the American Constitution, for it made good government vulnerable to the opinions of the uneducated masses. Repington entirely disapproved of America's apparent reluctance to accept her world responsibilities. The United States alone could redeem Europe 'from all the terrible troubles which my inquiries ... have made poignantly manifest to me'.[6]

He warned of Japan's overweening ambitions as an imperial and military power. The Japanese threatened to take the place of the Germans as the greatest threat to universal peace. The USA needed to wake up to the dangers implicit in the rise of this ambitiously aggressive Asiatic power.[7] He declared in the preface of *After the War*, 'when judging the future direction of foreign policy in a world where all has changed, it is useless to content oneself with archaic notions'. He acknowledged the inevitability of change in every generation and took his own admonition to heart. Yet it is impossible to ignore the nostalgic spirit that permeates his account; his regret for old days and old ways gone beyond recall. A similar spirit had informed the latter part of his war diaries. A visit to Vienna enhanced his pessimistic mood. 'The old glory has departed for ever', he wrote. 'There is no fashion, taste or elegance. It is the end of a period.'[8]

Before his new diary was published his mind had been fixed upon several, other projects to rescue his finances. He had long thought he might write a play. He had been very much impressed by Edward Brewster Sheldon's *Romance* (1913). One of his favourite actresses, Doris Keane,[9] had enjoyed her greatest success in Sheldon's play. It had been a phenomenal West End stage hit earning the author the best part of 50,000 pounds at the box office in one season.[10] Repington was convinced that in the story of Mary Queen of Scots and her tempestuous love for the Earl of Bothwell he had discovered a compelling mixture of passion, intrigue and high romance that could not fail to attract hordes of theatrical patrons. His researches suggested Tudor grandees would also provide the ideal subject for the series of popular lectures he planned. Scarcely had he returned from America than he was off again across the Atlantic, full of enthusiasm, forgetting how 'infernally stuffy' he had found American hotels and how the whole country had behaved as though 'consumed by an impossible, unending rush'. His lecture tour of the American Midwest in February 1922 was a success. He said he had undertaken it 'in an attempt to find out what sort of people they were', but his real *raison d'être* was to raise more funds. He was an accomplished and experienced public speaker and addressed small and large audiences with equal facility. He told his New York publishing contact, Ferris Greenslet, he found American audiences 'very attractive, kindly and appreciative'.[11] His published recollections are similarly generous, but his immediate observations in letters home to Mary were less so. The public mask occasionally slipped to reveal behind the urbane civilities an increasingly weary irascibility. He reminded himself, 'On these tours one must be immune from fatigue. Everywhere there are people [mostly perfect strangers] to meet as kindly as if one had known them all one's life . . . One must place oneself in their hands.' He admired Americans for their optimism, their unceasing, youthful energy. But as his own energy levels perceptibly diminished sometimes the readily assumed familiarity of individuals he scarcely knew irritated a raw nerve.

He completed his play, *The Life and Death of Marie Stuart* (Edinburgh, 1923). It was published but never staged. The skills that had served Repington well as a journalist did not equip him to write convincingly for the stage. He determined the text should be written in blank verse supposing its rhythms and cadences best served his noble theme. With compelling understatement Mary later wrote she was certain 'blank verse was unlikely to add to the chances his play would be produced'. She did what she could to dissuade him 'but all was in vain'.[12]

Policy and Arms (1924) was a collection of original essays and articles he had recently published in journals in America and Britain, an eclectic yet elegant *réchauffé* of old quarrels and stale issues together with an inspired glimpse of the future that demonstrated Repington had not entirely lost his cunning as a defence analyst and prophet. Why this hasty appearance of yet another book by Repington, the fifth in as many years? The answer, as always, was the hopeless pursuit of funds to restore his much desired but unrealisable financial equilibrium. Also, at least in part, *Policy and Arms* was called into the lists to take up the gage thrown down by Churchill in *The World Crisis* (1924). An unrepentant 'Easterner', not for the first or the last time Churchill sought to make the case for the Dardanelles expedition as a viable, strategic alternative to the unimaginative 'tactical and strategic catalepsy' of the British high command. As an unrepentant 'Westerner', Repington asked how politicians could suppose the way to beat the Germans was to go where they were not to be found? Only a fool would seek a decision anywhere but in France. Yet that was just what a 'little knot of politicians persuaded themselves for they believed they were great intellectuals and soldiers narrow minded dolts'.[13] It was another already too familiar reworking of a stale issue. This, however, was not true of Repington's critique of the proposal to construct a huge naval base at Singapore. Given his earlier declared opinion – a belligerent Japan threatened any power with interests in or around the Pacific – it made perfectly good sense to suggest Australia offered a more secure anchorage for the British Grand Fleet. He also noted Singapore's defences were exclusively concentrated to repel a seaward attack. The peninsula was, therefore, vulnerable to invasion from the mainland. His accurate premonition of future military humiliation and naval disaster at the hands of the Japanese was ignored.

While still attending the Naval Conference, Repington had written to tell Burnham he would be 'glad to quit America'. He had no reason to complain about the generosity of his hosts, who were 'too kind for words'. He likened the way his table was 'littered with invitations' to 'a London Season before the War'. But he had 'lost the taste for this sort of thing'. He had written in a similar spirit to Ian Hamilton the previous year. At the time he had been laid up for a couple of weeks in a London nursing home with a sharp attack of neuralgia. He had been feeling 'a bit of an old crock', his mood not helped by realising forty-one years earlier to the day he had first crossed into Afghanistan as a keen young soldier aching for action. The years of frenetic activity were finally catching up with him. Despite his best efforts there was no longer sufficient money to extend the lease on the service flat he had held for eighteen very pleasant months. He moved to Hove where, with Mary and Laetitia, he lived comfortably but in considerably reduced circumstances. His life was now quiet, ordered, free of excess, save when occasionally he ventured to London or sometimes further afield to visit old friends. But he was never far or for long away from his small, book-lined study. There he worked at his regular contributions for the *Daily Telegraph* on a wide range of topics. Inevitably he was drawn back to the familiar personalities and events of the 1914–18 war. This 'new' life revealed a resigned Repington, nowhere better demonstrated than in his generous appreciation of Henry Wilson written for the *Telegraph* after the field marshal's assassination by two IRA thugs on the steps of his Eaton Place home. He acknowledged Wilson's 'very considerable abilities and great flexibility of mind' and how this had 'uniquely equipped him to be the precursor of a new kind of soldier'. Modern democratic politics required the government's chief military adviser 'to work efficiently and in harmony with the Cabinet'. He concluded that Field Marshal Sir Henry Wilson had possessed such intellectual qualities and skills in abundance.[14]

Early in 1924 Repington experienced persistent pain in his heart. Following a particularly acute bout he was persuaded to see the family physician. The prognosis was not favourable. Apparently his heart was severely damaged. It was thought better to reveal this to Mary alone. Repington was persuaded to take life even more steadily, though it was never an injunction he obeyed readily. In the course of the year he appeared to make a good recovery. He visited Lord French, laid up in a nursing home in Vincent Square, and was touched by the invalid's obvious pleasure at the visit. They yarned together affectionately, about old times, colleagues and campaigns. Shortly afterwards, when the fatally stricken French died, Repington wrote a fine appreciation of his old friend and comrade-in-arms, published by the *Daily Telegraph* on Saturday 23 May 1925.

On Monday 25 May, having completed that day's work for the *Telegraph*, Repington, who had started to write a letter, suddenly suffered a cerebral haemorrhage. He lapsed into unconsciousness. Five hours later he was dead. He was 67 years of age. His funeral service, at the local Anglican church, St Barnabas, was attended by Mary,[15] his three daughters and a small company of neighbours and friends. His simple coffin was draped with the Union Jack. There were no military honours, nor was there any formal military representation. Viscount Burnham represented the *Telegraph;* no one from *The Times* or the *Morning Post* saw fit to attend. He was buried in Hove cemetery.[16]

23   A fractured reputation

The epitaph carved on Repington's tomb reads, 'The most brilliant military writer of his day, his pen was entirely devoted to the service of England and the Army he loved.' The obituary notices in the national, provincial and world's press, at considerable length and with detail confirmed the truth of that engraved tribute. Only one newspaper chose to damn him with faint praise. *The Times* insisted 'defects of temperament and judgment detracted from his talent'. They did not deign to call him a liar, but instead dismissed as 'entirely imaginary' his claim that he quit Printing House Square in 1918 because of undue and unreasonable editorial interference. They scolded the published diaries of his wartime experiences as '*chroniques scandaleuses*, replete with reckless statements and attributions of motive that cannot be condoned'. Finally, grudgingly, they did allow that his last book had been 'an attempt to return to his better self' and had contained 'some useful information'. Yet it had 'disappointed the anticipation raised by its ambitious title'. *The History of The Times* adopted a similarly superior and carping tone. Dillon's generous compliment in the House to 'the famous Colonel Repington . . . the twenty-third member of the Cabinet' was dismissed as 'quite undeserved'. Incorrectly it asserted 'from the beginning of the war' Repington had been 'in constant disagreement with Dawson, his foreign editor Steed and with the office about his articles'. The validity of Dawson's final, prejudiced and deliberately incorrect explanation of why Repington had resigned from Printing House Square was accepted without question. Finally, it was asserted his tenure at PHS had depended 'entirely upon him learning to advertise himself', and that was how he impressed Northcliffe, who was 'insensitive to his vanity'.[1] The portrait drawn was neither flattering nor was it honest.

Repington's departure from PHS in January 1918 had prompted Dawson's raw contempt. He was convinced greed alone explained why Repington had quit *The Times*. He wrongly supposed Repington long before his departure from PHS had negotiated his engagement to the

Morning Post at an increased salary. Concerned only to satisfy his greed, he had been uncaring of the duty he owed his former employer and colleagues. It was not so. Repington sincerely believed, with England engaged in a war of national survival, he owed his greatest duty to his country, not his employer. Earlier, Garvin had deliberately sought to undermine Repington's reputation by blatant misrepresentation. Dawson had sought to defame his former colleague by knowingly falsifying his record of events. Both shabby actions were prompted out of loyalty to Milner and indirectly at his prompting.

Repington's self-confidence on occasion must have been insufferable; such complacency, such arrogant self-assurance. It offends this generation's sense of social propriety, but a modish snobbery was a characteristic affectation of Repington's class and generation. He too readily discounted the scale of the injuries his acerbic tongue and pen inflicted upon those less thick-skinned than himself. He believed, from time to time, to suffer the scourge of some outraged opponent was inevitable. Such stripes he counted the necessary price to be paid by anyone engaged in the rough trade of journalism. But whatever the cost, he was unfailingly loyal to what he honestly considered were the best interests of the army, nation and empire. Woe betide anyone who mistakenly supposed loyalty would curb his criticism of anyone or anything he had reason to believe deserving of his censures. Not everyone subscribed as readily as he to this credo. Many in authority believed that to criticise them or the social and political status quo was to indulge a gross and dangerous disloyalty.

On becoming a military correspondent, Liddell Hart had been warned by Ivor Maxse, 'Generals are more sensitive than prima donnas.' Before the war, when Maxse commanded a brigade at Aldershot, senior officers would often say to him, 'Did you see what that awful fellow Repington said in his latest article? He ought to be barred.' But sometime later their tone would often change. 'Isn't Repington a friend of yours? Do ask him to dinner so that I could get his support for a scheme I wish to suggest to him.' Liddell Hart noted how 'Generals in those days, though fond of scoffing at the press, tended to take an exaggerated view of its influence – especially on their own careers.'[2] This explains why Repington's relationships with so many of his former colleagues who had risen to the highest ranks, could be coloured by caution. He was undoubtedly a useful ally but too much the independent critic ever to be entirely let off the rein.

Many of Repington's former colleagues had hoped for, indeed expected his reinstatement in the army; a few feared that possibility. Whatever marshal's baton he might have carried in his mental knapsack as a young, ambitious soldier, he had long abandoned such daydreams.

He entertained no illusions about the difficulties of high command. He was amused and flattered but thought Churchill's suggestion absurd when, in 1916, at a critical time in the nation's military fortunes, Winston suggested Repington's services and brilliant military brain were desperately required and could best be utilised in high command. Repington dismissed the idea as a flattering but silly conceit.

As a journalist his relationship with those he spoke to, whether he wished it were so or no, was instrumental. He was as Max Beerbohm unerringly caricatured him.[3] People had long known why 'dear, sweet Colonel Repington always carried that funny little note-book with him'. They also understood what purpose the notes were intended to serve. Frequently, those he spoke to thought to turn the conversation to their advantage, but in doing so more often than not they unintentionally revealed more to their perceptive auditor than they supposed or intended. Repington was charming, his manner disarming, and above all he was a very good listener, a rare quality possessed by few men. His conversation was informed and amusing. Liddell Hart, at his first meeting with Repington in 1924, immediately formed the impression of a 'most enter-taining' conversationalist. He particularly warmed to the friendly interest the older man showed in his views, 'which in many respects differed as widely from his as did our respective ages'. But what Hart most appre-ciated was how Repington 'treated [him] as a colleague rather than as a novice ... in the field where he had made such an outstanding mark'.[4]

As a military writer, critic and propagandist Repington flourished and was most influential in the decade or so before the war, 'the years of preparation'.[5] Particularly after he joined *The Times* his writing not only stimulated thought in British political circles concerning the art of war but helped to promote, publicise and support a raft of crucial, revolutionary, military and administrative reforms introduced by Lord Esher and Richard Haldane. Repington worked purposefully and with missionary zeal. He sought to fit the army for the entirely new responsibilities that modern warfare would inevitably impose. Not all was satisfactorily achieved; but that so much was in so short a time emphasises the value of his contribution. He lobbied relentlessly in the background, chivvied away at ministers, civil servants and soldiers by letter and conversation. In *The Times*, he sought to convince a wider audience of opinion and policy makers, by advertisement, explanation, endorsement and instruction. He championed the abolition of the post of Commander-in-Chief and the setting up of the Army Council; promoted the General Staff and its expansion to embrace an imperial dimension; above all, he encouraged joint, co-ordinated planning between the services. With good reason he retained reservations about the success of all these schemes. Similarly, he

Fig. 15 Repington and his little book: as caricatured by Max Beerbohm
(© The Estate of Max Beerbohm)

considered the army still 'unfit for purpose' in 1914 because until
Kitchener settled the matter on becoming war minister and announcing
his plans, the politicians refused to recognise the true implication of war
between the Great Powers in Europe. Moreover, the public refused to
acknowledge, if Britain wished to retain its international status as a Great
Power and remain secure at home and abroad, then it was necessary they
become, as Haldane had required, a nation-in-arms. The clash of mass,
conscripted armies would painfully reveal the inadequate size of the
British regular army no matter how well trained and equipped. Despite
Repington's constant efforts he failed to overcome the national prejudice
against conscription. Before 1914 he had wanted to spell this out but
found it hard to tell such a dreadful truth bluntly. He hoped against hope
that public opinion would finally comprehend why a small, volunteer

army, no matter how well equipped, trained and led, was not enough to resist the kaiser's massive, conscripted forces.

How much influence anyone exercises shaping a minister's legislative plans must be uncertain, but Repington's contribution as an initiator as well as supporter of Haldane's Territorial scheme[6] certainly may be traced from June 1903. Nor should the significant part he played in bringing about the military *pourparlers* with France be forgotten. To that extent he certainly helped shape military policy in the pre-war years. He consistently made efforts to encourage the British public to acknowledge the true nature of the commitment to France; a nominal entente but an alliance in reality. Only five days before Britain declared war against Germany he repeated in *The Times* the same argument he had consistently employed since 1905: 'We must support France.' He demonstrated that it was German ambitions that posed the greatest threat to British national and imperial interests. The Radicals always pointed out how the *Reichstag* was full of peace-loving German Socialists. Repington did not deny that Socialism might well determine the spirit of German domestic policy, but Germany's foreign policy was altogether different. It was driven primarily by the ambitions of the kaiser. Its associated military policy was predicated on the demands and ambitions of von Moltke and the German High Command. Repington understood why they intended to follow Schlieffen's master scheme. When the time came for the German armies to strike, they would respect neither Belgium's boundaries nor international treaty obligations. As they had long planned, they would debouch over the borders in a redoubtable torrent and pour irresistibly towards Paris until it was engulfed. With the French broken and defeated in double-quick time, the backs of Germany's armies would be secure. Now they might safely turn east to savage Russia. They would successfully have avoided the need to fight simultaneously on two fronts.

The military historian Jay Luvaas has correctly emphasised that those traits, loyalties and prejudices to which Repington had stuck constantly and consistently were not altered but rather intensified by the war. He held no principles that he had not previously rehearsed and demonstrated a thousand times before in his pre-war writings. In 1914, after the short war of movement came the seemingly endless static warfare on the western front. These circumstances, where the defensive enjoyed a huge advantage over the offensive, were new, yet Repington offered no novel solution. Like the commanders in the field, he too was a Victorian soldier of empire. The wars with which he was familiar were small wars, wars of movement. Now, asked to fight a modern, entrenched war against a major European power, this was a task for which their previous experience in the field scarcely fitted them. Nonetheless, Repington expected the politicians unquestioningly to provide the military with the resources they demanded, to allow them to determine the strategy, and at all times in all circumstances to afford them carte blanche to get on with their job. There should be no interference by 'amateurs'. When it came to waging war, Repington shared the generally poor opinion soldiers commonly held of the capacity of politicians. War was a soldier's business; they were the professionals and in such concerns, all others were amateurs.Whatever politicians claimed to the contrary, Repington believed none of them, not even Lloyd George, possessed strategic genius.

A die-hard 'Westerner', Repington opposed side-shows. The authority of Clausewitz supported his insistence that victory would be found only in overwhelmingly defeating Germany in France. Alienated from Lloyd George, earlier his ally in the shell crisis of 1915, he became the whole-hearted supporter and advocate of Robertson and Haig. In that process he buried (though he did not lose) his long-held reservations about Haig's capacity to command. What GHQ required, Repington demanded; whether it was more shells, high explosive rather than shrapnel, more and yet more bigger calibre guns, and always, greater reserves – more, ever more infantry. Britain was engaged in a war of attrition: killing Germans was the name of the game. Until the last hundred days, suc-cesses on the western front were few, the price in dead and wounded inordinately high. Yet, he never changed his message. His dominant demand was always 'more men', 'more bayonets'. A war of attrition meant more and better *materiel de guerre*; bigger guns, heavier guns, a vast expenditure of ammunition, many fewer 'duds'. All these he relent-lessly demanded.

Repington was as unapologetically a man of his times as he was of his social class. He cared not at all what posterity might think of him. He supposed such concerns presumptuous. That was as well, for posterity has not chosen to deal kindly with his reputation. In February 1918 he told Lady Randolph Churchill, whatever others might think, he har-boured no regrets about the way he had conducted his life. 'We agreed that if we could begin again at 17 we should do the same as we had done then, only more so. Then we decided we could not have done more if we tried.'[7] Caring little for what tomorrow might bring them, both had seized their day.

After the war Repington would suffer the judgment of those whose selective recollection omitted their own failings while happily exaggerat-ing his. The embittered conservative critic Harold Begbie, referring to the *War Diaries* wrote, 'To read these volumes is to discover the unthinkable and the impossible. Nowhere will you find a sentence of which you could say, "*There, that is what we fought for!*" The Cause finds no expression.'[8]

Repington would not have denied Begbie's complaint. He had seen no reason to go out of his way to suggest Britain had gone to war with Germany to serve some noble, altruistic purpose. His explanation was as simple as it was unambiguous: war had been unavoidable; a harsh necessity, a case of *real politik*. Germany had determined its own harsh fate by its political, territorial and economic actions. Just as the ambitions of Carthage eventually determined the destruction of the Carthaginian state at the hands of Rome – *Delenda est Carthago* (Carthage must be destroyed) – so war and the destruction of Germany answered a practical imperative that no Englishman could afford to ignore. Germany's restless ambition had posed a real and ever-growing threat to European integrity in general and British sovereignty in particular. If Britain and her empire were to flourish, Germany had to be extirpated – *Delenda est Germanica.*

Repington was well aware he would suffer unrelenting criticism for daring to express his own, unvarnished opinions honestly. Spending a weekend at Coombe, he recorded a conversation with Rosamund, Viscountess Ridley. 'We agreed we should be considered rather callous to go on with our usual life when we were reading of 3,000 to 4,000 casualties a day.' Among his own social class he recorded 'the only visible signs of war' were that white tie and tails were no longer de rigueur for gentlemen in the evenings; dinners, like men's jackets, were shorter, servants fewer and less competent, and there was a want of taxis. He had not expected a bouquet for such observations, nor did he receive one, particularly from those who were only too anxious to hide the reality that the creature comforts of their own very comfortable lives had been comparatively unaltered by the war. The middle classes, he perceived, had been 'the greatest sufferers, especially the humble gentlewomen with fixed incomes, and those who have lost husbands and sons'.[9] His honest, complacent, unimaginative listing of the war's 'hardships' borne by civilians appalled St Loe Strachey. He likened it to 'looking under a flat stone in the garden ... ugly and disgusting but intensely interesting'. Massingham in the *Nation* saw only 'arrogance and stupidity'.[10]

Repington did not necessarily condone all that he reported; nor was he averse, on occasion, to allow his prejudices free rein. He particularly enjoyed doing so when writing about certain, notorious, society figures. A journalist once perceptively noted of his candour, 'What he writes may be true, but it is as though a naughty child were repeating things he should not.'[11] Not only 'victims' questioned the propriety of Repington publishing the content of private conversations. Repington's own social class thought he had overstepped the mark. Their disapproval, however, did not stop them reading and retailing with relish the indiscretions of those who had proved less discreet than themselves.

The final nail in the coffin of Repington's pre-war reputation was the changed perception of the war's nature reflected in books like C. E. Montague's *Disenchantment* (1922) or Philip Gibbs's *The Realities of War* (1920). The poems and books of the soldier poets, 'the voice of outraged protest' from the 'lost generation', associated Repington with their fathers, the conservative elders, the politicians, and above all, 'the scarlet faced' generals. He was damned and 'criticised by association'. Thus Montague wrote of 'Colonel Repington's friends with their scented baths, prime vintages and their mutinous chatter ... the air stank of bad work in high places'.[12] Youth, according to T. E. Lawrence, won the war, but it was taken away from them by age seeking to remake the world in its former likeness.[13] Repington was branded an elderly thruster who, secure in his Hampstead hideaway, like the other Abrahams of his generation knowingly led their sons to the altar and then took a knife and slew them.[14]

A century has elapsed since the First World War. Perceptions of that epic struggle have constantly changed. Those who first recounted the story – poets, artists, musicians, writers, diarists, soldiers, civilians, politicians – lived through and personally experienced the war. They were very different personalities who found themselves in wildly disparate circumstances. It is scarcely surprising, therefore, that they experienced and remembered the war in very different ways and that the 'truths' they perceived about the war's essential nature should have varied widely. Knowledge not of one but many truths about what happened and why it happened was passed on to posterity.

Interest in the First World War has not faded with time, nor has questioning ceased. Subsequent generations in pursuing their own versions of the war, have extolled and emphasised those aspects of the story that best satisfy their interests, prejudices and predilections. In 1991 Professor Brian Bond wrote, 'The time is surely approaching ... when the First World War can be studied as history without polemic intent or apologies.'[15] More than two decades have already elapsed since that forecast was confidently made, but arguments continue unabated. In these centenary years, is it too much to hope that the time has now arrived when one man and what he wrote about the war may receive fresh consideration without the burden of ancient prejudice? Is it possible we may at last see Repington for who and what he was and to read what he actually said, rather than readily and unquestioningly accept what has been said by those who, for their own reasons, deliberately chose to misrepresent him?

Biographical notes

William Lockett Agnew (1858–1917), a leading art dealer was a very close friend of Repington.

Aitken. *See* Beaverbrook.

Field Marshal Sir Henry Edward Hynman Allenby, 1st Viscount (1861–1936), was known as 'the Bull' for his furious temper. Repington thought very highly of his capacity to command. He was Inspector of Cavalry, 1910–14, Commander of Cavalry, 1914; GOC V Army Corps, 1915; GOC Third Army, 1915–17; and C-in-C Egyptian Expeditionary Force, 1917–19.

Leopold Charles Maurice Stennet Amery (1873–1955), a staff member of *The Times* from 1899 to 1909, was Unionist MP for South Birmingham, 1911–18, and a member of Milner's personal staff, 1917–18. He grew to distrust Repington, who had helped him with *The Times History of the War in South Africa* (1900–09).

Sir Ralph Norman Angell (1872–1967) was a journalist who originally worked for Northcliffe. A world-famous peace campaigner, his book, *The Great Illusion* (1911), though not original was most influential.

Lieutenant General Sir John Charles Ardagh RE (1840–1907), when made DMI in 1896 was considered the foremost politico-military officer in the British army. He served on a number of congresses and conferences as a technical adviser.

Hugh Oakley Arnold-Forster (1855–1909) was Unionist MP for West Belfast, 1892–1906, and Croydon, 1906–09. He was Secretary of State for War, 1903–05. An able politician and polemicist, he was betrayed by his health and an over-confidence in his own abilities. Despite their differences, Repington admired him.

Prince William Patrick Albert Arthur, 1st Duke of Connaught and Strathearn (1850–1942), was the godson of Wellington and Victoria's third son. It was intended he would succeed Cambridge as Commander-in-Chief. He undertook a variety of posts in the army, reaching the rank of Field Marshal in 1902, and in 1904 was appointed Inspector General. Packed off to the Mediterranean command, he counted his contribution worthless and high-mindedly resigned in 1909, ending his active military career.

Sir George Compton Archibald Arthur (1860–1946) was Kitchener's private secretary, 1914–16, and author of his official *Life*.

Herbert Henry Asquith (1852–1928), cr. Earl 1925. He was Liberal MP for East Fife, 1896–1918, and by turns Home Secretary, 1892–95; Chancellor of the Exchequer, 1905–08; and thereafter Prime Minister until December 1916 when ousted by Lloyd George. A Liberal Imperialist, his abilities were not well suited to wartime leadership.

Margaret Emma Alice 'Margot' Asquith (née Tennant) (1864–1945), married Asquith as his second wife in 1892. She was fashionable, opinionated and shocked society with her *Autobiography* based upon her diaries. She was never reconciled to leaving 10 Downing Street in 1916.

Waldorf Astor, 2nd Viscount (1879–1952), immensely wealthy, was encouraged by his wife Nancy to enter politics. He became the hard-working, ambitious though somewhat maverick Tory MP for Plymouth from December 1910 to 1919, when reluctantly he resigned and entered the Lords. He was Lloyd George's PPS in December 1916. From 1911 he enjoyed effective control of the *Observer* as its influence grew under Garvin's editorship. He was the most enthusiastic and least critical Milnerite.

Admiral Sir Reginald Hugh Spencer 'Porky' Bacon (1863–1946), Fisher's naval assistant, director of naval ordnance and torpedoes 1907–09, became managing director of Coventry Ordnance. He was a pioneer of the submarine service, and was a dedicated Fisherite.

Norman Diehl Baker (1871–1937), Democrat politician, was persuaded by Woodrow Wilson to become American Secretary of State for War in March 1916. When the USA entered the war in April 1917, he presided over the selective service system, attracting criticism from Democrats and Republicans. A humane, reasonable and thoughtful politician, he backed Pershing's insistence to preserve the independence of his command and would not allow American troops to be employed piecemeal.

Arthur James Balfour (1848–1930), cr. Earl, 1922, a philosopher of sorts, was condemned by family connections to be leader of the Unionist Party at a particularly difficult time in its always difficult history. He succeeded his uncle Salisbury as Prime Minister, 1902–05. He took a genuine and informed interest in matters of defence and helped create the Committee of Defence. Repington was not particularly impressed by his grasp of strategy. Far too urbane and sophisticated for the taste of his MPs, he was replaced by Andrew Bonar Law. He was First Lord of the Admiralty, 1915–16, and Foreign Secretary, 1916–19.

Baring. *See* Cromer

Countess Lilias Margaret Frances Bathurst (1871–1965), proprietor of the *Morning Post*, 1908–24, generally allowed the editor H. A. Gwynne to have his own way. She distrusted Repington.

Prince Louis Alexander of Battenberg (1854–1921), cr. Marquess of Milford Haven, 1917, was appointed Director of Naval Intelligence, 1902–05, and First Sea Lord, 1912–14. He became a political victim of anti-German prejudice.

William Maxwell (Max) Aitken Beaverbrook, 1st Baron (1879–1964), was an Unionist MP, 1911–16, and Bonar Law's private secretary before being made Minister of Information in 1918, taking over the *Daily Express* the following year. He was a political fixer, propagandist, a manipulator of men, markets and ideas.

Harold Begbie (1871–1943) was a journalist who wrote novels, occasional biographies and works of Christian apologetics.

Charles Frederic Moberly Bell (1847–1911) was assistant manager of *The Times*, 1890–1908, then manager, 1908–11. Of the Printing House Square hierarchy, he was the most friendly towards Repington.

Hilaire Réné Belloc (1870–1953), who wrote much on a variety of subjects, was a Radical MP from 1906 to 1910. Repington scorned his commentaries on the war written for *Land and Water.*

Admiral Lord Charles William de la Poer Beresford (1846–1919), 'Charlie B', served as an Unionist MP between periods spent in various naval commands as C-in-C Atlantic, 1905, Mediterranean, 1905–07, and Channel, 1907–09. An ardent and dedicated critic of Fisher, he was associated with the Roberts–Repington invasion campaign. He was the subject of many amusing stories, some of which were true.

Francis Leveson Bertie, Viscount Bertie of Thame (1844–1919), was British Ambassador in Paris. Repington underrated his diplomatic skills.

General Sir James Frederick Noel 'Curly' Birch (1865–1939) was greatly admired by Haig who did much to further his military career. He was a leading figure in the development of the artillery.

Birkenhead. *See* F. E. Smith.

Augustine Birrell (1850–1933), lawyer, academic, Liberal MP, President of the Board of Education, 1905–07, was Chief Secretary for Ireland from 1907 until his resignation in 1916.

Henri Georges Stephan Opper de Blowitz (1825–1903) was a famed foreign correspondent. *Punch* in its obituary notice called him 'the prince of journalists'. Repington aspired to his job and legendary status as a foreign correspondent.

Paul Marie Bolo (d. April 1918), also known as Bolo Pasha, was the son of a café owner in Marseilles. He twice acted as a German spy. He was supposed by the extreme right in France and England to be the archetypal treasonable left-wing conspirator. Uncovered by the British Secret Service in 1917, Clemenceau used him to get at Caillaux. An amiable confidence trickster, he was executed as a spy at Vincennes by firing squad.

Horatio William Bottomley (1860–1933) was thought mistakenly to be the natural son of Charles Bradlaugh, the great Victorian freethinker. His reckless audacity, energy, extreme good fortune and unrivalled capacity to separate the credulous from their money, enabled him for a considerable time to indulge his prodigious appetite for sensual pleasure. A brilliant journalist, he founded then edited from 1906 to 1921 *John Bull*. Found guilty of fraudulent conversion, he served five years in prison, 1922–27, a harrowing experience from which he never fully recovered.

General Sir Henry Brackenbury (1837–1914) was a significant influence on Repington's career as a staff officer. He was Director of Military Intelligence, 1886–91, and Director General of Ordnance, 1899–1904.

Sir Reginald Herbert Brade (1864–1933) was successively Assistant Secretary, 1904–14, then Secretary to the War Office, 1914–20. He kept in close contact with Riddell and disliked Repington.

Aristide Briand (1862–1932) was France's longest-serving wartime prime minister, which office he combined with that of Foreign Secretary, October 1915–March 1917.

Admiral Sir Francis Charles Bridgeman (1848–1929) was C-in-C Home Fleet, 1907–09; First Sea Lord, 1911–12.

William St John Freemantle Brodrick, Viscount Midleton (1856–1942), Unionist MP for Surrey, 1880–1906, went to the Lords, 1907. Frequently crossed swords with Repington when Secretary of State for War, 1900–03. He was Secretary of State for India, 1903–05.

John Buchan, 1st Baron Tweedsmuir (1875–1940), novelist, propagandist, avid Milnerite and later imperial statesman, was Milner's private secretary in 1917, then appointed government Director of Information before it became a ministry. He was succeeded by Beaverbrook. He is now best remembered for his novels, particularly *The Thirty-Nine Steps* (1915). An early historian of the war, he was Haig's official biographer.

George Earle Buckle (1854–1935) was editor of *The Times*, 1884–1912.

General Sir Henry Redvers Buller VC (1839–1908) was C-in-C, Second Anglo-Boer War, 1899–1900, then replaced by Roberts. Repington served on his staff. He was not impressed by Buller's cautious style of leadership but was not unmindful of his good qualities as a commander and did not wish him unnecessarily or unfairly denigrated by Amery in his *History of War in South Africa* for faults that were not his responsibility.

Burnham. *See* Lawson.

Field Marshal Sir Julian Hedworth George Byng (1862–1935), cr. Viscount Byng of Vimy, 1926, commanded 3rd Cavalry Division, 1914–15; the Cavalry Corps, 1915; successively the IX and the XVII Army Corps, 1915–16, and the Canadian Corps, 1916–17, before being given command of Third Army, 1917–19.

Lugi Cadorna (1850–1928) was Italian Commander-in-Cheif from 1915, but replaced after humiliating defeat at Caporetto, November 1917.

William Elliot Cairnes (1862–1902) preceded Repington as military correspondent of the *Westminster Gazette*, and in his time made a significant contribution to military reform. He was the author of *An Absent-Minded War* (1900), an indictment of the War Office.

Major General Sir Charles Edward Callwell (1859–1928) was an old army colleague of Repington's in Intelligence; recalled from retirement and made DMO and I, 1914–16, then adviser on ammunition to the Ministry of Munitions, 1916–18. He was sympathetic as censor and a regularly supplied information to Repington.

Pierre Cambon (1843–1924) was French Ambassador to the Court of St James's, 1898–1920.

Sir Henry Campbell-Bannerman (1836–1908) was leader of the Liberal Party, 1899–1908, then Prime Minister, 1905–08. He managed the not inconsiderable task of uniting his party. He was not so great a Radical in matters of defence and foreign policy as the Radical Liberals liked to think.

Sir Edward Henry Carson (1854–1935) was Unionist MP for Dublin University, 1892–1918; Solicitor General, 1900–05; Attorney General, 1915–16; Lord of Appeal, 1921–35; First Lord of the Admiralty, 1916–17 and member of the War Cabinet until January 1918. He was leader of the Irish Unionists in the Commons, 1910–21.

Field Marshal Frederic Rudolph 'Fatty' Lambart Cavan, 10th Earl (1865–1946) succeeded Henry Wilson as CIGS. He demonstrated his qualities as a military leader at First Ypres, made an outstanding contribution at Loos with the Guards Division, and commanded the Tenth Army in Italy.

Lord Hugh Richard Heathcote 'Linky' Cecil (1869–1956) was Unionist MP for Greenwich, 1895–1906, and for Oxford University, 1910–37.

Robert Cecil. *See* Salisbury.

Sir Joseph Austen Chamberlain (1865–1937), was a leading Unionist. MP for East Worcester, 1892–1914, and for Birmingham East, 1914–37, he was Chancellor of the Exchequer, 1903–05. Together with Walter Long, he stood down in favour of Andrew Bonar Law as Unionist leader in 1911. Had he been less of a gentleman, he would almost certainly have been more effective as a politician.

Brigadier Sir John Charteris (1877–1946) was an Intelligence officer whose career owed much to Haig's patronage. He was accused of providing Haig with ridiculously optimistic forecasts of the suppose effect of Haig's attacks on the Germans. His post-war books defended Haig's reputation.

Sir Charles Ignatius Valentine Chirol (1852–1929) was a brilliant but narrowly opinionated authority on foreign affairs. He succeeded Mackenzie Wallace as head of *The Times*' Foreign Department in 1899. He opposed Repington's championing of Kitchener. He resigned from *The Times* in 1912 as he was opposed to the journalistic values Northcliffe espoused. A friend of Will Garstin's, he greatly disliked and distrusted Repington and judged his amorous adventures harshly.

Jeanette (Jenny) Churchill (née Jerome), Lady Randolph (1854–1921), the second, beautiful daughter of Clara and Leonard Jerome, American millionaire, was the mother of Winston Churchill. After her husband's death she married successively George Cornwallis-West and Montagu Porch and as well enjoyed a string of ardent young lovers and admirers. A friend of Repington's.

Sir Winston Leonard Spencer Churchill (1874–1965), first Unionist, then Liberal MP for Oldham, 1900–04 and 1904–06; Manchester, 1906–08; Dundee, 1908–22; Home Secretary, 1910–11; First Lord of the Admiralty, 1911–15; Chancellor Duchy of Lancaster, 1915; served on western front, 1915–16; Minister of Munitions, 1917–19; wrote an influential personal account of the First World War, 1923–31. Repington appreciated his vitality and courage if not always his political/strategic judgment.

Sir George Clarke (1848–1933) was created Baron Sydenham in 1913. From 1885 to 1901 he wrote on naval, military and imperial subjects for *The Times*. He was Secretary of the CID, 1904–07. Initially he supported Repington's appointment to PHS, but subsequently associated himself with Valentine Chirol as a major opponent. Repington for the most part admired and liked the irascible Sir George but regretted his good sense was so often undone by envy.

Karl Marie von Clausewitz (1780–1831) was a great military theorist whose works, particularly *Vom Kriege* (1833), were much valued by Repington.

Georges Clemenceau (1841–1929), was a journalist who was twice French Prime Minister, 1906–09 and 1917–20. A remorselessly aggressive, patriotic, leader he deserved his nickname 'Tiger'. Admired by Repington, he helped to sustain French and Allied morale.

Lieutenant General Sir Edwin Henry Hayter Collen (1843–1911), Secretary of the India Military Department, 1887–96, was a Member of the Viceroy's Council, 1896–1901.

Vice Admiral Philip Howard Colomb and Sir John Charles Ready Colomb (1831–99 and 1838–1909) were brothers who made important contributions to naval and imperial defence theory. Their more important works were the elder brother's *Essays* (1893) and *Naval Warfare* (1899) and the younger brother's *The Protection of our Commerce* (1867) and *The Defence of Great and Greater Britain* (1880).

Lord Leonard Henry Courtney (1832–1918) was an academic, journalist and Radical politician. A stern anti-Imperialist, he was opposed to Edward Grey. He was a noted constitutional authority. When Deputy Speaker, 1886–92, he was described as 'impartially unfair to both sides'.

Lieutenant General Sir John Steven Cowans (1862–1921), QMG throughout the war, was Repington's boon companion. His fondness for the ladies almost undid his fine career.

Captain James Craig (1872–1940), cr. Viscount Craigavon, was Ulster Unionist leader and MP for two County Down constituencies, 1906–21. He was an important Ulster contact of Repington.

John Adam Cramb (formerly Cram) (1861–1913), lecturer in history, Queen's College, London, was a fervent imperialist who helped shape anti-German attitudes with his influential little book, *Germany and England* (1914). He contributed to Roberts's *Fallacies and Facts* (1911) and was one of Roberts's speech writers. He was an early supporter of the NSL and compulsory military training.

Robert Offley Ashburton Crewe-Milnes, Marquis of Crewe (1858–1945), a Liberal politician, was appointed Secretary of State for India in 1910. He disapproved of the fanaticism of Edwardian politics. War brought him relief as it ended his political career. He behaved badly towards his family but was unfailingly polite to strangers.

Dr Hawley Harvey Crippen (1862–1910), an American resident in London, poisoned his second wife, Cora, and dismembered her body before fleeing in disguise with his lover, Ethel le Neve. He was recognised and captured by police after the first successful use of wireless telegraphy to apprehend criminal suspects. He was tried at the Old Bailey, found guilty and executed.

George Nathaniel Curzon (1859–1925), u. Earl in 1911, was frequently critised by Repington for not supporting Kitchener. He was Viceroy of India, 1898 to 1905, and a member of Lloyd George's War Cabinet.

Sir Charles John Darling (1849–1936) was a High Court judge. Whimsical and facetious, he was prone to lose the respect of his juries. He was judge in the bizarre trials of both Horatio Bottomley and Pemberton Billing.

George Geoffrey 'Robin' Dawson (1874–1944) had the surname Robinson until 1917. He was both a friend and disciple of Milner. Twice editor of *The Times*, he succeeded Buckle in September 1912 and resigned in February 1919 after constant difficulties with Northcliffe. Initially he enjoyed a close relationship with Repington, but this subsequently deteriorated forcing Repington's resignation in January 1918.

Théophile Delcassé (1852–1923) was the French foreign minister forced to resign in the first Moroccan crisis of 1905. He had been one of the principal architects of the Anglo-French entente, 1904. As minister for the navy, 1911–13, he agreed to concentrate the French fleet in the Mediterranean, leaving the defence of France's Atlantic coach to the British navy.

Edward George Villiers Stanley Derby, 17th Earl (1865–1948), was Director General of Recruiting, October 1915; Under Secretary at the War Office, July–December 1916; and Minister for War, 1916–18. To make way for Milner, he was appointed Ambassador to France from 1918 to 1920, when he returned to the War Office. He resented what he supposed was his 'betrayal' by Repington in *War Diaries*.

Sir Charles Wentworth Dilke (1843–1911), Radical Liberal MP for Chelsea, 1868–86, was later MP for the Forest of Dean, 1892–1911. A potential prime minister, his parliamentary career was ruined by a sexual scandal. One of the very few MPs informed and interested on defence matters. He liked Repington.

Major General Sir Stanley Brenton von Donop (1860–1941), gunner who served in South Africa, 1899–1902, was later Director of Artillery at the War Office, Master General of the Ordnance and 4th Military Member of the Army Council, 1913–16. He was savagely victimised by Lloyd George.

General Sir Charles Whittingham Horsley Douglas (1850–1914), Adjutant General, 1904–09; GOC Southern Command, 1909–12; Inspector General of Home Forces, 1912–14; replaced French as CIGS after the Curragh incident. Died from overwork in October 1914.

Admiral Adam Duncan, Viscount (1731–1804), when Admiral of the White, won a famous naval victory over the Dutch at the Battle of Camperdown, 1797.

Alexander William Charles Oliphant Murray Elibank, Viscount (1870–1920), was a politician and a businessman. Whilst Liberal Chief Whip, 1910–12, he was notoriously involved with Lloyd George and Reading in the Marconi Scandal. Extreme Unionists permanently associated his name with corrupt political practices.

Lieutenant General Sir Gerald Francis Ellison (1861–1947) was Secretary of the War Office Reconstruction Committee, 1904–05. As Haldane's private military secretary, 1905–08, he was crucial in designing Haldane's reforms. Appointed Director of Army Organisation, 1908–11, he was much admired by Repington.

Sir Harold Elverston (1866–1941) was a newspaper proprietor and Liberal MP for Gateshead, 1911–18.

Reginald Baliol Brett, 2nd Viscount Esher (1852–1930), was a life member of the CID, the committee that was essentially his own creation, 1905–18. He was the quintessential *eminence grise*. He was an important contact for Repington in his early years as military correspondent. Typically, Esher valued him only so long as he was useful to him.

General Sir John Spencer Ewart (1861–1930) was DMO, 1906–10; Adjutant General, 1910–14; and GOC Scotland, 1914–18. He was a thinking soldier for whom Repington had a high regard.

Erich von Falkenhayn (1861–1922) was Prussian War Minister, 1913, before succeeding Moltke as Chief of German Staff in September 1914. He was replaced after failure of the offensive strategy at Verdun in August 1916; thereafter, he commanded in Rumania, 1916–17, in Palestine, 1917, and in Lithuania, 1918.

Admiral Sir John 'Jacky' Arbuthnot Fisher (1841–1920) was the great naval reformer Repington first met at The Hague Peace Conference. He was twice First Sea Lord, 1904–10 and 1914–15, father of the *Dreadnought*, and creator of the modern Royal Navy. A great manipulator of the press, he totally misunderstood Repington.

Maréchal Ferdinand Foch (1851–1929) was from March 1918 Allied Commander. A resourceful general, courageous and optimistic, he described Versailles not as 'a peace treaty but a twenty-year armistice'. He is remembered for signalling to Joffre at the Marne, 'My centre is giving way, my right retreating, situation excellent, I am attacking.' He was liked by Repington and Henry Wilson.

Philip Staveley Forster (1865–1933) was an honorary major in the Staffordshire Yeomanry. He was Unionist MP for Stratford-upon-Avon, 1901–06, defeated by Kincaid-Smith; he was re-elected in 1909 after beating Kincaid-Smith in a by-election. He held on to the seat until his retirement in 1918.

Franz Ferdinand (1863–1914), Archduke of Austria, was nephew and from 1896 heir apparent to Franz Joseph I (1830–1916), the emperor of Austria, 1848, and king of Hungary, 1867. With his wife, Sophie, he was assassinated at Sarajevo in June 1914, precipitating the Great War. Austria used his assassination by Serbian nationalists to justify their attack on Serbia.

Lovat Fraser (1871–1926), editor of the *Times of India*, 1902–06, was a member of the editorial staff of *The Times*, 1907–22.

Field Marshal Sir John Denton Pinkstone French (1852–1925), cr. Viscount, 1915; Earl, 1921; CIGS, 1911–14; C-in-C of BEF, 1914–15; C-in-C Home Forces, 1916–18; Lord Lieutenant of Ireland, 1918–21. He was closely associated with Repington over the shells scandal of 1915. Repington much admired the dashing cavalry general. He liked the ladies and also shared Repington's careless attitude to money, but without the same disastrous personal consequences.

Sir William Edwin Garstin (1849–1925), a brilliant civil engineer, who planned and built the Aswan dam. He was the husband of Mary (Molly) née North whom he divorced for her adulterous liaison with Repington.

James Louis Garvin (1868–1947), 'Jim' or 'Garve', was an outstandingly brilliant Tory journalist and editor who made his name and that of his paper, the *Observer*, synonymous. A trenchant polemicist and propagandist, he was Fisher's strong advocate. At Milner's and his proprietor's request, he sought to discredit Repington in an article replete with misrepresentation.Though they frequently disagreed Repington, admired Garvin as a journalist and editor.

Sir Auckland Campbell Geddes (1879–1954), who enjoyed success in a series of disparate careers, as businessman, politician and professor of anatomy, was appointed minister of national service in 1917. Independently minded and industrious.

Sir Eric Campbell Geddes (1875–1937), before he was 40 had been appointed general manager of the London and North East Railway. His outstanding abilities as an administrator were recognised by Lloyd George. He dramatically improved the chaotic logistics of the BEF but was resented by the military, although Haig soon acknowledged his value. Inspector General of Transportation, 1916–17, he became Unionist MP for Cambridge, 1917–22, First Lord of the Admiralty in 1917, and a member of the War Cabinet in 1918. Repington reluctantly acknowledged his abilities and value.

David Lloyd George (1863–1945), cr. 1st Earl of Dwyfor, 1945, was a mercurial Welsh Liberal politician. Prime Minister, 1916–1922, he proved himself a great war leader with the capacity after the war and in peacetime to break the mould of domestic party politics. He is, perhaps, remembered most fondly for his early Radicalism. Many have chosen to write about him but few have succeeded in capturing convincingly this most enigmatic political genius. Courted then vilified by Repington, LG sought in his *War Memoirs* to pay back Repington, accusing him absurdly and unjustifiably of being a traitor to his country.

Sir Philip Armand Hamilton Gibbs (1877–1962) represented the *Daily Chronicle* and the *Daily Telegraph*, and was the best known of the British war correspondents. He was knighted in 1920 for his services to journalism. His changed perception of the nature of the First World War is reflected in his books with their ever-changing prefaces.

Major General Count Albert Edward Wilfred Gleichen (1863–1937) was military attaché in Berlin, 1903–06, in Washington, 1906; Assistant DMO, 1907–11; and Commander of the 15th Infantry Brigade.

Lieutenant General Sir Hubert de la Poer Gough (1870–1963), or 'Goughie', was a daring and brilliant cavalry officer who in 1914 commanded the 3rd Cavalry Brigade. His involvement in the Curragh incident did not hinder his career. Successively he was commander of the 2nd Cavalry Division, 1915; I Army Corps, 1916; and then the Fifth Army, 1916–18. Removed from his command, he was enthusiastically supported by Repington who blamed the politicians, not the generals, for the German breakthrough.

The Hon. Margaret Helen Greville (1867–1942), the most generous of hostesses, was a great friend of Repington. A millionaire in her own right, her money came from shipping and brewing. She always had a coterie of ambassadors, peers and politicians who adored her.

Sir Edward Grey (1862–1933), cr. Viscount, 1916, a Liberal imperialist MP since 1885, served as Foreign Secretary from 1905 to 1916. An honourable man, he was defeated by physical frailty.

Lieutenant General Sir James Moncreiff Grierson (1859–1914), DMO, 1904–06; Commander 1st Division, Aldershot, 1906–10; GOC Eastern Command, 1910–14; he died on active service, August 1914.

Edward William Macleay Grigg (1879–1955) was a member of the editorial staff at *The Times*, 1903–05 and 1908–13, whom Repington much admired. He was assistant editor of *Outlook*, 1905–06, and served throughout the war with the Grenadier Guards.

Emilie or Emily Grigsby (1876/80–1964), an American courtesan, was one of Repington's mistresses and also a loyal friend who proved a diligent and kindly godmother to his daughter, Laetitia. Among her other occasional lovers were Repington's friends Cowans and possibly French.

Howell Arthur 'Taffy' Gwynne (1865–1950) was editor of the *Standard*, 1904–11, before his appointment as editor of the High Tory *Morning Post*, 1911–37. An inveterate and incorrigible political plotter and anti-Semite, he gave a berth to Repington for two years after he left *The Times* despite his proprietor's reservations. Because of their close association, Repington was frequently accused of sins that were more often his editor's.

Field Marshal Sir Douglas Haig (1861–1928), cr. Earl, 1919; brought home from India where he had been Inspector General of Cavalry, 1903–06, he was successively Director of Military Training, 1906–07, then Director of Staff Duties, 1907–09. He returned to India as Chief of Staff, 1909–12, before his appointment as GOC Aldershot, 1912–14. Commander of the First Army, 1914–15, he replaced French as C-in-C of the BEF, 1915–19. He did not like Repington and Repington entertained serious reservations about his fitness to be C-in-C but nonetheless supported him.

Elizabeth Sanderson Haldane (1862–1937), founder of the Territorial Nursing Service, devoted much of her life to the care of her brother, Lord Haldane.

General Sir James Aylmer Lowthrop Haldane (1862–1950) was Lord Haldane's cousin and successively Commander of the 10th Infantry Brigade BEF, August–November 1914; of the 3rd Division, 1914–16; and finally VI Army Corps, 1916–19.

Mary Elizabeth Haldane (née Burdon Sanderson) (1825–1925) was the mother of Lord Haldane. He was absolutely devoted to her and they exchanged daily letters.

Richard Burdon Haldane (1856–1928), cr. Viscount, 1911, was the Liberal Imperialist MP for East Lothian, 1885–1912, Secretary of State for War, 1905–12 and Lord Chancellor, 1912–15. Close to Repington but not so close as to over-value his friendship, he was the political friend of Grey and Asquith and was effectively betrayed by latter. He transferred to the Labour Party to become their first Lord Chancellor.

General Sir Ian Standish Monteith Hamilton (1853–1947) was a brave, romantic soldier now best remembered for commanding the unsuccessful Dardanelles expedition in 1915. A fine writer, he was a friend of Repington. He was married to Jean Miller née Muir (1861–1941), daughter of an extremely rich Glasgow businessman. She befriended Mary, although she never liked Repington.

Sir Maurice Pascal Alers Hankey (1877–1963), cr. Baron, 1939, was Secretary to the CID. This former Royal Marine officer was a powerful and influential figure in foreign and defence politics.

Lewis Vernon 'Loulou' Harcourt, 1st Viscount (1863–1922), was opposed to any increase in military or naval expenditure and resisted the idea Britain was under any moral obligation to support France in arms against Germany. He was close to Esher. A proven and sound administrator he buried himself under the pall of his father's disappointed ambitions recorded in his two-volume hagiographical biography.

Charles Hardinge, 1st Baron Hardinge of Penshurst (1858–1944), was a distinguished diplomat and Permanent Undersecretary at the Foreign Office, 1906–10, before his appointment as Indian Viceroy, 1910–16.

Harmsworth. *See* Northcliffe.

Sir Robert Leicester Harmsworth (1870–1937), Northcliffe's younger brother, the fifth of the eleven surviving Harmsworth children and the fifth of eight brothers, was an undistinguished Liberal MP who represented Leicester for twenty years but scarcely ever spoke in the House.

Austin Frederic Harrison (1873–1928) was a newspaper journalist who took over the *English Review*'s editorship from Ford Maddox (Heuffer) Ford. In several pre-war books he warned of Germany's aggressive intentions. These included *England and Germany* (1907), which particularly impressed Northcliffe. He applauded Repington's 'shell campaign', but opposed Lloyd George's punitive peace terms. He became an early supporter and advocate of the League of Nations.

Lieutenant General Sir David Henderson (1862–1921) was distinguished both as a soldier and an important figure in the development of the Royal Flying Corps. He remained in overall command of the RFC until October 1917. He was once considered a candidate for the post of CIGS.

Reginald Herbert, 15th Earl of Pembroke (1880–1960), was Repington's cousin.

Sir Gordon Hewart (1870–1948), cr. Viscount, a lawyer, was Liberal MP for Leicester East, 1918–22. He became successively Solicitor General, 1916–19, then Attorney General until his elevation to Lord Chief Justice in 1922.

Field Marshal Paul von Beckendorff von Hindenburg (1847–1934), C-in-C on the German Eastern Front, 1914–16, was chief of the German Army General Staff, 1916–18, and Germany's president, 1925–34.

Francis Wrigley Hirst (1873–1953) was the editor of the *Economist*. A Radical Liberal, his ideas were shaped by the Boer War. He enjoyed little influence after the 1914–18 war. He helped Morley write his *Life of Gladstone*.

General Victor Jacques-Marie Huguet (1858–1925) was the French military attaché. A long-standing friend of Repington's, together they were instrumental in beginning the Anglo-French military *pourparlers*.

Lieutenant General Henry Doveton 'Hutch' Hutchinson (1847–1924) was Director of Staff Duties at the War Office, 1904–08. Repington had a poor opinion of his abilities.

Lieutenant General Sir Edward Thomas Henry 'Curly' Hutton (1848–1923) commanded the Dominion Militia, 1898–1900, was Australian Military Forces Commander, 1901–04, and Commander of Eastern Command, 1905–06, before retiring. He was a spokesman on military subjects, particularly conscription, and Repington thought highly of his abilities and wanted him to become an MP.

Admiral Sir John Rushworth Jellicoe (1859–1935) cr. Viscount, 1918 and Earl, 1925; was 2nd Sea Lord, 1912–14; C-in-C Grand Fleet, 1914–16; 1st Sea Lord, 1916–17; and Chief of the Naval Staff, 1917.

General Joseph Jacques Césare 'Papa' Joffre (1852–1931) was the rotund C-in-C of the French armies from May 1914 and was effectively Allied military supreme commander in 1915. He planned the Somme with Haig and when it failed was replaced by Nivelle. French complained Joffre treated him as though he were a corporal, but Repington, who thoroughly approved of 'Papa' thought him impressive.

General Sir Thomas Kelly-Kenny (1840–1914), as Adjutant General, 1901–04, presided with Roberts at Repington's 'trial' and pronounced him guilty of breaking his parole, requiring him to resign his commission. He was a sound but essentially dull and old-fashioned officer who thoroughly disliked and distrusted Repington.

Lieutenant General Sir Launcelot Edward 'Kigge' Kiggell (1862–1954) was a friend of Repington's. From December 1915 to January 1918 he served as Haig's Chief of Staff, his advancement owing everything to ability and nothing to influence. He was hard-working, loyal and thoroughly professional, but almost certainly too self-effacing and not sufficiently assertive when 'advising' Haig.

Thomas Malcolm Harvey Kincaid-Smith (1874–1938) as a regular cavalry officer served with the 9th Lancers, 1894–1901. He was Liberal MP for Stratford-upon-Avon from 1906 until March 1909 when he took the Chiltern Hundreds to fight a by-election on compulsory military training and was heavily defeated.

Field Marshal Sir Horatio Herbert Kitchener (1850–1916), cr. Earl 1914, 'K' or 'K of K', was Britain's greatest serving soldier when in 1914 Asquith appointed him Secretary of State for War. He devised the New Armies and dominated British strategy. Though he was not unaware of his failings, Repington admired him. He was drowned at sea in January 1916 when his ship hit a mine.

Sir Francis Knollys (1837–1924), cr. Viscount, 1911, was private secretary to Edward both as Prince of Wales and king, and to George V until 1913, when he completed forty-three years of royal service.

Lambart. *See* Cavan.

George Lambert, 1st Viscount (1866–1958), a Devonshire farmer and Liberal politician who was appointed Civil Lord at the Admiralty.

Henry Charles Keith Petty-Fitzmaurice Lansdowne, 5th Marquess (1845–1927), was Secretary of State for War, 1895–1900; Foreign Secretary, 1900–05, responsible for the Anglo-French entente, 1904; and the author of the Peace Memorandum, November 1916.

Sir Philip Alexius László de Lombos László (1869–1937), the Hungarian-born British painter. Enjoyed an international reputation as an outstanding portraitist. He was a victim of DORA.

Andrew Bonar Law (1858–1923) was Unionist MP for Glasgow Blackfriars, Central, Dulwich and Bootle. He succeeded Balfour as Unionist leader, 1911–23. Colonial Secretary, 1915–16, he was made Chancellor of the Exchequer, 1916–18, and Leader of the House, 1916–21. He was Prime Minister from 1922 to 1923. Always a hard-line supporter of Ulster, he was coached on military problems by Repington as well as Henry Wilson.

General Sir Herbert Alexander 'Lorenzo' Lawrence (1861–1943) resigned twice from the army, in 1903 and 1916, before being given the command of 66th Division in France in March 1917. More independently minded than Kiggell, in February 1918 he succeeded him as Haig's Chief of Staff. Lawrence, a fine and clever soldier became indispensible to Haig.

Harry Lawson Webster Levy-Lawson (1862–1933), cr. Viscount Burnham, was the owner of the *Daily Telegraph* but not so successful as his father, Edward Levy-Lawson, 1st Baron Burnham (1833–1916). The *Telegraph* struggled to retain its sales under his leadership. He finally sold in 1927 to the Berry brothers and Iliffe. His viscountcy recognised his work for the Territorial Army. He became Repington's employer after leaving the *Morning Post*. For years he was the highly respected and acknowledged spokesman for the newspaper industry.

Arthur Hamilton Lee, Viscount Lee of Fareham (1868–1947), was by turns soldier, Unionist MP, patron of the arts and national benefactor. His wife's great wealth allowed him a high degree of political independence. Appointed First Lord of the Admiralty, in LG's post-war administration he gave Chequers as a grace and favour residence for use of the Prime Minister and the Courtauld Institute to London University.

Colonel Herman Le Roy-Lewis (1860–1931), the British military attaché in Paris from 1915 to September 1918, was clever and mischievous. He was disliked by Haig but liked by Esher because he had a poor opinion of Bertie, the ambassador. Something of a man of mystery, he proved a very useful contact for Repington.

Sir John Randolph 'Shane' Leslie (1885–1971), author, poet, biographer, Irish Catholic apologist, cousin of Winston Churchill, did not like Repington.

Basil Henry Liddell-Hart (1895–1970) was a military journalist and historian who succeeded Repington as military correspondent of the *Daily Telegraph*.

Theresa Susey Helen Vane-Tempest-Stewart Londonderry, 6th Marchioness (1856–1919), otherwise known as 'Nellie', was a grand political hostess, relentless string-puller and a great friend of Repington who brought him nothing but joy.

Walter Hume Long, 1st Viscount (1854–1924), was a Unionist politician and most certainly not the booby squire some took him to be. In forty years in Parliament he represented seven different constituencies. He sought to become the major arbiter of opposition policy in Ireland. He abandoned his own claim to the leadership of his party in 1911 in favour of Bonar Law, and retired as First Lord of the Admiralty.

Simon Joseph Fraser Lovat, 14th Baron (1871–1933), was a founder member of the NDA and was closely associated with Repington in all pre-war invasion inquiries. Independently minded, he commanded the Highland Mounted Brigade at Gallipoli.

General Sir Neville Gerald 'NG' Lyttelton (1845–1931), although a brave soldier, was not a success as CGS, 1904–08. He was undoubtedly the best cricketer in the army but the least intellectually capable of the Lyttelton brothers. Repington acknowledged his faults as CGS, but personally was very fond of him.

General Sir George Mark Watson Macdonogh (1865–1942) was an Intelligence officer with the BEF from 1914 to 1916 when he became DMI at the War Office. He was able but cautious by disposition. Haig disapproved of Macdonogh's, caution referring to him as 'defeatist'. On occasion he was an important source of information for Repington. He was Adjutant General, 1918–22.

Alfred Thayer Mahan, USN (1840–1914), was a most influential naval historian and theorist; he wrote *The Influence of Sea Power upon History, 1600–1812* (1890–92), which had a considerable, world-wide effect upon naval strategic thinking. His work was frequently misunderstood and misrepresented.

General Charles Marie Emmanuel Mangin (1866–1925) was sacked by Nivelle after the Aisne attack in 1917 but restored to his command by Foch who admired 'the butcher's' aggression.

Colonel Raymond John Marker (1867–1914) was ADC for Curzon, 1899–1900, for Kitchener, 1902–06, and private military secretary to Arnold-Forster. He was the most important conduit of information in the early years at PHS between Repington and Kitchener. He died of his wounds soon after reaching France.

Henry William Massingham (1860–1924) was a brilliant journalist with a great passion for Nonconformity, Liberalism and literature. He disapproved of Repington's militarism.

Major General Sir Frederick Barton Maurice (1871–1951) was a great friend of 'Wully' Robertson's. The two men were particularly closely associated after 1915 as CIGS and DMO. In his 'Letter', published in certain newspapers in 1918, he questioned Lloyd George's figures concerning troop strengths, but was rebutted in Parliament. He was accused incorrectly of plotting against the government and of being influenced by Repington. He was effectively dismissed from the army. Lloyd George never forgave him. He was the son of Sir John Frederick Maurice (1842–1912), who was Wolseley's protégé and loyal supporter. As a teacher at Camberley of military history and tactics, he was an important military mentor of Repington's.

General Sir Frederick Ivor Maxse (1862–1958) was commander of the 1st Guards Brigade, 1914; of 18th Division, 1915–17; of XVIII Army Corps, 1917–18; Inspector General of Training, France, 1918; and GOC-in-C Northern Command, 1919–23. Repington thought highly of his qualities as a soldier.

Leopold James Maxse (1864–1932), the uncompromising ultra-Tory editor/owner of the *National Review*, was a great and indiscriminate hater, as anxious to get rid of Balfour as he was of Haldane. Frequently before the war he gave a home to Repington's articles that Dawson or Buckle did not want for *The Times*.

Admiral Sir William Henry May (1849–1930) was C-in-C Atlantic, 1905–07; and Second Sea Lord, 1907–09.

Reginald McKenna (1863–1943), Liberal MP for Monmouthshire, 1895–1918, succeeded Tweedmouth as First Lord of the Admiralty, 1908–11. He was thereafter successively Home Secretary, 1911–15, and Chancellor of the Exchequer, 1915–16. Both he and his wife for a time were friends of Repington's.

Midleton. *See* Brodrick.

Milford Haven. *See* Battenberg.

Alfred Milner (1854–1925), cr. Viscount, 1902, was High Commissioner for South Africa, 1897–1905; member of Lloyd George's War Cabinet, 1916–18; War Minister, 1918–19; and Colonial Secretary. He inspired a generation of imperialists identified as his *Kindergarten*. He did not like criticism and inspired Garvin's attack upon Repington in the *Observer*. He was an outstanding administrator but no democrat.

Gilbert John Elliot-Murray-Kynynmound, 4th Earl of Minto (1845–1914), was successively Governor General of Canada, 1891–1904, then of India, 1905–10. His character and integrity compensated for his lack of intellectual brilliance, even as his wife's sensitivity and knowledge of India helped to smooth his relations with John Morley.

Helmuth von Moltke (1800–91) was Chief of the German Staff, 1858–88 during which period he reorganised the Prussian army. He planned the successful campaigns against Denmark, 1863–64; Austria, 1866; and France, 1870–71.

Helmuth Johannes Ludwig von Moltke (1848–1916) lacked his uncle's military genius. Nevertheless he succeeded Alfred von Schlieffen (1833–1913), author of the 'Plan' for a swift German victory in the west before tackling the Russians. Chief of the German Staff, 1913, after a nervous breakdown in September 1914 he was replaced by Erich von Falkehayn.

Charles Edward Montague (1867–1928), journalist, wrote for the *Manchester Guardian*. His books, *Disenchantment* (1922), *Fiery Particles* (1925) and *Rough Justice* (1926) were seen as condemnatory of people like Repington. Essentially, they are critiques based upon his personal experience of the war's conduct and the lack of generosity and decency in the post-war years.

John Morley (1838–1923), cr. Viscount, 1908, was Liberal MP for Newcastle-upon-Tyne, 1893–95, and Montrose Burghs, 1896–1908; Secretary of State for India, 1905–10; and Lord President of the Council, 1910–14. In August 1914 he resigned from the Cabinet as a protest against the war. A nominal Radical, Repington was surprised at his support for Grey, especially in relation to Russia and Germany.

Mottistone. *See* Seely.

Murray. *See* Elibank.

General Sir Archibald James Murray (1860–1945) was Deputy CIGS, then CIGS, 1915, before taking the Egyptian Command in 1916–17. He was GOC-in-

C Aldershot, 1917–19. 'Old Archie' was a much valued friend of Repington's and frequently a source of useful information.

Lieutenant General Sir James Wolfe Murray (1853–1919), Master General of the Ordnance and Fourth Member of the original Army Council, 1904–07, was appointed CIGS, October 1914 to September 1915.

Field Marshal Sir William Gustavus 'Old Nick' Nicholson (1845–1918) was an outstanding staff officer whose qualities Repington unjustifiably mistrusted. He was appointed QMG, 1905–07; Chief of the General Staff; then first CIGS, 1908–12.

Harold George Nicolson (1886–1968) was a man of extraordinary talents, by turn civil servant, diplomat, journalist, failed politician, broadcaster, novelist, historian, biographer and diarist. He was married to Vita Sackville-West, poet and novelist, like him an extremely promiscuous homosexual. Their garden at Sissinghurst, now maintained by the National Trust, stands as a delightful joint memorial. He was a useful source of information and opinion for Repington during the Versailles Peace Conference.

Alfred Charles William Harmsworth Northcliffe (1865–1922), cr. Baron, 1905, and 1st Viscount, 1917, was the outstanding newspaper proprietor of the age. He founded the *Daily Mail* in 1896. An inventive and brilliant journalist he was a most successful businessman. As chief proprietor of *The Times*, 1908–22, he was not responsible for Repington leaving Printing House Square in 1918 for the *Morning Post*. He sympathised with Repington's irregular domestic ménage for he too was somewhat overburdened with mistresses and illegitimate issue.

Frederick Scott Oliver (1864–1934) was associated with Roberts's campaign for National Service and also with other right-wing enterprises. An anti-democrat and passionate Milnerite, he wrote *Ordeal by Battle* (1915).

Vittorio Emmanuele Orlando (1860–1952) was a Sicilian lawyer who became Italy's prime minister after Caporetto. At Versailles he failed to extract sufficient territorial concessions to satisfy Italian expectations. He resigned and retired from politics after Mussolini's rise to power in 1925.

Rear Admiral Sir Charles Langdale Ottley (1858–1932) was Assistant Secretary CID, 1904; DNI, 1905–07; and Secretary to the CID, 1907–11. A good servant of the CID, he was always a loyal 'interpreter' of Fisher.

General Sir Arthur Henry Fitzroy Paget (1851–1928), or 'AP', was GOC Ireland, 1911–14. His behaviour and actions during the Curragh incident blighted the rest of his military career. As GOC Southern Command, 1914–18, he and his wife were great friends of Repington's, who was a frequent weekend guest at their country home.

Paul Painlevé (1863–1933), as an independent Socialist, was Minister for War, March–September 1917, then Prime Minister of France until November 1917, when he was succeeded by Georges Clemenceau.

Palmer. *See* Selborne.

Sir Cyril Arthur Pearson (1866–1921), the newspaper and periodical proprietor, founded *Pearson's Weekly* and the *Daily Express*. He unsuccessfully aspired to the ownership of *The Times*. He later founded St Dunstan's and was President of the National Institution for the Blind.

Pembroke. *See* Herbert.

General John Joseph Pershing (1860–1948) was C-in-C of the American Expeditionary Force. His experience in the field before 1917 was limited but he proved a thoroughly sound and professional soldier. 'Black Jack' was very conscious of his responsibility to the American nation, something Haig, who grew increasingly exasperated, did not appreciate. He was inexcusably condescending supposing Pershing's gentlemanly bearing the unusual for an American'. Repington admired Pershing.

Marshal Henri Philippe Benoni Omer Joseph Pétain (1856–1951), Commander of the French Second Army in charge of the besieged city of Verdun, was made Chief of the General Staff in April 1917, then from May 1917 until November 1918, C-in-C. He was an important French contact for Repington, who admired his professionalism and steely determination.

Field Marshal Sir Herbert Charles Onslow 'Plum' Plumer (1857–1932), cr. Viscount, was QMG, 1904–05; GOC Northern Command, 1911–14; Commander of the Second Army, 1915–17 and again in 1918; GOC Italy, 1917–18; and GOC Army of the Rhine, 1918–19. He was a successful but scarcely brilliant general. His lugubrious appearance did not belie his nature.

Arthur Ponsonby, 1st Baron (1871–1946), a Liberal Radical who became a Labour MP, was a leading pacifist and founding member of the UDC. A highly principled but sadly ineffectual politician, he sought unavailingly to change British foreign policy. He was one of A. J. P. Taylor's 'Troublemakers'.

Archibald Philip Primrose, 5th Earl of Rosebery (1847–1929), succeeded Gladstone as Liberal Prime Minister, 1894–95, before resigning leadership of the Liberals in 1896. He was a political busted flush after Campbell-Bannerman became Prime Minister in December 1905, despite his leadership of the Limp faction. He was probably admired by Repington as much for his stable and his 'Classic' winners as for his political skills and influence as an imperialist statesman.

General Sir William 'Putty' Pulteney (1861–1941) was one of Repington's closest Ulster friends and was GOC III Corps from 1914 to 1918.

Grigory Efimovich Rasputin (*c.* 1870–1916), the Russian mystic known as the 'Mad Monk' who exercised considerable influence at the Russian court, was assassinated by noblemen led by Prince Yusupov.

General Sir Henry Seymour 'Rawly' Rawlinson (1864–1925), an early military friend of Repington's, was appointed Commandant of the Staff College, 1903–06. He commanded the 3rd Cavalry Division, 1914; IV Corps,

1914–15; First and Fourth Armies, 1915–18, and was British Representative at the Supreme War Council, 1918. His cautious 'bite and hold' method of attack proved costly in 1916 and was not looked upon with favour by Haig, but in different conditions it enjoyed success in 1918.

John Edward Redmond (1856–1918), the Irish politician who had led the small Parnellite minority in the Commons, was elected chairman of the new Nationalist Party after reunion in 1900. His more powerful colleagues, such as Dillon, Devlin and Healy, never allowed him to exercise his full authority. Aloof and reclusive, his conciliatory agenda was sacrificed for political survival and party unity. The Easter Rising of 1916 finally crushed his endeavours.

Thomas Henry Ribblesdale, 4th Baron (1854–1925), soldier, politician, huntsman and author of *The Queen's Hounds* (1897), was the subject of an iconic portrait painted by John Singer Sargeant (1902). His first wife, 'Charty' Monckton Tenant, the sister of Margot Asquith, was a fine horsewoman and as strikingly handsome as her husband. She died in 1911 whereupon Ribblesdale decamped to Rosa Lewis's Cavendish Hotel. In 1919 he married Ava, the American widow of John Jacob Astor. He was a friend of Repington's and a fellow Rifleman. A Liberal whip until 1911, he was the epitome of the late Victorian gentleman. Both his sons were killed on active service.

Lieutenant General Sir George Lloyd Reily Richardson (1847–1931), a veteran from the Indian army, was appointed, at Roberts's instigation, Commander of the Ulster Volunteer Force.

Sir George Allardice Riddell (1865–1934) was created 1st Baron in 1920. A solicitor who was chairman of the *News of the World*, 1903–34, he was the intimate of Lloyd George. His diaries are an important source for the politics of the period.

Lady Rosamund Cornelia Gwladys Ridley (née Guest), widow of 2nd Viscount Ridley (d. 1916) (1874–1947), was a frequent dinner companion of Repington's whom he favoured for her spirit, level-headedness and common sense. She once told Repington that she despaired only if deprived of cigarettes and biscuits.

Field Marshal Sir Frederick Sleigh Roberts, VC (1832–1914), 'Bobs', was cr. Earl in 1901. A hero of the Indian Mutiny, he was C-in-C South Africa, 1899–1900, and Commander in Chief, 1901–04. After his retirement until his death he was the foremost public advocate of conscription.

Edmund Robertson, 1st Baron Lochie (1845–1911), was a Liberal politician whose 'true Scottish tenacity for arithmetical calculations' was much admired by Radicals.

Field Marshal Sir William 'Wully' Robert Robertson (1859–1933) was CGS of the BEF from January to December 1915, when he was appointed CIGS, 1915–18. Repington's single, most important contact at the War Office was in this latter period.

Robinson. *See* Dawson.

Rosebery. *See* Primrose.

Leopold de Rothschild (1845–1917) was the youngest of Baron Lionel de Rothschild's three sons. From 1906 Haig was a great friend. His generosity was much appreciated by Haig's staff for he kept them well supplied with champagne, brandy, cigars and delicacies from Fortnum & Mason.

Robert Arthur Talbot Gascoyne-Cecil, 3rd Marquis of Salisbury (1830–1903) was a Conservative politician who became party leader and Prime Minister. He was one of the greatest Foreign Secretaries.

John Sattersfield Sandars (1853–1924), 'Jack', was Political Private Secretary to Balfour, 1892–1905, until 1911 his confidential aide, and then, for a short period, 1914–15, acted as his secretary. He was an important organiser of a news service at Unionist Central Office.

General Paul Maurice Emmanuel Sarrail (1856–1929), GOC of the French Third Army, was dismissed by Joffre in 1915 and appointed GOC of the French Army of the Orient and sent to Salonika in 1916, only to be dismissed by Clemenceau in 1917.

Sir Philip Albert Gustave David Sassoon (1888–1939), Unionist MP for Hythe, 1912–39, was Haig's private secretary, 1915.

George Saunders (1859–1922) was the deservedly famed Berlin correspondent of *The Times*. He repeatedly warned his readers of German foreign policy's true intent. He was afforded the kaiser's ultimate accolade when referred to as 'a first class swine'.

Major General Sir Henry Jenner Scobell (1859–1912) was Repington's brother-in-law. His brilliance as a junior cavalry leader made him a favourite of French's, but he disappointed his mentor, was publicly rated and his active career destroyed.

Sir Samuel Edward Scott (1873–1943) was Unionist MP for Marylebone, 1898–1922. As a major he served at Gallipoli and in Egypt. As Repington's friend he financed the research for the 1907 invasion inquiry.

John Edward Bernard Seeley (1868–1947), otherwise known as 'Galloping Jack', cr. Baron Mottistone, 1933, a Unionist then Liberal MP, was by turns Under Secretary for War, 1911–12, and an undistinguished War Minister, 1912–14. He was required to resign over the Curragh incident. He served as a Major General with the Canadian Cavalry Corps. Repington admired him more for his physical courage and good nature than for his application and intellect.

Sir John Allsebrook Simon (1873–1954), Liberal MP, was an outstanding lawyer who resigned as Home Secretary in 1916 in opposition to conscription and became leader of the Liberal rump. He was appointed Lord Chancellor, 1940–45.

Vice Admiral William Sowden Sims USN (1858–1936) commanded all anti-submarine warfare vessels in European water. He was good friend of Britain and a far-seeing naval officer.

Admiral Sir Edmund John Warre Slade (1859–1928) succeeded Ottley as DNI, 1907–09, before an appointment as C-in-C East Indies, 1909–12. He advised Balfour on naval matters at Versailles, 1919–20. Open-minded, he supported Repington's demand for shared strategic planning.

Frederick Edwin Smith, 1st Earl of Birkenhead (1872–1930), was a Tory MP and brilliant lawyer who became Lord Chancellor, 1919–1924. He proved a failure as Censor. Despite the bitterness of party politics of the period, he retained friendships across the party divide. He was associated with Repington, particularly in Ulster.

Sir Hubert Llewelyn Smith(1864–1945) was an outstanding civil servant of marked Radical sympathies, 'a statesman in disguise'. His contribution to Whitehall's response to the economic and administrative challenges that war posed was crucial, and he helped in organising Lloyd George's Ministry of Munitions and largely shaping wartime manpower policy.

General Sir Horace Lockwood Smith-Dorrien (1858–1930) was a general whom Repington much admired for his outstanding qualities as a leader. Unfortunately he quarrelled with French. He was GOC Aldershot, 1907–12; GOC Southern Command, 1912–14; II Corps and Second Army, 1914–15; and was thereafter sidelined. He saved the BEF on 26 August 1914 with his unsanctioned stand at Le Cateau.

Jan Christian Smuts (1870–1950) was the South African statesman and soldier who commanded Imperial forces in East Africa in 1916 and was appointed to the War Cabinet, 1917–18. He enjoyed a respect and reputation for his military judgment, which he did not deserve.

John Alfred Spender (1862–1942) was editor of the *Westminster Gazette*, 1896–1922, the doyen of Liberal editors, and Repington's first newspaper editor and journalistic mentor.

William Thomas Stead (1849–1912) was the distinguished editor of the *Pall Mall Gazette* and founder of the *Review of Reviews*, the mentor of both Esher and Milner as journalists. He always thought well of Repington's qualities as a journalist.

Henry Wickham Steed (1871–1956) joined *The Times* in 1896 and was successively an outstanding foreign correspondent in Berlin, Rome and Vienna. Appointed Foreign Editor, 1914, he replaced Dawson as editor, 1919–22. He was much put about and upon by the increasingly bizarre behaviour of Northcliffe. Astor replaced him as editor. He was too independently minded for the new owner, who reverted to his fellow Milnerite, Dawson. Steed did not like Repington. A brilliant and knowledgeable critic he was underestimated and undervalued.

Giles Lytton Strachey (1880–1932), literary critic, biographer and essayist, was best known for his biographical collection *Eminent Victorians* (1918). A literary bombshell in its own time for its mocking challenge to Victorian values, it no longer shocks modern readers for what then was novel now is commonplace. His lively letters reveal many affectionate qualities that endeared him to his friends.

John St Loe Strachey (1860–1927) was a brilliant journalist who was both editor and proprietor of the *Spectator*, 1896–1925. An influential Unionist free-trader, his interest in volunteers, rifle shooting and Germany's aggressive intent before 1914 brought him close to Repington.

Admiral Sir Frederick Charles Doveton Sturdee (1859–1925), Assistant DNI, 1900–02, was Beresford's Chief of Staff, 1905–07, before becoming Edward VII's ADC.

Prince Charles Maurice de Talleyrand–Périgord (1754–1838) was a cynical clergyman who became a famed French statesman and diplomat with something of the character of the Vicar of Bray.

André Tardieu (1876–1995) was a popular journalist who wrote for *Le Temps*, a newspaper supposedly close to the thinking of the French Foreign Office. He argued for conversion of the Anglo-French Entente into an alliance and considered British adoption of universal military service a necessary preliminary.

Sir William Beach Thomas (1868–1957), journalist and author, specialised in rural stories. During the 1914–18 war he found himself, rather like Waugh's Boot of the *Beast*, unwittingly designated a war correspondent. A dedicated Northcliffian, his reports were invariably optimistic and full of patriotic sentiment that did wonders for civilian morale but were laughed at by soldiers. He was rewarded for his sterling efforts as a war correspondent when knighted in 1920.

Sir James Richard Thursfield (1840–1923) was a leader writer for *The Times* as well as a naval and literary expert. A favoured vehicle for Fisher to 'inspire', he became an opponent of Repington.

Edward Majoribanks Tweedmouth (1849–1909) as First Lord of the Admiralty, 1905–08, was involved in the Fisher–Beresford quarrel and the notorious Kaiser–Tweedmouth correspondence that Repington tried to exploit to his advantage.

Tweedsmuir. *See* Buchan.

Sir William George Tyrrell (1866–1947) was an outstanding diplomat. Tommy Sanderson's private secretary, he was by turn secretary to the CID, 1903–04; the private secretary and confidant of Sir Edward Grey and, like Eyre Crowe, an important anti-German figure at the Foreign Office. He was Minister Plenipotentiary at the Peace Conference. His dislike of Germans, Curzon, Lloyd George and paperwork all endeared him to Repington, but not his overfondness for alcohol. His many journalist friends included Leo Maxse and Taffy Gwynne.

Brigadier General Cyril Moseley Wagstaff (1878–1940) joined the army in India in 1897 and served throughout the war as a staff officer on Haig's staff, where he was attached to USAEF.

Arthur Fraser Walter (1846–1910) was the second son of John Walter (1819–94). The two men were successively proprietors of *The Times*. 'AF', a friend of Repington's, was chairman of The Times Publishing Co., 1908–10.

Herbert George Wells (1866–1946) was a distinguished novelist, commentator and speculator upon the past, present and future. A Socialist, he was the casual friend and neighbour of Repington's. They shared a phenomenal appetite for pretty women who were not married to them.

Sir George Stuart White, VC (1835–1912) succeeded Sir William Penn Symons (1843–99) as commander in Natal after Penn was killed attacking Talana Hill.

Herbert Spenser Wilkinson (1853–1937) was a distinguished writer who influenced a generation of army officers. From 1895 to 1914 he was a staff member of the *Morning Post* writing on military and diplomatic subjects; Chichele Professor of Military History, All Souls, Oxford University, 1909–23; he eschewed theory, emphasising the practical, but sadly, by 1914 was very much yesterday's man.

Admiral Sir Arthur Knyvet Wilson, VC (1842–1921) was known as ''ard 'eart'. He was C-in-C Channel Fleet, 1905–07, a member of the CID from April 1909, and became Fisher's successor as First Sea Lord, January 1910. Fisher thought very highly of him, but Churchill removed him in November 1911 when he lost the strategic argument with Henry Wilson after Agadir. Repington had no good opinion of him as a strategist.

Field Marshal Sir Henry Hughes Wilson (1864–1922) was Commandant of the Staff College, 1907–10; DMO, 1910–14; Assnt. CGS, 1914–15; liaison officer with the French army, 1915; Commander IV Corps, 1916; British Representative at Supreme War Council, 1917–18; and CIGS, 1918–22. He was an Ulster Unionist MP when assassinated in 1922. He won the all-important strategic argument with the Admiralty in 1911 and as DMO was crucial in the preparation of the BEF for action in France. Once a close colleague of Repington, although both men shared many similar ideas they grew to dislike and distrust each other intensely. Repington blamed Wilson for his dismissal from the army.

President Thomas Woodrow Wilson (1856–1924) was elected President of the United States of America in 1912 and brought to the presidency an unusual degree of high-minded intellectualism; re-elected in 1916, his hopes to keep the US out of the war were sunk by the German U-boat policy. He realised he could have greater influence over the peace-making as a belligerent. America's entry into the war was an enormous boost to the Allied cause. In January 1918 he pronounced his 'Fourteen Points', a scheme for a new world order and international arbitration enforced by the League of Nations – a noble vision that deserved to succeed but failed; Repington was scathing and thought Wilson 'knew as much about European politics as a Hindu about skates'. Undone by Cabot Lodge and the Republicans in the Senate, Wilson's political credit had already evaporated before in 1919 he suffered a debilitating stroke.

Field Marshal Sir Garnet Joseph Wolseley (1833–1913), cr. Viscount, 1885, was the original 'modern Major General'. He was Commander-in-Chief of the British army, 1895–1900.

Field Marshal Sir Henry Evelyn Wood (1838–1919) was always distrustful of Kitchener. A supporter of Haig, he made it his business to see Amery was supplied with information critical of Roberts, Kitchener and Buller for *The Times History of the War in South Africa*.

Major General Edward 'Eddy/Eddie' James Montagu-Stuart-Wortley (1857–1934) was a friend of Repington's who became notorious for his *Daily Telegraph* interview with the kaiser. Both he and Repington served on Buller's staff. He was GOC 4th Division, 1914–16, but was sacked after his failure at Gommecourt on the first day of the Somme.

Notes

Unless otherwise indicated, the place of publication is London.

Introduction

1. The surname Repington was added in October 1903, when on his father's death he succeeded to the Amington estate. Its addition was required to satisfy the terms of an ancient will.
2. Further details on persons mentioned in the text can be found in the Biographical Notes *ante*.
3. For a more detailed account of Repington's life before 1902, with source references, see *The Letters of Lieutenant-Colonel Charles à Court Repington CMG*, Army Records Society (Stroud, 1999), pp. 1–10. Hereafter this book is cited as *Correspondence*.
4. à Court Repington was his full correct surname, Repington having been assumed upon his father's death. Except in a formal context he was and is more usually referred to as Repington.
5. Quoted in A. E. Sullivan, 'Colonel Repington', *Army Quarterly* (October 1968), p. 92.
6. See Hamilton to Repington, 14 November 1919, and Repington to Hamilton, 27 November 1919, Military Archives, King's College London, Hamilton MSS, 13/89.
7. H. H. Asquith, *Memories and Reflections 1852–1927* (1928), vol. I, p. 224.
8. Mary Repington collected contemporary reviews of Repington's published work in two large scrapbook folio volumes, from which volumes this quotation and the others have been taken.
9. See Derby to Stamfordham, 23 September 1920, Royal Archives, Geo. V O 1431/31. See also Hardinge to Curzon, 29 March 1922: 'Repington has committed the inexcusable fault of publishing a diary containing private conversations with individuals that show a lack of taste that is absolutely inexcusable and pernicious ... I did not believe he could be either such a cad or such a fool.' Cambridge University Library, Hardinge Papers, vol. 45, p. 64. For the conversations Hardinge complained about, see Colonel Repington, *The First World War 1914–1918: Personal Experiences of Lieutenant-Colonel à Court Repington*, 2 vols. (1920) (hereafter *War Diaries*), vol. II, pp. 21–6, 7–10 August 1917.

344 Notes to pages 8–24

10. See Admiral Sir Reginald Bacon, *From 1900 Onward* (1940), p. 181.
11. See Esher to Stamfordham, 23 September 1920, RA Geo. V O 1431/31.
12. The Very Rev. J. G. McCormick to Henry Wilson, 27 December 1921, Imperial War Museum, Wilson MSS, 2/91/89.
13. Quotations taken from Ian Beckett, 'Frocks and Brasshats', in Brian Bond (ed.), *The First World War and British Military History* (Oxford, 1991), p. 104.
14. Review notice, quoted in K. Jeffery, *Field Marshal Sir Henry Wilson* (Oxford, 2006), p. 292.
15. A notable exception is W. M. Ryan. See his, *Lieutenant-Colonel Charles à Court Repington* (New York, 1987).

1   A new profession

1. Deeply conventional, Chirol, a friend of Sir William Garstin, had been in Cairo when Repington's liaison with Mary Garstin was *the* subject of social gossip in the British community. His sense of moral outrage was further excited by the Garstin divorce and the fact that Mary and Repington subsequently flouted convention by living together. As his de facto wife, she called herself Mrs Repington.
2. A Court(Repington) to Sir George White, 9 March 1901, British Library, Oriental and India Office Collections, MSS EUR, F108/66.
3. A Court (Repington) to Moberly Bell, 2 January 1902, Times Archive.
4. See J. A. Spender, *Life, Journalism and Politics*, 2 vols. (1927), vol. I, p. 96 and vol. II, p. 74; and Spender to Tweedmouth, 6 March 1908, Ministry of Defence, Naval Library, Tweedmouth MSS, B/126.
5. Quoted Hamilton Fyfe, *Northcliffe: An Intimate Biography* (1930), p. 68.
6. Quoted Stephen E. Koss, *The Rise and Fall of the Political Press in Britain*, 2 vols. (1981 and 1984), vol. I, pp. 418–19.
7. Sir George Clarke to Chirol, 4 April 1905, Times Archive.
8. A Court Repington to Churchill, 5 December 1903, in *Correspondence*, p. 48.
9. Same to same, 29 April 1903, Churchill Archive Centre, Cambridge, Churchill MSS, CHAR 1/38/28.
10. Same to same, 1 May 1903, Churchill MSS, CHAR 3/4/83.
11. Repington to Churchill, 5 December 1903, in *Correspondence*, pp. 47–8.
12. H. O. Arnold-Forster to A. J. Balfour, 28 May 1908, British Library, Balfour Add. MSS, 49723, fos. 254–55.
13. See Repington's essay, 'A Plea for History', *The Times*, 10 September 1904.
14. The quotations are from Repington's essay. This paragraph owes much to the writing of Ian Beckett, and particularly to his 'War, Truth and History', in *The Victorians at War* (2003), pp. 83–92.
15. See Repington to Esher, 18 September 1904, in *Correspondence*, pp. 53–5.
16. *Vestigia: Reminiscences of Peace and War* (1919), p. 257. See also 'Statecraft and Strategy', *The Times*, 10, 12 and 27 June 1908.
17. See Bell to Repington, 19 December 1904, Times Archive; and Repington to Bell, 18 December 1904, in *Correspondence*, pp. 58–9.

18. See further R. F. Mackay, *Balfour: Intellectual Statesman* (Oxford, 1985), pp. 126ff. See also J. K. Dunlop, *The Development of the British Army, 1899–1914* (1938), pp. 153–55 and 225.
19. Repington to Bell, 11 January 1905, Times Archive.

2   Kitchener's champion

1. Repington to Buckle, 8 March 1906, *The Times*, 9 March 1906.
2. Repington to Marker, 14 July 1904, British Library, Kitchener-Marker Add. MSS, 52277B, fo. 1.
3. See for example, Repington to Esher, 26 and 29 July 1907, Churchill Archive Centre, Cambridge, Esher MSS, ESHR 5/23.
4. Repington to Marker, 19 August 1904, Kitchener-Marker Add. MSS, 52277B, fos. 2–3.
5. Same to same, 26 January 1906, Kitchener-Marker Add. MSS, 52277B, fos. 84–8.
6. Chirol to Moberly Bell, 20 January 1906, Times Archive.
7. See Chirol to Bell, 10 November 1905, Times Archive.
8. Repington to Marker, 25 May 1906, in *Correspondence*, pp. 93–4.
9. See Repington to Dawson, 26 February 1913, Times Archive.
10. Sir Valentine Chirol, *Fifty Years in a Changing World* (1927), p. 228.
11. See Kitchener to Marker, 15 February 1905, Kitchener-Marker Add. MSS, 52277A; George Clarke to Chirol, 11 November 1907 and 7 May 1908, BM, Add. MSS, 50832, fos. 62–3 and 171–79.
12. After the divorce from Sir William Garstin, for the rest of her life Mary styled herself as Mary Repington or Mrs Repington. Her friends called her Molly.
13. Repington to Marker, 5 July 1906, in *Correspondence*, pp. 95–9.
14. Ecclesiastes 1: 2 and 4. 'Vanity of vanities, saith the Preacher ... all is vanity ... One generation passeth away and another generation cometh.'
15. At a meeting of the subcommittee of the Defence Committee in 1907 that reported on India's military requirements, Clarke's cross-examination of the Chief of India's General Staff revealed that General Beauchamp Duff had no idea how the extra troops in the field he had requested were to be supplied. Clarke demonstrated that to keep 155,000 men for a year required the services of more than 5 million camels – an impossible number.
16. Repington to Marker, 5 July 1906, in *Correspondence*, pp. 95–9.
17. Repington to Marker, 2 January 1906, *ibid.*, pp. 73–9.
18. Repington to Marker, 26 January 1906, *ibid.*, pp. 84–8.
19. Quoted Keith Robbins, *Sir Edward Grey* (1971), p. 160.
20. Repington to Marker, 29 June 1906, Kitchener-Marker, Add. MSS, 57722B, fos. 66–71.
21. Same to same, 3 August 1906, Kitchener-Marker Add. MSS, 52277B, fos. 98–102.
22. Curzon to Barrow, 30 November 1906, Barrow Papers, MSS EUR, E420/20.
23. Morley to Minto, 13 January 1909, MSS EUR, D573/4.
24. Morley to Minto, 3 October 1907, MSS EUR, D573/4. Morley's uncharacteristic anger during this period had much to do with domestic

worries. In November 1907 his stepson was tried and sentenced to ten years' penal servitude for forging Morley's signature in an attempt to extort money.

25. Minto to Morley, 29 November 1907, MSS EUR, D 573/2.
26. See further, J. McDermott, 'The Revolution in British Military Thinking from the Boer War to the Moroccan Crisis', in Paul Kennedy (ed.), *The War Plans of the Great Powers, 1880–1914* (1979), pp. 99–117.
27. Repington to Marker, 11, 13 and 14 April 1909, Kitchener-Marker Add. MSS, 52277B, fos. 157–61.
28. See further on the Kitchener legend, G. H. Cassar, *Kitchener: Architect of Victory* (1977), pp. 179–82.
29. See Chirol to Morley, 10 September, Morley to Crewe, 17 October, and Crewe to Morley, 19 October 1911, Cambridge University Library, Crewe Papers, c/37.
30. *Vestigia*, p. 254.
31. Chirol, *Fifty Years in a Changing World*, p. 228.

3   Esher's War Office reforms

1. Gary Mead, *The Good Soldier: The Biography of Douglas Haig* (2007), p. 126.
2. James Lees-Milne, *The Enigmatic Edwardian* (1986), p. 168.
3. Esher to Knollys, 10 August 1903, RA W38/110. There were of course other intelligent soldiers with relevant experience to whom Esher could and did turn for advice, e.g. Douglas Haig. Repington's great advantage was that he was no longer a serving officer.
4. Repington to Esher, 25 September 1904, ESHR 10/24. See also Sir Sidney Lee, *King Edward VII: A Biography* (1927), vol. II, p. 197.
5. 'The Royal Commission on the War in South Africa'. The chairman was Victor Alexander Bruce, 9th Earl of Elgin.
6. See Esher to Balfour, 15 December 1903, in Maurice V. Brett (ed.), *Journals and Letters of Reginald Viscount Esher*, 2 vols. (1934–38), vol. II, p. 33.
7. See Esher to Knollys, 16 January 1904, Royal Archives, W32/22. See also, Esher to M. V. Brett, 26 November 1903, in Brett (ed.), *Journals and Letters of Esher*, vol. II, p. 31.
8. See *The Times*, 1 February 1904.
9. See Repington to Esher, 4 February 1904, in *Correspondence*, pp. 49–50.
10. See Repington to Marker, 25 August 1904, *ibid.*, pp. 52–3.
11. Edward thought French insufficiently senior for the post of CGS. French apparently was delighted to get out of the job. See French to Esher, 24 February 1904, quoted Richard Holmes, *The Little Field Marshal: Sir John French* (1981), pp. 126–27.
12. Repington to Esher, 9 February 1904, in *Correspondence*, pp. 51–2.
13. Repington to Esher, 24 August 1906, *ibid.*, pp. 106–09.
14. He told Esher that he really did not think he could do the job. 'I should fail. I think I know ... what are my limitations.' Kitchener to Esher, 14 August 1905, in Brett (ed.), *Journals and Letters of Esher*, vol. II, p. 98. See also Cassar, *Kitchener*, p. 155.

15. Repington to Marker, 21 July 1907, Kitchener-Marker Add. MSS, 52277B, fos. 142–44.
16. See *Observer* (April–May 1910).
17. Henry Wilson's diary, entry for 10 and 11 February 1904, quoted C. E. Callwell, *Field Marshal Sir Henry Wilson: His Life and Diaries*, 2 vols. (1927), vol. I, p. 55.
18. Repington to Marker, 25 August 1904, in *Correspondence*, pp. 52–3.
19. See Cmd. 1932, Report of the War Office (Reconstitution) Committee (Part I), 1904.
20. Cicero, *De Legibus*, 3.3.8. 'The well-being (or safety) of the people is the supreme law.'
21. Repington to Leo Maxse, 27 February 1906, in *Correspondence*, pp. 89–91.
22. Esher to Repington, 19 May 1905 (draft), ESHR 10/25.
23. Repington to Esher, 5 October 1906, in *Correspondence*, pp. 109–12.
24. Esher to Repington, 6 October 1906, ESHR 10/25.
25. Clarke to Esher, 20 October 1906, ESHR 10/39.
26. See Repington to Maxse, 17 and 27 February 1906, in *Correspondence*, pp. 88–91.

4   Arnold Forster lays the foundation for the General Staff

1. See Repington to Churchill, 5 December 1903, in *Correspondence*, p. 47.
2. Repington to Esher, 9 February 1904, *ibid.*, pp. 51–2.
3. *Vestigia*, p. 82.
4. Repington to Esher, 18 July 1905, in *Correspondence*, pp. 64–5.
5. *The Times*, 25 May 1905.
6. Repington to Esher, 25 May 1905, ESHR 10/25. Repington's claim was untrue.
7. Wilson's diary, 10 July 1905, quoted John Gooch, *ante*, p. 85.
8. Arnold Forster to Balfour, 10 October 1905, quoted, John Gooch, *The Plans of War: The General Staff and British Military Strategy c. 1900–1916* (1974), p. 90.
9. See *The Times*, 25 November 1905. Hannah Glasse (née Allgood) (1708–70). Her book, *The Art of Cookery made Plain and Easy, by a Lady* (1746), contains a well-known recipe for jugged hare that begins, 'Take your hare when it is cased'. This is familiarly misquoted as 'First catch your hare'.
10. Repington to Esher, 6 March 1910, ESHR 5/33.
11. *Vestigia*, pp. 259–60.

5   Anglo-French military conversations

1. Repington to Marker, 16 June 1905, Kitchener-Marker Add. MSS, 52277B, fos. 23–4. See also, G. W. Monger, *The End of Isolation* (Edinburgh, 1963), ch. 8, *passim*.
2. Or Three Emperors League, 1875, Bismarck's attempt to stabilise the European balance of power to Germany's advantage by keeping Austria-Hungary and Russia in harmony under German tutelage.

3. Repington to Marker, 2 January 1906, in *Correspondence*, pp. 73–9.
4. See *Vestigia*, p. 262.
5. See *The Times*, 27 December 1905.
6. Repington to Sir Edward Grey, 29 December 1905, in *Correspondence*, pp. 71–2.
7. Repington to Esher, 29 December 1905, and Esher to Clarke, same date, quoted Nicholas d'Ombrain *War Machinery and High Policy: Defence Administration in Peacetime Britain 1902–1914* (Oxford, 1973), p. 84.
8. Repington to Esher, 14 January 1906, in *Correspondence*, pp. 79–81.
9. See Holmes, *Little Field Marshal*, p. 140. 'French became a planner by accident and there is no evidence he had any aptitude for the task.'
10. See Spender, *Life, Journalism and Politics*, vol. II, pp. 67–8. On Fisher and the notion of the preventive attack and whether he was merely pulling the royal leg, see Ruddock F. Mackay, *Fisher of Kilverstone* (Oxford, 1973), pp. 319–21. When he made the same suggestion a second time a few years later, Edward was not unreceptive.
11. Repington to Marker, 2 January 1906, in *Correspondence*, pp. 73–9.
12. Grey to Repington, 30 December 1905, *ibid.*, p. 299 n. 20.
13. Repington to Edward Grey, 3 January 1906, Public Record Office, E. Grey Papers, FO. 800/110. Repington as military attaché a few years earlier had been engaged in conversations with the Belgian military authorities: 'Grey does not think the Belgians would enter into any arrangement with Germany permitting the latter to cross their territory.' See Clarke to Esher, 9 January 1906, ESHR 10/38.
14. Repington to Esher, 14 January 1906, in *Correspondence*, pp. 79–81.
15. Repington to Marker, 14 June 1906, Kitchener-Marker, Add. MSS, 52277B, fos. 60–4.
16. In four volumes, *Projets et tentatives de débarquement aux Iles Britanniques*. The project was not finally abandoned until 1908.
17. Repington to Esher, 14 January 1906, in *Correspondence*, pp. 79–81.
18. Same to same, 18 January 1906, *ibid.*, p. 82.
19. See Lord Ponsonby of Shulbrede's contemporary memoir of Campbell-Bannerman subsequently used by Francis Hirst for his idealised portrait of Sir Henry, *In the Golden Days* (1947), *passim*, but particularly p. 265, 'He kept the faith to the end'.
20. *War Diaries*, vol. I, p. 12.
21. Repington to Esher, 18 January 1906 (second letter), in *Correspondence*, p. 83.
22. Repington to Esher, 19 February 1906, ESHR 10/26.
23. Clarke to Esher, 9 January 1906, ESHR 10/38.
24. Repington to Marker, 5 July 1906, in *Correspondence*, pp. 95–9.
25. This was one of a number of incidents in Morocco in the autumn of 1908. Six Foreign Legion deserters had taken refuge in the German consulate but were carried off by force. Public opinion was roused and the military made plans for war which neither the German nor the French government wanted. Even before it was referred to The Hague Court of Arbitration, the matter was settled amicably.
26. Repington to Esher, 20 January 1909, *ibid.*, p. 150 and n. 88, pp. 306–07.

27. See entry in General Ewart's diary, 21 June 1908, Scottish Record Office, Ewart MSS, RH/4/64/4.
28. *Ibid.*, 14 January 1907. This entry from his diary is incorporated in Ewart's unpublished autobiography.
29. Repington to Knollys, 15 December 1906, in *Correspondence*, pp. 114–15.

6   Finding suitable generals

1. Repington to Knollys, 15 December 1906, in *Correspondence*, pp. 114–15.
2. Repington to Marker, 2 January 1906, *ibid.*, pp. 73–9.
3. Same to same, 15 March 1906, Kitchener-Marker Add. MSS, 52277B, fos. 46–9.
4. See Repington to Marker, 22 August 1906, Kitchener-Marker Add. MSS, 52277B, fos. 115–18.
5. See Same to same, 29 June 1906, Kitchener-Marker Add. MSS, fos. 66–71: these comments arose in the context of Repington telling Haldane that ideally he would have Kitchener as CGS. Same to same, 25 July 1906, Kitchener-Marker Add. MSS, fos. 92–7.
6. Haldane to S. Wilkinson, 6 January 1906, Army Museums Ogilby Trust, Wilkinson MSS, 13/32.
7. Repington to Esher, 24 August 1906, ESHR 10/27.
8. Repington to Marker, 27 August 1906, Kitchener-Marker Add. MSS, 52277B, fos. 119–21.
9. Same to same, 22 August 1906, Kitchener-Marker Add. MSS, fos. 115–18.
10. See Repington to Esher, 24 August 1906, in *Correspondence*, pp. 106–09.
11. 'Military Notes', *The Times*, 30 October 1906.
12. 'John French: An Appreciation', *Daily Telegraph*, Saturday 23 May 1925.
13. Repington to Esher, 14 October 1907, ESHR 5/23.
14. Repington to Esher, 24 August 1906, in *Correspondence*, pp. 106–09.
15. Repington to Marker, 25 July 1906, Kitchener-Marker Add., MSS, 52277B, fos. 92–7.
16. See Repington to Esher, 19 August 1906, in *Correspondence*, pp. 105–06.
17. See Repington to Esher, 18, 19 and 24 August 1906, ESHR 10/26; Repington to Marker, 22 August 1906, Kitchener-Marker Add. MSS, 52277B, fos. 115–18.
18. The Mediterranean Command was based on Malta and combined Crete, Gibraltar, Cyprus, Egypt and Malta. Although it constituted a strategic group, a C-in-C was really superfluous as his duties were more or less confined to the inspection of troops. Connaught, recognising it as a hopeless backwater, resigned. Haldane then offered the command to Kitchener, who rejected it because he supposed it to be too narrow for his talents. See Cassar, *Kitchener*, pp. 159ff.
19. See *The Times*, 15 August 1907; Noble Frankland, *Witness of a Century* (1993), p. 249; Clarke to Chirol, 11 November 1907, British Library, Sydenham Papers, Add. MSS, 50832, fos. 62–3.
20. Repington to Marker, 14 June 1906, Kitchener-Marker Add. MSS, 52277B, fos. 60–4.

21. Repington to Esher, 30 September 1907, in *Correspondence*, pp. 121–22.
22. See Repington to Esher, 30 September and 7 October 1907, in *Correspondence*, pp. 121–25.
23. See Holmes, *Little Field Marshal*, pp. 127–28. See also Repington to Esher, 29 July 1907, ESHR 5/23.
24. Quoted Holmes, *Little Field Marshal*, p. 137.
25. See Repington to Esher, 20 September 1908, ESHR 5/27. Cf. French to Knollys, 10 September 1908, RA W28/56–7.
26. Repington to Esher, 8 August 1910, ESHR 5/35.
27. See Army Order 233 'Organisation of the General Staff', 12 September 1906, WO 123/48.
28. Repington to Esher, 7 October 1907, ESHR 5/23.
29. Esher to Repington, 10 October 1907 (typed copy), ESHR 5/23.
30. Repington to Esher 14 October 1907, ESHR 5/23.
31. Repington to Esher, 20 January 1907, ESHR 5/22.
32. Same to same, 16 January 1907, ESHR 5/23.
33. Repington to Marker, 24 January 1907, Kitchener-Marker Add. MSS, 52277B, fos. 131–32.
34. Same to same, 18 December 1906, Kitchener-Marker Add. MSS, 52277B, fos. 129–30.

7   Invasion

1. See Francis Hirst, G. H. Perris et al., *The Burden of Armaments* (1905), p. 126.
2. Fisher to J. Sandars, 23 July 1904, Balfour Add. MSS, 49710, fo. 150.
3. Fisher claimed Repington was (Leo) Maxse's 'chosen apostle lying on his bosom'. The pun on lie was intentional. Dalgetty is a disreputable character in Scott's *Legend of Montrose*. See further A. J. Marder (ed.), *Fear God and Dread Nought: The Correspondence of Admiral of the Fleet Lord Fisher of Kilverstone*, 2 vols. (London, 1952–59), vol. II, p. 146 and n. 2.
4. Arnold Forster to Balfour, 28 May 1905, Balfour Add. MSS, 49723, fos. 252–57.
5. *Vestigia*, p. 277.
6. Repington to Roberts, 20 November 1907, in *Correspondence*, p. 131.
7. Repington to Marker, 5 July 1906, *ibid*, pp. 95–9.
8. Fisher to Arnold White, 10 February 1910, quoted Admiral Bacon, *From 1900 Onward*, vol. II, p. 120.
9. Spender, *Life, Journalism and Politics*, vol. II, p. 67.
10. Repington to Esher, 14 August 1906, ESHR 10/26; same to same, 24 August 1906, in *Correspondence*, pp. 106–09.
11. Repington to Marker, 25 July 1906, Kitchener-Marker Add. MSS, 52277B, fos. 92–7.
12. Fisher to Esher, 12 September 1907, in Marder (ed.), *Fear God and Dread Nought*, vol. II, p. 134.
13. *Vestigia*, p. 280.
14. Repington to Esher, 22 November 1906, in *Correspondence*, pp. 112–13. In this section on the Channel Tunnel I have relied primarily on Keith Wilson's

excellent monograph, *Channel Tunnel Visions, 1850–1945: Dreams and Nightmares* (Hambledon, 1994), *passim*. Clarke to Esher, 3 January 1907, ESHR 10/40.

15. See exchanges between Clarke and Repington in Letters to the Editor of *The Times*, published in October and November 1907.

16. Fisher to Corbett, 28 September 1907, in Marder (ed.), *Fear God and Dread Nought*, vol. II, pp. 137–38.

17. All the relevant correspondence is contained in CAB 3/2/42A.

18. Repington to Esher, 22 October 1907, ESHR 5/23.

19. See Beresford to Repington, 17 November 1907, Army Museums Ogilby Trust, Roberts MSS, R62/23.

20. Repington to Bell, 21 April 1907, Times Archive.

21. See Repington to Roberts, 11 and 12 November 1907, Roberts MSS, R62/17/19–20; Esher thought the list absurdly long. See his journal, 16 November 1907, in Brett (ed.), *Journals and Letters of Esher*, vol. II, p. 257.

22. Asquith's reputation as 'Squiff' or 'Sozzle' was attributed largely to the malice of political opponents. See, S. E. Koss, *Asquith* (1976), p. 187; see also pp. 139–40 and 255–56.

23. See Brett (ed.), *Journals and Letters of Esher*, vol. II, p. 263.

24. Repington to Roberts, 29 November 1907, in *Correspondence*, pp. 133–34.

25. Esher's journal, 21 and 28 November 1907, ESHR 2/10.

26. Repington to Roberts, 29 November 1907, in *Correspondence*, pp. 133–34.

27. Repington to Roberts, 2 January 1908, Roberts MSS, R62/35.

28. 'So much the worse for them'.

29. Repington to Esher, 4 January 1908, in *Correspondence*, pp. 138–39.

30. Sir Edmund Slade, diary, 15 February 1908, National Maritime Museum.

31. Repington to Esher, 5 November 1907, ESHR 5/24.

32. See Slade's *Diary, supra*, 29 January 1908.

33. See Fisher to king Edward, 8 March 1908, and Edward to Fisher, 10 March 1908, in Marder (ed.), *Fear God and Dread Nought*, vol. II, pp. 167–68.

34. For the Kaiser's letter and related diplomatic correspondence, see, G. P. Gooch and H. Temperley, *British Documents on the Origins of the War, 1898–1914*, 11 vols. (1926–38) (hereafter cited as *BD*), vol. VI, p. 132f.

35. See Buckle to Thursfield, 8 March 1908, Times Archive.

36. Repington to Esher, 14 March 1908, ESHR 10/53.

37. Leading article, *The Times*, 6 March 1908.

38. Repington to Esher, 5 March 1908, ESHR 10/53.

39. Repington to Maxse, 11 March 1908, in *Correspondence*, pp. 144–45.

40. *Ibid.*

41. Repington to Sir Charles Dilke, 10 March 1908, *ibid.*, pp. 142–43.

42. J. S. Sandars to Maxse, 27 March 1908, West Sussex Record Office, Chichester, Maxse MSS 458, fo. 671.

43. H. O. Arnold-Forster to L. J. Maxse, 27 July 1907, Maxse MSS 457, fos. 552–56. As Lambert was a Devon farmer, presumably he was the better qualified professionally to distinguish between a battleship and a cow.

44. J. A. Spender to Tweedmouth, 6 March 1908, Tweedmouth MSS, B/126.

45. See *Vestigia*, p. 256.

46. See Repington to Roberts, 15 November 1908, Roberts MSS, R62/48.
47. Repington to Haldane, 18 November 1908, National Library of Scotland, Haldane MSS, 5908, fo. 75.
48. Same to same, 20 November 1908, Haldane MSS, 5908, fo. 76.
49. Repington to Ellison, 19 November 1908, in *Correspondence*, p. 149.
50. Repington to Roberts, 30 November 1908, Roberts MSS, R62/59.

8   Repington helps Haldane

1. See Repington to Hutton, 26 December 1904, in *Correspondence*, p. 60.
2. Rosebery's struggling ministry was brought down by a snap vote over insufficient supplies of cordite. There was no constitutional reason for Rosebery to quit but he had lost the will to fight and resignation was a more comfortable solution.
3. Repington, *'Ex Libris'* draft MSS, n.d. (1925?), in author's possession.
4. Repington to Esher, 5 October 1906, in *Correspondence*, pp. 109–12.
5. Repington to Marker, 15 December 1905, *ibid.*, pp. 68–70.
6. Not strictly true, but when he wrote *Vestigia* his recollection was suffused with the warm feelings induced by victory.
7. Repington to Mrs Mary Elizabeth Haldane, 27 February 1908, *ibid.*, pp. 141–42.
8. Repington to Marker, 25 July 1906, Kitchener-Marker Add. MSS, 52277B, fos. 92–7.
9. Repington to Marker, 1 June 1906, Kitchener-Marker Add. MSS, 52277B, fos. 54–9.
10. Repington to Esher, 7 January 1907, ESHR 5/22.
11. Repington to Ellison, 19 November 1908, in *Correspondence*, p. 149. Hasten slowly.
12. On this aspect of Haig's character, see G. J. De Groot, *Douglas Haig, 1861–1928* (1988), pp. 24–5. Haig until he married enjoyed a reputation as a misogynist. See Mead, *Good Soldier*, pp. 26, 57–8, 80, 105 and 139.
13. Repington to Marker, 6 August 1906, Kitchener-Marker Add. MSS, 52277B, fos. 103–10.
14. Same to same, 1 June 1906, Kitchener-Marker Add. MSS, 52277B, fos. 54–9.
15. General Sir Patrick MacDougall, a leading military writer and committed reformer, as chairman of the critical 'localization committee' insured that Cardwell's reforms reflected the thinking of the leading supporters of reform among senior army officers at the time, including Wolseley.
16. Repington to Marker, 6 August 1906, Kitchener-Marker Add. MSS, 52277B, fos. 103–10.
17. Repington to Esher, 28 September 1906, ESHR 10/26.
18. Same to same, 2 October 1906, ESHR 10/26.
19. The full council in session.
20. Repington to Esher, 7 January 1907, ESHR 5/22.
21. *Vestigia*, p. 266.

22. See for example, Repington to Esher, 5 October 1906, in *Correspondence*, pp. 109–12.
23. Repington to Marker, 25 July 1906, Kitchener-Marker Add. MSS, 52277B, fos. 92–7.
24. Repington to Marker, 5 July 1906, in *Correspondence*, pp. 95–9.
25. Same to same, 19 July 1906, Kitchener-Marker Add. MSS, 52277B, fos. 86–91.
26. *Vestigia*, pp. 267–69. Repington's article on the cost of the army was published in *The Times*, 5 July 1906.
27. See Repington to Buckle, 8 May 1908, Times Archive.
28. Repington to Elizabeth Haldane, 26 June 1908, in *Correspondence*, pp. 147–48.
29. 'The Cabinet and the Army', *The Times*, 3 July 1908.
30. The Strike Force had been renamed the Expeditionary Force at Repington's suggestion. He thought it would be less alarming or likely to arouse Radical sensibilities – or prejudices as he would describe them.
31. Haldane to J. A. Spender, 24 January 1911, British Library, Spender Add. MSS, 46390, fo. 167.
32. *Vestigia*, pp. 274–75.
33. See E. M. Spiers, *Haldane: An Army Reformer* (Edinburgh, 1981), pp. 59–63.
34. See Repington to Marker, 5 July 1906, in *Correspondence*, pp. 95–9.
35. *The Times*, 16 July 1906.
36. Repington to Marker, 19 July 1906, Kitchener-Marker Add. MSS, 52277B, fos. 86–91.
37. Haldane to his Mother, 12 July 1906, quoted Spiers, *Haldane*, p. 61.
38. Repington to Esher (n.d.) (Monday, February? 1907), ESHR 5/22.
39. Repington to Esher, 5 October 1906, in *Correspondence*, pp. 109–12.
40. Repington to General Hutton, 13 March 1907, *ibid.*, pp. 116–17.
41. See *The Times*, 5 March 1907.
42. Repington to Marker, 19 April 1907, Kitchener-Marker Add. MSS, 52277B, fos. 135–36. See also his earlier letter to same correspondent, 17 April 1907, in *Correspondence*, pp. 117–18.
43. See Repington to Marker, 14 April 1907, in *Correspondence*, pp. 117–18.
44. Repington to Haldane, 17 and 19 April 1907, *ibid.*, pp. 118–21.
45. Repington to Marker, 21 August 1907, Kitchener-Marker Add. MSS, 52277B, fos. 145–47.
46. Repington to Haldane's sister, 19 July 1907, Haldane MSS, 6020, fos. 92–3.
47. See Repington to Mrs Haldane, 27 February 1907, in *Correspondence*, pp. 141–42.

9   Conscription

1. Repington to Marker, 5 July 1906, in *Correspondence*, pp. 95–9.
2. See same to same (incomplete typescript with handwritten marginal comments), 16 May 1905, Kitchener-Marker Add. MSS, 52277B, fo. 164.
3. See Repington to Roberts, 26 March 1909, in *Correspondence*, p. 151.
4. Same to same, 14 April 1909, *ibid.*, pp. 152–53.

5. Roberts to Balfour, 7 April 1909, Balfour Add. MSS, 49725, fos. 288–90.

6. *The Times*, 10 May 1909. The following month Esher distributed £500 to the Legion of Frontiersmen. The source of this money is a mystery. See further R. Pocock (ed.), *Frontiersman's Pocket Book* (1909); and R. Pocock, *Chorus to Adventurers* (1931); and also the unpublished biography, G. Pocock, *The Road for the Rest*.

7. J. L. Garvin to Dr E. J. Dillon, 12 May 1909 (copy), Humanities Centre, University of Texas, Garvin MSS.

8. See John Grigg, *Lloyd George, the People's Champion: 1902–1911* (1978), p. 264 and appendix A, pp. 362–68.

9. Repington to Esher, 14 August 1910, ESHR 5/35.

10. Editorial note at conclusion of Esher to Asquith, 12 July 1910, in Oliver, Viscount Esher (ed.), *Journals and Letters of Reginald Viscount Esher* (1938), vol. III, pp. 9–10. See also Roberts to Esher, 21 July 1910, *ibid.*, pp. 10–11.

11. Repington to Esher, 8 August 1910, in Esher (ed.), *Journals and Letters of Esher*. The *World* cost six pence per part.

12. George Geoffrey Dawson, formerly Robinson, took the surname Dawson by royal licence in 1917 in order to satisfy the terms of inheritance from his Aunt, Mary Jane Dawson.

13. Repington to Dawson, 2 September 1912 (postcard), Times Archive.

14. See *Nation*, 24 October 1912.

15. *Daily Mail*, 28 October 1912.

16. *Evening Standard*, 30 October 1912.

17. See Bromley Davenport to H. A. Gwynne, 29 October 1912. The letter was published in the *Daily News* on the next day.

18. Repington to Dawson, 11 December 1912, in *Correspondence*, pp. 196–97. The previous two paragraphs are based upon notes he provided Dawson, 27 November 1912, that Dawson used in his leader on the Territorial Force, *The Times*, 10 December 1912.

19. Repington to Dawson, 11 December 1912, in *Correspondence*, pp. 196–97.

20. Dawson to Repington, 11 December 1912, Times Archive.

21. Repington thought of all social benefits as bribes intended to attract the votes of Socialist and Radical slackers.

22. Repington to Dawson, 11 December 1912, Times Archive.

23. Lovat Fraser to J. L. Garvin, 30 October 1912, Garvin MSS.

24. See Repington to Dawson, 8 November 1912, in *Correspondence*, p. 191.

25. Same to same, 5 November 1912, *ibid.*, pp. 190–91.

26. Dawson to Repington, 5 November 1912, Times Archive.

27. Dawson to Chirol, 9 January 1913, Times Archive.

28. Dawson to Steed, 6 November 1912, Times Archive.

29. But cf. Jeffery, *Field Marshal Sir Henry Wilson*, pp. 103–05.

30. Repington to Haldane, 27 November 1912, in *Correspondence*, pp. 192–93.

31. See Dawson to Repington, 2 March 1913, Times Archive.

32. See *Vestigia*, p. 293; Repington to Dawson, 3 March 1913, Times Archive.

33. See Dawson to Northcliffe, 2 March 1913 (copy), Times Archive; Dawson to George Saunders, 21 February 1913, in *Correspondence*, p. 315 n. 132.

34. See Repington to Saunders, 7 March 1913; also Saunders to Repington, 9 March 1913 (copy), and Saunders to Dawson, 9 March 1913, in *Correspondence*, pp. 204–06.

35. Repington to Dawson, 11 February 1913, Times Archive.

36. Panouse to Minister of War, 15 March 1913, French Military Archives, Box 7 N 1228, *Attaché Militaire Grande Bretaigne*. 'Open the eyes of British opinion to see the need to accept conscription.'

37. See 'A Policy of Procrastinators', *The Times*, 12 February 1913; Repington to Dawson, 11 February 1913, Times Archive.

38. Repington to Seely, 11 February 1913, Nuffield College Library, Oxford, Mottistone MSS, MOT 20, fo. 153.

39. Repington to Dawson, 1 February 1913, Times Archive.

40. For the opposing arguments, see S. R. Williamson, Jnr, *The Politics of Grand Strategy* (Cambridge, MA, 1969), p. 306 (Wilson/Repington); and H. R. Moon, 'The Invasion of the United Kingdom, 1888–1914', unpublished Ph.D (1970), p. 433 (Churchill).

41. Memorandum, 17 October 1912, quoted A. J. Marder, *The Road to War, 1904–14* (Oxford, 1961), pp. 352–53.

42. See particularly his articles in *The Times*, 5 and 13 May 1913. As early as 12 February, Repington had stated the inquiry was inspired by a Radical intrigue.

43. See Repington to Dawson, 13 April 1913, in *Correspondence*, p. 207.

44. For Memorandum, dated 30 March 1913, OA 25, pp. 1–15, in CAB 16/28B. Also Repington to Dawson, 13 April 1913, in *Correspondence*, p. 207.

45. According to Wilson's diary, the damascene moment had been fully six months earlier and due to his, not Repington's, persuasive powers.

46. See Jeffery, *Field-Marshal Sir Henry Wilson*, p. 110.

47. Repington to the Editor of *The Times*, 14 April 1913.

48. See various comments from Wilson's diary, 21 and 23 February, 4 March, 5 August and 9 December 1913.

49. Repington to Dawson, 13 April 1913, in *Correspondence*, pp. 207–08.

50. See Appendix to Final Report of the subcommittee, CAB 16/28A, pp. 371–86.

51. Cf. Repington's description of the Territorials in his 12 February article: 'an abjectly weak mob of men with rifles and antiquated guns, lacking cohesion and without trained officers'.

52. See Appendix to Final Report of the subcommittee, CAB 16/28A, pp. 390–91.

53. Esher to Asquith, 25 June 1913 (copy), Balfour Add. MSS, 49719, fos. 244–45; Esher (ed.), *Journals and Letters*, vol. III, pp. 134–35.

54. Repington to Dawson, 6 July 1913, in *Correspondence*, p. 209.

55. Same to same, 17 July 1913, *ibid.*, p. 210.

56. Hankey to Stamfordham, 18 July 1913, CAB 17/35, fos. 210–13.

57. Hankey to Balfour, 27 August 1913, Balfour Add. MSS, 49703, fos. 14–15.

58. See Report of 13th meeting, pp. 144–69 and Col. 7250.

59. See Repington to Dawson, 17 July 1913, Times Archive.

60. See initial hearing on 1 July 1913, CAB 16/28A, pp. 96–118.

61. Bridgeman to Sandars, 28 July 1913, Bodleian Library, Sandars MSS, 765, fos. 131–33.
62. Sandars's memorandum of his conversation with Bridgeman, 29 July 1913, Sandars MSS, 765, fos. 134–35.
63. See Thursfield to Dawson, 13 February 1913, quoted in P. H. S., *History of 'The Times'*, vol. IV, pt. 1, *The 150th Anniversary and Beyond, 1912–1920* (1952), p. 96.
64. Repington to Buckle, 7 January 1912, in *Correspondence*, pp. 180–82. Repington was right. As with the CID, there had to be a joint approach to problems of national defence.
65. Repington to Dawson, 30 November 1911, *ibid.*, p. 179.
66. See *Vestigia*, pp. 294–95; Letters to the Editor, *The Times*, 2 and 8 September 1913.
67. CAB 16/28A, at p. 315.
68. See Hankey to Stamfordham, 30 November 1913, CAB 17/35, fos. 304–07.
69. See Jeffery, *Field Marshal Sir Henry Wilson*, p. 126.
70. Repington to Dawson, 18 June 1914, Times Archive.

10   Northcliffe and *The Times*, Repington and the *Army Review*

1. The issue of the Parnell forgeries is most conveniently and briefly set in its context and explained in Koss, *Rise and Fall of the Political Press in Britain*, vol. I, pp. 297–98. See also Paul Bew, *C. S. Parnell* (Dublin, 1980), pp. 100–07.
2. The convoluted history of *The Times* for this period is well chronicled and explained in P. H. S., *The History of The Times*, vol. III, *The Twentieth Century Test, 1884–1912* (1947), chs. 16–19, pp. 509–600.
3. Repington to Esher, 4 January 1908, in *Correspondence*, p. 138. As far as I could discover, nothing came of Esher's idea.
4. Brett (ed.), *Journals and Letters of Esher*, vol. II, pp. 275–76 (17 January 1908).
5. See Fisher to Northcliffe, quoted R. Pound and G. Harmsworth *Northcliffe* (1959), p. 320.
6. Northcliffe to Steed, 6 September 1908, Times Archive.
7. Repington to Northcliffe, 7 July 1908, in *Correspondence*, p. 148.
8. Same to same, 29 June 1911, *ibid.*, pp. 167–68.
9. Repington to Esher, 29 November 1906, ESHR 10/27.
10. See F. J. Hudleston's marginal annotation in the War Office Library's copy of *Vestigia*, p. 303.
11. Edmonds in his entry on Repington in the *Dictionary of National Biography* asserted without qualification that Repington's appointment was intended as a step towards his official reinstatement in the army. In his *Memoirs*, Edmonds stated: 'it was seriously proposed to reinstate Repington, but Wilson organised opposition'; see ch. 20, pp. 27–9. Liddell Hart Military Archives, King's College, London, Edmonds MSS, III/5.
12. See Jeffery, *Field-Marshal Sir Henry Wilson*, pp. 89–90, nn. 27 and 28. Wilson's last assertion alone was true.
13. See Repington to Northcliffe, 29 June 1911, in *Correspondence*, pp. 167–68.

14. See Northcliffe to Buckle, 27 May 1911, British Library, Northcliffe Dep., 4890/1.
15. Repington to Northcliffe, 29 June 1911, Northcliffe Dep., 4890/1.
16. See Repington to Hamilton, 11 June 1912, Liddell Hart Military Archives, King's College, London, Hamilton MSS, 5/1/42.
17. Repington to Northcliffe, 29 June 1911, Northcliffe Dep., 4890/1.
18. Repington to Northcliffe, 9 July 1911, in *Correspondence*, p. 168.
19. See Repington to Dawson, 20 July 1911, *ibid.*, p. 169.
20. See Repington to Buckle, 7 January 1912, *ibid.*, pp. 180–82.
21. *Vestigia*, p. 303.
22. See Gooch and Temperley, *BD*, vol. VI, pp. 594–95. See also Repington's article, 'The Debate on Defence', *The Times*, 7 April 1911. See Matthew S. Selligmann (ed.), *Military Intelligence from Germany, 1906–14*, Army Records Society, vol. XXXIV (Stroud, 2014), pp. 126, 137–39 and 160–61.
23. See Gooch and Temperley, *BD*, vol. VI, pp. 645, 652–55 and 703–05. See also C. H. D. Howard (ed.), *Edward Goschen's Diary* (1980), p. 248.
24. Repington to Dawson, 28 February 1912, in *Correspondence*, p. 184.
25. *Ibid.*
26. Repington to Buckle, 7 January 1912, *ibid.*, pp. 180–82.
27. Repington to Churchill, 21 and 27 March 1912, in R. S. Churchill, *Winston S. Churchill Companion* (1969), vol. II, pt. 3, *1911–1914*, pp. 1527–28 and 1532.
28. See Fisher to Arnold White, November 1911, in Marder (ed.), *Fear God and Dread Nought*, vol. II, pp. 416–17.
29. For Ballard's and Hankey's comments, see, Churchill, *Churchill Companion*, vol. II, pt. 3, pp. 1532–35.
30. Repington to Churchill, 2 May 1912, *ibid.*, p. 1548.
31. Repington to Esher, 15 July 1912, ESHR 5/41.
32. Repington to Northcliffe, 22 July 1912, Northcliffe Add. MSS, 62254, fo. 18.
33. Nicholson to Repington, 26 July 1912, Times Archive.
34. Repington to Dawson, 7 August 1912, in *Correspondence*, pp. 188–90.
35. Repington to Northcliffe, 1 June 1912, Northcliffe Add. MSS, 62253, fo. 12; Northcliffe to Repington, 2 June 1912, *ibid.*, fo. 14.
36. Same to same, 3 June 1912, Northcliffe Add. MSS, 62253, fo. 15. No more was heard of this extraordinary proposal.
37. Repington to Northcliffe, 4 June 1912, Northcliffe Add. MSS, 62253, fo. 16
38. Northcliffe to Repington, 4 July 1912, Northcliffe Add. MSS, 62253, fo. 17; Repington to Esher, 4 July 1912, ESHR 5/41.
39. See Repington to Esher, 3, 5 and 6 August 1912, ESHR 5/41.
40. See Repington to Dawson, 29 August, 2 and 6 September 1912, Times Archive. The *Army Review* did not long outlast Repington's editorship, ending with the outbreak of war in 1914. Its subsequent revival was obstructed and prevented by the Treasury who decreed that in future, such an exercise was better left to private enterprise.
41. Northcliffe to Repington, 20 August 1913, in *Correspondence*, pp. 210–11.
42. Repington to Northcliffe, 22 August 1913, *ibid.*, pp. 211–12.

11   The Curragh incident

1. See Repington to J. E. B. Seely, 30 December 1913, in *Correspondence*, pp. 214–15.
2. Repington to Haldane, *ibid.*, pp. 192–93.
3. *The Times*, 10 April 1912, quoted P. Jalland, *The Liberals and Ireland* (Brighton, 1980), p. 77.
4. See *Vestigia*, p. 310.
5. For Dawson's attitude, particularly on exclusion, see P. H. S., *History of 'The Times'*, vol. IV, pt. 2, *1921–48*, appendix 2, S. xiii, pp. 1108–09.
6. Dawson to Repington, 2 July 1913, Times Archive.
7. Repington to Dawson, 3 July 1913, in *Correspondence*, pp. 208–09.
8. Henry Wilson's diary, 6 November 1913. See also Holmes, *Little Field Marshal*, pp. 169–70; Jeffery, *Field Marshal Sir Henry Wilson*, p. 117.
9. Ian Colvin, *The Life of Lord Carson* (London, 1936), vol. II, pp. 132–33. But cf. Henry Patterson, *Class Conflict and Sectarianism* (Belfast, 1980), pp. 89–90.
10. See *The Times*, 18 and 19 March 1914; also Repington to Dawson, 4 March 1914, in *Correspondence*, p. 217.
11. Same to same, 9 March 1914, *ibid.*, p. 218.
12. Asquith to Venetia Stanley, 21 March 1914, in M. and E. Brock (eds.), *H. H. Asquith: Letters to Venetia Stanley* (Oxford, 1982), pp. 58–9.
13. *Ibid.*, commentary, p. 58. The Prime Minister considered Balfour the only Unionist 'with a quick mind among that ill-bred lot'. He thought Balfour's words alone 'touched the spot'. See his letter to Venetia Stanley, 23 March 1914, *ibid.*, p. 60.
14. See entry for 1 April in the diary of Charles Hobhouse, in Edward David (ed.), *Inside Asquith's Cabinet* (1977), p. 168.
15. See Lord Riddell, *More Pages from my Diary* (1934), pp. 210–11.
16. See HC Deb. (5th series), 1914, vol. 40, c. 176.
17. See Asquith to Churchill, 22 March 1914, Churchill MSS, CHAR 2/63/19.
18. Repington to Lewis Harcourt, 20 March 1914, Bodleian Library, Harcourt MSS, Dep. 444, fo. 78.
19. Asquith to Venetia Stanley, 30 March 1914, in Brock and Brock (eds.), *Asquith*, p. 62.
20. Repington to Dawson, 18 June 1914, in *Correspondence*, pp. 223–24.
21. *The Times*, 27 March 1914.
22. See above articles in *The Times*; also Dawson to Repington, 10 March 1914, Times Archive; Repington to Dawson, 13 March 1914, in *Correspondence*, p. 219.
23. Repington to Dawson, 9 April 1914, in *Correspondence*, p. 220.
24. Repington to Captain James Craig, 25 March 1914, quoted St John Ervine, *Craigavon; Ulsterman* (1949), p. 260.
25. Repington to Dawson, 9 April 1914, in *Correspondence*, p. 220.
26. See Repington to Craig, 25 March 1914, in St John Ervine, *Craigavon*, p. 260.
27. Repington to Dawson, 9 April 1914, in *Correspondence*, p. 220. To write 'Derry' not 'Londonderry' was deliberate.

28. See Repington to Dawson, 13/14 April 1914, in *Correspondence*, pp. 221–22. *The Times*, 18 April 1914. The same day the *Daily Mail* published its story of the Unionist 'plot' to attack Ulster.
29. *The Times*, 27 April 1914.
30. *Ibid.*, 21 April 1914.
31. *The Times*, 27 April 1914. When the government subsequently claimed that Paget had misunderstood his orders and that the Curragh incident was the inevitable consequence of Paget's incompetence, both claims were laughed out of court by Bonar Law.
32. See Robert Blake, *The Unknown Prime Minister: The Life and Times of Andrew Bonar Law 1858–1923* (1955), ch. 12, *passim*. Also Jalland, *Liberals and Ireland*, pp. 222ff. Jalland earlier states at p. 207, 'The source material now available *suggests* [my emphasis] that there was no sinister conspiracy.'
33. Asquith to Venetia Stanley, 22 March 1914, in Brock and Brock (eds.), *Asquith*, p. 59
34. See Morley's comment to Esher, cited in Esher (ed.), *Journals and Letters of Esher*, vol. III, p. 167.
35. L. S. Amery, *My Political Life* (1953–55), vol. I, p. 454.
36. *Vestigia*, p. 310.
37. See Richard S. Grayson, *Belfast Boys* (2009), ch. 1, *passim*.
38. Repington to Dawson, 18 June 1914, in *Correspondence*, pp. 223–24.

12   Are the army and navy prepared for war?

1. See *Vestigia*, p. 293.
2. See Fisher to White, 17 March 1913, in Marder (ed.), *Fear God and Dread Nought*, vol. II, p. 484 n. 3.
3. See *Vestigia*, pp. 295ff.
4. *Ibid.*, p. 295.
5. Repington to Roberts, 3 February 1914, in *Correspondence*, pp. 215–16, 'a maid for all tasks'.
6. See *Vestigia*, pp. 298–99.
7. See Ian Hamilton to Winston Churchill, 28 July 1914, Churchill MSS, CHAR 2/64/1.
8. German surface vessels also bombarded the north and east coast of England with impunity. Two German crusers evaded a British force, escaped from the Adriatic and safely reached Constantinople. Meanwhile, in the Indian and Atlantic Oceans the *Emden* and the *Karlshue* sank or captured 150,000 tons of Allied shipping in a period of three months.
9. Fisher to White, 13 March 1913, in Marder (ed.), *Fear God and Dread Nought*, vol. II, p. 484
10. See 'New Wars for Old', *Blackwood's Magazine* (May and June 1910). See also *Vestigia*, pp. 295–97.
11. Fisher to Arnold White, November 1911, in Marder (ed.), *Fear God and Dread Nought*, vol. II, pp. 415 and 417. For Repington's enthusiastic support of oil and his support of the Royal Commission's recommendations, see Repington to Robinson, 18 June 1914, in *Correspondence*, pp. 223–24.

12. This was a concept Repington pursued energetically once more after the Italian super-dreadnought building programme was announced in September 1913. But see Dawson to Repington, 27 February 1914, Times Archive.

13. Cf. Repington to Roberts, 3 February 1914, in *Correspondence*, pp. 215–16.

14. Repington to Dawson, 18 June 1914, *ibid.*, pp. 223–24.

15. See Repington to Esher, 12 July and 3 August 1912, ESHR 5/41.

16. See Wilson's diary, 14 and 16 March 1912, in Jeffery, *Field Marshal Sir Henry Wilson*, p. 102.

17. Sir James Edmonds, *Autobiography* (unpublished), ch. 23, p. 25.

18. See 'Report on Army Manoeuvres, 1912', cited J. P. Harris, *Douglas Haig and the First World War* (Cambridge, 2008), p. 52 and n. 69, p. 555.

19. Edmonds, *Autobiography*, ch. 22, p. 12.

20. Hamilton to Repington, 30 September 1912 (copy), Hamilton MSS, 5/1/42.

21. Brigadier General John Charteris, *Field-Marshal Earl Haig* (1929), p. 66.

22. See 'The Manoeuvres Conference', *The Times*, 21 September 1912.

23. See Wilson's diary, 26 September 1913, Imperial War Museum, Wilson MSS.

24. French to Esher, 1 October 1913, in the Hon. Gerald French (ed.), *Some War Diaries, Addresses and Correspondence* (1937), p. 136. The description better fitted his own behaviour.

25. Repington to Dawson, 9 October 1913, in *Correspondence*, p. 212.

26. See *The Times*, 10 October 1913.

27. See Ian Beckett's fascinating essay, 'Gough, Malcolm and Command on the Western Front', in Bond et al., *Look to your Front* (Staplehurst, 1999), pp. 1–12.

28. Repington to Dawson, 1 November 1913, in *Correspondence*, p. 213.

29. Repington to Howell, 26 October 1913, Liddell Hart Military Archives, King's College London, Howell MSS, IV/c/2/40.

30. See Repington to Roberts, 8 February 1914, and Repington to Dawson, 3 February 1914, in *Correspondence*, pp. 215–17.

31. See Nicolson to British Ambassador in Vienna, 6 July 1914, *BD*, vol. XI, p. 46.

32. Esher to Repington, 15 July 1914 (typed copy), ESHR 4/5.

33. Same to same, 20 July 1914 (typed copy), ESHR 4/5.

34. See Repington to Ian Hamilton, 27 July 1914, in *Correspondence*, p. 225. See also *War Diaries*, vol. I, p. 18 Hamilton enclosed Repington's letter with his to Churchill, 28 July 1914, Churchill MSS, CHAR 2/64/1. For an account revealing Germany's part in the Austrian ultimatum to Serbia, see Fritz Fischer (trans. Marian Jackson), *War of Illusions: German Policies from 1911 to 1914* (1975), pp. 461–515.

35. See Repington to Esher, 14 January 1906, in *Correspondence*, pp. 79–81.

36. *The Times*, 30 July 1914.

37. See in particular his articles on 'Military Policy', *The Times*, 6 and 7 February 1913; cf. Jay Luvaas, *The Education of an Army* (1965), pp. 312–14.

38. See Leon O' Broin, *The Chief Secretary: Augustine Birrell in Ireland* (1969), p. 103.

39. See E. Wrench, *Geoffrey Dawson and Our Times* (1955), p. 104.

40. See Dawson's diary, 31 July 1914, Times Archive, Dawson MSS, 64, fos. 68–74.
41. Northcliffe to Repington, 31 July 1914, BL, Northcliffe Add. MSS, 62253, fo. 22. 'The War Day by Day', a daily account of the war, was reprinted in the *New York Times*. Repington's writing was important as British propaganda as it helped to sway American 'uneducated public opinion' to support the Allied cause. See Willert to Dawson, 18 August 1914, Times Archive.
42. See his *War Diaries*, vol. I, p. 19.
43. See 'The War Day by Day', 3 August 1914. Here he is clearly arguing that the arrival of the BEF would make all the difference.
44. Most of the wartime hassles between the press and the Censor concerned the Unionist Press. It was assumed that the censorship was politically motivated. See A. J. P. Taylor, *Politics in Wartime* (1964), *passim*.
45. See P. H. S., *History of The Times*, vol. IV, pt. 1, p. 220, quoted Koss, *Rise and Fall of the Political Press in Britain*, vol. II, p. 241. This sweeping generalisation is not altogether fair, certainly not to the intention of the censors who were put in an impossible position. Koss, *Rise and Fall*, ch. 7, pp. 238–73. 'Declaration of War' is a splendid guide to this difficult subject.
46. See Repington to Roberts, 22 October 1914, in *Correspondence*, pp. 227–28.
47. 'The War Day by Day', *The Times*, 1 August 1914.
48. *Ibid.*, 3 August 1914.
49. *The Times*, 4 August 1914.
50. 'The War Day by Day', 5 August 1914. The bravado of the words echo sentiments similar to those expressed at the opening of so many wars.
51. Repington to J. S. Sandars, 15 August 1914, in *Correspondence*, p. 226.

13   The 1915 shells scandal

1. See *War Diaries*, vol. I, p. 26; Repington to Roberts, 19 October 1914, in *Correspondence*, p. 227.
2. Dawson to Leo Maxse, 13 August 1918, quoted, P. H. S., *History of The Times*, vol. IV, pt. 1, p. 217 n. 2. Repington had proposed Kitchener as Secretary of State for War on a number of occasions in the previous decade.
3. *War Diaries*, vol. I, p. 20.
4. See *ibid.*, pp. 85, 87 and 275.
5. See *ibid.*, pp. 20–21.
6. See Repington to Dawson, 22 and 27 January and 4 February 1913, Times Archive. Also articles by Repington in *The Times*, 6 and 7 February 1913.
7. See Sir Ernest Swinton, *Eyewitness* (1932), pp. 62–3.
8. Clarke's criticism of Repington is a classic example of the messenger being blamed for the message. In reporting Kitchener's judgment, Repington had neither agreed nor disagreed.
9. Clarke to Dawson, 16 August 1914, Times Archive.
10. See *War Diaries*, vol. I, p. 24. But cf. Brock and Brock (eds.), *Asquith*, p. 156 n. 6.

11. See *The Times*, 15 December 1914. Cf. Alan Clark (ed.), *A Good Innings* (1974), p. 134.
12. Repington to Roberts, 19 and 22 October 1914, in *Correspondence*, pp. 227–28; 2 November 1914, R62/72, and *War Diaries*, vol. I, p. 26.
13. Selborne to Dawson, 20 October 1914, in D. George Boyce (ed.), *The Crisis of British Unionism, 1885–1922* (1987), pp. 116–17.
14. Haldane to Churchill, 19 October 1914, quoted Martin Gilbert, *Winston S. Churchill*, vol. III, *1914–1916* (1971), p. 133. See also, French to Churchill, *ibid.* 'You did splendid work at Antwerp ... For God's sake don't pay attention to what the rotten papers say.'
15. See Hamilton to Repington, 2 November and 9 December 1914 (typed copies), Hamilton MSS, 6/12.
16. See *War Diaries*, vol. I, pp. 56–7.
17. J. M. McEwen (ed.), *The Riddell Diaries, 1908–1923* (1986), entry for 1 April 1915, p. 104.
18. 'Problems of Defence', *The Times*, 14 January 1915.
19. Dawson to Repington, 3 January 1915 (typed copy), Times Archive.
20. Walter Long to Fitzgerald, 4 January 1915, Fitzgerald Correspondence, Imperial War Museum.
21. Robertson to Wigram, 17 May 1915, RA, Geo. V, Q2522/3/172.
22. See *War Diaries*, vol. I, p. 29.
23. See McEwen (ed.), *Riddell Diaries*, p. 108.
24. Dawson to Repington, 3 January 1915 (typed copy), Times Archive.
25. See Gerald French, *Life of Sir John French* (1931), pp. 288–89.
26. See Repington to Bonar Law, 24 November 1915, in *Correspondence*, pp. 240–45.
27. *The Times*, 2 and 20 April 1915; *War Diaries*, vol. I, p. 42.
28. French to Kitchener, 14 May 1915, quoted Holmes, *Little Field Marshal*, p. 289.
29. See *War Diaries*, vol. I, pp. 34–5.
30. 20 April 1915. See Brock and Brock (eds.), *Asquith*, pp. 558–59 nn. 1–5. See Lady Cynthia Asquith, *Diaries 1915–18* (1968), pp. 34–5 and 44. Repington in *The Times*, 27 April 1915, slipped past the Censor that it was 'want of artillery ammunition' that hampered the army, 'and there is not a man in the army who is not aware of the fact'.
31. Repington to Dawson, 11 May 1915, in *Correspondence*, pp. 229–31. *War Diaries*, vol. I, p. 37, incorrectly dates the communication about the shells to go to the Dardanelles as 15 May. The letter stated 'marked "passed by censor" but he will not have seen it', implying the Censor had agreed to connive in the deception.
32. Sir Edward Cook's diary, 18 May 1915, quoted Cameron Hazlehurst, *Politicians at War, July 1914 to August 1915* (1971), p. 248 n. 4.
33. Brigadier-General Sir C. E. Callwell, *Experiences of a Dug-Out, 1914–1918* (1920), pp. 323–24.
34. Kitchener to French, 14 May 1915, Kitchener MSS, PRO 30/57/50.
35. See Riddell's diary, 16 May 1915, in McEwen (ed.), *Riddell Diaries*, p. 111.
36. See Robert Blake (ed.), *The Private Papers of Douglas Haig 1914–1919* (1952), p. 93.

37. See Field Marshal French, *1914* (1919), pp., 358–61. This is plausible but very contrived. French dictated this 'explanation' to Lovat Fraser, Sir John's 'ghost' writer, when *1914* was being 'written' after the war. Then, it was generally accepted as a 'fact' that Repington's revelation had triggered the First Coalition and the reconstruction of Asquith's cabinet, and so French emphasised the political reaction. But the intended victim of his attack had been Kitchener, which explains why Northcliffe was associated with him. He subsequently spoiled their 'plot' by over-enthusiastically attacking Kitchener in the *Daily Mail*.

38. See *War Diaries*, vol. I, pp. 39–40.

39. See Riddell's diary entry for 24 April 1915, in McEwen (ed.), *Riddell Diaries*, p. 109.

40. He chose not to mention the briefing Lloyd George had earlier received from Guest and Fitzgerald. Repington's puzzlement at how little Lloyd George appeared to know was understandable. It was a pose that allowed LG to claim, when writing to Asquith (19 May), for months the War Office (Kitchener) had deliberately failed to tell him the truth about the insufficient supply of shells to the western front.

41. Repington to Lloyd George, 17 May 1915, in *Correspondence*, pp. 231–33.

42. 'Fount and beginning' – a cliché even in classical times – but the claim surely *deserves* a cliché!

43. Duncan Crow, *A Man of Push and Go* (1965), p. 114.

44. See H. Llewellyn Smith to Lloyd George, 21 and 22 May 1915, Parliamentary Archives, Lloyd George MSS, C7/5/21–22.

45. Lord Beaverbrook, *Politicians and the War, 1914–1916* (1960), pp. 94 and 97. Beaverbrook's account drew heavily from a memo by J. L. Garvin. See Hazlehurst, *Politicians at War*, p. 233 n. 2.

46. See Stamfordham to George V, 19 May 1915, RA, GV K.770/3.

47. John Dillon to Augustine Birrell, 15 May 1915, Trinity College, Dublin, Birrell MSS, 10:3:8.

48. See *War Diaries*, vol. I, p. 41.

49. Entitled, 'More Shells', Repington's *Times'* despatch was reprinted in the *Daily Mail*, 15 May 1915. However, the Censor struck out all mention of this article from a letter written by a London Scottish private that the *Mail* wished to publish

50. See in particular the *Daily Mail* editorial headlined 'The Tragedy of the Shells. Lord Kitchener's Grave Error'. The editorial categorically asserted it had been Kitchener who had starved the army of shells. 'For that reason he must go.'

51. See J. Lee Thompson, *Northcliffe: Press Baron in Politics 1865–1922* (2000), pp. 240–42.

52. See Koss, *Rise and Fall of the Political Press in Britain*, vol. II, p. 280, and n. 1.

53. B. Fitzgerald to Selborne, 27 May 1915, Fitzgerald Correspondence, IWM.

54. See HC Deb. (5th series), vol. 77, c. 259.

55. Esher's journal, 21 and 22 May 1915, in Esher (ed.), *Journals and Letters of Esher*, vol. III, pp. 240–43.

14 How do we secure the necessary troops?

1. See Repington to Lloyd George, 20 May 1915, in *Correspondence*, pp. 233–37.
2. See *The Times*, 2 April 1915.
3. Repington to Ian Hamilton, 8 January 1916, Hamilton MSS, B/89. See *War Diaries*, vol. I, pp. 104–05 and p. 211
4. When Bulgaria joined with Germany and Austria in October 1915, the Greeks mobilised supposing the Bulgars coveted Macedonia. They requested Allied help. A combined French–British force landed at Salonika. Eventually Bulgaria sued for peace in September 1918. Things turned out in Salonika as Repington said they would. (See his surveys in *Correspondence*, pp. 239–45 and 253–60.) Repington bewailed Salonika as 'This Tomfool expedition that has cost lives uselessly.' He knew from his old schoolfriend 'Fatty' Wilson, who commanded a division that was 'at 50% strength' owing to malaria and dysentery. Another friend 'Bockus' Nicol had been sending back '1000 sick a week'. The Germans shared Repington's contemptuous opinion of the Salonika campaign and thought of it as little more than an internment camp. It was kept in play because General Maurice P. E. Sarail (1856–1929), the French commander, enjoyed considerable political influence. Clemenceau finally dismissed him in December 1917.
5. See Repington to Lloyd George, 3 July and 18 September 1915, in *Correspondence*, pp. 237 and 239; *War Diaries*, vol. I, p. 45, entry dated Wednesday 29 September 1915.
6. Repington to Northcliffe, 2 September 1915, in *Correspondence*, pp. 238–39.
7. See *War Diaries*, vol. I, pp. 65–6.
8. *Quod erat demonstrandum* meaning, 'what was to be proved'. His article 'Trade or Victory', in *The Times*, 27 December 1915, was excoriated in the *Daily News*, 28 December 1915.
9. See *War Diaries*, vol. I, p. 101.
10. See *Hampstead and Highgate Express*, 11 March 1916. See also various issues for January–March 1916 of the *Hampstead Record* and the *Hampstead, St John's Wood and Kilburn Advertiser*.
11. See *War Diaries*, vol. I, p. 297.
12. See *ibid.*, p. 144.
13. *Ibid.*, pp. 135–36. Entries for Friday 25 February and Thursday 2 March 1916.
14. See *ibid.*, p. 120.
15. The figures were requested by the Local Government Board, June 1916. See copy in Borough Council Minutes, vol. 55 (1915–16), pp. 371–72, Archive Series B/HA/M/1. The last meeting Repington attended was little more than a week before the war's end, Friday 1 November 1918.
16. See diary entry for 19 March 1916, Hampstead Borough Council Library.
17. See *War Diaries*, vol. I, pp. 146–47.
18. See for his visit to France, *ibid.*, pp. 151–77.
19. Asquith emerged from the vote considerably weakened. See Hankey's diary, 2 May 1916, quoted R. J. Q. Adams and Philip P. Poirier, *The Conscription Controversy in Britain,1900–18* (1987), p. 168.

20. Robertson to Gen. Sir A. J. Murray, 18 May 1916, in D. R. Woodward (ed.), *The Military Correspondence of Field-Marshal Sir William Robertson, Chief of the Imperial General Staff, December 1915–February 1918*, Army Records Society (1989), pp. 48–9.
21. See *The Times*, 8 May 1916; *War Diaries*, vol. I, pp. 187–88 and 196.
22. See *War Diaries*, vol. I, pp. 192, 204 and 206.
23. *Ibid.*, p. 208.
24. See *ibid.*, pp. 214–15.

15   Changing the old guard

1. The second occasion Kitchener 'informed' Sir John that he was expected as far as possible to conform to Joffre's plans. See Kitchener to French, 31 August 1914, Kitchener MSS, PRO 30/57/49.
2. See Blake (ed.) *Private Papers of Haig*, p. 95.
3. See Gary Sheffield and John Bourne (eds.), *Douglas Haig: War Diaries and Letters, 1914–1918* (2005), p. 130.
4. See Philip Gibbs, *Adventures in Journalism* (1923), p. 232.
5. See *War Diaries*, vol. I, pp. 56–7.
6. See *Correspondence*, pp. 228 and 237–38. Also *War Diaries*, vol. I, pp. 52–3 and 60.
7. Quoted Mead, *Good Soldier*, p. 209.
8. Philip Gibbs, *Bapaume to Passchendaele, 1917*, p. 21, quoted Stephen Badsey, 'Haig and the Press', in B. Bond and N. Cave (eds.), *Haig: A Reappraisal 70 Years on* (Barnsley, 1999), p. 182.
9. See Blake (ed.), *Private Papers of Haig*, pp. 93 and 95.
10. W. B. Thomas, *A Traveller in News* (1925), p. 105, quoted M. J. Farrar, *News from the Front* (Stroud, 1998), p. 77. Much of this paragraph is based on Farrar's chapter on Loos, pp. 80–96.
11. See Dawson's 'Rough Diary of a Visit to GHQ, October 1916', Dawson MSS, 66, fos. 130–31.
12. See Harris, *Haig and the First World War*, p. 182.
13. Haig to Lady Haig, 24 October 1915, quoted Holmes, *Little Field Marshal*, p. 307. See also Haig's diary, Sunday 24 October 1915, in Sheffield and Bourne (eds.), *Haig: War Diaries and Letters*, pp. 166–67.
14. See Haig's diary, entry for Wednesday 14 July 1915, in Sheffield and Bourne (eds.), *Haig: War Diaries and Letters*, p. 130.
15. See further Harris, *Haig and the First World War*, pp. 178–203.
16. Repington to Andrew Bonar Law, 16 November 1915, in *Correspondence*, pp. 239–40.
17. *War Diaries*, vol. I, p. 70, Friday 19 November 1915.
18. See Callwell, *Experiences of a Dug-Out*, p. 233. But cf. Esher's *Journal*, entry dated 18 November, Esher (ed.), *Journals and Letters of Esher*, vol. III, p. 281.
19. See Holmes, *Little Field Marshal*, pp. 310–13.
20. See *War Diaries*, vol. I, pp. 92 and 95.
21. See *ibid.*
22. See *ibid.*, p. 138, Friday 10 March 1916.

23. Quoted R. Blake, *The Unknown Prime Minister: The Life and Times of Andrew Bonar Law 1858–1923* (1955), p. 275.
24. Asquith to Lloyd George, 3 November 1915, quoted Robert Blake, *The Unknown Prime Minister: The Life and Times of Andrew Bonar Law, 1858–1923* (1955), p. 270.
25. See *War Diaries*, vol. I, pp. 64–5, 8 and 10 November 1915.
26. See *ibid.*, pp. 67–8, Wednesday 17 November 1915.
27. *Ibid.*, p. 69, Friday 19 November 1915.
28. See Repington to Bonar Law, 16 November 1915, in *Correspondence*, pp. 239–45.
29. James Stuart (1633–1701) attempting to flee his kingdom on 11 December 1688, dropped the Great Seal into the Thames with the intention of thwarting legitimate government.
30. See *War Diaries*, vol. I, p. 77, Friday 3 December 1915.
31. See *ibid.*, p. 99, entry for 4 January 1916.
32. See *ibid.*, pp. 83–6.
33. Repington to Dawson, 22 December 1915, in *Correspondence*, pp. 246–48.
34. There seems to be some uncertainty over whether Haig's instructions made him less or more independent than French had been, or if there was very little difference. Cf. Cassar, *Kitchener*, p. 458, and John Terraine, *Douglas Haig: The Educated Soldier* (1963), p. 181; *War Diaries*, vol. I, pp. 21.

16   The Somme

1. Letter of F. S. Oliver, 22 June 1916, quoted J. P Grigg, *Lloyd George: From Peace to War, 1912–1916* (1985), p. 359. Oliver's claim was exaggerated.
2. There is a most interesting alternative telling of this story from entries in Lady Lee's diary for June and July 1916. See Alan Clark (ed.), *A Good Innings* (1974), pp. 156–57.
3. See Lady Asquith, *Diaries*, p. 202. She had thought the story 'quite incredible' because she made a mistake identifying the lady in question.
4. *War Diaries*, vol. I, pp. 274–75.
5. See *ibid.*, p. 277.
6. See Grigg, *Lloyd George*, p. 394.
7. W. Robertson, *Soldiers and Statesmen, 1914–1918* (1926), vol. I, p. 179.
8. Repington to H. G. Wells, 6 March 1917, in *Correspondence*, pp. 262–64.
9. See for example, *War Diaries*, vol. I, p. 368, entry for Thursday 19 October 1916.
10. See *ibid.*, pp. 284–85, entry for 19 July 1916.
11. The Indian army opposed in Mesopotamia a combination of Turks, Arabs and Kurds. The original British involvement had been small – to guard the oil wells at the head of the Persian Gulf. From Basra the British pushed up the Tigris and Euphrates, lured north by the prospect of Baghdad. After early success at Kut al Imara, despite a limited tactical success at Ctesiphon, Townshend's force was beleaguered. The war in Mesopotamia was as much about supplies as fighting, the Allies finally succeeding under Maude, but the campaign exhausted Allied strength without commensurate military

gains. The losses – dead, wounded and missing – exceeded 100,000. The economic (oil) and political prizes were realised after the war.

12. In his *War Memoirs* (1938), not notable for the generosity of his appreciation of British generals, Lloyd George praised Cowans. It was not his intention to damn Jack with faint praise when he described him as 'the most capable soldier thrown up by the war in our army'. See also A. J. P. Taylor (ed.), *Lloyd George. A Diary by Frances Stevenson* (1971), p. 113, entry for 8 August 1916.

13. *War Diaries*, vol. I, p. 293, entry for 29 July 1916.

14. See *ibid.*, p. 360, entry for 12 October 1916. The other two members of the court were Mr Justice Aitkin, a High Court judge, and Donald Maclean, a Liberal MP.

15. See *ibid.*, p. 398, entry for Saturday 25 November 1916. Repington observed that 'An illustrious person' (the king) had condemned the use of the letters as 'outrageous'. The king informed Lloyd George, in his opinion Cowans had done nothing to justify being dismissed.

16. See *ibid.*, p. 400.

17. See Taylor (ed.), *Stevenson*, p. 130, entry for 30 November 1916.

18. Lieutenant General Sir Frederick Thomas Clayton (1855–1933), in 1915 was Inspector General of Communications, BEF. He resented Geddes being sent out by LG to assist over communications. Haig approved telling Geddes he was 'glad to have practical help from anyone capable of advising'. See Blake (ed.), *Private Papers of Haig*, p. 161, entry for 24 August 1916. Taylor (ed.), *Stevenson*, p. 115, offers a different version of the same story.

19. See *War Diaries*, vol. I, p. 428. At least Stuart-Wortley had one supporter, the French military attaché who 'deplored' the departure of 'an officer who had done so well as Director of Movements'! See pp. 445–46.

20. See *ibid.*, p. 414.

21. See *ibid.*, p. 372, entry dated Wednesday 25 October 1916. Fifteen months later, 22 January 1918, Lloyd George told Stamfordham that the army had 'lost confidence in Brass Hats generally'. The army showed 'a lack of organisation and a want of brains; the best men are not employed'. See RA, GV/ F1259/4.

22. *War Diaries*, vol. I, pp. 422 and 428. Civilians replacing soldiers, especially in his department, had concerned Cowans as much as Repington. On a visit to Haig, 14 October 1916, Cowans made a point of impressing the C-in-C that Lloyd George wanted to put civilians into the military machine wherever possible to replace soldiers but 'especially in the QMG's branch'. Sheffield and Bourne (eds.), *Haig: War Diaries and Letters*, p. 241. Haig realised the need for civilian expertise to be employed in the army. See diary entry for 27 October 1916, pp. 248–49.

23. The key features of the Court of Inquiry are conveniently covered in Grigg, *Lloyd George: From Peace to War, 1912–1916, ante*, pp. 368–69 and footnotes. Grigg's summary is based upon the reports of the Court in the Lloyd George Papers.

24. See *War Diaries*, vol. I, p. 263 n.

25. See *ibid.*, pp. 263–65 and 283–85.

26. See Robert Blake (ed.), *Haig's Diaries 1914–1919*, p. 84, entry for 22 January 1915.
27. But cf. Jeffery, *Field-Marshal Sir Henry Wilson*, pp. 142–44.
28. See *inter alia*, Robertson to Haig, 5 and 7 July 1916, quoted Harris, *Haig and the First World War*, p. 243.
29. See *ibid.*, vol. I, pp. 281–82.
30. See Robertson to Haig, 29 July 1916, and Haig to CIGS, 1 August 1916, in Sheffield and Bourne (eds.), *Haig: War Diaries and Letters*, pp. 213–14.
31. See *War Diaries*, vol. I, pp. 283–98.
32. See Grigg, *Lloyd George*, p. 376
33. A contemporary newspaper article, reprinted in Northcliffe, *At the War*, p. 63.
34. See Taylor (ed.), *Stevenson*, p. 111, entry for 2 August 1916.
35. See Brigadier General John Charteris, *At G.H.Q.* (n.d. [1931]), p. 164, entry for 12 August 1916; *War Diaries*, vol. I, p. 308.
36. See *War Diaries*, vol. I, p. 319, entry for 31 August 1916.
37. See in particular, his surveys in *Correspondence*, to Bonar Law, 16 November 1915, pp. 239–45; and to Steed, 11 October 1916, pp. 253–60; *War Diaries*, *passim*, but particularly entry for Monday 9 October 1916, vol. I, p. 357.
38. See Callwell, *Wilson: His Life and Diaries*, vol. I, p. 292.
39. Sheffield and Bourne (eds.), *Haig: War Diaries and Letters*, p. 232, entry for 17 September 1916.
40. See Wilson (ed.), *Rasp of War*, pp. 189–90, nn. 1–3.
41. See *War Diaries*, vol. I, pp. 353–54, entry for Tuesday 3 October 1916.
42. See Taylor (ed.), *Stevenson*, pp. 119–20, entry for 24 October 1916.
43. Robertson to Haig, 27 September 1917, in Woodward (ed.), *Military Correspondence of Robertson*, pp. 228–29. See also, for this section, the splendid essay by John Gooch, 'Soldiers, Strategy and War Aims in Britain, 1914–1918', in his *The Prospect of War: Studies in British Defence Policy, 1847–1942* (1981), pp. 124–45, where Robertson's letter is cited.
44. See *War Diaries*, vol. I, pp. 371–74, entry for Wednesday 25 October 1916.
45. See *ibid.*, pp. 358–59, entry for Tuesday 10 October 1916.
46. Lloyd George stated, 'I have never questioned your authority . . . in all matters affecting strategy'. D. Ll. George to General Sir William Robertson, 11 October 1916, in Woodward (ed.), *Military Correspondence of Robertson*, pp. 93–96.
47. See *War Diaries*, vol. I, pp. 350–51.
48. Victor Bonham Carter, *Soldier True: The Life and Times of Field Marshal Sir William Robertson* (1963), p. 189.
49. See *The Times*, 24 August 1916.
50. See Taylor (ed.), *Stevenson*, p.115, entry for 12 October 1916.
51. Mead, *Good Soldier*, p. 264.
52. See *The Times*, 29 November 1916.
53. See report of Lloyd George's conversation with Stamfordham, 22 January 1918, RA, GV/F1259/4.
54. See *War Diaries*, vol. I, p. 383, entry for Saturday 11 November 1916.
55. *Ibid.*, pp. 391–93, entry for Wednesday 22 November 1916.

56. *Ibid.*, p. 392.
57. The question of training was equally vital as an exchange with General Tom Bridges demonstrated. See *ibid.*, p. 412, entry for Monday 18 December 1916.
58. See *ibid.*, p. 420.

17   Repington leaves *The Times*

1. G. S. Freeman had been in charge while Dawson was in France. See exchange between the Assnt. Editor and Repington, 8–11 October 1916, in *Correspondence*, pp. 250–52.
2. See Memorandum, 11 October 1916, *ibid.*, pp. 253–60.
3. See Repington to Northcliffe, 13 October 1916, *ibid.*, pp. 252–53.
4. See *War Diaries*, vol. I, pp. 454–59.
5. See Blake (ed.), *Private Papers of Haig*, p. 155.
6. See *Daily Mail*, 13 October 1916; entry for 13 October 1916, in Jean Hamilton's *Diary*, vol. IX, and Repington to Northcliffe, 13 October 1916, in *Correspondence*, pp. 252–53.
7. Repington to Northcliffe, 19 October 1916, Northcliffe Papers in the BM, now BL, Add. MSS 62253, fo. 97.
8. Northcliffe to Repington, 18 October 1916 (copy), Northcliffe Add. MSS 62253, fo. 96.
9. Quoted in R. Pound and G. Harmsworth, *Northcliffe* (London, 1959), p. 477.
10. See *War Diaries*, vol. I, p. 535. Despite Repington's clear desire to help, Haig could not forbear from criticising Repington writing in his diary he thought his guest, 'A very conceited man'.
11. Repington to Northcliffe, 27 April 1917, in *Correspondence*, pp. 266–67.
12. Almost as strange were the proprietors. Julias Elias, later Lord Southwood (1873–1946), acquired the *National News* from its two Belgian owners, who had left England on the outbreak of war. Elias sold it on to Sir Henry Dalzeil (1868–1935), from whom Horatio Bottomley (1860–1933) secured it with dud funds. Later, to further his career as a newspaper tycoon, he merged it with the *Sunday Evening Telegraph*.
13. See D. Ayerst, *Garvin of the 'Observer'* (1985), pp. 166–67.
14. See *War Diaries*, vol. II, p. 151, Tuesday 11 December 1917.
15. He was killed on 23 July 1916 at Bazentin-le-Petit. For Garvin's feelings, see Katharine Garvin, *J. L. Garvin: A Memoir* (1948), pp. 85ff. See also M. Pootle and J. G. G. Ledingham, *We Hope To Get Word Tomorrow* (2009).
16. See *War Diaries*, vol. I, pp. 368–69. Repington's first long leader for the *Observer* attracted considerable, widespread and favourable comment.
17. Steed was biased; he had reason to dislike both Repington and Dawson. See 'Note of a conversation with Steed by M. R. D. Foot, 4 January 1950', HWS/3, Times Archive. In September 1916, Dawson told Corbett that since the war's beginning he had 'scrapped a very large number of Repington's articles'. Repington was 'a brilliant but very uneven writer'. He admitted whether to pull a contribution was often 'rather difficult to adjudicate'.

18. A. M. Gollin, *Proconsul in Politics: A study of Lord Milner in Opposition and in Power* (1964), p. 324.
19. Koss, *Rise and Fall of the Political Press in Britain*, vol. II, p. 207.
20. *Nation*, 24 February 1917. On Milner's *Kindergarten*, his 'young men intent on running the Empire', see John Marlowe, *Milner: Apostle of Empire* (1976), pp. 258–59.
21. See *War Diaries*, vol. II, pp. 30–32.
22. Speech at Caxton Hall, 1 January 1917, quoted, Gollin, *Proconsul*, p. 447.
23. See Steed's comments, Times Archive, HWS/3. 'During one year of the war (according to Freeman) Dawson was away from the office for sixty working nights in addition to his holidays. He made a point of disappearing when a crisis was boiling up.'
24. Gollin, *Proconsul*, p. 451.
25. See *War Diaries*, vol. I, p. 429.
26. See Derby to Esher, 25 November 1917, in Randolph Churchill, *Lord Derby, 'King of Lancashire'* (1959), pp. 293–94.
27. See Haig's diary, Monday 14 January 1918, Sheffield and Bourne (eds.), *Haig: War Diaries and Letters*, pp. 371–72.
28. *War Diaries*, vol. II, p. 50, Monday 17 September 1917.
29. *Ibid.*, pp. 55–6, Tuesday 25 September 1917.
30. Plumer's support was not based on Charteris's optimism about which he was 'sarcastic'.
31. *Ibid.*, pp. 98–104.
32. *Ibid.*, pp. 82–3.
33. *Ibid.*, pp. 106–07, Tuesday 23 October 1917.
34. *Homme brûlé* is a man who has lost his reputation.
35. Repington to Dawson, 4 November 1917, in *Correspondence*, p. 271.
36. See *War Diaries*, vol. II, pp. 128–29. Monday 5 November to Wednesday 7 November 1917.
37. *Ibid.*, pp. 126–34. Friday 2 November to Friday 16 November 1917. See on Rapallo Conference, Lord Hankey, *The Supreme Command* (1961) vol. II, pp. 716–19.
38. *War Diaries*, vol. II, p. 139. Tuesday 20 November 1917.
39. See *ibid.*, p. 149, Friday 7 December 1917.
40. Dawson claimed, it was not just the uninformed public that regretted the outcome of the Battle of Cambrai, but 'the unanimous verdict of officers of all ranks returning from the Front'. Wrench, *Dawson and our Times* (1955), p. 160.
41. Esher to Hankey, 20 December 1917; passed on by Hankey to Lloyd George, 24 December 1917, Lloyd George MSS, F/23/1/35.
42. *War Diaries*, vol. II, p. 164, Monday 31 December 1917.
43. *Ibid.*, p. 165, Wednesday 2 January 1918.
44. See *ibid.*, pp. 173–81, 6–10 January 1918.
45. See Repington to Dawson, 11 January 1918, in *Correspondence*, pp. 272–74.
46. It may be the letter was never sent. There is no mention of it in Repington's *War Diaries*. The original remains in the Times Archive.
47. See HC Deb. (5th series), vol. 101, cc. 58–86.

48. See Peter Fraser, *Lord Esher* (1973), p. 376.
49. See *War Diaries*, vol. II, pp. 183–87, 14–16 January 1918, and Esher to Haig, 18 January 1918, quoted Fraser, *Esher*, pp. 376–77.
50. Dawson kept a pocket diary in which he recorded little more than names and random, abbreviated notes on this thoughts or mood at the time. He later wrote up certain episodes in greater detail. A third source is provided by letter diaries designed to inform a particular individual. There is such a letter diary covering Repington's departure from PHS, written to Haig. Although dated at its opening, 30 January 1918, the letter was continued to cover events into mid February 1918. This source was used exclusively by the historian of *The Times* for his account of these events. See Dawson MSS, Dep. 67, fos. 160–72.
51. See *War Diaries*, vol. II, pp. 187–88, Wednesday 16 January 1918.
52. Repington wrote to Northcliffe on 16 January (see *Correspondence*, p. 275). At no time in his letters to anyone did Repington suggest Northcliffe was responsible for his resignation. The responsibility was Dawson's alone. Months later, when the heat and hurt of departure were somewhat abated, F. E. Smith asked Repington whether it was Northcliffe or Dawson he had fallen out with. Repington insisted, 'I had no personal disagreement with Northcliffe, my quarrel was with Dawson.' See *War Diaries*, vol. II, p. 245 and also p. 503.
53. See Repington to Corbett, 16 January 1918, *ibid.*, pp. 275–76.
54. Geoffrey Dawson, *Diary*, 1918, vol. 24, Wednesday 16 January, Geoffrey Dawson MSS.
55. *Ibid.*, Thursday 17 January 1918.

18   At odds with DORA

1. See *War Diaries*, vol. II, p. 191.
2. See Repington to H. A. Gwynne, 19 January 1918, in *Correspondence*, pp. 276–77.
3. Milner to Lloyd George, 18 January 1918, Lloyd George MSS, P38/3/4.
4. See Gwynne to Rawlinson, 30 January 1918, in K. Wilson (ed.), *The Rasp of War* (1988), pp. 240–41.
5. *Nolo episcopari* is the formula by which a bishopric is declined. It is said bishops refuse twice but modestly acquiesce at the third asking. The phrase suggests a false modesty.
6. See Strachey to Repington (copy), 26 January 1918; Repington to Strachey, 29 January 1918, Parliamentary Archives, J. St Loe Strachey MSS, S/12/1/2.
7. See Austen to Ida Chamberlain, 25 January, 8 and 15 February 1918, University of Birmingham, A. Chamberlain MSS, AC5/1/57, 59 and 60.
8. Esher most fully developed this concept in his book, *After the War* (1919). See further, Esher to Haig, 14 February 1918, Churchill College, Cambridge, Esher MSS, ESHR 4/9.
9. See Esher to Stamfordham, 22 January 1918, RA, Geo. V, Q724.
10. Repington's resignation was spoken of in the *New York Times* as though the departure were that of a Cabinet minister, not a journalist. A variety of

character sketches of Repington and interviews with him appeared in the press. See in particular Repington to Gwynne, 21 January 1918. Bodleian Library, Oxford, Gwynne MSS, Dep. 21.

11. Repington to Gwynne, 20 January 1918, Gwynne MSS, Dep. 21. War Office figures, although they came through the DMO's department, were compiled by the Adjutant General's department.

12. Gwynne to Repington, 22 January 1918, Gwynne MSS, Dep. 21

13. See *The Times*, 23 January 1918; Dawson's Private Secretary to Repington, 23 January 1918(copy), Times Archive, Repington File.

14. See *War Diaries*, vol. II, p. 198, and Repington to Gwynne, 24 January 1918, Gwynne MSS, Dep. 21 (Repington 1917–21).

15. How the spirit, intention and content of Repington's article could be entirely misrepresented is clear from, for example, Dawson's letter to Haig, 30 January 1918, Dawson MSS, 67, fos. 55–8.

16. See Repington to Gen. Sir Ian Hamilton, 23 January 1918, Hamilton MSS.

17. Lloyd George to Derby, 24 January 1918, Lloyd George MSS, F/14/5/4.

18. Derby to Lloyd George, 29 January 1918, Lloyd George MSS, F/14/5/6.

19. Jeffery, *Field Marshal Sir Henry Wilson*, p. 217. The generals would have argued the new body contravened a great principle of the science of war, that committees are incapable of making sound decisions about strategy.

20. See Robertson to Gwynne, 7 February 1918, in Wilson (ed.), *Rasp of War*, pp. 242–43.

21. He had met with members of the mission and conversed at length on two occasions with Major General Sidney Clive.

22. See *War Diaries*, vol. II, pp. 204–09. A version of Richard III's, 'six Richmonds in the field' of whom he slew five that day – but not the Henry Richmond who replaced him as king. The idea was an invention by Shakespeare. See Shakespeare's *Richard III*, Act 5, scene 6.

23. See Ethel Smyth to H. A. Gwynne, 15 February 1918, and Gwynne to Ethel Smyth, 25 February 1918, Gwynne MSS, Dep. 21.

24. Leo Amery to Lloyd George, 3 February 1918, Lloyd George MSS, F/2/1/15; Amery to Mrs Amery, 3 February 1918, in John Barnes and David Nicholson (eds.), *The Leo Amery Diaries*, vol. I, *1896–1929* (1980), p. 205. That same day Amery told Milner of his bright idea. 'Milner knows he could do it better than anyone.' Amery, diary entry for 3 February 1918, *ibid.*, vol. I, p. 205.

25. Repington to Gwynne, 5 February 1918, Gwynne MSS, Dep. 21 (Repington 1917–21).

26. See *Morning Post*, 8 February 1918.

27. Quoted Lloyd George, 'German General Staff Memorandum', in *War Memoirs*, vol. II, p. 1669.

28. See *War Diaries*, vol. II, pp. 278 and 304.

29. See Robertson to Repington, 31October 1916, in Woodward (ed.), *Military Correspondence of Robertson*, pp. 100–01; *War Diaries*, vol. I, pp. 376–77.

30. See *Correspondence*, pp. 249 and 322 n. 192.

31. See *Morning Post*, 11 February 1918.

32. Lloyd George, *War Memoirs*, vol. II, p. 1676. For Ananias, see Acts 5: 1–6.

33. See Keith Middlemas (ed.), *Thomas Jones: Whitehall Diary* (1969), vol. I, p. 52, entry for 12 February 1918.

34. Esher to Haig, 13 February 1918, quoted Wilson (ed.), *Rasp of War*, p. 245 n. 2. Repington provides a variation of Esher's story. See *War Diaries*, vol. II, p. 244, entry for 14 March 1918. The Repington article elicited great excitement in Paris. See H. Le Roy-Lewis to Esher, 15 February 1918, Esher MSS, ESHR 5/55.

35. Gordon Hewart to Lloyd George, 11 February 1918, Lloyd George MSS, F/ 24/4/2. Regulations imposed by the Defence of the Realm Acts, 1914–15 (DORA) made dramatic inroads into personal liberties. Several well-informed people did not think it wise to prosecute, including Bertie, the British Ambassador in Paris. See his *Diaries*, edited by Lady Lennox (1924), vol. II, p. 259.

36. Lloyd George made the patently false claim that the lesser charge of a breach of DORA regulations was to avoid 'giving further publicity to the Versailles plans and thus aggravate the mischief'. *War Memoirs*, vol. II, p. 1679. Robert Sanders, an unofficial Tory whip who suspected Lloyd George, thought Repington was conspiring with Asquith (for there were rumours going about Westminster that the military correspondent had been seen with McKenna) and believed the government would have to sue the *Morning Post* and Repington, otherwise it would be thought of as weak. See J. Ramsden (ed.), *Political Diaries of Robert Sanders, 1910–1935* (1984), p. 101, entry for 13 February 1918.

37. See *War Diaries*, vol. II, pp. 197–98.

38. Jean, Lady Hamilton, *Diary*, 12 February 1918, vol. XI, Nov. 1917–Jan. 1919.

39. See Colvin, *Life of Lord Carson*, vol. III, p. 320.

40. See *War Diaries*, vol. II, pp. 230–31.

41. See Parliamentary Report in *The Times*, 13 February 1918.

42. Cynthia Asquith, *Diaries*, p. 411, Wednesday 13 February 1918. The *Manchester Dispatch* the previous day reported Repington had been arrested while *The Times* insinuated that he ought to have been, so perhaps Lady Cynthia's mistake was excusable.

43. Dawson to Corbett, 14 February 1918, Times Management File.

44. See *War Diaries*, vol. II, pp. 230–31.

45. At 8 p.m. the previous evening a member of the press brought Robertson an official note from the Press Bureau stating that the government had accepted his resignation. Robertson told him that he had NOT resigned. The best contemporary coverage from Robertson's point of view of this tortuous disagreement is in David Woodward's edition of Robertson's military correspondence as CIGS (Army Records Society 1989), ch. 5, pp. 245–308. There are also two memoranda by Gwynne that he enclosed in a letter to Lady Bathurst, 5 March 1918, summarising the events, in Wilson (ed.), *Rasp of War*, pp. 254–58. For a persuasive, concise contrary view, see Jeffery, *Field Marshal Sir Henry Wilson*, pp. 215–18.

46. See Jean, Lady Hamilton, *Diary*, entry for 19 February 1918; *War Diaries*, vol. II, pp. 233–35 and 237, entries for 18–20 February and 24, 25 and 27 February 1918.

47. See Gwynne to Lady Bathurst, 21 February 1918, in Wilson (ed.), *Rasp of War*, pp. 251–52; Sir Edward Cook, *The Press in Wartime* (1920), p. 89 n. 1.
48. See *War Diaries*, vol. II, p. 234; Repington to Maurice, 24 February 1918, Maurice MSS, 3/5/70.
49. See 'Introduction', in Blake (ed.), *Private Papers of Haig*, pp. 48–9.
50. Allenby to Repington, 4 February 1918 (received after the trial), in *War Diaries*, vol. II, pp. 236–37.

19   Repington discredited

1. See Repington to Dawson, 22 December 1915, in *Correspondence*, pp. 246–48.
2. See Maurice's diary, Saturday 26 January 1918, in Nancy Maurice (ed.), *The Maurice Case* (1972), p. 66.
3. *Ibid.*, p. 76.
4. See *Morning Post*, 16 March 1918. In the four weeks from 21 March to 18 April 1918 there were 70,000 more British casualties than in the fourteen weeks of the Battle of Passchendaele.
5. See *War Diaries*, vol. II, pp. 254–60, entries from 21 to 31 March 1918.
6. H. A. Gwynne to Repington, 7 March 1918, Gwynne MSS, Dep. 21.
7. Same to same, 28 February 1918, Gwynne MSS, Dep. 21.
8. See Repington to Gwynne, 7 March 1918, Gwynne MSS, Dep. 21.
9. The name given to the secretariat Lloyd George established on becoming premier. Many were appointed on the recommendation of Milner. Members of Lloyd George's secretariat occupied temporary huts constructed in the garden of 10 Downing Street; hence the nickname.
10. See *War Diaries*, vol. II, p. 240.
11. Repington to Gwynne, 1 April 1918, Gwynne MSS, Dep. 21.
12. During this period Haig twice examined the divisions who were holding the front and examined and approved the British defences. He expressed eagerness the Germans should attack, expecting a series of probes that probably would fall most heavily upon the French. Haig also was given the unexpected and unwelcome news late in the day by 'Curly' Birch, his chief artillery adviser, that there was a considerable shortfall in artillery ammunition.
13. See *War Diaries*, vol. II, pp. 267–70. For Gough's own account of the battle and Lloyd George's speech – 'ungenerous', 'inaccurate', 'disparaging', 'a cruel travesty of the facts' – see Hubert Gough, *Soldiering On* (1954), pp. 176ff. See also Nancy Maurice, 'The Defeat of the Fifth Army, July 1918', reprinted in Maurice (ed.), *Maurice Case*, pp. 208–19.
14. See *War Diaries*, vol. II, pp. 272–74.
15. *Ibid.*, p. 282, entry for Wednesday 24 April 1918.
16. See Repington to Maurice, 17 May 1918, Maurice MSS, 4/9/34.
17. See Blake's claim in *The Unknown Prime Minister* (1955), p. 367.
18. There are three references only to Repington in Maurice's diary and they all refer to the trial. See Maurice (ed.), *Maurice Case* (1972), pp. 70–71.
19. See Nancy Maurice, 'The Story of the Crisis of May 1918', *ibid.*, pp. 91–116.

20. HC Deb. (5th series), vol. 105, cc. 851–53.
21. Robertson knew of Maurice's intended action. He said nothing to Repington, which strongly implies the three were men were not engaged in a conspiracy.
22. *War Diaries*, vol. II, p. 296. Maurice's guileless, noble rectitude sounds almost too good to be true, but he was the soul of military honour, deeply sensible of his duty and responsibility to his country. He had hoped that his self-immolation would force Parliament to set up an inquiry to reassess ministerial policy before it was too late and was fully prepared to pay the full price professionally for his action. Maurice behaved consistently – in his own words – 'according to my lights in an upright and patriotic manner'. (See Maurice to Milner 18 May 1918.) Undoubtedly he was hounded by a vengeful and vindictive establishment and must have known that the government, fighting for its political life, would not hesitate to pull every stroke in the game.
23. See Jean Hamilton's *Diary*, 16 May 1918, Hamilton MSS, 20/1/3. Cf. Esher's opinion of Maurice, Esher to Hankey, 9 May 1918, who dismissed Maurice as 'an ass'. See Fraser, *Esher*, p. 394.
24. Lloyd George, *War Memoirs*, vol. II, pp. 1781–82.
25. See Gollin, *Proconsul*, pp. 513–14.
26. See A. Geddes to Lloyd George, 22 April 1918, and Lloyd George to Auckland Geddes, 23 April 1918 (my emphasis), Lloyd George MSS, F/17/5/15–16.
27. See *War Diaries*, vol. II, pp. 300–01, Friday/Saturday 10/11 May 1918.
28. See *Morning Post*, 19 and 26 April 1918; Gollin, *Proconsul*, pp. 510 and 515; *War Diaries*, vol. II, pp. 277 and 285.
29. Gollin, *Proconsul*, p. 516.
30. For their most recent altercation, see, *War Diaries*, vol. II, p. 151, Tuesday 11 December 1917.
31. This and all subsequent quotations in this section not otherwise attributed are taken from Garvin's 12 May 1918 *Observer* article: 'An Exposure, *Naturalised News* and Military Scandal, Chapter and Verse'.
32. This was the preferred and easiest stick with which to hit Repington. 'That unprincipled scoundrel, Repington was primarily responsible for fostering the prejudice against Wilson.' Repington was not unique in his poor opinion of Wilson; it was shared by almost all members of the British High Command. See Milner to Northcliffe, 22 April 1918, Northcliffe Add. MSS, 62339, fos. 172–74.
33. Ayerst, *Garvin*, p. 165.
34. Luvaas, *Education of an Army*, p. 322.
35. Repington, preaching the importance of the French armies and the BEF adopting the defensive exaggerated the destructive powers of the Russian mass armies once properly mobilised. His ideas were shared by French in particular, and these views were generally held until the end of 1914, ideas which Garvin seems to have forgotten that he too shared at the time. It was the policy of *The Times*, in the autumn of 1914, to emphasise the weight and irresistible force of the Russian armies.
36. See Ayerst, *Garvin*, p. 166.

37. In the index entry for Maurice in his *War Memoirs*, Lloyd George describes him as 'an instrument, the tool of astute men', and one whose mind was 'apparently unhinged'.
38. Asquith, the Liberal leader and former prime minister, together with the remnants of the Liberal Party, were the intended political beneficiaries of the plot to oust LG using the disclosures in Maurice's letter.
39. Gollin, *Proconsul*, p. 519.
40. Milner to Robertson, 18 May 1918, Lloyd George MSS, F/38/3/33.
41. Milner to Lloyd George, 19 May 1918, Lloyd George MSS, F/38/3/35.
42. André Cheradame, 'The Fundamentals of the Situation', *National Review* (May 1918), pp. 306ff.
43. See Austin Harrison to Editor of the *Morning Post*, 13 and 14 May 1918 and H. A. Gwynne to Harrison, 14 May 1918, Gwynne MSS, Dep. 21.
44. See Gwynne to Lady Bathurst, 22 May 1918, in Wilson (ed.), *Rasp of War*, pp. 281–82.
45. Gwynne to Lady Bathurst, 15 and 22 May 1918, *ibid.*, pp. 280–82.
46. Same to same, 18 March and 15 May 1918, *ibid.*, pp. 260 and 281.
47. Same to General Rawlinson, 30 January 1918 (my emphasis), *ibid.*, p. 240.
48. See Keith Wilson's entry on Gwynne in *ODNB*, vol. xxiv, pp. 366–68.
49. Gollin, *Proconsul*, p. 517.
50. Jean, Lady Hamilton's diary, 12 May 1918, Hamilton MSS, 11 (Nov. 1917–Jan. 1919).
51. See Gollin, *Proconsul*.

20   A consummation devoutly to be wished

1. See *War Diaries*, vol. II, p. 86.
2. Though comprising the same number of battalions – twelve – as the traditional British division, each battalion was of a thousand bayonets, so that by 1917/18 the American division was more than twice the size of its British, French or German equivalents. The Americans placed great emphasis upon the infantry as the arm of decision.
3. Robertson to Gen. A. J. Murray, 13 February 1917, in Woodward (ed.), *Military Correspondence of Robertson*, p. 149.
4. One among a number of versions of advice generally attributed to Charles-Maurice de Talleyrand-Périgord (1754–1838) that might be translated, 'Above all else do not be too earnest.'
5. See *War Diaries*, vol. II, pp. 86–96, entries for Tuesday to Thursday, 9–11 October 1917.
6. Repington, *Policy and Arms* (1924), p. 115.
7. For this section, see *War Diaries*, vol. II, pp. 393–403.
8. When Haig asked to increase the divisions in the American Corps, Pershing said he could not 'because his losses had been heavy, though *not so heavy as the British and French had been accustomed to suffer*' (my italics). Later figures suggest the number was an underestimate by as much as 50 per cent. Sheffield and Bourne (eds.), *Haig: War Diaries and Letters*, p. 479, entry for 23 October 1918.
9. See *War Diaries*, vol. II, p. 459, entry for Tuesday 8 October 1918.

10. Bonham Carter, *Soldier True*, p. 373.
11. See *War Diaries*, vol. II, p. 344 and pp. 355–56.
12. See *ibid.*, pp. 375–76, entry for 3 September 1918.
13. See *ibid.*, pp. 378–82.
14. Repington to Mary, 19 and 23 July 1918, in author's possession.
15. General Pershing would confirm in June 1919 that Repington's articles were, and always had been, 'widely read in America'. See *ibid.*, p. 545.
16. See Reading to D. Lloyd George, 19 September 1918, together with the attached note, Lloyd George MSS, F/43/1/19.
17. Repington to Mary, 19, 23 and 26 July 1918, in author's possession.
18. Repington to Gwynne, 29 July 1918, Gwynne MSS, Dep. 21. Repington 1917–21. Lt Col. Fabry wrote for the journal *Oui*. Repington rated him 'the best of the military critics in France'. Bidou wrote for *Débats*.
19. See Repington to Mary, 30 July 1918, *War Diaries*, vol. II, p. 347.
20. Repington to Gwynne, 19 September 1918, Gwynne MSS, Dep. 21. The battlefield description is from *War Diaries*, vol. II, p. 397.
21. The Germans did not show the same confidence in their artillery to judge from a notice found in a captured trench. It read, 'We fear nothing but God and our own Artillery.' See *War Diaries*, vol. II, p. 365.
22. Churchill had been recalled to office in July 1917, a bold stroke by LG because the Tories in the government hated Winston. He was a great success as Minister for Munitions.
23. *Ibid.*, p. 456.
24. See *ibid.*, pp. 460–62, entry for 9 October 1918.
25. See further, Gary Sheffield, *Forgotten Victory* (2002), pp. 237–63.
26. See *War Diaries*, vol. II, pp. 463–67, entries for Saturday 12 October to Friday 25 October 1918.
27. See *ibid.*, pp. 468–75. 'Woe to the vanquished' from Livy's *Ab Urbe Condita*.
28. See *The Times*, 15 and 16 January 1915.
29. *War Diaries*, vol. II, p. 391.

21   Peace poses its own problems, 1918–1920

1. See *Morning Post*, 11 November 1918.
2. See *War Diaries*, vol. II, p. 509.
3. For a very different view, see Andrew Rothstein, *The Soldiers' Strikes of 1919* (1980).
4. *War Diaries*, vol. II, p. 491, entry for Monday 6 January 1919. For previous quotations in this paragraph not cited, see *ibid.*, pp. 481–91.
5. There was an unbridgeable divide on the peace settlement between France and the USA. America wished the settlement to be based on Wilson's Fourteen Points whereas France wanted permanent guarantees against German revival and for them to enjoy greater influence in south-east Europe. Repington set out his arguments for ratification two months later in the *Morning Post*.
6. See *ibid.*, p. 527; Repington to Gwynne, 22 May and 17 July 1919, Gwynne MSS, Dep. 21.

7. See *Morning Post*, January and February 1919, especially, 15, 18 and 26 February.

8. Repington to Mary, 27 to 31 July1919, courtesy of Mrs Stapleton.

9. See *War Diaries*, vol. II, pp. 542–43.

10. See Repington to Mary, 3, 12 July and 12, 26 August 1919, courtesy Mrs Stapleton.

11. Repington to Gwynne, 14 May 1919, Gwynne MSS, Dep. 21.

12. See Repington to Gwynne, 17 August 1919; Gwynne to Repington (copy), 18 August 1919, Gwynne MSS, Dep. 21.

13. See Ribblesdale to Repington, 26 August 1919, in author's possession.

14. Throughout the 1920s and 1930s there was a lively, inconclusive debate concerning the Official Secrets Act 1911 (amended 1920) involving the memoirs of soldiers and statesmen. A good starting point to examine this fascinating and important legal and literary minefield is Ian Beckett's cogent and clear account, 'Frocks and Brasshats', in Brian Bond (ed), *The First World War and British Military History* (Oxford, 1991), pp. 90–112.

15. See *War Diaries*, vol. II, p. 539, entry for Monday 9 June 1919.

16. 'But what would you have me do when the one (LG) supposes he is Napoleon and the other (Wilson) thinks he's Jesus Christ.' Nicolson first told this story to his wife, 20 May 1919. The letter is quoted in James Lees-Milne, *Harold Nicolson, a Biography* (1980), vol. I, *1886–1929*, p. 119. The story is retold in *War Diaries*, vol. II, p. 544, entry for Tuesday 10 June 1919.

17. See Gwynne to Repington, 17 June 1919, and Repington to Gwynne, 20 June 1919, Gwynne MSS, Dep. 21.

18. See *War Diaries*, vol. II, pp. 523–24.

19. See Repington to General Sir A. F. H. Paget, 21 May 1919, BL, Add. MSS 51250, fo. 208.

20. This was a reference not only to Steed's long-time interest in Balkan nationalism but also to his mistress Madam Rose, a mysterious Yugoslav lady.

21. See *War Diaries*, vol. II, p. 503.

22. Repington to Gwynne, 5 and 9 November 1919, Gwynne MSS, Dep. 21.

23. H. A. Gwynne to Repington, 17 December 1919, Gwynne MSS, Dep. 21.

24. See Repington to Gwynne, 13(?) April 1920, and Gwynne to Repington, 14 April 1920, Gwynne MSS, Dep. 21.

22   Last post, 1920–1925

1. See Mary Repington to Jean Hamilton, 19 April 1920; fragment in letters in Hamilton MSS.

2. See *Daily Telegraph*, 7, 8, 10, 11, 12 and 13 January 1921.

3. See 'The German Army Today', *Living Age*, 16 July 1921, at p. 179.

4. See 'Colonel Repington's Epigrams', *New York Tribune*, 2 April 1922.

5. 'Disarmament and the State of Europe', *Atlantic Monthly*, p. 667.

6. See *ibid.*, p. 466.

7. These opinions were expressed in his writing for the *Daily Telegraph* in the autumn of 1921. His regular contributions on the Washington Conference

were in turn syndicated in the *New York Times*, to which newspaper on 2 December 1921 he contributed a long article on the conference.

8. See *After the War*, p. 151.
9. It is probable that for a short time Repington enjoyed her sexual favours.
10. See *War Diaries*, vol. I, pp. 116 and 322–23.
11. See Repington to Ferris Greenslet (n.d.) (February 1922).
12. See Repington, *Thanks for the Memory*, pp. 283–84.
13. Luvaas, *Education of an Army*, quoting Repington.
14. See 'Sir Henry Wilson, some reflections', *Daily Telegraph*, 24 June 1922. See also Jeffery, *Field Marshal Sir Henry Wilson*, p. 289.
15. Mary's presence has caused some confusion in the historical record. In the newspaper reports of the funeral she was listed leading the mourners as Mrs Repington. That indeed was her name (as registered by deed poll and by common usage). However, it has been wrongly assumed (for example, in the essay on Repington in the *DNB* by J. Edmonds, *Supplement, 1922–30*, pp. 717–18) that Repington's wife, from whom he had never been divorced, Mrs Melloney Catherine à Court Repington (née Scobell), 1860–1938, attended the funeral. Edmonds wrongly supposed Repington 'had sometime previously been reconciled to his wife'. This mistake prompted Mary to write to J. R. H. Weaver (the editor) at Oxford, to point out the error. Subsequently it led to her writing *Thanks for the Memory* (1938), her attempt to put straight the record of her story and that of Repington.
16. See accounts in *Brighton Herald* and *Sussex Daily News*, Saturday 30 May 1925.

23   A fractured reputation

1. See P. H. S., *History of the Times*, vol. IV, pt. 1, *The 50th Anniversary and Beyond 1912–1948* (1952), pp. 231ff.
2. See B. H. Liddell Hart, *Memoirs* (1965), vol. I, p. 81.
3. Beerbohm's brilliant caricature is entitled 'A Chiel, 1914–1918'. 'Chiel' features in Burns's poem,'Of the late Captain Grose's Peregrinations through Scotland'. The pertinent line is, 'A chiel's among you taking notes and faith he'll prent it.' See Samuel Hynes, *A War Imagined* (London, 1990), pl. 20, p. 306.
4. *Ibid.*, p. 75.
5. The title Jay Luvaas gives to part 4 of his *Education of an Army*.
6. Consider his article 'Home Defence', *Blackwood's Magazine* (June 1903). His outline of the Territorial Army matches Haldane's original bill. W. G. St Clair, in his obituary notice of Repington in the *Times of Ceylon*, 2 June 1925, quoted an exchange of correspondence he had had with Spenser Wilkinson on this subject. Wilkinson wrote he had 'learned for the first time the extent of Lord Haldane's indebtedness to Col à Court Repington'. He verified St Clair's statement.
7. *War Diaries*, vol. II, p. 235.
8. E. H. Begbie, *The Glass of Fashion* (1921), p. 32, quoted, Hynes, *War Imagined*, p. 290.

9. See *War Diaries*, vol. II, pp. 3–4, Sunday 22 July 1917.
10. *Spectator*, 2 October 1920; *Nation*, 25 September 1920; both quoted Hynes, *War Imagined*.
11. See *Newcastle Chronicle*, 28 May 1925.
12. See Montague's *Disenchantment* (1922), p. 47.
13. See Hynes, *War Imagined*, p. 384 and p. 502 n. 3.
14. See Genesis 22.
15. Brian Bond, 'Introduction', in his *First World War and British Military History*, p. 12. See also Bond's Lees Knowles Lectures for 2000, in his *The Unquiet Western Front: Britain's Role in Literature and Society* (Cambridge, 2002), particularly ch. 4, pp. 75ff.

Select bibliography

A short, select list of books, suggested for further reading and arranged by subject. Many contain bibliographies. Unless otherwise indicated, the place of publication is London, and works by Repington are listed in date order.

Publications by Charles à Court Repington

The War in the Far East (1905)
Imperial Strategy (1906)
Peace Strategy (1907)
The Foundations of Reform (1908)
The Future of Army Organization (1909)
Essays and Criticisms (1911)
Vestigia: Reminiscences of Peace and War (1919)
The First World War, 1914–1918: Personal Experiences (two vols., 1920)
After the War: A Diary (1922)
The Life and Death of Marie Stuart (Edinburgh, 1923)
Policy and Arms (1924)

Studies of Repington

Morris, A. J. A. 'Repington, Charles à Court (1858–1925)'. *Oxford Dictionary of National Biography*, vol. xlvi (Oxford, 2004)
Morris, A. J. A. (ed.). *The Letters of Lieutenant-Colonel Charles à Court Repington CMG*, Army Records Society, vol. xv (Stroud, 1999)
Repington, Mary. *Thanks for the Memory* (1938)
Ryan, W. Michael. 'Lieutenant-Colonel Charles à Court Repington: A Study in the Interaction of Personality, the Press and Power'. Ph.D. dissertation, University of Cincinnati, 1976
Lieutenant–Colonel Charles à Court Repington (New York, 1987)

The press – history

Blumenfeld, R. D. *The Press in my Time* (1933)
Koss, S. E. *The Rise and Fall of the Political Press in Britain: The Twentieth Century*, 2 vols., *The Nineteenth Century* and *The Twentieth Century* (1981 and 1984)

Lee, A. J. *The Origins of the Popular Press 1855–1914* (1976)
P. H. S. *The History of The Times*, volume III, *The Twentieth-Century Test, 1884–1912* (1947), and volume IV, part 1, *The 150th Anniversary and Beyond, 1912–1920* (1952)

Newspaper proprietors, editors and journalists

Ayerst, D. *Garvin of the 'Observer'* (1985)
Fritzinger, L. B. *Diplomat without Portfolio: Valentine Chirol, his Life and 'The Times'* (2006)
Fyfe, Hamilton H. *Sixty Years of Fleet Street* (1949)
Gibbs, Philip A. H. *The Pageant of the Years* (1946)
Gollin, A. M. *'The Observer' and J. L. Garvin, 1908–14* (1960)
Harris, Wilson. *J. A. Spender* (1946)
Steed, H. W. *Through Thirty Years, 1892–1922: A Personal Narrative*, 2 vols. (1924)
Thompson, J. Lee. *Lord Northcliffe and the Great War* (Kent, OH, 1999)
   Northcliffe: Press Baron in Politics, 1865–1922 (2000)
Wilson, K. (ed.). *The Rasp of War* (1988)
Wrench, J. E. *Geoffrey Dawson and our Times* (1973)

Foreign policy issues

Hale, O. J. *Publicity and Diplomacy, 1890–1914* (New York, 1940)
Hinsley, F. H. (ed.). *British Foreign Policy under Sir Edward Grey* (Cambridge, 1963)
Howard, G. H. D. *Splendid Isolation* (1967)
Kennan, George F. *The Fateful Alliance* (New York, 1984)
Kennedy, Paul. *The Rise of the Anglo-German Antagonism, 1860–1914* (1980)
Monger, G. W. *The End of Isolation* (Edinburgh, 1963)
Steiner, Zara. *Britain and the Origins of the First World War* (1977)

Naval officers and naval issues

Bennett, G. *Charlie B* (1968)
Beresford, Lord Charles. *The Betrayal* (1912)
Chatfield, Lord. *The Navy and Defence* (1942)
Clarke, G. S. and Thursfield, J. *The Navy and the Nation* (1897)
Graham, G. S. *The Politics of Naval Supremacy* (Cambridge, 1965)
Herwig, Holger H. *Luxury Fleet: The Imperial German Navy, 1888–1918* (1980)
Mackay, Rudock. *Fisher of Kilverstone* (Oxford, 1973)
Marder, Arthur (ed.). *Fear God and Dread Nought: The Correspondence of Admiral of the Fleet Lord Fisher of Kilverstone*, 3 vols. (1952–59)
   From Dreadnought to Scapa Flow 1904–19, 5 vols. (Oxford, 1961–70)
Pudeston, W. D. *Mahan* (1939)
Roskill, Stephen. *Earl Beatty* (1980)

Steinberg, Jonathan. *Yesterday's Deterrent* (1965)
Woodward, E. L. *Great Britain and the German Navy* (Oxford, 1935)

Soldiers and military/political issues

Adams, R. J. Q. and Poirier, P. P. *The Conscription Controversy in Great Britain, 1900–18* (1987)
Beckett, Ian F. W. *The Army and the Curragh Incident 1914*, Army Records Society (Stroud, 1986)
Beckett, Ian and Simpson, Keith (eds.). *A Nation in Arms* (Manchester, 1985)
Bond, Brian. *The Victorian Army and the Staff College* (1972)
  Liddell Hart, 2 vols. (1977)
Bond, Brian (ed.). *The First World War and British Military History* (Oxford, 1991)
Bond, Brian et al., *Look to your Front: Studies in the First World War by the British Commission for Military History* (Staplehurst, 1999)
Callwell, C. E. *Stray Recollections*, 2 vols. (1923)
Cassar, George H. *Kitchener's War: British Strategy from 1914 to 1916* (Washington, DC, 2004)
  The Tragedy of Sir John French (Newark, DE, 1985)
Dockrill, Michael and French, David (eds.). *British Policy During the First World War* (1996)
Dunlop, J. K. *The Development of the British Army 1899–1914* (1938)
French, David. *British Economic and Strategic Planning 1905–15* (1982)
  British Strategy and War Aims 1914–1916 (1986)
Gooch, John. *The Plans of War: The General Staff and British Military Strategy* (1974)
  The Prospect of War (1981)
Guinn, Paul. *British Strategy and Politics, 1914–1918* (Oxford, 1965)
Hamer, W. S. *The British Army: Civil–Military Relations 1889–1905* (Oxford, 1970)
Harris, J. P. *Douglas Haig and the First World War* Cambridge, 2008)
Holmes, Richard. *The Little Field Marshal: A Life of Sir John French* (1981)
Howard, Michael. *The Continental Commitment* (1972)
Jeffery, Keith. *Field Marshal Sir Henry Wilson: A Political Soldier* (Oxford, 2006)
Keegan, John. *The Mask of Command* (1987)
Kennedy Paul (ed.). *The War Plans of the Great Powers, 1880–1914* (1979)
Lee, John. *A Soldier's Life: General Sir Ian Hamilton, 1853–1947* (2000)
Luvaas, Jay. *The Education of an Army* (1965)
Maurice, Nancy (ed.). *The Maurice Case* (Barnsley, 1972)
Mead, Gary. *The Good Soldier: The Biography of Douglas Haig* (2007)
Ombrain, Nicholas d'. *War Machinery and High Policy, 1902–1914* (Oxford, 1973)
Philpott, William. *Anglo-French Relations and Strategy on the Western Front 1914–1918* (1996)
  Bloody Victory: The Sacrifice on the Somme (2009)
Sheffield, Gary. *Forgotten Victory: The First World War, Myths and Realities* (2001)

Sheffield, Gary and Bourne, John (eds.). *Douglas Haig: War Diaries and Letters 1914–18* (2005)
Simkins, Peter. *Kitchener's Army: The Raising of the New Armies, 1914–16* (Manchester, 1988)
Spiers, Edward M. *The Late Victorian Army, 1868–1902* (Manchester, 1992)
Strachan, Huw. *The Politics of the British Army* (Oxford, 1997)
Williams, Rhodri. *Defending the Empire: The Conservative Party and British Defence Policy, 1899–1915* (New Haven, CN, 1991)
Williamson, S. R., Jnr. *The Politics of Grand Strategy* (Cambridge, MA, 1969)
Wilson, Trevor. *The Myriad Faces of War* (Cambridge, 1988)
Woodward, D. R. *Lloyd George and the Generals* (Newark, DE, 1983)

Politicians and other panjandra

Amery, Leo S. *My Political Life*, 3 vols. (1953)
Arnold-Forster, H. O. *Military Needs and Military Policy* (1908)
Asquith, Cynthia. *Diaries 1915–18* (1968)
Asquith, Herbert Henry. *The Genesis of the War* (1923)
Balfour, Michael. *The Kaiser and his Times* (1964)
Beckett, Ian and Gooch, John (eds.). *Politicians and Defence* (Manchester, 1981)
Blake, R. *Andrew Bonar Law: The Unknown Prime Minister* (1955)
Bonham-Carter, Violet. *Winston Churchill as I knew him* (1965)
Brock, M. G. and Brock, E. (eds.). *H. H. Asquith: Letters to Venetia Stanley* (Oxford, 1982)
Fraser, Peter. *Lord Esher: A Political Biography* (1973)
Gollin, A. M. *Proconsul in Politics* (1964)
Grigg, John. *Life of Lloyd George*, volumes II–IV (1978–2002)
Hankey, Lord. *The Supreme Command*, 2 vols. (1961)
Koss, Stephen E. *Asquith* (1976)
    Lord Haldane: Scapegoat for Liberalism (New York, 1969)
Lewis, Geoffrey. *Carson: The Man who Divided Ireland* (Hambledon, 2005)
Mackay, Rudock. *Balfour: Intellectual Statesman* (Oxford, 1985)
Nicholls, David. *The Lost Prime Minister: A Life of Sir Charles Dilke* (Hambledon, 1995)
Robbins, Keith. *Sir Edward Grey: A Biography of Lord Grey of Fallodon* (1971)
Ronaldshay, Earl of. *The Life of Lord Curzon*, 3 vols. (1928)
Roskill, Stephen. *Hankey: Man of Secrets*, 2 vols. (1970)
Spiers, Edward M. *Haldane: An Army Reformer* (Edinburgh, 1981)

Finally, a short, extremely useful and convenient work of reference for the 1914–18 war together with a concise guide to further reading:

Bourne, J. M. *Who's Who in World War One* (2001)

Index

CPSIA information can be obtained
at www.ICGtesting.com
Printed in the USA
LVOW13s1803050118
561979LV00013B/191/P